GRAN FURY

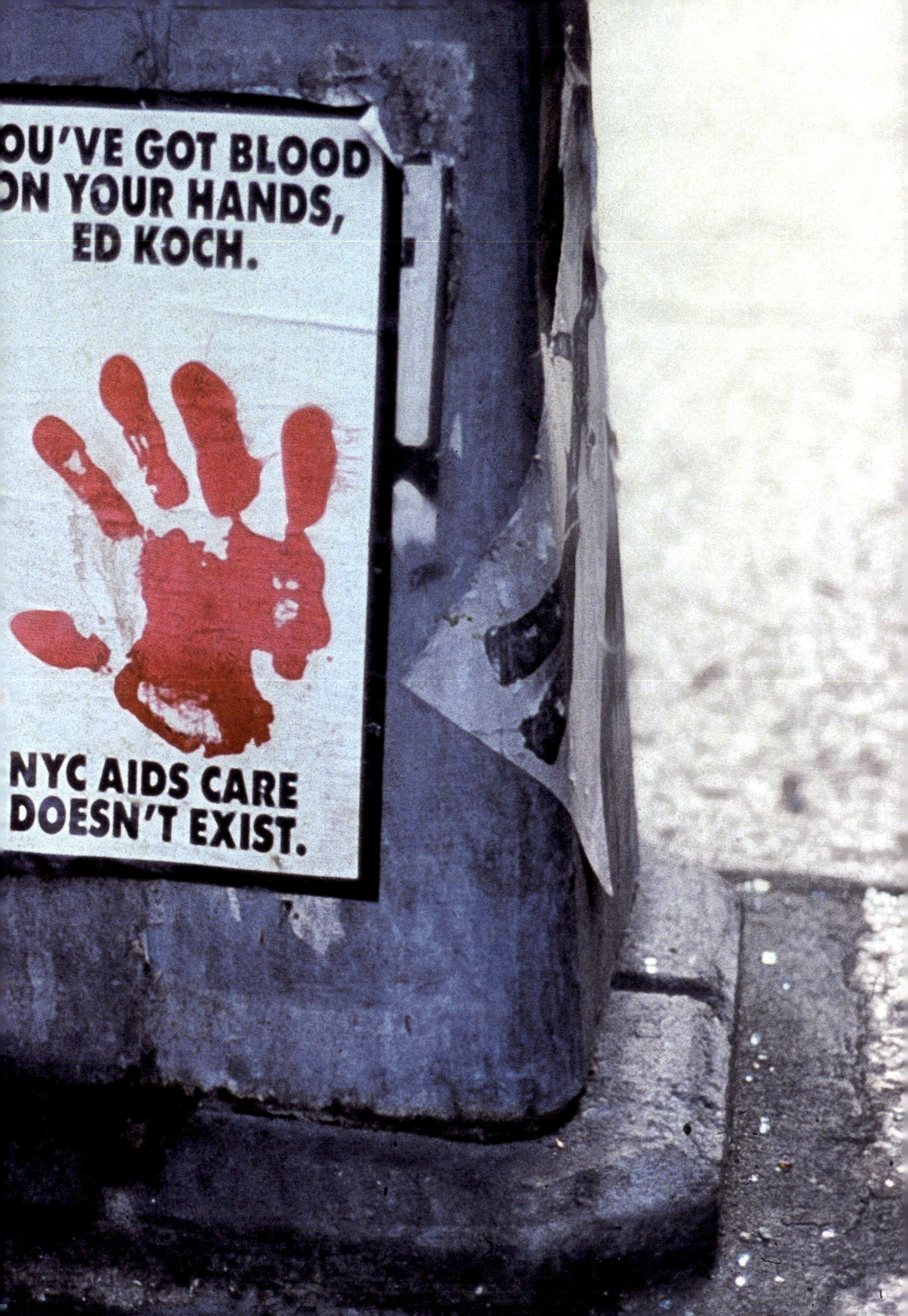
OU'VE GOT BLOOD
ON YOUR HANDS,
ED KOCH.
NYC AIDS CARE
DOESN'T EXIST.

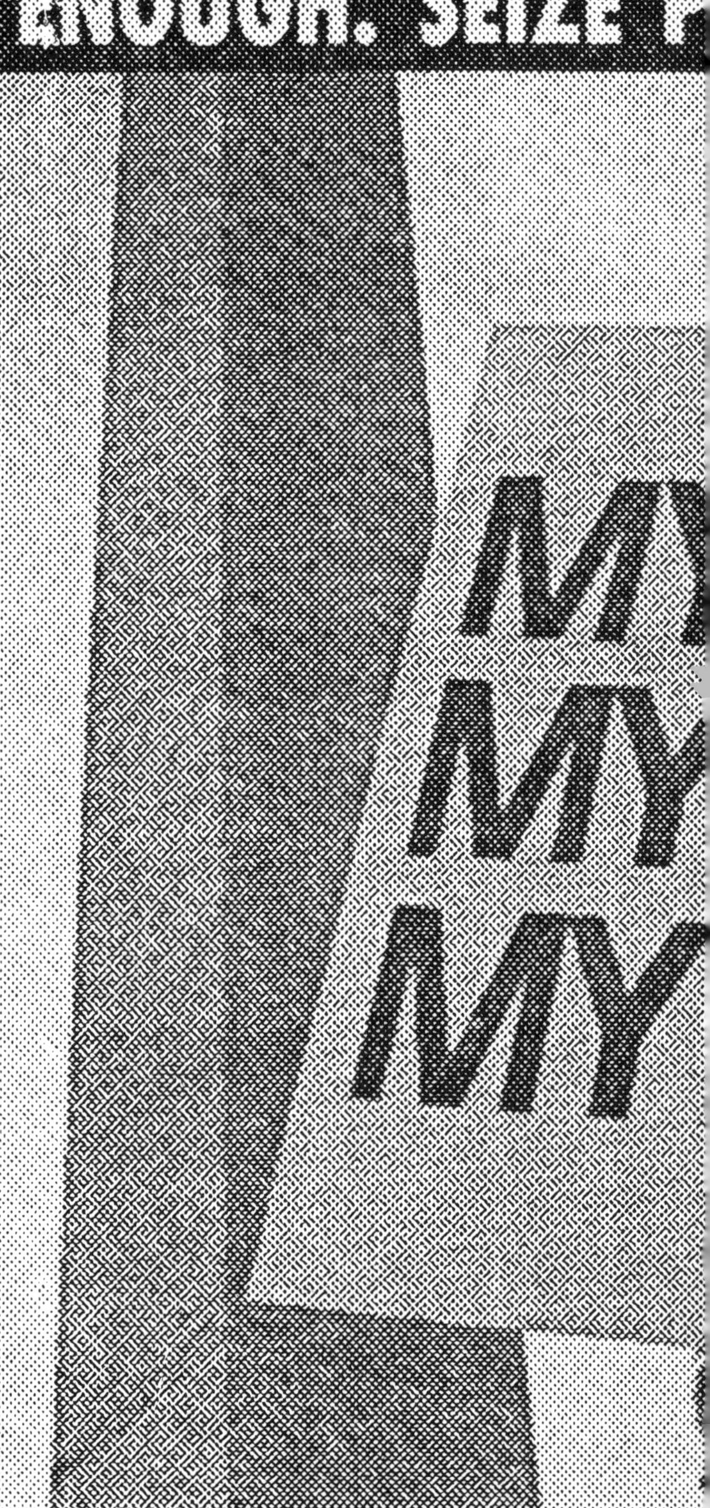

ART IS NOT ENOUGH. SEIZE P
MY
MY
MY

VER THROUGH DIRECT ACTION.

BODY
MIND
CHOICE

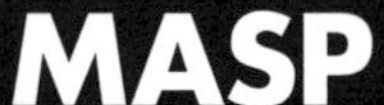

MASP MUSEU DE ARTE
DE SÃO PAULO
ASSIS CHATEAUBRIAND

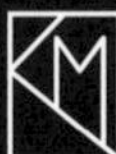

Edited by
ADRIANO PEDROSA
ANDRÉ MESQUITA

Curated by
ANDRÉ MESQUITA

With the assistance of
DAVID RIBEIRO

Texts by
ANDRÉ MESQUITA
DAVID DEITCHER
DOUGLAS CRIMP
GRAN FURY
MARCOS MARTINS AND **VINÍCIUS FRANCO**

Production

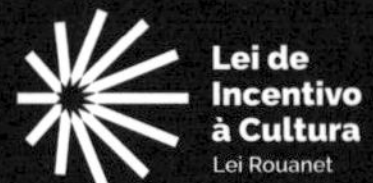

Lei de
Incentivo
à Cultura
Lei Rouanet

MINISTÉRIO DA
CULTURA

GOVERNO FEDERAL
BRASIL
UNIÃO E RECONSTRUÇÃO

GRAN FURY

ART IS NOT ENOUGH

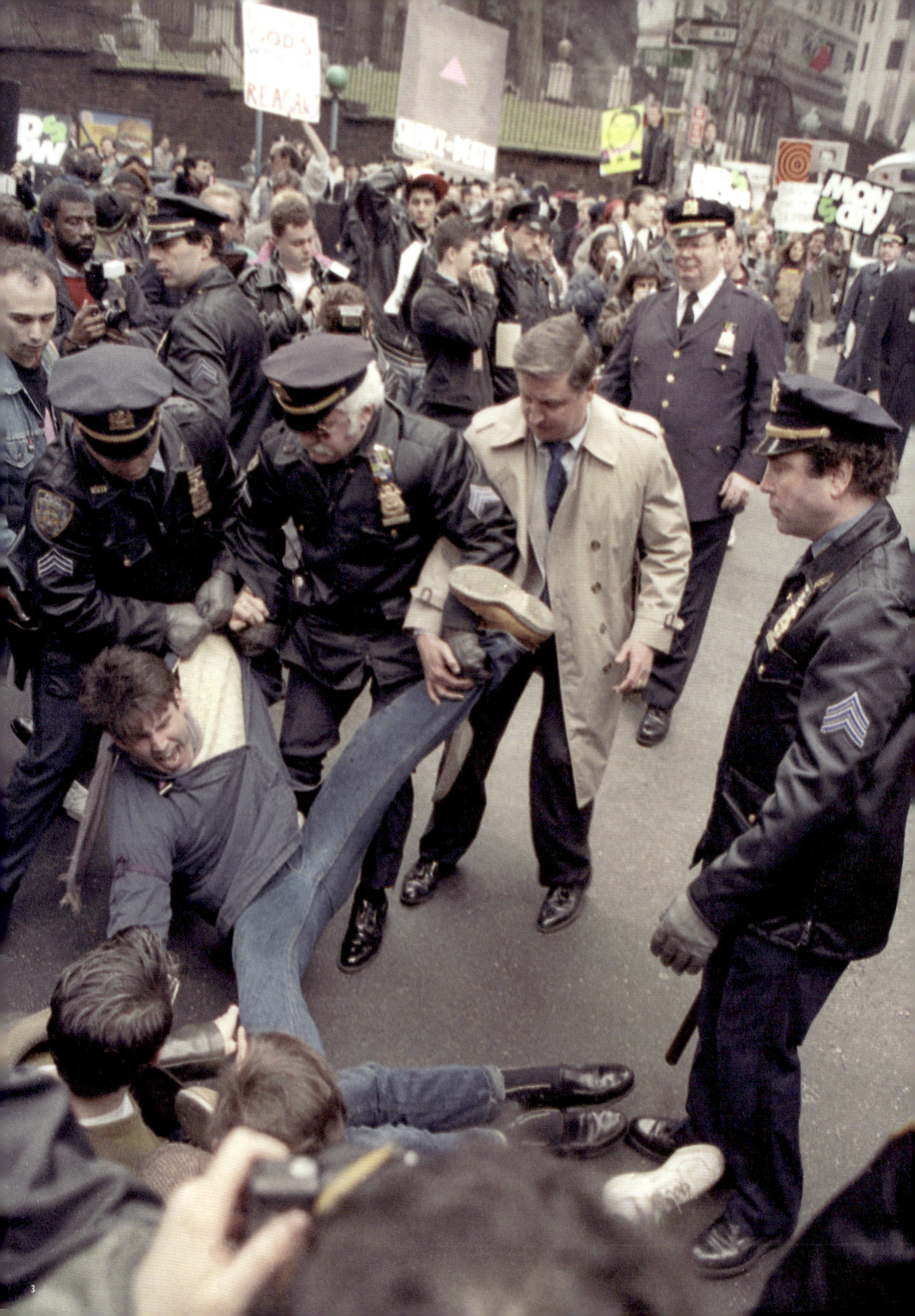

GOD'S
WRATH
REAGAN
SILENCE=DEATH
MON
DAY

CONTENTS

GRAN FURY AT MASP

It is a pleasure for the Museu de Arte de São Paulo Assis Chateaubriand (MASP) to present the first exhibition dedicated to the work of the Gran Fury collective in Latin America, as well as the first book dedicated to the group.

The exhibition is contextualized within a year-long program at MASP devoted to the *Queer Histories*, which includes exhibitions by Francis Bacon (1909–1992), Catherine Opie, Leonilson (1957–1993), Lia D Castro, Mário de Andrade (1893–1945), Serigrafistas Queer, as well as the major group show *Queer Histories*, and exhibitions in the Video Room dedicated to Kang Seung Lee, Manauara Clandestina, Masi Mamaní/Bartolina Xixa, Tourmaline, and Ventura Profana.

With a total of 76 works, the exhibition at MASP is titled *Art Is Not Enough*. The phrase is found in one of Gran Fury's posters [img. 57], and it refers to the impact and effectiveness of the collective's campaigns, pointing towards the strategic role of art in HIV and AIDS queer-led activism, in direct response to the epidemic crisis.

Formed in New York in 1988, Gran Fury emerged from ACT UP (AIDS Coalition to Unleash Power), a group of artists, activists, and collectives committed to exposing the US government's neglect in regards to the HIV/AIDS crisis in the late 1980s and early 1990s, at the height of the epidemic. The collective redefined the role of art by engaging in direct action, challenging the art system and questioning the role of museums, artists, and institutions in confronting the crisis. Gran Fury supported ACT UP with the production of graphic campaigns and public interventions in demonstrations and civil disobedience activities, which eloquently challenged the inertia of public authorities and demanded awareness of the epidemic.

Gran Fury took part in the *Aperto* section of the Biennale di Venezia in 1990, at the Corderie dell'Arsenale, the first edition of the Italian show that I myself visited at a very young age. The group's participation caused a huge controversy, with two large posters juxtaposing the image of Pope John Paul II with that of an erect penis, alongside a text criticizing the position of the Catholic Church, which rejected the use of condoms, so essential for the fight against AIDS at the time. Personally, and since then, Gran Fury's work has been a fundamental artistic reference, like that of another North American collective, the Guerrilla Girls. After presenting Guerrilla Girls' work at the museum in 2017, in the year dedicated to the *Histories of Sexuality*, it is a great pleasure to now be able to present Gran Fury's, curiously in the same year that I curate the show that is now the equivalent of *Aperto* at the Biennale di Venezia, which also has a focus on queer artists. I witnessed the most acute years of the AIDS crisis, when we lost many friends, artists, and intellectuals, deeply marking an entire generation. Gran Fury's extraordinary work reminds us not only of that painful period—for everyone, but especially for those of us in the LGBTQIA+ community—and also draws attention to the importance of queer art and activism.

We are extremely grateful to Gran Fury for allowing this exhibition to take place and for supporting it. We thank the members of the collective, Richard Elovich, Avram Finkelstein, Tom Kalin, John Lindell, Loring McAlpin, Marlene McCarty, Donald Moffett, Michael Nesline, Mark Simpson (*in memoriam*), and Robert Vazquez-Pacheco, for all the work and support. Many thanks to ACT UP and the artists responsible for key photographic records included in this book: Catherine McGann, Donna Binder, Ellen B. Neipris, Lola Flash, Tom McKitterick, and T. L. Litt. We would like to express our gratitude to the other photographers and institutions who provided us with images for this publication: Bill Stamets, Bruno Jakob, Collection Eugene Gordon/The New-York Historical Society, Katherine Foran, Lisa Howe-Ebright, The New York Public Library, and Paula Goldman.

The exhibition at MASP is curated by André Mesquita, curator, with the assistance of David Ribeiro, Mediation and Public Programs supervisor, and we are grateful to both of them for all their valuable work and dedication to this project. Many thanks to the authors, Marcos Martins and Vinícius Franco, who, like Mesquita, wrote an essay for our publication. We would also like to express our gratitude to Bloco Gráfico, who conceived the book's graphic design, and to all the museum's teams who worked on the project in some way—particularly the Production team, led by Marina Moura, the Architecture team, coordinated by Juliana Ziebell, and the Editorial team, led by Carol Ribas. Special thanks to Karen Marta and Todd Bradway, from KMEC Books in New York, who have partnered with us in the English version on this book, as well as its international distribution.

Finally, our special thanks to MASP's board members and patrons, and to our strategic partner, Itaú, whose essential support allows us to develop all our programs at the museum.

ADRIANO PEDROSA, Artistic Director, MASP

ART IS NOT ENOUGH

André Mesquita

What can art do in the face of a pandemic? It is likely that many of us have asked this question following the countless deaths caused by COVID-19 and the responses coming from our governments, the media, and scientific research in the context of a serious epidemiological crisis.

We continue to grapple with the devastating consequences of this pandemic, including the physical and psychological aftermath that has affected those who were in quarantine and infected by the coronavirus. Pushed to the brink by neoliberal and extractivist policies, we have rediscovered how to navigate the maintenance of life and essential care. The world post-pandemic—which has violently devastated the most vulnerable populations and communities—will never be the same.

The reworking of social events in the public sphere, alongside broader movements, to articulate a historical memory that accounts for the trauma and scars of death and grief still etched on many bodies is essential, impelling emancipatory struggles to defend the most basic, human, and dignified rights of our existence—health, education, food, housing, land protection, and knowledge.

But within a complex scenario of instability, alarming numbers of infected and deceased individuals, uncertainty, neglect, pain, and collapse, is art enough?

More than three decades before the onset of COVID-19, the Gran Fury collective (1988–1995) posed this very question in the context of the AIDS crisis in the United States, which began with the first documented case in 1981 and quickly evolved into a global epidemic.[1] Invited by The Kitchen, an independent experimental art and performance institution in New York, in 1988, to design the cover of the space's calendar, Gran Fury responded with a poster [img. 4] that included event dates as a mere detail. The poster featured the declaration that "With 42,000 Dead, Art Is Not Enough," and urged, in bold letters: "Take Collective Direct Action to End the AIDS Crisis." The statement can be read as a provocation for the art world. What does it mean to engage in direct action? What role do museums, cultural institutions, artists, critics, and curators play in the face of the alarming death tolls resulting from HIV infection? What does art have to do with it?

Gran Fury's solo exhibition, presented in 2024 at the Museu de Arte de São Paulo Assis Chateaubriand (MASP) and this accompanying publication, which both respond to the museum's curatorial framework of *Queer Histories*, borrows part of this declaration as the exhibition's

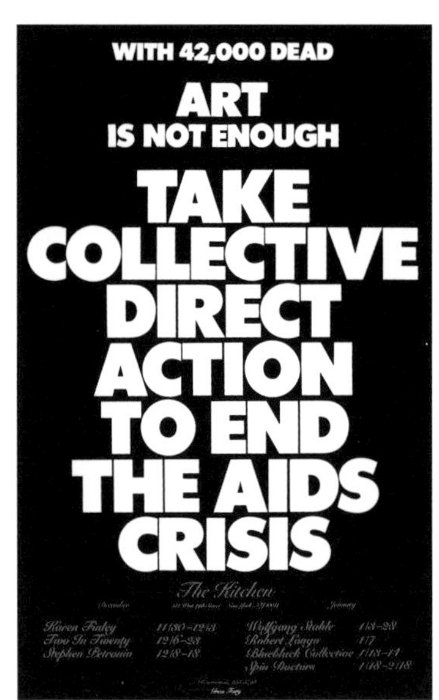

4

4
Gran Fury
Art Is Not Enough, 1988
Offset print on paper,
54.5 × 34.5 cm
Poster for a series of
events at The Kitchen,
New York, United States

title: *Art Is Not Enough*. The show aims to explore the boundaries and impact of the collective's activism through graphic design, as well as the concept of art more broadly as a strategic instrument within queer-led HIV/AIDS[2] activism movements, and histories of direct action in the social and political arena in a context of epidemic. It generates new ways of seeing, feeling, living, intervening, and transforming reality.

Gran Fury's work became a fundamental reference for artistic activism in the 1980s and 1990s. Notably, the notion of artistic activism is associated with "approaches to creating aesthetic forms and relationships that prioritize social action over the conventional pursuit of the autonomy of art"[3] and that do not rely on artistic institutions. Instead of merely depicting politics or social injustices,

> the activist artist can be distinguished by an unyielding focus on agitation and protests as an artistic medium. Typically, these practitioners operate collectively, working with other artists, but also in collaboration with "non-art" political activists and on occasion they do manage to bring about a degree of positive societal change.[4]

As Douglas Crimp (1944–2019) aptly noted, beyond just commemorating a form of cultural renaissance in the field of art, the movement of artistic activism played a pivotal role in fostering cultural practices that actively engaged "in the struggle against AIDS," stating, "We don't need to transcend the epidemic, we need to end it."[5] The history of the HIV/AIDS activism movement is one of permanence, a tale of the necessity for powerful images and marginalized groups born out of micropolitical, anti-authoritarian, and community actions that gradually gained momentum, support, exposure, discussion, space, and influence in the public sphere.

This exhibition provides an opportunity to revisit the not-so-distant past and examine the present, reflecting on how these movements have progressed, what has changed since then, and what still needs to be transformed, confronted, and resisted. One of Gran Fury's works embodies this spirit of confrontation during the HIV epidemic's most critical years, linking a militant past with the disputes of that era that continue to inspire contemporary LGBTQIA+ movements. For them, it was no longer sufficient to simply replicate "AIDS" as a concrete symbol of existence and presence, as the Canadian collective General Idea had done by proliferating the acronym AIDS in screen prints, paintings, and installations (*AIDS*, 1987) [img. 5], evoking Robert Indiana's (1928–2018) iconic letter arrangement in the painting *LOVE* (1970).

Gran Fury responded to General Idea's work by infusing it with a revolutionary perspective, employing an even more pertinent term for the moment: *RIOT* (1988) [img. 37]. Later, the painting was transformed into a sticker that evoked the insurgent memory of the Stonewall Riots that occurred twenty years before [img. 35].[6] Gran Fury believed that rebellion was necessary, injecting energy and hostility into activism to propel the movement forward, react, and confront the epidemic.

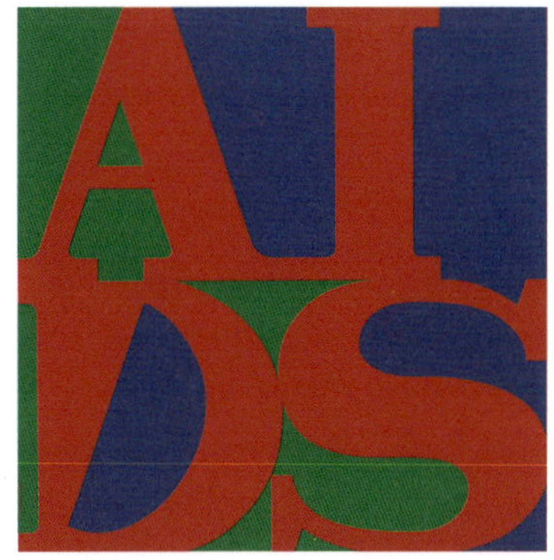

5

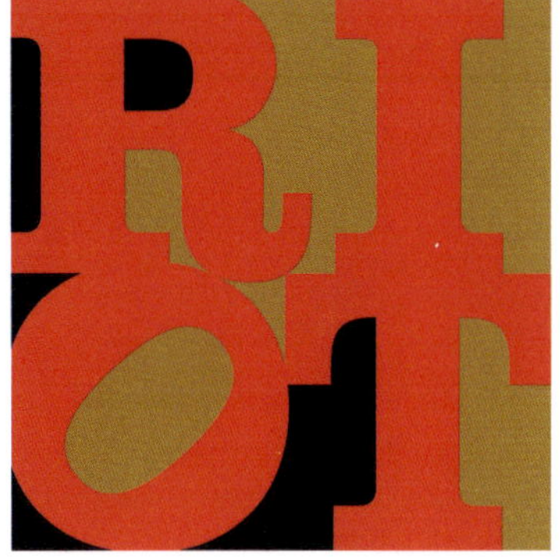

6

FROM SILENCE TO ACTION

The histories of Gran Fury and HIV/AIDS activism in the United States can be recounted through numerous personal and collective accounts. One of these tales begins with an anonymous poster. In 1987, the streets of New York were adorned with an image. Set against a black background, an equilateral pink triangle occupied the poster's center. Below it, a phrase inscribed in white and capitalized letters, using the Gill Sans Bold Extra Condensed font, conveyed the equation: *SILENCE = DEATH* [img. 7]. This triangle represented an activist reinterpretation of a well-known symbol from one of the darkest episodes of the twentieth century: a reference to the pink triangle that the Nazis stitched onto the garments that identified those deemed to be homosexuals imprisoned in their concentration camps. In contrast to the faded pink of the Nazi symbol, the triangle on the poster was printed in vibrant fuchsia. The poster drew a parallel between Nazism and the HIV epidemic as two historical moments of persecution and eradication of homosexuals, urging an intervention for their survival. A significant conceptual change in this image is the positioning of the vertices of the pink triangle. While the triangle used by the Nazis appeared to point downward, the triangle in this first, anonymous activist poster pointed upward. This simple graphic inversion, as Marcelo Expósito pointed out,

> transforms a symbol of stigmatization into a symbol of affirmation: the same type of reappropriation that movements based on identity politics have been using since the 1970s–80s to resignify the negative words and symbols that stigmatize certain individuals for our ethnic origins or sexuality (poofter, n****r, fag, dyke…), thus transforming them into labels that are positively adopted with the pride of a publicly—and tactically—declared identity.[7]

The proposal to create a poster that positively summoned the gay and lesbian community of New York to confront the government and the media's silence on the HIV/AIDS epidemic emerged as a collective and tactical response to grief. The group behind the poster's creation, established in 1986 and known as the Silence = Death Project, consisted of Avram Finkelstein, Brian Howard, Charles Kreloff, Chris Lione, Jorge Soccarás, and Oliver Johnston (1952–1990). Their collaboration encapsulated personal accounts of solitary and irrevocable loss. They witnessed the death of close companions and friends due to the opportunistic diseases affecting those living with HIV. Their devastation led them to create a consciousness-raising group aimed at discussing and sharing the anguish of survival and the often-isolating experience of grappling with the fear of eventually dying as a result of AIDS. As Finkelstein noted in a 1986 diary entry, "the closet," symbolizing the concealment of one's public acknowledgment of homosexuality, had turned into a "coffin."[8]

Finkelstein came up with the concept for *SILENCE = DEATH* by drawing inspiration from the political art of feminist activism and the civil rights movements, referencing a well-known poster by the Art Workers' Coalition (AWC), where the photograph depicting the My Lai massacre in

5
General Idea
AIDS, 1987
Three-colour poster
(red, green & blue),
68.5 × 68.5 cm
Art Metropole
Collection, gift
Jay A. Smith, 1999,
National Gallery of
Canada, Ottawa

6
Gran Fury
RIOT, 2019
Digital illustration,
10 × 10 cm

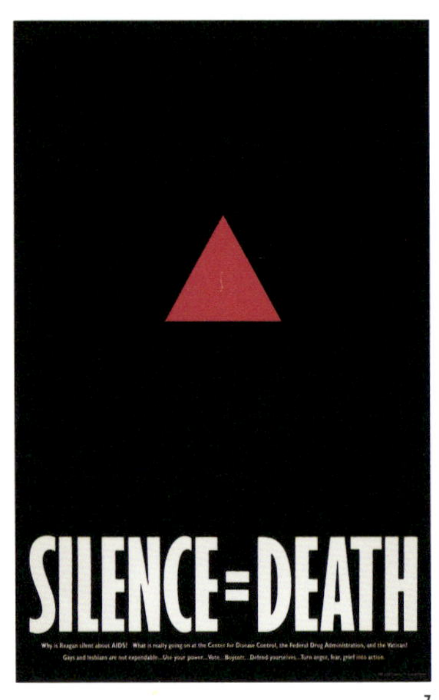

7

Vietnam was printed alongside the phrase "Q. And babies? A. And babies" [img. 8].[9] AWC and the Guerrilla Art Action Group took the posters to the Museum of Modern Art in New York, staging a protest in 1970 in front of *Guernica* (1937) to denounce the killings by US forces in Vietnam, using the photograph as a tool for criticism. Both the 1970 and 1987 posters were designed with concise text and impactful imagery to convey information through effective visual synthesis. The dominant black void in the *SILENCE = DEATH* poster symbolizes the lack of answers in the face of the epidemic. Why did Ronald Reagan (1911–2004) and the mainstream media remain silent about the HIV/AIDS crisis? Appearing during Reagan's second term in office, the poster was revealed during a new wave of conservatism that embroiled the arts and the press within a wave of culture war and calls for artist censorship.

The HIV epidemic led to a representation crisis for minority groups and democratic processes. In 1983, HIV was identified as a transmissible virus, with the Centers for Disease Control and Prevention (CDC) reporting that it was not spread through the air, casual contact, water, or food. Despite diagnoses in heterosexual patients, HIV transmission continued to be associated primarily with the homosexual community.[10] Access to public policies, information, and healthcare for people living with HIV was severely limited and, in some cases, denied. The acronym "AIDS" was rarely spoken of, and Reagan's first public mention of the acquired immunodeficiency syndrome (AIDS) did not occur until 1985, in response to reporters' inquiries. His first speech about AIDS did not come until 1987.[11] In response to Reagan's speech, the Silence = Death Project created the *AIDSGATE* poster (1987) [img. 123], framing the HIV epidemic as a political scandal by drawing parallels between the government's negligence to the Watergate case,[12] demanding urgent investigation. Activist artist Donald Moffett's poster, *He Kills Me* (1987) [img. 124], also portrayed the president as a genocidal figure.

More conservative factions condemned people living with HIV, perceiving the infection as a form of divine punishment. The church vehemently opposed the use of condoms and disposable clean needles as preventive measures. Estimates of the number of fatalities and infections, as well as strategies to contain the epidemic, were largely disregarded and overlooked by the government. The fatality count was rising exponentially. Fear, stigmatization, and biased or veiled discussions surrounding HIV transmission spurred community organizations to advocate for the rights of gays, lesbians, and those living with HIV/AIDS, leading to efforts to combat homophobia and intolerance. The phrase at the bottom of the *SILENCE = DEATH* poster called for a tactical shift: "turn anger, fear, grief into action."

Soon after *SILENCE = DEATH* appeared on the streets, a gathering took place on March 10, 1987, at the Lesbian and Gay Community Services Center (now the Lesbian, Gay, Bisexual & Transgender Community Center) in New York. Playwright and activist Larry Kramer (1935–2020) urged the audience to form a militant group. By that time, the United States had upwards of 32,000 cases of people living with HIV.[13] Two days later, ACT UP, an abbreviation for AIDS Coalition to Unleash Power [img. 9], was founded by approximately three hundred individuals, who together formed a decentralized organization. ACT UP operated based

16

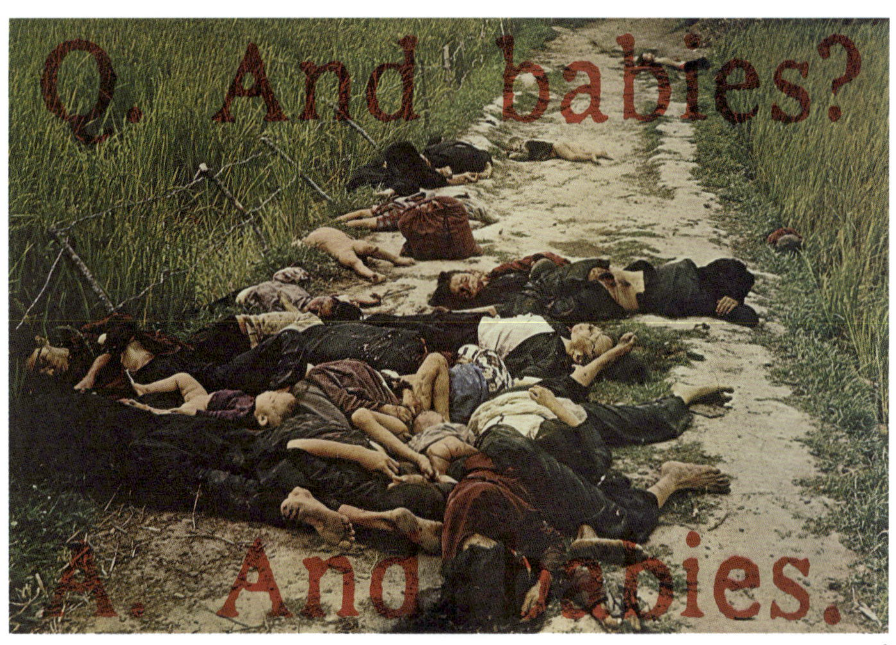

8

on principles of solidarity and mutual support, maintained a non-partisan stance, employed a cellular structure, and comprised various autonomous affinity groups, such as Wave 3, which played a significant role within the organization.[14] These groups collaborated on collective demonstrations and the execution of specific actions and projects using visual and performative strategies. Their objective was to draw critical attention to the US government's negligence in the spread of HIV, pressuring state agencies to develop public policies and provide free healthcare. ACT UP challenged the pharmaceutical industry and corporations profiting from the epidemic, while advocating for free and more accessible antiviral medications. The members of the Silence = Death Project attended the meeting where Kramer spoke and revealed themselves as the creators of the anonymous poster. They offered the poster to the audience, which swiftly adopted the image and the *SILENCE = DEATH* slogan as their emblem.

Since its inception, ACT UP has maintained *SILENCE = DEATH* as the official image of HIV/AIDS activism. This image has helped foster unity within the diversity of the coalition, serving as a direct and visual representation of ACT UP in the media and on the streets, and reinforcing its symbolic and political influence as a dynamic and highly organized group.[15] Prior to the advent of the internet and the widespread sharing of images on social networks, the pink triangle and equation of *SILENCE = DEATH* was organically disseminated by ACT UP on T-shirts, banners, stickers, and buttons, extending its reach beyond the activist community to diverse audiences and contexts. It appeared everywhere; donned by actors and actresses wearing T-shirts and buttons with the image in interviews and on TV, adorning the covers of punk band albums,[16] and featured prominently in artworks such as Keith Haring's (1958–1990) drawings [img. 12] and Group Material's *AIDS Timeline* (1989)—a multimedia installation that served as a real-time analysis of the HIV/AIDS epidemic in the United States, presented in a chronological timeline featuring a variety of images, posters, videos,

---

8
Irving Petlin, Jon Hendricks, Frazer Dougherty, Ronald L. Haeberle, Emilio Ambasz (Art Workers' Coalition)
Q. And babies?
A. And babies., 1970
Offset print on paper, 63.5 × 96.5 cm
Courtesy of the Estate of Irving Petlin (www.irvingpetlin.com) and The Museum of Modern Art, gift Benefit for Attica Defense Fund, New York, United States

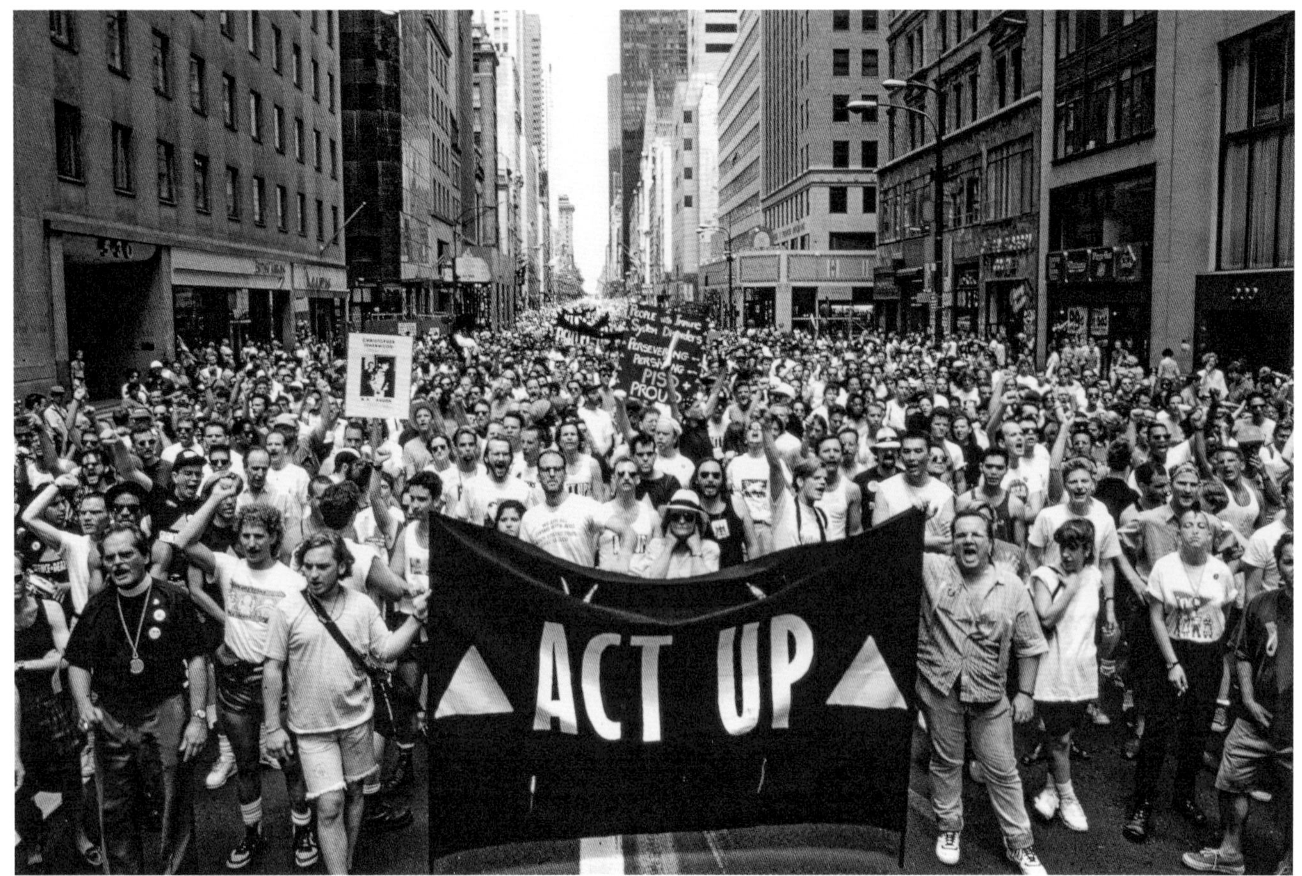

9

newspaper clippings, and objects [imgs. 10, 11]. Perhaps one of the most poignant displays of the iconic pink triangle occurred on the jacket of artist David Wojnarowicz (1954–1992) during an ACT UP-organized event in October 1988 in front of the Federal Food and Drug Administration (FDA) building, where the image was featured beneath the text: "IF I DIE OF AIDS—FORGET BURIAL—JUST DROP MY BODY ON THE STEPS OF THE FDA."[17]

ACT UP played a crucial historical role in advancing HIV-related issues in the United States. Recognizing that taking to the streets alone was not enough, the group actively worked to disseminate its image and message nationally and internationally through various media channels and by infiltrating centers of governmental, corporate, and institutional power. This process involved establishing connections with culturally and politically influential figures and employing strategies that involved both institution-building and antagonism, challenging the hegemonic power dynamics and being actively present within social relations,[18] akin to what we observe today in powerful movements such as Black Lives Matter. Within ACT UP's decentralized structure, a diverse array of visual artists, architects, filmmakers, designers, and cultural producers participated in the organization's weekly meetings in New York, held every Monday at The Lesbian and Gay Community Services Center. Several other artistic activism collectives emerged from within ACT UP, including Art Positive, Gang, DIVA TV (Damned Interfering Video Activists), House of Color, LAPIT (Lesbian Activists Producing Innovative Television), Little Elvis, and Testing the Limits. These groups engaged in the production of videos,

9
T. L. Litt
ACT UP at the New York City Pride, United States, March 1989
Collection of the artist, Medford, Massachusetts, United States

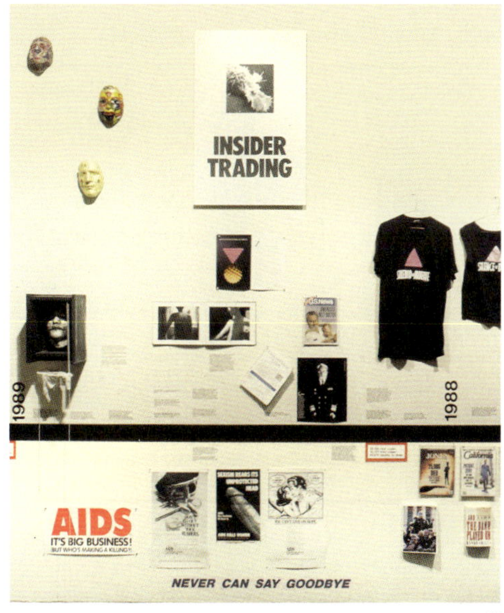

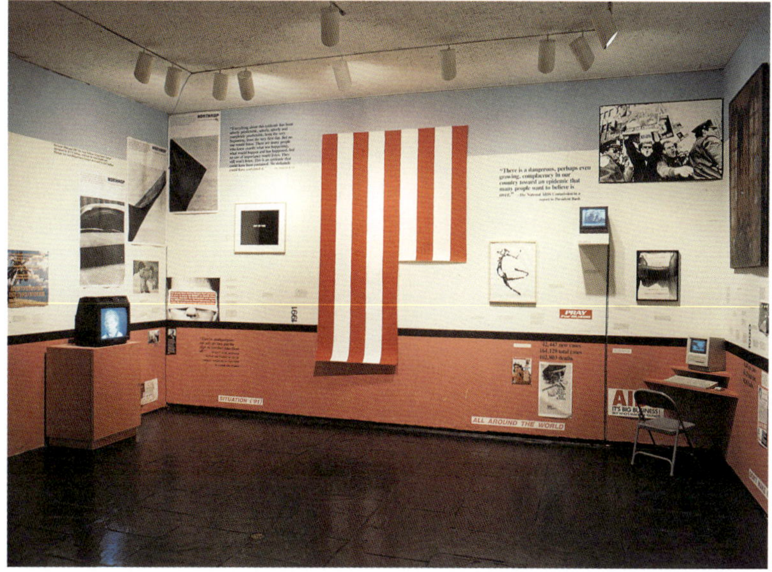

10   11

protest documentation, posters, banners, T-shirts, stickers, and billboards, autonomously occupying and intervening in the city, thus fostering a punk, do-it-yourself spirit of creating and making things. These activist artists were part of a generation that spent their twenties and thirties attending the funerals of partners and friends every week. They intimately cared for their loved ones until their final moments. People were dying quickly. Urgent action was needed; there was no time to waste. According to Chicago-based sociologist and ACT UP activist Deborah B. Gould:

> Through their emotion work, AIDS activists gave shape to the affective experience of the disjuncture, naming as outrage what might have been experienced more amorphously as a mixture of incredulity, disappointment, and frustration that the government and mainstream society could be so unaware and uncaring about life for queers amid the AIDS crisis.[19]

The emotional and mobilizing work of HIV/AIDS activism is often fueled by a collective anger that permeates, spreads, and reinforces the struggle within a shared space, where the crisis experienced as a personal ordeal by different individuals is collectively positioned as a potential public conflict.[20] Among those who attended the weekly ACT UP meetings, a group of individuals decided to engage in direct graphic action in urban spaces, aiming to bring about meaningful changes and a profound shift in the perception of the HIV epidemic. This effort included interventions in the processes of social subjectivation and advocacy for healthcare as a human right. Some of them had participated in an initiative proposed by an ACT UP committee to occupy the New Museum's outside windows upon the invitation of Bill Olander (1950–1989), the institution's senior curator and ACT UP member. Titled *Let the Record Show...* [imgs. 125, 126] (1987), the installation juxtaposed photographs from the Nuremberg Trials and silhouettes of "AIDS criminals" in the United States alongside their damning declarations, further expanding the analogy between Nazism and the epidemic. Subsequently, a group of activists began discussing the creation of

10
Group Material
AIDS Timeline, 1989
Installation view, University Art Museum, University of California, Berkeley, United States
Courtesy Group Material and Four Corners Books

11
Group Material
AIDS Timeline (New York, 1991)
Installation view, Whitney Museum of American Art, New York, United States
Courtesy Group Material and Four Corners Books

posters like *SILENCE = DEATH* for rapid dissemination throughout the city. They proposed adopting the name of the Plymouth sedan used by the New York Police Department to establish a collective dedicated to ACT UP, referred to by Douglas Crimp and Adam Rolston as "an unofficial propaganda ministry and guerrilla graphic designers."[21] The collective came to be known as Gran Fury—a name that evoked a sense of collective outrage.

ANGER IS AN ENERGY

Gran Fury was formed in January 1988, initially conceived as an open, fluid, and autonomous collective that welcomed ideas from various participants and proposals from ACT UP activists, before later choosing to operate from within a fixed internal membership. The group defined itself as "a band of individuals united in anger and committed to exploiting the power of art to end the AIDS crisis"—a statement featured on their first poster [img. 33]. Rejecting the label of artists or individual creators and aiming to avoid traditional art spaces, the group declined invitations to participate in institutional exhibitions and have their work confined to museums and galleries.

However, in 1990, Gran Fury agreed to participate in the Venice Biennale, as part of a section titled *Aperto* dedicated to the work of emerging artists. At the event, they boldly criticized the Catholic Church's stance on HIV-related topics, which opposed the use of condoms and clean needles as effective means of preventing HIV transmission.

In Venice, Gran Fury initially proposed to display a banner in the city, but the Biennale's artistic direction rejected the idea. Consequently, the collective showcased the installation *The Pope and The Penis* (1990) at the exhibition. It consisted of two billboards: a triptych featuring a photograph of Pope John Paul II with an accompanying text criticizing the Catholic Church's stance on HIV education and prevention [img. 90], and a second panel displaying a photo of an erect penis accompanied by uppercase text advocating for the use of condoms by men as a preventive method [img. 91].

The panels caused a stir, with the Biennale director of visual arts, Giovanni Carandente (1920–2009) threatening to resign if they were exhibited, arguing they were not artworks. The panels were temporarily held at airport customs. Carandente went as far as to claim that HIV and "AIDS did not exist in Italy, that it was a New York problem"[22] during a conversation with Gran Fury. The members responded by holding a press conference, garnering support from other artists at the exhibition. The action nearly led to the arrest and charging of Gran Fury members by Italian authorities for blasphemy. The press dubbed the incident "the Biennale scandal," juxtaposing Gran Fury's images with reports on the number of people living with HIV in Italy [img. 98]. Eventually, the panels were authorized for display after a thorough analysis by a magistrate specially called in by the director, who confirmed that the content did not constitute blasphemy. Carandente did not resign.

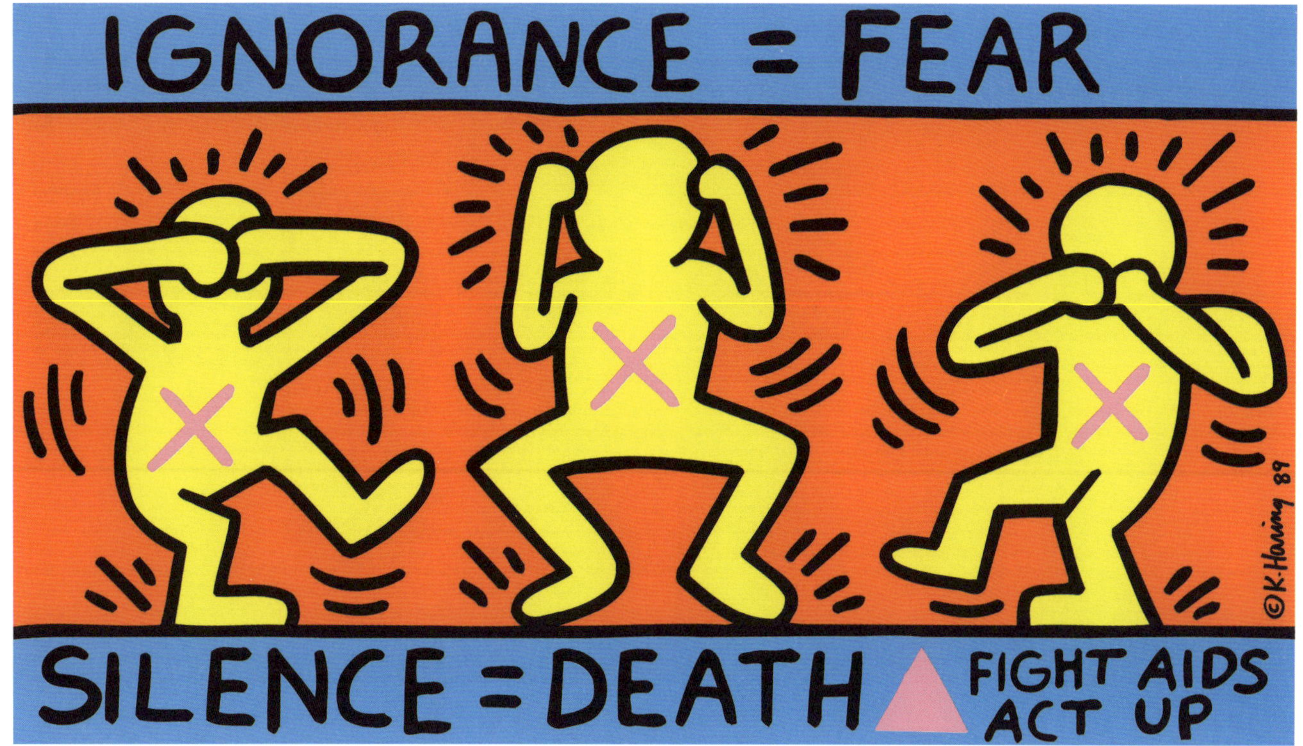

Throughout much of its existence, Gran Fury consisted of Avram Finkelstein, Donald Moffett, John Lindell, Loring McAlpin, Mark Simpson (1950–1996), Marlene McCarty, Michael Nesline, Richard Elovich, Robert Vazquez-Pacheco, and Tom Kalin. Additionally, other ACT UP activists, including Amy Heard, Anthony Viti, Don Ruddy, John Keenan, Leonard Bruno, Mark Harrington, Neil Spisak, Richard Deagle, Steven Barker, Terry Riley, and Todd Haynes, participated in actions alongside the group.

A guiding principle from which this MASP exhibition borrows its name, "direct action" emerges as a pivotal concept for understanding ACT UP's demonstrations and its collaborations with Gran Fury as methods of agitation and protest. Direct action can be broadly defined as collective actions devised to change established conditions through various means, whether violent or non-violent. It stands as a fundamental component of a counter-history of opposition and social activism, emphasizing the rejection of traditional forms of political representation. As activists in Latin America would say, direct action is like *poner el cuerpo* [putting the body in], which means to organize, block, occupy. It signifies the call to "embody your feelings," and "perform your politics."[23] These practices are based on the principles of anarchism, encompassing proactive forms of action that value self-organization without representatives, as well as reactive forms of action that emphasize the power to resist, occupy, and use all available means to enact change.[24]

Among the array of Gran Fury's projects, I have chosen to focus on graphic actions featured in this exhibition that highlight the radical occupation of public spaces and the media, often in collaboration with ACT UP. Gran Fury is a crucial part of the history of activism that uses communication tools for political purposes and challenges mainstream

12
Keith Haring
Ignorance = Fear /
Silence = Death, 1989
Offset print on paper,
61 × 109.5 cm
© Keith Haring
Foundation, New York,
United States

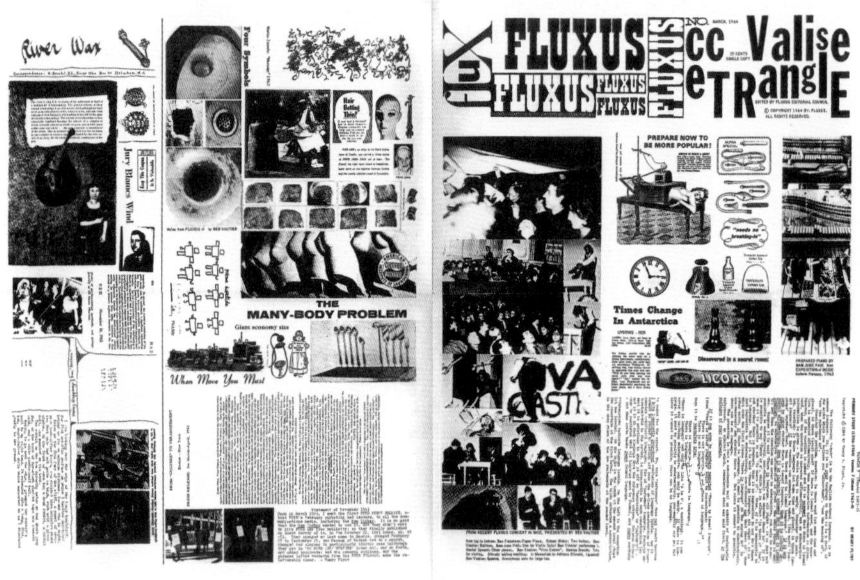

13

images and discourses, paving the way for what was later recognized in the 1990s as "tactical media" among activist art collectives and social movements.[25]

There is an extensive and detailed research available on this subject and its contemporary developments. However, it is worth considering the notion proposed by theorists and activists that tactical media empowers marginalized or excluded groups and individuals to produce a new form of dissident aesthetics by engaging in temporary and inclusive initiatives, using diverse modes of cultural dissemination and semiotic intervention in public spaces, and employing different visual mediums.

As an exercise of *détournement*, a tactic advocated by the Situationist International and propagated in the 1960s for appropriating pre-existing elements and subverting them within a revolutionary framework,[26] Gran Fury produced thousands of counterfeit copies of a four-page newspaper. The prints featured texts from ACT UP along with their own comprehensive news coverage and graphics, presenting some truths about power and emulating the visual style of *The New York Times*' front page. Finkelstein had the idea of making a fake newspaper after visiting a Fluxus exhibition at the MoMA library which encouraged visitors to "make your own newspaper and hand it out on a street corner." "So, we talked about it and decided that the AIDS reporting wasn't sufficient, it didn't address the issues, so we would write our own newspaper."[27] *The New York Crimes* [imgs. 70–72] rectified the misrepresentation and misinformation prevalent in *The New York Times*' reporting on the disease, including the claim that control over the spread of HIV had already been established. This information was published on June 29, 1989, in an editorial by *The New York Times* titled "Why Make AIDS Worse Than It Is?" Gran Fury and ACT UP activists retaliated by taking to the streets of New York during the night, opening the delivery boxes of *The New York Times*, removing the original copies, and replacing the front pages with the counterfeit newspaper. In the morning, readers were met with a more accurate and realistic coverage of the HIV epidemic.

13
FLUXUS
*Fluxus cc Valise
eTRanglE
(Fluxus newspaper #3)*,
March 1964
Offset print on paper,
58 × 87 cm

22

In a project commissioned by the Art Against AIDS: On the Road[28] initiative, titled *Kissing Doesn't Kill* (1989–90) [imgs. 77–81], Gran Fury strategically repurposed the corporate multiculturalism of the renowned campaigns produced by the Italian clothing company Benetton. By subverting its visual and semantic codes and its seductive imagery, the project showcased photographs of three interracial couples kissing. These couples were formed by members of Gran Fury and ACT UP (Robert Vazquez-Pacheco and Heidi Dorow, Mark Simpson and Jose Fidelino, Julie Tolentino and Lola Flash)—in an attempt to also highlight the diversity within ACT UP, beyond the prevalent presence of white gay men in their thirties.[29]

The *Kissing Doesn't Kill* poster was displayed on the sides of buses and in subway stations in San Francisco, Chicago, New York, and Washington D.C. In Chicago, the installation was defaced and covered in black paint.[30] The anti-advertisement strategy of *Kissing Doesn't Kill* achieved what gained popularity in the 1990s as "culture jamming," involving the subversion, manipulation, or symbolic disruption of advertising messages in both the media and urban spaces. This practice updated the Situationist concept of *détournement* for a new generation of semiotic activists eager for rebellion. The poster's image, also replicated in short videos produced by Gran Fury [imgs. 82–86], did not promote any product. Instead, it challenged the (still) prevalent misconception at that time that kissing was a risky behavior and saliva was a potential transmission fluid for HIV. Essentially, the kiss was perceived by ACT UP as a political gesture of affection, pride, pleasure, and trust.

In their creative process, Gran Fury often skillfully appropriated hegemonic discourses, as seen in their use of George H. W. Bush's (1924–2018) presidential campaign tagline, "Read My Lips: no new taxes," for the poster titled *Read My Lips* (1988) [img. 48]. The poster, created for a kiss-in organized by ACT UP, featured a photograph of two sailors kissing—another version of the poster featured a couple of women kissing [img. 50]. The text on the poster was designed in a style reminiscent of Barbara Kruger's work [img. 113]. The collective frequently repurposed and revisited images from earlier works in new projects, such as the image of an erect penis featured in the *Sexism Rears Its Unprotected Head* poster [img. 53] (1988), which was later revisited in *The Pope and The Penis*.

Tactical media projects such as *New York Crimes*, *Read My Lips* and *Kissing Doesn't Kill*, according to Alessandra Renzi, "are expressions of dissent that rely on artistic practices and do-it-yourself (DIY) media created from readily available, relatively cheap communication and technology."[31] Renzi's definition further underscores what Loring McAlpin highlights about Gran Fury's graphic interventions as influential tactical media actions that were fast, instantaneous, and achievable with whatever resources are available: "If anyone is angry enough and has a Xerox machine and has five or six friends who feel the same way, you'd be surprised how far you can go."[32] Gran Fury embraced McAlpin's suggested blueprint for creating an effective form of anti-capitalist graphic activism. On March 24, 1988, ACT UP organized a second demonstration on Wall Street, protesting

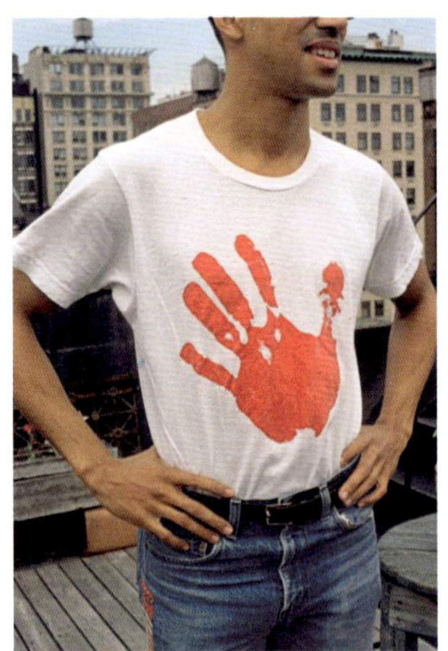

14, 15
Gran Fury
*The Government Has
Blood on Its Hands*, 1988
Silkscreen on fabric

the pharmaceutical industry's monopoly and the exorbitant price of the only FDA-approved HIV treatment drug at the time, AZT (Azidothymidine), manufactured by a single company, Burroughs Wellcome. The cost of AZT treatment amounted to approximately $10,000 (USD) per patient annually, with no generic version of the drug available, and its effectiveness was limited. Gran Fury reproduced hundreds of $10, $50, and $100 counterfeits, virtually identical to the genuine bills, save for the collective's name replacing the official Treasury signature. The reverse side of the notes featured a green background with messages such as: "FUCK YOUR PROFITEERING. People are dying while you play business"; "WHY ARE WE HERE? Because your malignant neglect KILLS"; and "White Heterosexual Men Can't Get AIDS... DON'T BANK ON IT" [imgs. 41–47].

During the Wall Street demonstration, ACT UP activists organized themselves into different groups, or "waves" to disrupt traffic.[33] Some participants sat on the ground to block the flow, while another wave, which included members of Gran Fury, handed out the forged bills to people stuck in traffic and affixed them to car windshields.[34]

A total of 111 demonstrators were arrested but later released. The following year, on September 14, 1989, an affinity group known as Power Tools, comprised of seven ACT UP activists, returned to Wall Street. Disguised in suits and equipped with fake IDs, they infiltrated the stock exchange building, concealing posters and cameras beneath their clothes. Positioned on a mezzanine on the trading floor, the protesters threw the counterfeit bills at the traders, temporarily halting the day's trading. This intervention calls to mind a similar event in the countercultural history of artistic activism, which occurred on August 24, 1967, when the Yippies (Youth International Party) led by Abbie Hoffman (1936–1989), staged an action at the New York Stock Exchange to disrupt US politics and capture the attention of national newspapers. From the balcony, the Yippies showered the trading floor with 200 dollars in $1 bills. For Hoffman, it was an impromptu situation akin to guerrilla theater, unfolding without a script and using all available means. Distracted, the traders abandoned their work, scrambling to collect the money as it fell, which significantly impacted stock quotes. The press covered the incident as the day's major event.[35] The ACT UP action on Wall Street not only revived but also introduced an updated political perspective to the countercultural legacy of guerrilla theater groups like the San Francisco Mime Troupe, the Diggers, and the Yippies from the 1960s. These groups protested the Vietnam War and the government, capturing significant public and media interest. "[Throwing the fake bills during trading] was like throwing a wrench in the gears of capitalism,"[36] remarked Tom Kalin. Following the event, Burroughs Wellcome decreased the price of AZT by 20%.[37]

The "bloody hand" drawing emerged across New York City, marking walls, street signs, subway cars, and mailboxes [img. 63]. Created with red ink and rubber gloves, the symbol was propagated throughout the city by members of Gran Fury and ACT UP. It was as powerful and precise as the *SILENCE = DEATH* pink triangle, accusing the genocidal government that spread misinformation about the number

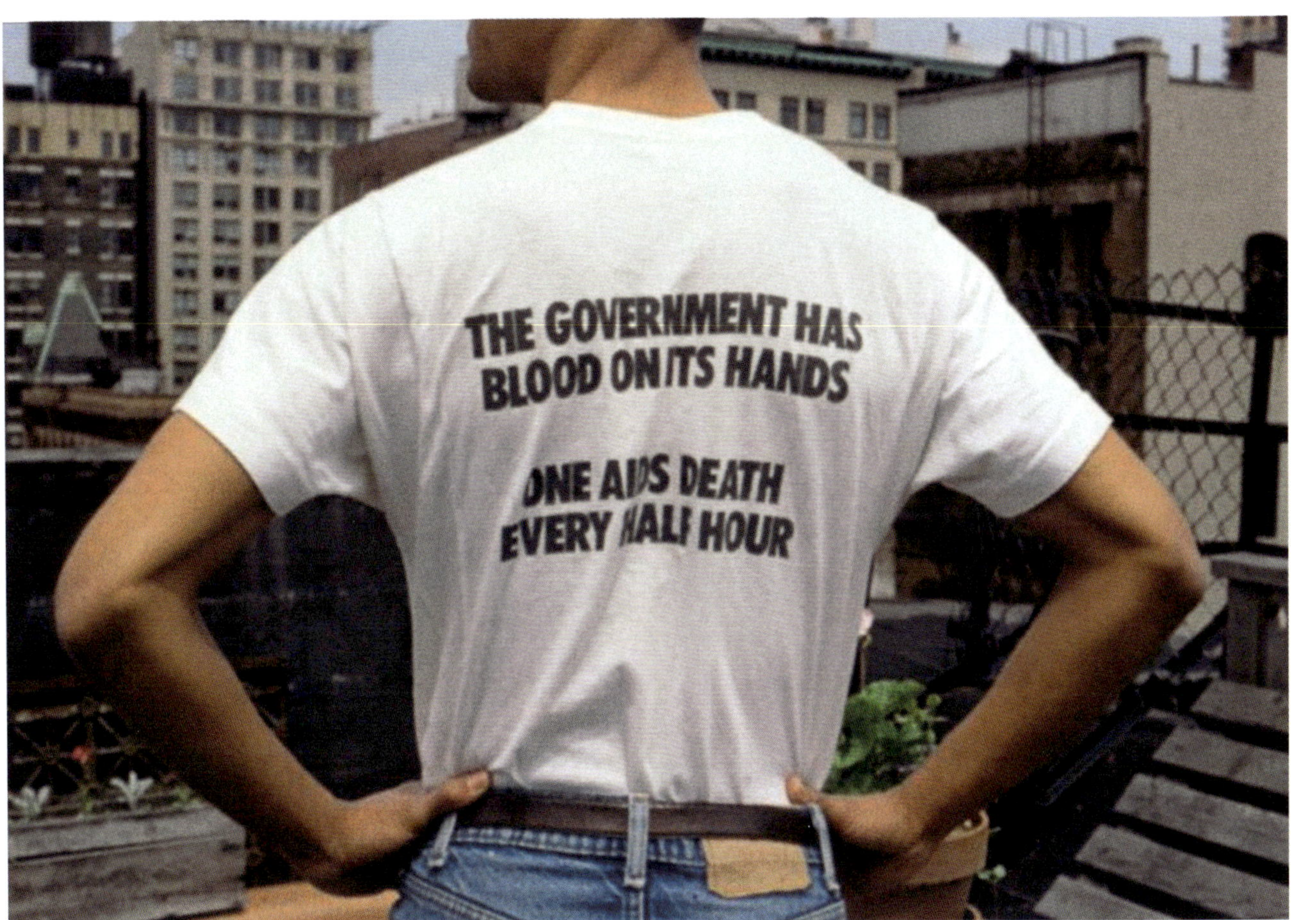

15

of HIV-positive individuals of having blood on its hands. The New York City health commissioner, Stephen Joseph, claimed that only 50,000 New Yorkers were living with HIV, significantly underreporting the actual number of 250,000, and showed reluctance to invest in basic healthcare during the epidemic for those living with the virus. The hand symbol was used to target Joseph and was printed on posters [img. 65] and later adapted and incorporated into the widely attended demonstration on October 11, 1988, known as Seize Control of the FDA, organized by a coalition of ACT UP activists from around the country called AIDS Coalition to Network, Organize, and Win (ACT NOW). The statement accompanying the red hand—featured on stickers, buttons, and T-shirts— gained national attention: "The Government Has Blood on Its Hands. One AIDS Death Every Half Hour" [img. 61]. Succinct phrasing paired with bold imagery: this is what Gran Fury relied on to create synoptic, fast, and effective visual devices as tools for public denunciation.

In *Art Is Not Enough*, there are pamphlets and photographs showcasing some of the demonstrations organized by ACT UP, including images from the Seize Control of the FDA protest. A striking image taken by photographer and ACT UP member Tom McKitterick [img. 16] depicts activists holding signs that read *The Government Has Blood on Its Hands*, *AIDSGATE*, and *SILENCE = DEATH*, while others engage in a die-in, a protest tactic used by ACT UP where demonstrators lie on the ground, reminiscent of a direct action tradition promoted by the antinuclear movement in the early 1980s.[38] The stretched bodies, outlined in white chalk, along with the image of the bloody hand brandished on posters

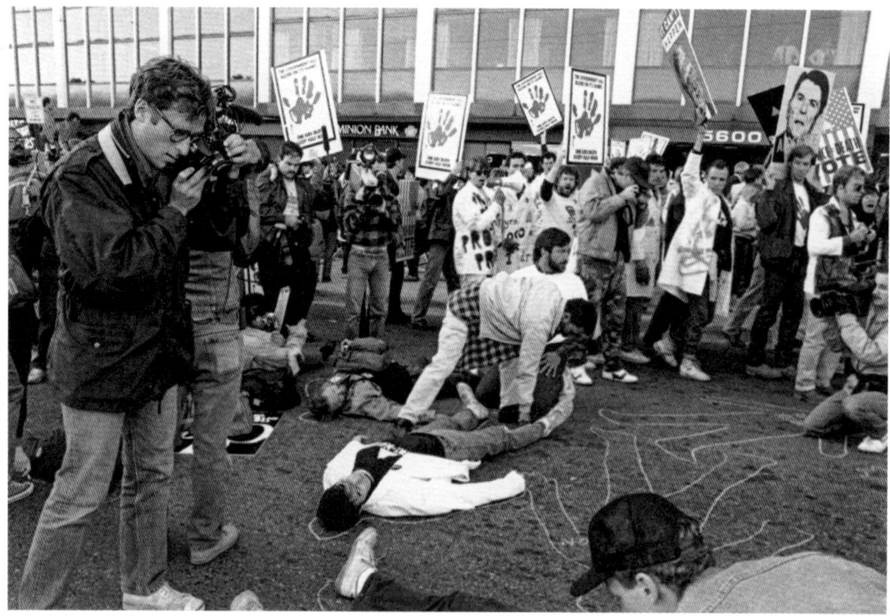

16

held by the protesters, serve as a testament to collective memory and the experience of loss. The image from the FDA event is visually and politically linked to another context of social and political struggle for remembrance and justice, namely the Third March of Resistance held in Argentina in September 1983 by the Mothers of Plaza de Mayo and other human rights organizations. During this event, a graphic action known as *Siluetazo* invited the relatives of those who disappeared during the military dictatorship in Argentina to *poner el cuerpo* [put the body in] the ground, as they lay on paper and drew life-size silhouettes, symbolizing the 30,000 missing [imgs. 17, 18].[39]

The *Siluetazo* reiterated the mothers' plea for their sons and daughters to reappear alive. Silhouettes, die-ins, pink triangles, and bloody hands reaffirm the presence of absence and are part of a collection of expressive forms that are open and available for use; they are biopolitical matrices that challenge the power of the state, which dictates who can live and who must die. Today, we are also experiencing these processes of pandemic brutality and state violence, termed by Achille Mbembe as "necropolitics."[40]

Seize Control of the FDA garnered significant national attention and press coverage, propelling ACT UP activists into negotiations with government agencies, involving them in discussions and decisions concerning treatments and the approval of new medications. In Rockville, Maryland, 1,500 activists marched to the FDA headquarters, demanding an expedited review and approval of new HIV treatment drugs, mandatory public campaigns on HIV treatment, and the assurance of essential care for all groups affected by HIV, including women, non-white individuals, children, hemophiliacs, people who use drugs, gay men, and low-income individuals in clinical trials. Gran Fury's poster *All People with AIDS Are Innocent* (1988) [img. 55] addresses the issues of ensuring care and respect for all people living with HIV, effectively challenging the prevailing moral narrative that some individuals deserved AIDS diagnosis more than others and the unjust hierarchy that stigmatized certain vulnerable groups such as gays, sex

16
Tom McKitterick
Seize Control of the FDA, action at the Food and Drug Administration Headquarters in Rockville, Maryland, United States, Oct. 11, 1988
Black & white analog photograph, photographic print on paper
Collection of the artist, New York, United States

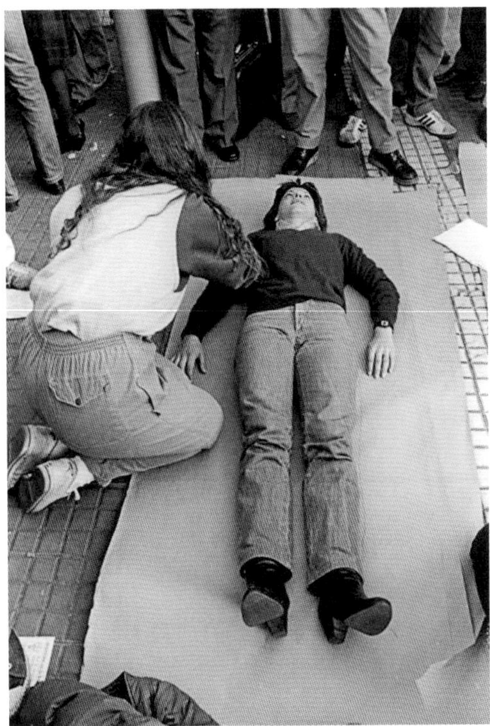

17

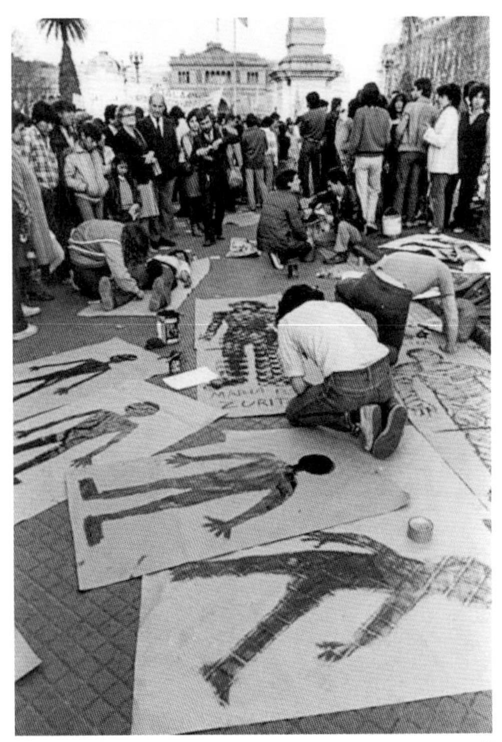

18

workers, and people who use drugs as guilty of transmitting the virus, while portraying others like children, hemophiliacs, and heterosexuals living with HIV as innocent. Gran Fury's message urged society to treat all people living with HIV equally, advocating for the right to receive equal care and assistance.

Gran Fury disbanded in 1995, before witnessing the collective impact of scientific and governmental progress on HIV care. The collective bid farewell with an essay published in a 1995 handbill, *Good Luck, Miss You*.[41] On it, Gran Fury reflects on the action they took and puts us a question: did activism adapt and accept the permanency of AIDS? To Marlene McCarty, Gran Fury "[...] fought for people have to say the words AIDS on television, people have to see a same-sex couple kissing."[42] After that, the topic of AIDS was addressed in another way, says McCarty: "The demographics of AIDS changed, the pharmaceuticals of AIDS changed. This is not what Gran Fury does. We decided it was time to stop."[43]

Its members continued to pursue their careers as artists, graphic designers, teachers, art directors, and filmmakers, and many maintained their involvement in HIV/AIDS activism within ACT UP and other organizations. The legacy of Gran Fury remains accessible, with their entire graphic body of work in the public domain, and their archives housed at the New York Public Library in New York City.[44] Their activist and provocative graphics continue to serve as a resource for future generations, with the ongoing incidence of HIV demanding continued attention. In creating this publication, we draw inspiration from the extensive work of Jim Hubbard and Sarah Schulman, who compiled an archive of 187 interviews with ACT UP activists and accounts from Gran Fury for the "ACT UP Oral History Project."[45] We have preserved the spirit of these testimonies and included two interviews with Gran Fury conducted at different times, highlighting the collective voice of the group.

17
Eduardo Gil
Silueteando I.
El Siluetazo, Buenos Aires, Argentina, Sept. 21–22, 1983
Black & white analog photograph, photographic print on paper, Collection of the artist, Buenos Aires, Argentina

18
Eduardo Gil
María Zurita.
El Siluetazo, Buenos Aires, Argentina, Sept. 21–22, 1983
Black & white analog photograph, photographic print on paper
Collection of the artist, Buenos Aires, Argentina

Acknowledging that "art is not enough" does not signify a complete renunciation of art in favor of activism, nor does it imply that artistic practices are ineffective in driving social change. On the contrary, Gran Fury's assertion suggests that simply creating art *about* a crisis is no longer enough. Rather, periods of challenge present revolutionary moments for radical imagination and the confrontation of hegemonic and oppressive systems. Their graphic work encourages us to recognize the urgent need for artists, activists, and cultural agents to unite as a solid political force towards direct action that aligns with protest movements.

Translated from the Portuguese by Adriana Francisco

ANDRÉ MESQUITA, curator, MASP

NOTES

1 Due to space constraints, I will not address the topic of the HIV epidemic and HIV/AIDS activism in Brazil in this essay. However, it is worth noting that during the 1980s, amidst the country's process of democratization, various groups were formed by activists and healthcare professionals to mobilize sectors of society in demanding better treatment conditions and awareness efforts, as well as the establishment of public policies to address HIV and AIDS properly at the municipal and state levels. Notable among these efforts were the establishment of non-governmental organizations such as the Grupo de Apoio à Prevenção da aids [Support Group for AIDS Prevention] (GAPA), founded in São Paulo in 1985, and the Associação Brasileira Interdisciplinar de aids [Brazilian Interdisciplinary AIDS Association] (ABIA), founded in Rio de Janeiro in 1986. For further information on this topic, please refer to the text by anthropologist Richard Parker, "AIDS Crisis and Brazil," 2020. Available at https://oxfordre.com/latinamericanhistory/display/10.1093/acrefore/9780199366439.001.0001/acrefore-9780199366439-e-865. Retrieved Oct. 5, 2023.

2 According to the Centers for Disease Control and Prevention, HIV attacks the body's immune system. If left untreated, it can lead to AIDS (Acquired Immunodeficiency Syndrome). It's important to remember that not all people living with HIV are diagnosed with AIDS. According to the United Nations Programme on HIV/AIDS (UNAIDS) Terminology Guidelines, "AIDS describes a syndrome of opportunistic infections and diseases that can develop as immunosuppression deepens along the continuum of HIV infection (from acute infection to death). [...] [AIDS] is an epidemiological definition based on clinical signs and symptoms. It is caused by HIV, the human immunodeficiency virus. HIV destroys the body's ability to fight off infection and disease, which can ultimately lead to death. Antiretroviral therapy slows down replication of the virus and can greatly extend life and enhance quality of life, but it does not eliminate HIV infection." See the UNAIDS guidelines at https://www.unaids.org/sites/default/files/media_asset/2015_terminology_guidelines_en.pdf. Retrieved Nov. 11, 2023.

3 Ana Vidal, Jaime Vindel and Marcelo Expósito, "Activismo artístico." In: Red Conceptualismos del Sur, *Perder la forma humana: Una imagen sísmica de los años ochenta en América Latina* (Madrid: Museo Nacional Centro de Arte Reina Sofía, 2012), 43.

4 Gregory Sholette, *The Art of Activism and the Activism of Art* (London: Lund Humphries, 2022), 12.

5 Douglas Crimp, "Aids: Cultural Analysis/Cultural Activism." In: *Aids: Cultural Analysis/ Cultural Activism*. (Cambridge, Massachusetts: MIT Press, 1988), 3.

6 Refers to an uprising that took place on June 28, 1969, in reaction to a police raid at the Stonewall Inn, a gathering place for the often-persecuted LGBTQIA+ community in New York City.

7 Marcelo Expósito, *Walter Benjamin, productivist* (Bilbao: consonni, 2013), 19. According to Avram Finkelstein, "turning [the triangle] upside down was another gesture of reinvention that was inadvertent but worked out in our favor. Chris [Lione], who had recently visited Dachau, was certain it pointed upward. Oliver volunteered to 'research' it and later confirmed the direction without actually checking it. We discovered it was incorrect after the printing, but decided it answered one of our concerns, superimposing an activist stance by borrowing the 'power' intonations of the upward triangle in New Age spirituality, further skewing its relationship to the death camps." Avram Finkelstein, "SILENCE = DEATH: How an Iconic Protest Poster Came into Being." December 1, 2017. Available at https://lithub.com/silence-death-how-an-iconic-protest-poster-came-into-being. Retrieved Oct. 2, 2023.

8 Quoted in Jack Lowery, *It Was Vulgar and It Was Beautiful: How AIDS Activists Used Art to Fight a Pandemic* (New York: Bold Type Books, 2022), 19.

9 On March 16, 1968, U.S. Army soldiers executed hundreds of civilians, mostly women and children, in the village of My Lai. The massacre is considered the largest civilian massacre to take place in the Vietnam War. The photograph used by the Art Workers' Coalition was taken by Ronald L. Haeberle, a photographer for the U.S. Army.

10 Tommaso Speretta, *Rebels Rebel: AIDS, Art and Activism in New York, 1979–1989* (Ghent: MER. Paper Kunsthalle, 2014), 113.

11 Ibid., 115.

12 The Watergate case, the greatest political corruption scandal in the

United States, took place in June 1972 and led to the resignation of then-president Richard Nixon (1913–1994).

13 Jack Lowery, 2022, op. cit., 52.

14 Wave 3 was an affinity group formed by ACT UP activists engaged in direct action tactics at demonstrations. The group dedicated itself to working on training meetings and discussions about HIV/AIDS research and treatment.

15 Ibid., 57.

16 Such as the back cover of the *Dark Days Coming* (1989) album by the band Three, where *Silence = Death* appears below in the bottom left corner. Available at https://www.discogs.com/master/9764-3-Dark-Days-Coming. Retrieved Oct. 2, 2023.

17 David Wojnarowicz died in 1992. ACT UP organized a political funeral in his honor. On this occasion, protesters carried a banner through the streets with the phrase "David Wojnarowicz died of AIDS due to government neglect." On October 13, 1996, an action was carried out by ACT UP in Washington D.C., and Wojnarowicz's ashes were scattered on the lawn of the White House.

18 Marcelo Expósito, 2013, op. cit., 19.

19 Deborah B. Gould, *Moving Politics: Emotion and ACT UP's Fight against AIDS* (Illinois: The University of Chicago Press, 2009), 235.

20 Marcelo Expósito, 2013, op. cit., 19.

21 Douglas Crimp and Adam Rolston, *AIDS Demo Graphics* (Seattle: Bay Press, 1990), 16.

22 Jack Lowery, 2022, op. cit., 239.

23 John Jordan, "El arte de la necesidad: la imaginación subversiva del movimiento de oposición a las carreteras y Reclaim the Streets." In: Paloma Blanco, Jesús Carrillo, Jordi Claramonte and Marcelo Expósito (eds.), *Modos de hacer: arte crítico, esfera pública y acción directa* (Salamanca: Ediciones Universidad de Salamanca, 2001), 372.

24 Cindy Milstein, *Anarchism and its Aspirations* (Oakland: AK Press, 2010), 70.

25 See David Garcia and Geert Lovink, "The ABC of Tactical Media," 1997. Available at http://www.nettime.org/Lists-Archives/nettime-l-9705/msg00096.html. Retrieved Oct. 2, 2023.

26 See Guy Debord and Gil J. Wolman, "A User's Guide to Détournement," 1956. Available at https://www.cddc.vt.edu/sionline/presitu/usersguide.html. Retrieved Oct. 2, 2023.

27 Gran Fury, *Gran Fury: Read My Lips* (New York: 80WSE Press, 2011), 25.

28 Art Against AIDS: On the Road was a public art project carried out between 1989 and 1990, which included the commissioned production of panels installed on the sides and backs of buses with information and reflections on HIV/AIDS. The project was curated by Ann Philbin for amfAR (American Foundation for AIDS Research) and involved the participation of around 30 artists, with their panels on public transport in the cities of San Francisco, Chicago, New York, and Washington D.C.

29 Jack Lowery, 2022, op. cit., 207.

30 As reported by Tom Kalin in his presentation for the seminar Histories of Sexuality at MASP: "*Kissing Doesn't Kill* was slated to appear on buses and subways in Chicago but Alderman Robert Shaw argued that the Chicago Transit Authority (CTA) should not promote a 'particular lifestyle,' and that the posters were directed at children for the purposes of 'recruitment.' In June 1990, the Illinois Senate barred the CTA from displaying 'any poster showing or simulating physical contact or embrace in a homosexual or lesbian context where persons under twenty-one could view it.' The ACLU protested, stating that it was unconstitutional. Concurrently, the Chicago Gay Pride parade marched with our banner and a 'kiss-in' was organized outside the CTA. The Illinois House of Representatives defeated the bill and in August 1990, *Kissing Doesn't Kill* was belatedly installed." Tom Kalin,

"O pornógrafo moral." In: Adriano Pedrosa and André Mesquita (eds.), *Histórias da sexualidade: antologia* (São Paulo: Museu de Arte de São Paulo Assis Cheateaubriand, 2017), 360.

31 Alessandra Renzi, "The Space of Tactical Media." In: Megan Boler (ed.), *Digital Media and Democracy. Tactics in Hard Times* (Cambridge: MIT Press, 2008), 71.

32 Quoted in Mark Dery, "Culture Jamming: Hacking, Slashing, and Sniping in the Empire of Signs," 1993. Available at https://www.markdery.com/books/culture-jamming-hacking-slashing-and-sniping-in-the-empire-of-signs-2. Retrieved Oct. 2, 2023.

33 Jack Lowery, 2022, op. cit., 112.

34 Ibid.

35 André Mesquita, *Insurgências poéticas: arte ativista e ação coletiva* (São Paulo: Annablume/FAPESP, 2011), 80.

36 Gran Fury, 2011, op. cit., 24.

37 Jack Lowery, 2022, op. cit., 3.

38 Yates McKee, *Strike Art. Contemporary Art and the Post-Occupy Condition* (New York: Verso, 2016), 42.

39 I am particularly grateful to Marcelo Expósito for initially pointing out the connections between ACT UP, Gran Fury, and *Siluetazo* in his essay *Walter Benjamin, productivist*. Marcelo Expósito, 2013, op. cit.

40 See Achille Mbembe, *Necropolitics* (Durham: Duke University Press, 2019).

41 See *Good Luck, Miss You*, in this publication.

42 Emily Colucci, "Is Art Enough? Gran Fury in Perspective," 2012. Available at https://hyperallergic.com/46881/gran-fury-read-my-lips-80-wse-nyu/. Retrieved Oct. 18, 2023.

43 Ibid.

44 Access the archive here: https://digitalcollections.nypl.org/collections/gran-fury-collection#/?tab=navigation. Retrieved Oct. 2, 2023.

45 All accounts can be accessed here: https://actuporalhistory.org. Retrieved Oct. 2, 2023.

MOVEMENTS IN MOVEMENT

———

Marcos Martins and Vinícius Franco

CURRENT FURY

Political activism and artistic avant-garde movements tend, over time, to lose their initial vitality. Exhibitions such as *Gran Fury: Art is not enough* at Museu de Arte de São Paulo Assis Chateaubriand (MASP) invite us to undertake the vital task of asserting their relevance and recovering their rebellion for present-day movements. We must also remember that the museum's free span has been the starting point for countless rallies and political demonstrations since the building's founding in 1968. It is, therefore, with this legacy of local demonstrations in mind that we look back at activist movements within Brazil in conversation with those that occurred in the United States during the 1980s and 1990s.

From the outset, the slow response of the Ronald Reagan (1911–2004) administration to the HIV/AIDS public health crisis in the 1980s—then a matter of life or death—and the movement that responded to that administration's inaction is echoed in the still-vivid memory of how Jair Bolsonaro's administration handled the COVID-19 pandemic in Brazil. The insidious fables and false truths with which Bolsonaro's administration attempted to justify its inaction, and the movement that formed as a reaction to that negligence is a story that resonates with the struggle of Gran Fury against the United States government's public policies during the HIV/AIDS epidemic. Going back a little further, we might also recall the furious Jornadas de Junho [June Journeys] of 2013, and the activism of the groups Mídia NINJA and Coletivo Projetação. Gran Fury's activism may also remind us of the political action of Brazilian artists from the 1960s–1970s during the military dictatorship that dominated the country from 1964 to 1985, as can be seen in works by artists such as Antonio Manuel and Cildo Meireles. In tracing the history and legacies of these movements and their similarities, we reach across space and time to recover fertile material for today's activists, tilling the soil for the seeds of movements to come.

CIRCLING

A major challenge for AIDS Coalition to Unleash Power (ACT UP)—the organization from which Gran Fury originated—was speed. Reacting, without delay, to the approval of retrograde laws, appalling statements by politicians, or the publication of biased news in the media implied the rapid preparation of demonstrations and their respective graphic materials. For Douglas Crimp (1944–2019), ACT UP's strategy was distinguished by its

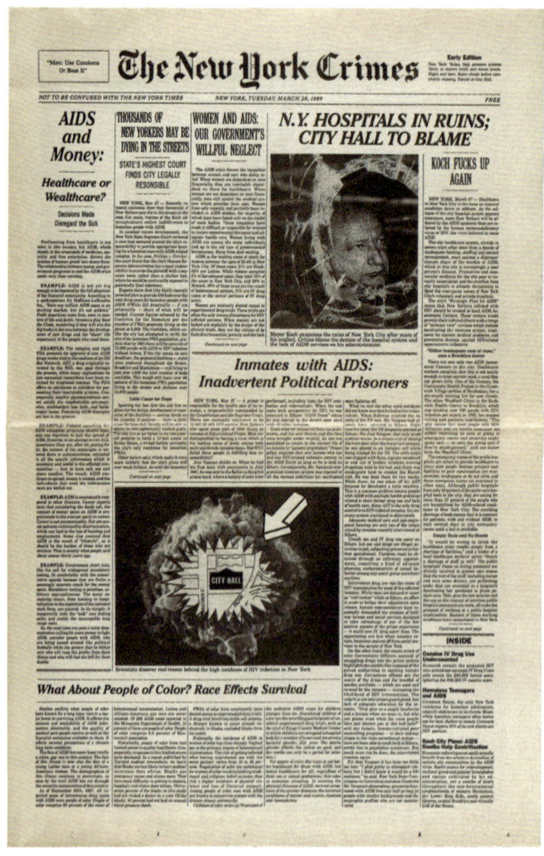

adept utilization of mechanical print reproduction technologies in order to respond quickly to shifts in the political discourse around the HIV/AIDS crisis.[1] Posters that were wheatpasted on the walls of New York, and later in Chicago, San Francisco, and other cities, multiplied the reach of their protest messages.

Gran Fury inherited and greatly expanded this use of mechanical printing methods, infiltrating graphic productions into the everyday urban flow. The work *The New York Crimes* (1989) [img. 19] is exemplary. Synchronized with a demonstration in March 1989 organized by ACT UP, members of Gran Fury designed a doctored version of the cover of *The New York Times*. This piece contained "more accurate AIDS reporting […] than has appeared cumulatively in nine years of the *Times*."[2] Gran Fury member Avram Finkelstein remembers that the collective was subdivided into smaller groups that "followed the trucks in the middle of the night […] with rolls of quarters" to open the newspaper's vending machines. While one member acted as a lookout, others removed the front page of that day's newspapers and replaced them with the doctored ones. "For a couple of rolls of quarters, we seized the voice of authority in New York," recalls Finkelstein.[3]

In Brazil, the artist Antonio Manuel also had to be strategic to create the series *Clandestinas* [Clandestines] (1973), a work that bears several similarities to *The New York Crimes*. In this series, the artist infiltrated the printing press of *O Dia*, a large-circulation newspaper in Rio de Janeiro, to change the printing matrices. Manuel was assisted by his accomplice, Ivan Chagas Freitas (1946–1984), son of the newspaper owner (and governor of Rio de Janeiro) Antônio de Pádua Chagas Freitas (1914–1991), who upon discovering the transgression, interrupted it.

19
Gran Fury
The New York Crimes,
1989
ACT UP; Target City
Hall Demonstration,
United States
Offset print on
newsprint, 58 × 38 cm

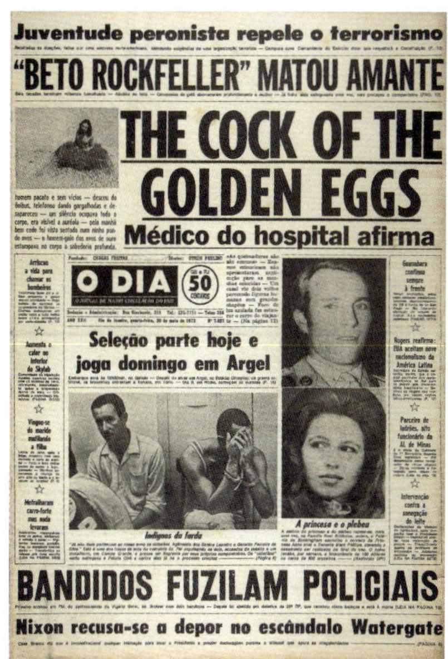

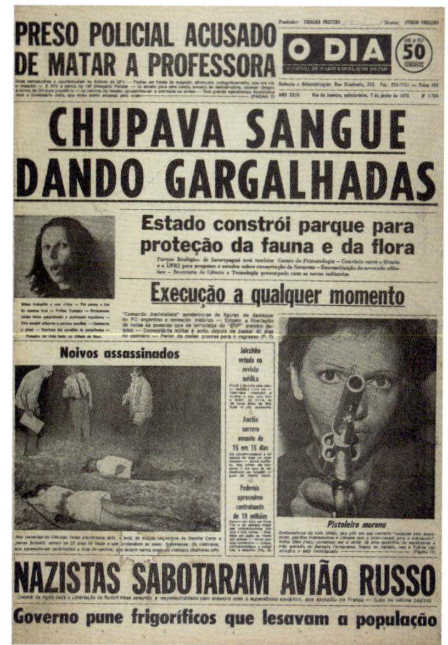

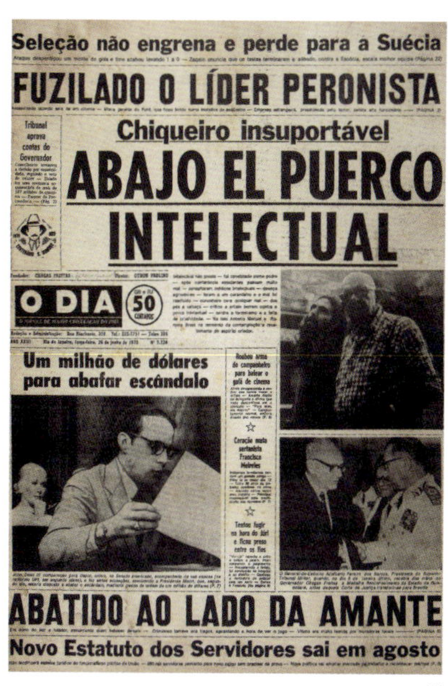

20   21   22

While Freitas was able to run *Clandestinas*, Manuel managed to change some of the headlines and front page photos for titles and texts with different subjects. For example, "The Cock of the Golden Eggs" [img. 20] and "Chupava sangue dando gargalhadas" [Sucked blood while laughing] [img. 21] emulate the typical sensationalism of the news cycle. His headline interventions also introduced blunt criticism (although not entirely explicit) of the complicity between the media and the Brazilian dictatorship, as in the headline "Chiqueiro insuportável/Abajo el puerco intelectual" [Unbearable pigsty/Down with the intellectual pig] printed on the same page that featured a photo of the newspaper owner handing over a medal to a general [img. 22].

It is true that these works by Antonio Manuel are more linked to the artist's poetics, and serve as a broader criticism of the art and political systems, diverging from Gran Fury's instrumentalization of graphic matter for a specific cause. In the *Clandestinas* series, Manuel intended to subvert and question the power of an institutionalized means of communication, while also attacking the art medium itself:

> When I created *Clandestinas*, I wanted […] to react to the political system, to the aesthetic system, taking the work to the streets, outside of official institutions […]. I did this by "piggybacking" on the newspaper and, in some way, distorting its real content.[4]

However, it is not difficult to associate, mutatis mutandis, Antonio Manuel's performance in the oppressive context of the military dictatorship with the work of the US collective. This means highlighting that, in both cases, the artists take on the untouchable structures of mass media by coopting their information dissemination circuit and occupying, for a moment, their "voice of authority." Communication media, besides being vehicles for propagating protest messages aimed at a larger audience, become a target themselves.

The series *Inserções em circuitos ideológicos* [Insertions into Ideological Circuits] (1970–76) [imgs. 23, 24], by Cildo Meireles, divided into two projects, *Coca-Cola* and *Cédula* [Banknote], reveals similar

20–22
Antonio Manuel
Clandestinas
[Clandestines], 1973
Offset print on paper,
55.5 × 37.5 cm
Collection of the artist,
Rio de Janeiro, Brazil

33

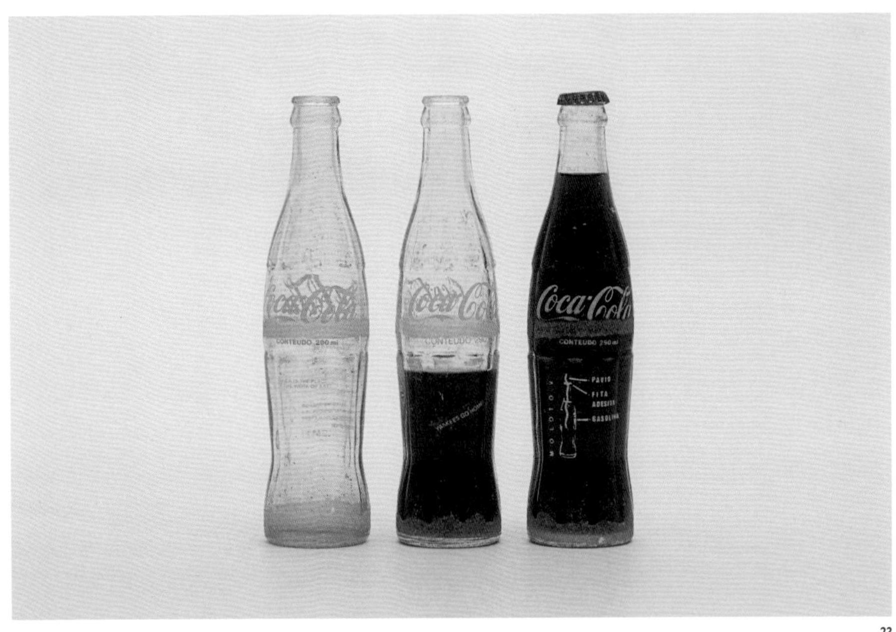

23

strategies and effects. In the first project, started in 1970, Meireles applied glazed paint decals to Coca-Cola bottles, which were then put back in circulation with messages such as "Yankees go home"; a definition of the project itself: "to register information and critical opinions on bottles and return them to circulation"; or even instructions on how to make a Molotov cocktail-type bomb. In *Cédula*, Meireles stamped the question "Quem matou Herzog?" [Who killed Herzog?], in reference to the murder of journalist Vladimir Herzog (1937–1975) disguised as a suicide that occurred in a room at the Department of Information Operations — Internal Defense Operations Center (DOI-CODI).

Meireles defined the work as follows:

1) there are certain circulation mechanisms (circuits) in society;
2) these circuits evidently convey the producer's ideology, but at the same time are capable of receiving insertions in their circulation;
3) this happens whenever people trigger them.[5]

The artist's interferences are made within exchange "circuits" that already exist in the capitalist system. His work uses these channels both to send subversive messages and to denounce the ideological nature of everyday objects. There is also an evident reconsideration of the traditional art object, which gives way to an action that becomes more relevant than the product: "we were no longer working with metaphors (representations) of situations, but with the situation itself, real."[6] In *Cédula*, the banknotes and the circuit formed by their circulation were real, and the artist's action took place, therefore, on a real object.

Meanwhile, in Gran Fury's work *Wall Street Money* (1988) [imgs. 25, 26], the banknotes they printed for their performance were photocopies of $10, $50, and $100 bills: they were evidently fake. While the "message" in Cildo Meireles' *Cédula* was stamped directly on real banknotes, Gran Fury's was printed on the back of their counterfeit bills, in bold typography, on a flat green background. It was possible to read, for example: "FUCK YOUR PROFITEERING. People are dying while you play business."

23
Cildo Meireles
Inserções em circuitos ideológicos: Projeto Coca-Cola [Insertions into Ideological Circuits: Coca-Cola Project], 1970
Coca-cola bottles, transfer with glazed paint, 24.5 × 5.5 × 2.5 cm (each)
Courtesy of the artist, Rio de Janeiro, Brazil

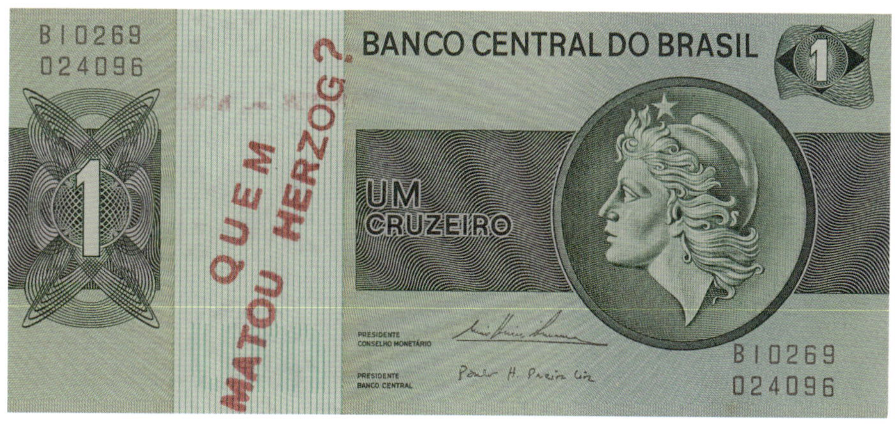

24

Instead of circulating as money, they were performatively dumped into the New York Stock Exchange, disrupting brokerage and attracting widespread media attention.[7] At first, this difference concerning the authenticity of these two currencies seems to drive the works apart; however, within the register of signification, the reception of the familiar image of the banknote of both works is consistent, bringing them closer together. Both rely on the recognition of the unchanged sign of (true or false) banknotes.

This condition of possibility brings Gran Fury's work closer to that of Cildo Meireles and Antonio Manuel. Despite the many differences between them, from the audience's point of view, the intended effect is quite similar: capturing an unsuspecting audience by surprise, through an encounter with a commonly used consumer good that carries a message that subverts expectations. These works are based on the premise that it is important to be familiar with the "normal" state of the medium in order to be surprised by the transgression, whether that be advertising, the layout of a newspaper, a Coca-Cola bottle, or currency notes. In this sense, they belong to a time when it was still possible to distinguish, within the "normalcy" of a given system, that which had been tampered with, which draws attention and generates surprise.

ATTENTION

Historically, visual expressions of counterculture sought to shock common sense, challenging conventional aesthetic norms. A genealogy of this subversion can be traced from Dadaism at the beginning of the twentieth century, through the psychedelia of the 1960s, to punk in the 1970s.[8] From the 1980s onwards, graphic subversion turned to advertising aesthetics. Collectives like Guerrilla Girls, Adbusters, and Gran Fury appropriated the predominant language in posters and advertisements to disseminate a counter-hegemonic discourse. During this period, mass communication was still strongly linked to the "one-to-many" model, with large media corporations controlling the parameters of what could and could not circulate. Against this power, the dispute over the advertising space language to promote a progressive political agenda has become a radical and effective tactic.

The emergence of the internet brought optimism, given the possibility that a new type of media and communication could escape centralization

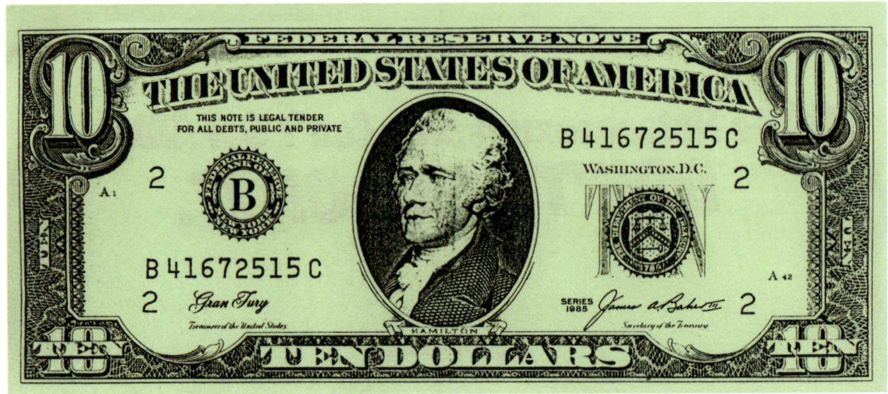

25

26

and subservience to corporate interests. However, what was observed after its popularization was exactly the opposite: new corporations quickly emerged and surrounded what was supposed to be a large digital public square with invisible fences. The advent of new forms of control and manipulation on social media has frustrated the positive expectations that drove the dreams of digital activists. They have subjected globalized communication to algorithmic logic, which has resulted in the extreme commodification of our online and offline habits. Social media forms the new terrain where the battle for attention on the internet is fought.

Loring McAlpin, a member of Gran Fury, comments that one of the group's objectives was precisely "to fight for attention as hard as Coca-Cola fights for attention."[9] Years after the collective was formed, attention was further consolidated as the main commodity of late capitalism.[10] The business model of social media that took over the web in the 2010s is summed up by the now famous saying: "if you are not paying for the product, then you are the product." The fight for attention on the internet involves keeping users (the new name for consumers) online for as long as possible, exposing them to advertisements published there. This exposure is automated by the behavior of people who, when interacting with a variety of content and users, indicate what they want to see and consume. In the new virtual "public" squares, we find advertising spaces that replace billboards and posters: "pop-ups," "bumpers," and "ads" are new names for old practices.

In this context, subverting a system in Gran Fury's way would be equivalent to, for example, hacking YouTube to display footage of a protest before a video. However, this hypothetical operation would not reach the core of the system, given that under digital capitalism

25, 26
Gran Fury
*Wall Street Money
(10 dollar bill)*, 1988
ACT UP; Wall Street
Demonstration, New
York, United States
Photocopy on paper,
9 × 21.5 cm

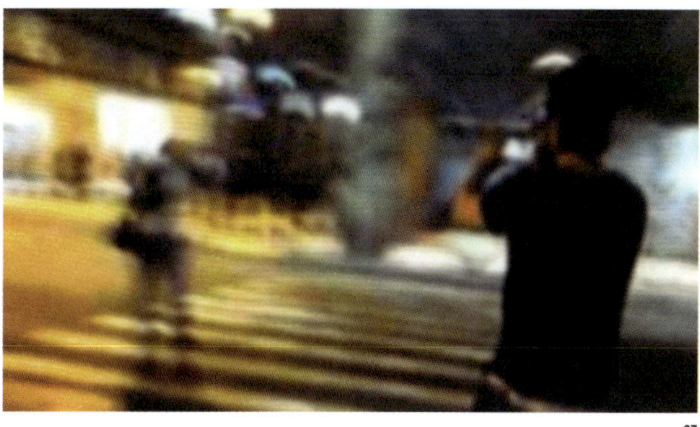
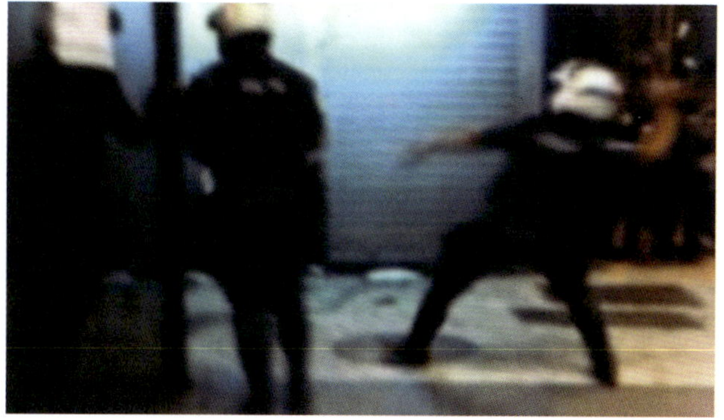

the content users publish is also advertising. The photo of a kitten, the recommendation of a new cosmetic product, the criticism of a political party: all are marketing of one kind or another. This scenario opens room for other possibilities of action.

Around the world, several movements have sought to use the internet as a tool for activism. In Brazil, collectives such as Mídia NINJA (an acronym in Portuguese for "Independent Narratives, Journalism, and Action") and Projetação were part of the Jornadas de Junho—a series of demonstrations that took over the country's streets in 2013, whose participants initially demanded a reduction in public transportation fares, and later expanded to new agendas following its viralization on the internet.

Just like Gran Fury, Mídia NINJA and Projetação competed for attention in a field already dominated by advertising. However, since advertising is no longer the exclusive privilege of advertisers, but is also present in amateur productions, this guerrilla warfare went beyond the realm of graphic language to establish itself in the field of content production. The challenge is no longer one of subverting established forms: how can we hack a newspaper when we ourselves already "are" the newspaper? What has always been—and continues to be—in dispute is people's attention.

Mídia NINJA [imgs. 27, 28] gained prominence precisely because it managed to capture attention by broadcasting live on the internet during the Jornadas de Junho. These broadcasts circulated on networks such as Twitter (now X) and Facebook and managed to compete with the mainstream media for the narrative about what was happening in the demonstrations. Thanks to videos filmed by the "ninjas," the country found itself amid a huge debate about the legitimacy of police actions and the black bloc tactic of attacking symbols of capitalism and public order, such as bank branches and street furniture. Thanks to the group's work, scenes of police violence, actions by undercover agents, and deliberate incrimination of innocent people became public. This confrontation, achieved with the use of mainstream media (in the case of Gran Fury, advertising; in the case of Mídia NINJA, social media) connects these phenomena over time.

However, June 2013 did not just take journalists to the streets; artists also sought to contribute to the fight for mobility and greater rights that shook the country. One of the most popular was the collective Projetação [img. 29], which used projectors to emit messages on walls and building facades. As with Gran Fury's, Projetação's performance reflects the

27, 28
Mídia NINJA
Frames of Mídia NINJA
live stream on July 11th,
2013, São Paulo, Brazil

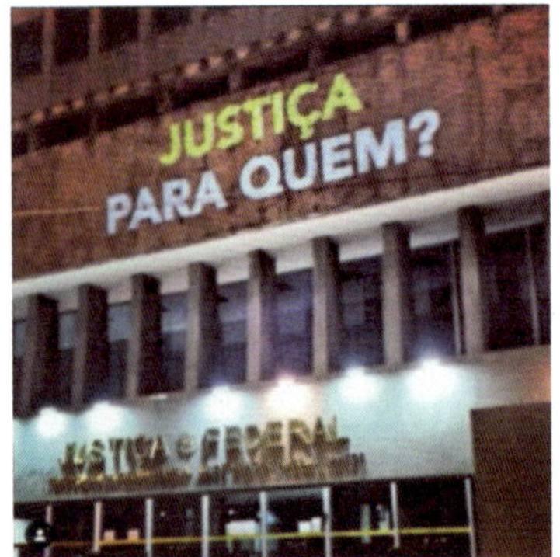

29

restlessness of artists led into the heat of street protest. A point of great similarity between the two collectives is that Projetação's visual language, despite not explicitly exploring an advertising aesthetic, is marked by the consistent use of stylized typography and image, typical of graphic design. On the other hand, like Cildo Meireles, Projetação chooses unforeseen spaces for their advertising: any building with good visibility would work. Furthermore, a significant difference is the fact that their projections are much more ephemeral than posters, flyers, or the sides of buses.

By observing the three collectives, and considering their respective historical contexts, we note that the main trait connecting Gran Fury, NINJA, and Projetação is their explicit, collective desire to compete with the official media in the search for attention, whether through the cooptation of established spaces or by opening new lines of communication within these same spaces.

MOVEMENT

From the origin of their name and logo—"stolen" from the name for a vehicle used by the New York City Police Department—to their advertisements installed on the sides of buses that mimicked the graphic style of Benetton advertisements, Gran Fury's activities have always been marked by both the displacement of the visual vocabularies of marketing and ad agencies and the production and distribution of images through mass media in the 1980s and 1990s. The production of Antonio Manuel and Cildo Meireles also operated with the intention to move their messages along pre-established channels. The newspaper inserts from the *Clandestinas* series were intended to enter the urban circulatory system to "piggyback" on the newspaper's reach. Cildo Meireles' stamped banknotes were conceived out of "the need to create a circulation system."[11] Mídia NINJA also circulated images as a result of the movement of activists' bodies, who followed the protests in real time. The Projetação collective made their projected image travel from a personal computer to the walls of buildings, in huge enlargements.

The movement of images is, therefore, an aspect that unites Gran Fury's tactics with the Brazilian examples of protest mentioned above. The Bolsonaro and Trump administrations liked to repress any movement other than that of their supporters. Largely elected, as we know, by mechanisms of viralization on social media, and going on to exercise their power amidst the isolation and immobility brought about by the COVID-19 pandemic, they seemed to convince us during their time in office that their paralyzing power was unbeatable.

The possibility of seeing Gran Fury's work today in the spirit of Brazilian protest movements in recent years encourages us to hope that today's activists can learn from successful movements like those in years past which took advantage of the prevailing modes of communication to deliver their messages, and that learning this history will inspire political action for the present moment. However, any such action will need to seek the wisdom to understand—just as Gran Fury did in its own historical context—contemporary forms of power, engendered in the circulation of texts, images, and videos, that today travel through the virtual space at

29
Projetação
Justiça para quem? [Justice for Whom?], projected on May 10, 2014, Rio de Janeiro, Brazil

30
Gran Fury
Kissing Doesn't Kill (ver. 1), billboard on bus, 1989-90
Four color bus poster, 76 × 355.5 cm
Commissioned work for the project Art Against AIDS: On the Road, San Francisco, United States

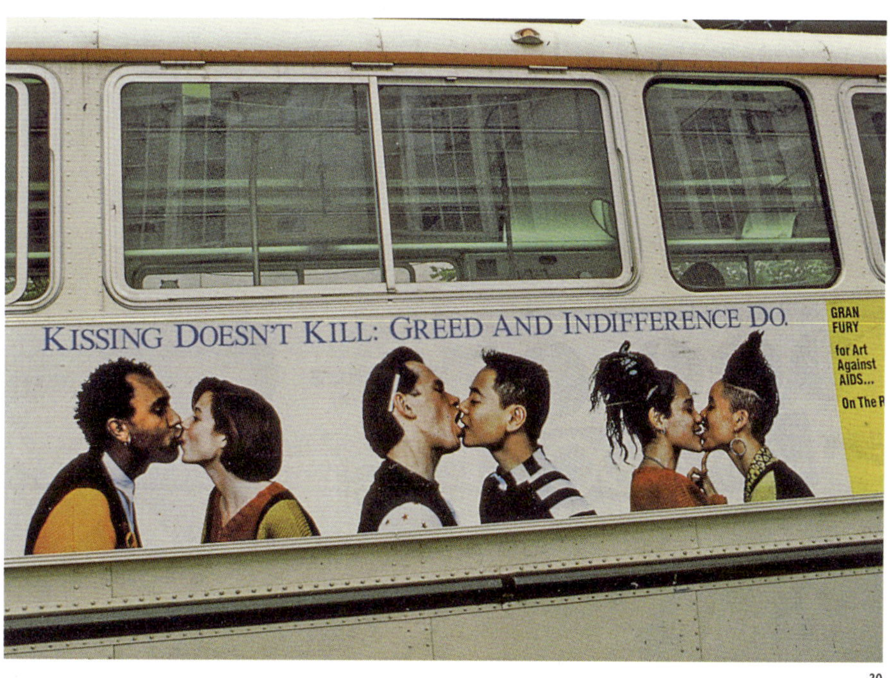

30

an infinitely greater speed than buses, newspaper editions, or consumer products. The Gran Fury exhibition at MASP provokes us to maintain a permanent reflection: what can movements achieve in a context where people today, instead of just consuming, are ourselves becoming consumer products and vehicles for political manipulation?

Translated from Portuguese by Lívia Prado Martins

MARCOS MARTINS is an interaction graphic designer, video artist and teacher at the Escola Superior de Desenho Industrial (ESDI) of the Universidade Estadual do Rio de Janeiro (UERJ).

VINÍCIUS FRANCO holds a Master's Degree in design from the Escola Superior de Desenho Industrial (ESDI) of the Universidade Estadual do Rio de Janeiro (UERJ) and is the design coordinator at the Globo platform of design and postgraduate education.

NOTES

1 Douglas Crimp and Adam Rolston, *AIDS Demo Graphics* (Seattle: Bay Press, 1990), 22.

2 Ibid., 95.

3 Gran Fury and Michael Cohen, *Gran Fury: Read My Lips* (New York: 80WSE Press, 2011), 25.

4 Antonio Manuel, *Exercício experimental da clandestinidade*. Nov. 24, 2015. Available at https://select.art.br/exercicio-experimental-da-cladestinidade/. Retrieved Oct. 3, 2023.

5 Cildo Meireles, "Inserções em circuitos ideológicos." In: André Mesquita, Charles Esche, and Will Bradley (eds.), *Arte e ativismo* (São Paulo: Museu de Arte de São Paulo Assis Chateaubriand/Afterall, 2021), 179.

6 Ibid.

7 Gran Fury and M. Cohen, 2011, op. cit., 22–25.

8 Madeleine Morley, "The Battle over the Visual Language of Counterculture, from Dada to the Digital Age." *Document Journal*, Dec. 29, 2020. Available at https://www.documentjournal.com/2020/12/aesthetics-of-counterculture-design/. Retrieved Dec. 14, 2023.

9 Richard Meyer, *Outlaw Representation: Censorship & Homosexuality in Twentieth Century American Art* (Oxford: Oxford University Press, 2002), 236.

10 Jonathan Crary, *24/7: Late Capitalism and the Ends of Sleep* (New York/London: Verso Books, 2013).

11 Cildo Meireles, 2021, op. cit., 178.

GOOD LUCK, MISS YOU

Gran Fury

Text reprinted from the *Good Luck, Miss You* handbill, 1995.
Created for *Temporarily Possessed: The Semi-Permanent Collection*
exhibition held at the New Museum of Contemporary Art, New York.

Life at the end of every century is typified by fear and anxiety. Apocalypse theories abound; nationalism and xenophobia encourage isolation. Urban violence, economic decline and AIDS have contributed to a reactionary environment where progressive thought is anathema.

The circumstances surrounding AIDS activism have radically changed since its beginning in 1986. Both the Executive Branch and the Congress have changed hands. America is in "decline." Communism is "dead." Internationally, politics have moved further to the right, and the citizenry of the United States has become more insular.

The lesbian and gay community has also changed. Embattled, fragmented and burned out, gay activists have adapted to the apparent permanence of the AIDS crisis. The notion that AIDS is here to stay threatens to overpowered the idea that it should be fought. This shift away from seeing AIDS as a political crisis gained momentum once it became obvious there would be no quick solution for it. Our horizons thus re-drawn, we are shunning the political questions and searching for new methods of coping: practical ones, personal ones.

Our culture is run on carefully crafted words and images. They are given tremendous authority, and have the power to shape society's responses. It is worth noting that the images which have endured through the AIDS crisis are not ones of activism. Rather, they are symbols of remembrance and reprieve: quilts, ribbons and angels. The symbols are symptoms of our acceptance of AIDS, our acceptance of death. Acceptance may be an appropriate response to the tragedy of AIDS. It is not a political response.

What does it mean when personal responses are confused with civic ones? In the case of AIDS, we are left without solutions for a constellation of woes far beyond the tragedy of human loss—such as the economics of health care, society's marginalization of individuals in need, the skewing of scientific research along lines of class, gender, and race, and the depletion of entire communities.

Our culture's acceptance of these images denotes a complicity between individual citizens, AIDS organizations and our government, where the responsibility for AIDS is consistently transferred elsewhere. Our government wants

the responsibilities privatized. When these images are backed
by philanthropic organizations, it enables the government to
steer responsibility for dealing with AIDS away from itself. In the
case of individuals, the desire is to transfer responsibility from
governments to Gods.

Since the beginning of the AIDS crisis, we've been reminded
by historians and spiritual leaders that death by plague is the
way of nature. But AIDS is not simply an act of nature, a fact
of life. It is also the business of government, the media world of
infotainment, the propaganda of religion, and the industry
of science.

In America, science and rationalism are paramount. When
privileged AIDS activists were introduced to scientists on the
battlefield of AIDS, they discovered a fellowship. By including
activists in the inner circles of the research establishment, the
system which activists set out to change neutralized their
dissent. Now, when scientists suggest there is no relief in sight
(an assertion based on limited scientific criteria) activists
working within the system concur.

Meanwhile, the media presents the picture that our society
has matured with respect to AIDS. Both film and television
have taken on the subject, although their analyses generally
ignore the political implications. Their spin is reductive, almost
irrelevant: that the human capacity to deal with loss is ennobling.
The cultural prognosis for AIDS is dismal. The drama of AIDS has
been replaced by its normalization. In terms of elections and
economics, the true determinants of our nation's soul, AIDS is
a very low priority. If we ever cared about it, we appear to have
given up on it. In inside circles, talk of a cure is rare.

If the original strategies of AIDS activism are in fact
outmoded, this is as much a by-product of the social context
as it is of the varied personal responses which have overtaken
the impulse which led to activism in the first place: the impulse
to stop the disease cold. What is not outmoded is the need for
action: action of all sorts and on all levels.

LET THE RECORD SHOW 2

In the Fall of 1987 Bill Olander [1950–1989] offered the window
of The New Museum For Contemporary Art to ACT UP to use as a
space for agit-prop. Individuals from within the group accepted
his offer and met to develop the installation *Let The Record
Show...* [imgs. 125–127]. Afterwards, many of us continued to meet;
the project's enthusiastic reception confirmed our feelings that
more work needed to be done exploring the political and social
dimensions of the AIDS crisis. Furthermore, the meetings allowed us
to utilize skills developed outside of ACT UP in a smaller group which
streamlined the process of working in the larger weekly meetings.

As a collective producing agit-prop around issues in the
AIDS crisis, we chose the name "Gran Fury" after the brand of

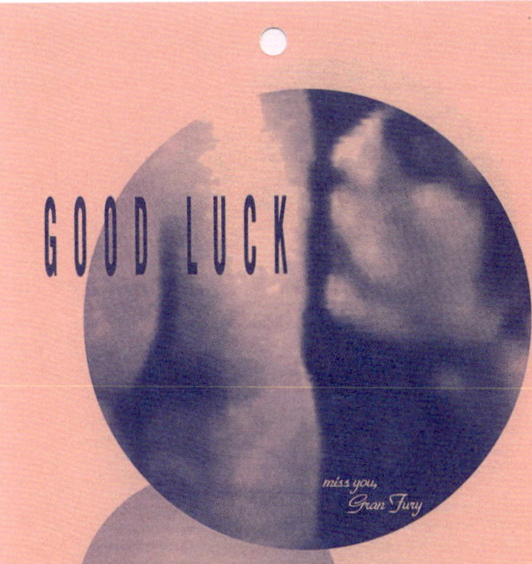

Life at the end of every century is typified by fear and anxiety. Apocalypse theories abound; nationalism and xenophobia encourage isolation. Urban violence, economic decline and AIDS have contributed to a reactionary environment where progressive thought is anathema.

The circumstances surrounding AIDS activism have radically changed since its beginning in 1986. Both the Executive Branch and the Congress have changed hands. America is in "decline". Communism is "dead". Internationally, politics have moved further to the right, and the citizenry of the United States has become more insular.

The lesbian and gay community has also changed. Embattled, fragmented and burned out, gay activists have adapted to the apparent permanence of the AIDS crisis. The notion that AIDS is here to stay threatens to overpowered the idea that it should be fought. This shift away from seeing AIDS as a political crisis gained momentum once it became obvious there would be no quick solution for it. Our horizons thus re-drawn, we are shunning the political questions and searching for new methods of coping: practical ones, personal ones.

Our culture is run on carefully crafted words and images. They are given tremendous authority, and have the power to shape society's responses. It is worth noting that the images which have endured through the AIDS crisis are not ones of activism. Rather, they are symbols of remembrance and reprieve: quilts, ribbons and angels. The symbols are symptoms of our acceptance of AIDS, our acceptance of death. Acceptance may be an appropriate response to the tragedy of AIDS. It is not a political response.

What does it mean when personal responses are confused with civic ones? In the case of AIDS, we are left without solutions for a constellation of woes far beyond the tragedy of human loss - such as the economics of health care, society's marginalization of individuals in need, the skewing of scientific research along lines of class, gender, and race, and the depletion of entire communities.

Our culture's acceptance of these images denotes a complicity between individual citizens, AIDS organizations and our government, where the responsibility for AIDS is consistently transferred elsewhere. Our government wants the responsibilities privatized. When these images are backed by philanthropic organizations, it enables the government to steer responsibility for dealing with AIDS *away* from itself. In the case of individuals, the desire is to transfer responsibility from governments to Gods.

Since the beginning of the AIDS crisis, we've been reminded by historians and spiritual leaders that death by plague is the way of nature. But AIDS is not simply an act of nature, a fact of life. It is also the business of government, the media world of infotainment, the propaganda of religion and the industry of science.

In America, science and rationalism are paramount. When privileged AIDS activists were introduced to scientists on the battlefield of AIDS , they discovered a fellowship. By including activists in the inner circles of the research establishment, the system which activist set out to change neutralized their dissent. Now, when scientists suggest there is no relief in sight (an assertion based on limited scientific criteria) activists working within the system concur.

Meanwhile, the media presents the picture that our society has matured with respect to AIDS. Both film and television have taken on the subject, although their analyses generally ignore the political implications. Their spin is reductive, almost irrelevant: that the human capacity to deal with loss is ennobling. The cultural prognosis for AIDS is dismal. The drama of AIDS has been replaced by its normalization. In terms of elections and economics, the true determinants of our nation's soul, AIDS is a very low priority. If we ever cared about it, we appear to have given up on it. In inside circles, talk of a cure is rare.

If the original strategies of AIDS activism are in fact outmoded, this is as much a by-product of the social context as it is of the varied personal responses which have overtaken the impulse which led to activism in the first place: the impulse to stop the disease cold. What is not outmoded is the need for action: action of all sorts and on all levels.

LET THE RECORD SHOW 2

In the Fall of 1987 Bill Olander offered the window of The New Museum For Contemporary Art to ACT-UP to use as a space for agit-prop. Individuals from within the group accepted his offer and met to develop the installation "Let The Record Show". Afterwards, many of us continued to meet; the project's enthusiastic reception confirmed our feelings that more work needed to be done exploring the political and social dimensions of the AIDS crisis. Furthermore, the meetings allowed us to utilize skills developed outside of ACT UP in a smaller group which streamlined the process of working in the larger weekly meetings.

As a collective producing agit-prop around issues in the AIDS crisis, we chose the name 'Gran Fury' after the brand of Plymouth automobile used as a squad car by the New York City police department. Gran Fury began in early 1988 and worked continuously until 1994 in various permutations with different members of a core group of about ten. Originally we kept the group open to anyone from ACT-UP, but after awhile, integrating new members proved to be too time consuming. Group members could participate or not depending on their availability and interest in specific issues. This stable group was an economical way for us to work. We understood each others' point of view and were comfortable tossing ideas around.

Our first projects were poster sniping (illegal wheat-pasting of posters on vacant signage) and Xeroxed flyers, a working method which grew out of an ACT-UP aesthetic and our limited funds. After about a year, our tactics changed as we questioned whether postering was the most effective means of reaching a large general audience. Also, we decided to become less dependent on ACT-UP for funding; loss of editorial control once a project came before the entire floor for approval lead to this move, although many of us continued to attend meetings as individuals. Both these shifts were influenced as well by the realization that art institutions would support our work. With their financial and institutional support, we adapted to strategies of intervention in advertising spaces.

As Gran Fury received increasing art world support, we did so with the condition that we receive the greatest possible public access to our work, in most cases exhibiting outside the art space itself. We decided not to produce work for the gallery market. Art institutions provided us with access to public spaces a group such as ours would otherwise never have had the resources to acquire; they profited through supporting AIDS work by an activist group which met their aesthetic standards and which was willing to observe certain boundaries of what was and was not allowable - explicit obscenity or critique of their sponsors.

Gran Fury was aware of the extent to which we were being used, but accepted the trade-off if our conditions were met. To its' credit, the art world was one of the few places outside of activism where such discussion about AIDS was allowed. The bulk of our funding came from art museums and foundations - The New Museum of Contemporary Art, The Whitney Museum of American Art, Los Angeles' MOCA and Creative Time to name a few. Additional funding came from lecturing at colleges, from AIDS organizations (though this was minimal) and finally from sales of T-shirts and stickers we had designed and sold through ACT UP, receiving a small portion of the profit. All of this went directly into funding the production of our projects, covering printing and the cost of advertising space; no one in the group received a salary.

Between 1989 and 1991 we were able to see our images circulate in a way we never imagined. Even if they didn't have the power to solve the crisis, they focused attention on it, and acted as a rallying cry, a point of identification for those inside the movement. Our projects developed a sec-

31

31
Gran Fury
Good Luck, Miss You,
1995
Offset print on paper,
55.5 × 14 cm
The New Museum
of Contemporary
Art, New York,
United States

43

Plymouth automobile used as a squad car by the New York City police department. Gran Fury began in early 1988 and worked continuously until 1994 in various permutations with different members of a core group of about ten. Originally we kept the group open to anyone from ACT UP, but after awhile, integrating new members proved to be too time consuming. Group members could participate or not depending on their availability and interest in specific issues. This stable group was an economical way for us to work. We understood each other's point of view and were comfortable tossing ideas around.

Our first projects were poster sniping (illegal wheat-pasting of posters on vacant signage) and Xeroxed flyers, a working method which grew out of an ACT UP aesthetic and our limited funds. After about a year, our tactics changed as we questioned whether postering was the most effective means of reaching a large general audience. Also, we decided to become less dependent on ACT UP for funding; loss of editorial control once a project came before the entire floor for approval lead to this move, although many of us continued to attend meetings as individuals. Both these shifts were influenced as well by the realization that art institutions would support our work. With their financial and institutional support, we adapted to strategies of intervention in advertising spaces.

As Gran Fury received increasing art world support, we did so with the condition that we receive the greatest possible public access to our work, in most cases exhibiting outside the art space itself. We decided not to produce work for the gallery market. Art institutions provided us with access to public spaces a group such as ours would otherwise never have had the resources to acquire; they profited through supporting AIDS work by an activist group which met their aesthetic standards and which was willing to observe certain boundaries of what was and was not allowable—explicit obscenity or critique of their sponsors.

Gran Fury was aware of the extent to which we were being used, but accepted the trade-off if our conditions were met. To its' credit, the art world was one of the few places outside of activism where such discussion about AIDS was allowed. The bulk of our funding came from art museums and foundations— The New Museum of Contemporary Art, The Whitney Museum of American Art, Los Angeles' MOCA and Creative Time to name a few. Additional funding came from lecturing at colleges, from AIDS organizations (though this was minimal) and finally from sales of T-shirts and stickers we had designed and sold through ACT UP, receiving a small portion of the profit. All of this went directly into funding the production of our projects, covering printing and the cost of advertising space; no one in the group received a salary.

Between 1989 and 1991 we were able to see our images circulate in a way we never imagined. Even if they didn't have the power to solve the crisis, they focused attention on it, and acted as a rallying cry, a point of identification for those inside the movement. Our projects developed a second life through the press coverage that accompanied them, so that their influence was greater than the physical spaces they occupied. The *Kissing Doesn't Kill* [1989–80] [imgs. 77–81] project got media coverage across the country through wire services and public radio stations, and even spawned a debate over representation of gays and lesbians on the floor of the Illinois State Senate.

Many of our strategies were incorporated into advertising. An ad campaign, however provocative, still has its AIDS message subservient to promoting a company name. In that relation, it loses the power of direct demand or exposure of facts. Bennetton went one step further by producing an issue of *COLORS* magazine to address AIDS. Many of the strategies they used were borrowed from projects we had done; we had been contacted by a researcher from Bennetton who asked for examples of our work, saying that they would be considered for inclusion in the magazine. That never happened; instead, they reworked our strategies, skewing them in a surreal direction with little or no context in which to interpret the images or statistics.

By 1993 the effort involved became too demanding for different members. Most people worked full-time if not more, running their own businesses. More importantly, for all the effort involved, it began to feel routine. We had settled too clearly into one way of working. As the AIDS epidemic had evolved, along with the governmental and institutional responses to it, the early solutions were no longer appropriate. As AIDS activists joined community-based organizations (CBOS) and governmental agencies, many activists moved inside institutions they had previously been excluded from. Many of these CBOS and AIDS organizations began to run media campaigns of their own, and even if they were not as politically sharp as Gran Fury's, they nonetheless occupied the "public space" that we had formerly filled. Finally, the issues—drug trial design and protocol, financing social services for PWAS, insurance industry fraud—became less readily communicable in sharp billboard copy. Gran Fury's original strategies were unable to communicate the complexities of AIDS issues in the mid-1990s.

At the same time, our work began to feel like a signature style, a convenient product for the art world to use to fulfill its desire to "do something" about the AIDS crisis. Gran Fury's status as flavor of the month in the American art world was over; interest in our work had shifted to Europe where we consistently felt handicapped by attempting to understand their specific issues, as well as by our inability to use colloquial slogans. In 1992 we designed a campaign for Montreal which utilized the symbols of Quebecois sovereignty to draw attention to AIDS issues— specifically a warning to conduct research and design programs that would apply to the Canadian situation [imgs. 105, 106]. The project backfired because the icon we chose to use was too potent—some did not recognize it as an AIDS campaign. In general, we found that we could only produce the most general messages, otherwise we ran the risk of misreading a local situation or creating something that would fail in translation.

Bill Clinton, while not providing strong leadership for the AIDS crisis, is not easily demonized, and does not make openly hostile or stupidly misinformed remarks about AIDS. [Ronald] Reagan's [1911–2004] blatant ignorance and hostility, and to a lesser degree [George H. W.] Bush's [1924–2018] as well, were easy targets for activism. Our early work was to draw attention to political and social issues of the AIDS crisis as we saw them. Those administrations initial lack of involvement made our work simple. Identifying aspects of the crisis as continued racism, sexism and homophobia was easy. The proliferation of issues, discourses, and the very expansion of efforts to end the AIDS crisis has meant that activism has changed. Though it may seem to many that the activism spawned by ACT UP had died, it has not. It has shifted focus. We have not ended the AIDS crisis, but work continues, and there is more to be done.

FUTURE SEX ACTS

The moment of early ACT UP has passed, and with it, large scale public demonstrations of outrage and anger. As AIDS awareness has spread into the mainstream, creating its own social sphere of community-based organizations, charitable institutions, even glossy magazines for the HIV and AIDS identified, many have organized to represent their particular interests—Latino, African-American, hemophiliac, I.V. drug users, children with AIDS, homeless PWAS. ACT UP grew from the gay and lesbian community, and now it may be appropriate to re-examine the particular needs of this community. Not that the larger goals which would affect all should be abandoned—reform is vitally important in light of the Clinton administration's inability to effect any substantive change in health care delivery. We simply need to recognize that our own community still has to fight for resources, representation, and the right to define strategies for fighting the epidemic.

Within the last two years, studies (conducted largely at the initiative of the gay and lesbian community) have revealed that the current efforts to prevent HIV transmission among self-identified gay men are failing, in spite of significant advances made to promote condom use. In San Francisco and New York, as many as an estimated 30% to 45% of HIV negative men between the ages of 18 and 25 reported engaging in unprotected anal intercourse within the previous six months. Many of these men know that wearing a condom prevents transmission; "wear a condom every time" and "safe sex is hot sex" campaigns fail to address the psychic resistance that leads some gay men to put themselves at risk even though they know better. Identification with HIV infected friends and lovers, the absence of a cure, the never ending toll of illness, the inability to imagine a time when ond life through the press coverage that accompanied them, so that their influence was greater than the physical spaces they occupied. "The Kissing Doesn't Kill" project got media coverage across the country through wire services and public radio stations, and even spawned a debate over representation of gays and lesbians on the floor of the Illinois State Senate.

Many of our strategies were incorporated into advertising. An ad campaign, however provocative, still has it's AIDS message subservient to promoting a company name. In that relation, it loses the power of direct demand or exposure of facts. Bennetton went one step further by producing an issue of COLORS magazine to address AIDS. Many of the strategies they used were borrowed from projects we had done; we had been contacted by a researcher from Bennetton who asked for examples of our work, saying that they would be considered for inclusion in the magazine. That never happened; instead, they reworked our strategies, skewing them in a surreal direction with little or no context in which to interpret the images or statistics.

By 1993 the effort involved became too demanding for different members. Most people worked full-time if not more, running their own businesses. More importantly, for all the effort involved, it began to feel routine. We had settled too clearly into one way of working. As the AIDS epidemic had evolved, along with the governmental and institutional responses to it, the early solutions were no longer appropriate. As AIDS activists joined community based organizations [CBO's] and governmental agencies, many activists moved inside institutions they had previously been excluded from. Many of these CBO's and AIDS organizations began to run media campaigns of their own, and even if they were not as politically sharp as Gran Fury's, they nonetheless occupied "public space" that we had formerly filled. Finally, the issues - drug trial design and protocol, financing social services for P.W.A.'s, insurance industry fraud - became less readily communicable in sharp billboard copy. Gran Fury's original strategies were unable to communicate the complexities of AIDS issues in the mid-1990's.

At the same time, our work began to feel like a signature style, a convenient product for the art world to use to fulfill its' desire to "do something" about the AIDS crisis. Gran Fury's status as flavor of the month in the American art world was over; interest in our work had shifted to Europe where we consistently felt handicapped by attempting to understand their specific issues, as well as by our inability to use colloquial slogans. In 1992 we designed a campaign for Montreal which utilized the symbols of Quebecois sovereignty to draw attention to AIDS issues - specifically a warning to conduct research and design programs that would apply to the Canadian situation. The project backfired because the icon we chose to use was too potent - some did not recognize it as an AIDS campaign. In general, we found that we could only produce the most general messages, otherwise we ran the risk of misreading a local situation or creating something that would fail in translation.

Bill Clinton, while not providing strong leadership for the AIDS crisis, is not easily demonized, and does not make openly hostile or stupidly misinformed remarks about AIDS. Reagan's blatant ignorance and hostility, and to a lesser degree Bush's as well, were easy targets for activism. Our early work was to draw attention to political and social issues of the AIDS crisis as we saw them. Those administrations initial lack of involvement made our work simple. Identifying aspects of the crisis as continued racism, sexism and homophobia was easy. The proliferation of issues, discourses, and the very expansion of efforts to end the AIDS crisis has meant that activism has changed. Though it may seem to many that the activism spawned by ACT UP had died, it has not. It has shifted focus. We have not ended the AIDS crisis, but work continues, and there is more to be done.

FUTURE SEX ACTS

The moment of early ACT UP has passed, and with it, large scale public demonstrations of outrage and anger. As AIDS awareness has spread into the mainstream, creating its own social sphere of community-based organizations, charitable institutions, even glossy magazines for the HIV and AIDS identified, many have organized to represent their particular interests - Latino, African-American, hemophiliac, I.V. drug users, children with AIDS, homeless PWA's. ACT UP grew from the gay and lesbian community, and now it may be appropriate to re-examine the particular needs of this community. Not that the larger goals which would affect all should be abandoned - reform is vitally important in light of the Clinton administration's inability to effect any substantive change in health care delivery. We simply need to recognize that our own community still has to fight for resources, representation, and the right to define strategies for fighting the epidemic.

Within the last two years, studies (conducted largely at the initiative of the gay and lesbian community) have revealed that the current efforts to prevent HIV transmission among self-identified gay men are failing, in spite of significant advances made to promote condom use. In San Francisco and New York, as many as an estimated 30 to 45% of HIV negative men between the ages of 18 and 25 reported engaging in unprotected anal intercourse within the previous six months. Many of these men know that wearing a condom prevents transmission. "wear a condom every time" and "safe sex is hot sex" campaigns fail to address the psychic resistance that leads some gay men to put themselves at risk *even though they know better.* Identification with HIV infected friends and lovers, the absence of a cure, the never ending toll of illness, the inability to imagine a time when sex will not automatically evoke death - these are the issues that prevention activists must address if they want to reduce HIV transmission among gay men.

The current sexual climate has never been more firmly aligned against a sex positive approach to HIV prevention. The New York City Office of HIV Prevention has never conducted a study to determine the infection rate of gay men, and has not developed a new prevention campaign for gay men in over two years. More specifically, Mayor Giuliani has targeted gay sex establishments in his effort to improve the "quality of life" in New York. Alliances between local law enforcement and frustrated gay activist who don't trust the gay community to regulate itself have meant that the potential for self-determination on these issue has been taken outside, to be hashed out in dailies like The Post and The Daily News - a desperate approach not likely to offer any realistic solutions.

Activist groups such as the AIDS Prevention Action League (APAL) and Community AIDS Prevention Activists (CAPA) have formed to readdress prevention needs and strategies from within the gay community. They have organized forums to encourage gay men to talk about when they do and do not practice safer sex; met with bar and club owners to discuss how they can assist prevention efforts, and have petitioned the city to allow the community to regulate itself, not the vice squad.

With discouraging reports of AZT's effectiveness in delaying the onset of AIDS at the 1992 Berlin AIDS conference and few encouraging developments in treatment, prevention has become the focus for many activists. Ten years of fighting AIDS has shown us that HIV education is not a conversion experience. Prevention must become an on-going effort that addresses not simply the mechanic of safe sex, but also our psychological needs. We must organize to develop our self-esteem within the community so that gay men feel that they have some stake in staying alive - especially for young men who may be in the middle of casting off internalized homophobia absorbed from their families and schools. During first sexual encounters, they must feel able to say "no" to partners who would but them at risk. They must realize their vulnerability to infection *in spite of their youth.*

Rather than simply printing up a list of "Do's and Don'ts", AIDS organizations need to recognize the importance of individuals weighing the risks of certain sexual acts against their needs for sexual pleasure and emotional intimacy. In spite of the fact that no doctor will guarantee that one cannot acquire HIV through oral sex, many have made their own evaluation from anecdotal evidence, and are willing to take the low risk associated with unprotected oral sex without ejaculation. If AIDS organizations fail to reflect these community norms when they do not pose serious health risks, they will lose credibility. Individuals must be allowed to make choices in those grey areas; AIDS organizations should provide information to facilitate these choices.

Prevention campaigns must recognize that punitive messages which demonize unsafe sex do not effectively reach those who are having it; they may even reinforce it by making men feel guilty. The reality of our sexual lives must be reflected in prevention efforts, even if it does not conform to the desired behavior change. Only by identifying our lapses will we begin changing them.

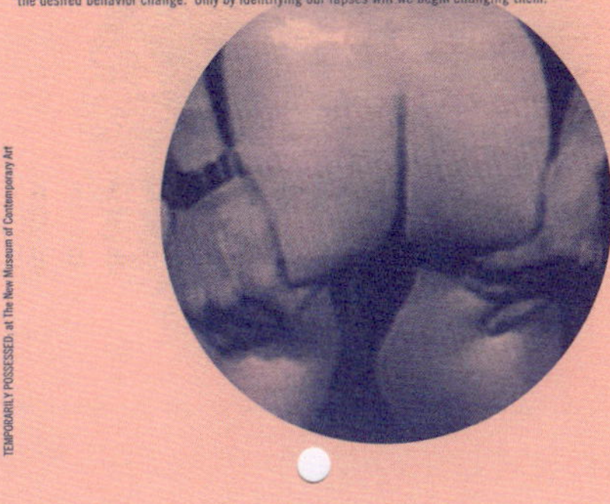

32
Gran Fury
Good Luck, Miss You,
1995
Offset print on paper,
55.5 × 14 cm
The New Museum
of Contemporary
Art, New York,
United States

sex will not automatically evoke death—these are the issues that prevention activists must address if they want to reduce HIV transmission among gay men.

The current sexual climate has never been more firmly aligned against a sex-positive approach to HIV prevention. The New York City Office of HIV Prevention has never conducted a study to determine the infection rate of gay men and has not developed a new prevention campaign for gay men in over two years. More specifically, Mayor Giuliani has targeted gay sex establishments in his effort to improve the "quality of life" in New York. Alliances between local law enforcement and frustrated gay activists who don't trust the gay community to regulate itself have meant that the potential for self-determination on these issues has been taken outside, to be hashed out in dailies like *The Post* and *The Daily News*—a desperate approach not likely to offer any realistic solutions.

Activist groups such as the AIDS Prevention Action League (APAL) and Community AIDS Prevention Activists (CAPA) have formed to readdress prevention needs and strategies from within the gay community. They have organized forums to encourage gay men to talk about when they do and do not practice safer sex; met with bar and club owners to discuss how they can assist prevention efforts, and have petitioned the city to allow the community to regulate itself, not the vice squad.

With discouraging reports of AZT's effectiveness in delaying the onset of AIDS at the 1992 Berlin AIDS conference and few encouraging developments in treatment, prevention has become the focus for many activists. Ten years of fighting AIDS has shown us that HIV education is not a conversion experience. Prevention must become an ongoing effort that addresses not simply the mechanics of safe sex, but also our psychological needs. We must organize to develop our self-esteem within the community so that gay men feel that they have some stake in staying alive—especially for young men who may be in the middle of casting off internalized homophobia absorbed from their families and schools. During first sexual encounters, they must feel able to say "no" to partners who would put them at risk. They must realize their vulnerability to infection in spite of their youth.

Rather than simply printing up a list of "Do's and Don'ts," AIDS organizations need to recognize the importance of individuals weighing the risks of certain sexual acts against their needs for sexual pleasure and emotional intimacy. In spite of the fact that no doctor will guarantee that one cannot acquire HIV through oral sex, many have made their own evaluation from anecdotal evidence, and are willing to take the low risk associated with unprotected oral sex without ejaculation. If AIDS organizations fail to reflect these community norms when they do not pose serious health risks, they will lose credibility. Individuals must be allowed to make choices in those grey areas; AIDS organizations should provide information to facilitate these choices.

Prevention campaigns must recognize that punitive messages which demonize unsafe sex do not effectively reach those who are having it; they may even reinforce it by making men feel guilty. The reality of our sexual lives must be reflected in prevention efforts, even if it does not conform to the desired behavior change. Only by identifying our lapses will we begin changing them.

REPRODUCTION OF WORKS

—

Gran Fury

AIDS: 1 in 61

One in every sixty-one babies
in New York City is born with AIDS
or born HIV antibody positive.

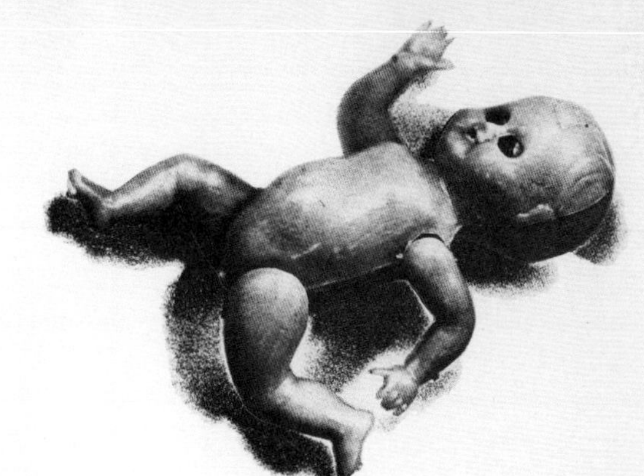

So why is the media telling us
that heterosexuals aren't at risk?

Because these babies are black.
These babies are Hispanic.

Ignoring color ignores the facts of AIDS.
STOP RACISM: FIGHT AIDS.

Uno de cada sesenta y uno de los bebés nacidos
en la ciudad de New York nacen con SIDA,
o con el anticuerpo HIV positivo.

¿Pero, por qué es que los medios de comunicación
nos dicen que los heterosexuales no corren riesgos?

Será porque estos bebes son negros,
o porque estos bebes son hispanos.

El SIDA no discrimina entre razas o nacionalidades.
¡PARE EL RACISMO! ¡LUCHE CONTRA EL SIDA!

ACT UP AIDS Coalition To Unleash Power (212) 533-8888   ACT UP is a diverse, non-partisan group of individuals united in anger and committed to direct action to end the AIDS crisis.

Gran Fury Gran Fury is a band of individuals united in anger and committed to exploiting the power of art to end the AIDS crisis.

33
AIDS: 1 in 61, 1988
ACT UP, Women's
Committee for the
Cosmopolitan Magazine
Demonstration
Offset print on paper,
56 × 43 cm

34

AIDS: 1 in 61 (Scared Fags Crap), 1988
Offset print on paper,
56 × 43 cm
Gran Fury Collection,
Manuscripts and
Archives Division,
The New York
Public Library,
United States

AIDS: 1 in 61.

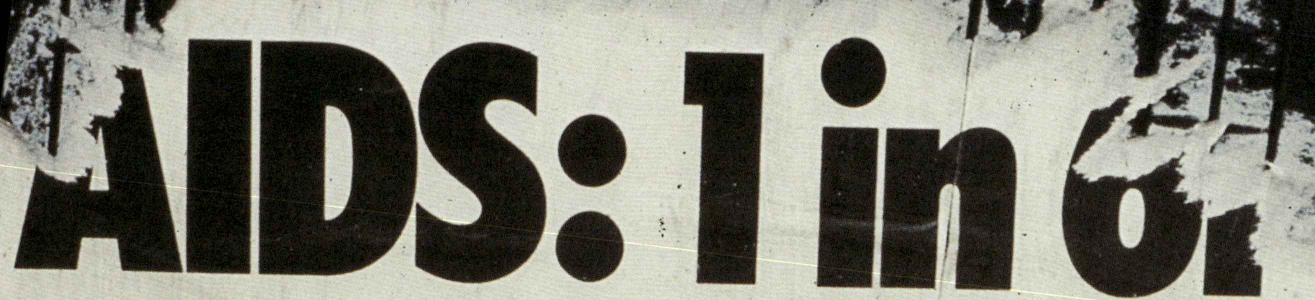

One in every sixty-one babies
in New York City is born with AIDS
or born HIV antibody positive.

Why is the media telling us
heterosexuals aren't at risk?

Because these babies are black.
These babies are Hispanic.

Ignoring color ignores the facts of AIDS.
STOP RACISM: FIGHT AIDS.

Uno de cada sesenta y uno de los bebés nacidos
en la ciudad de New York nacen con SIDA,
o con el anticuerpo HIV positivo.

¿Pero, por qué es que los medios de comunicación
nos dicen que los heterosexuales no corren riesgo?

Será porque estos bebes son negros,
o porque estos bebes son hispanos.

El SIDA no discrimina entre razas o nacionalidad.
¡PARE EL RACISMO! ¡LUCHE CONTRA EL SIDA!

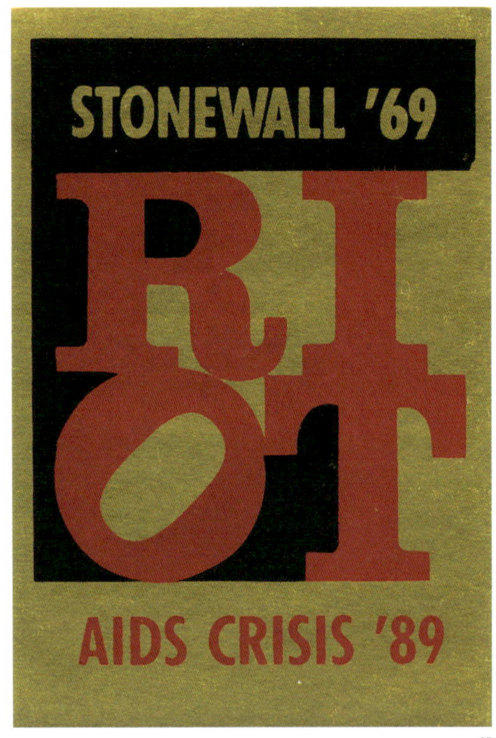

35

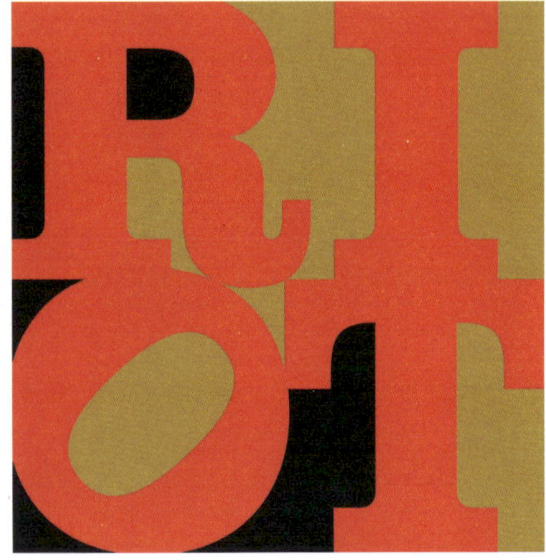

36

35
RIOT [Stonewall '69…
AIDS Crisis '89], 1989
Silkscreen on sticker,
13 × 9 cm
Gran Fury Collection,
Manuscripts and
Archives Division,
The New York Public
Library, United States

36
RIOT, 2019
Digital illustration,
10 × 10 cm

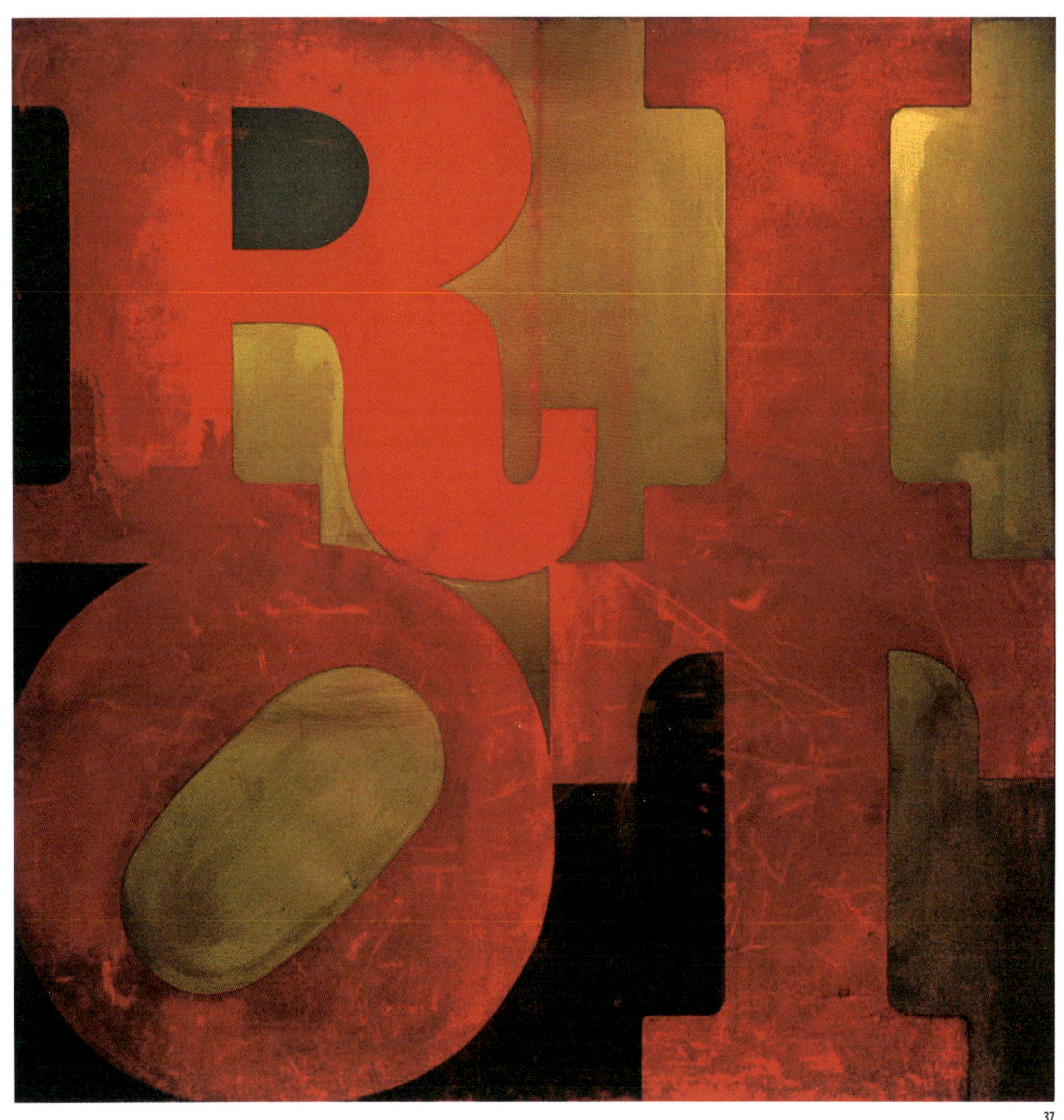

37

RIOT, 1988
Oil and dried pigment
on canvas,
183 × 183 cm
Private Collection,
courtesy neue
Gesellschaft für
bildende Kunst,
Berlin, Germany

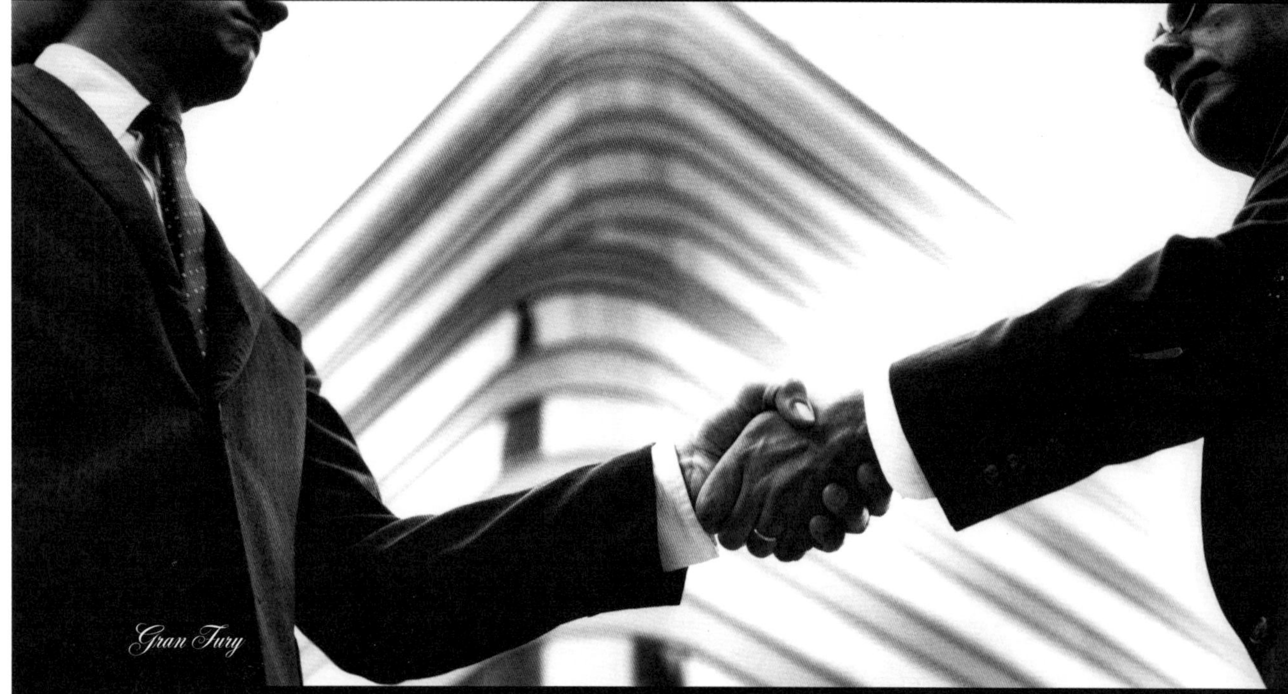

38

When a Government Turns Its Back on Its People, 1988
Offset print on paper, installed in the subway, 228.5 × 305 cm
Commissioned work for the *Full Blown Image AIDS: An Art Exhibition about Living and Dying*, neue Gesellschaft für bildende Kunst, Berlin, Germany

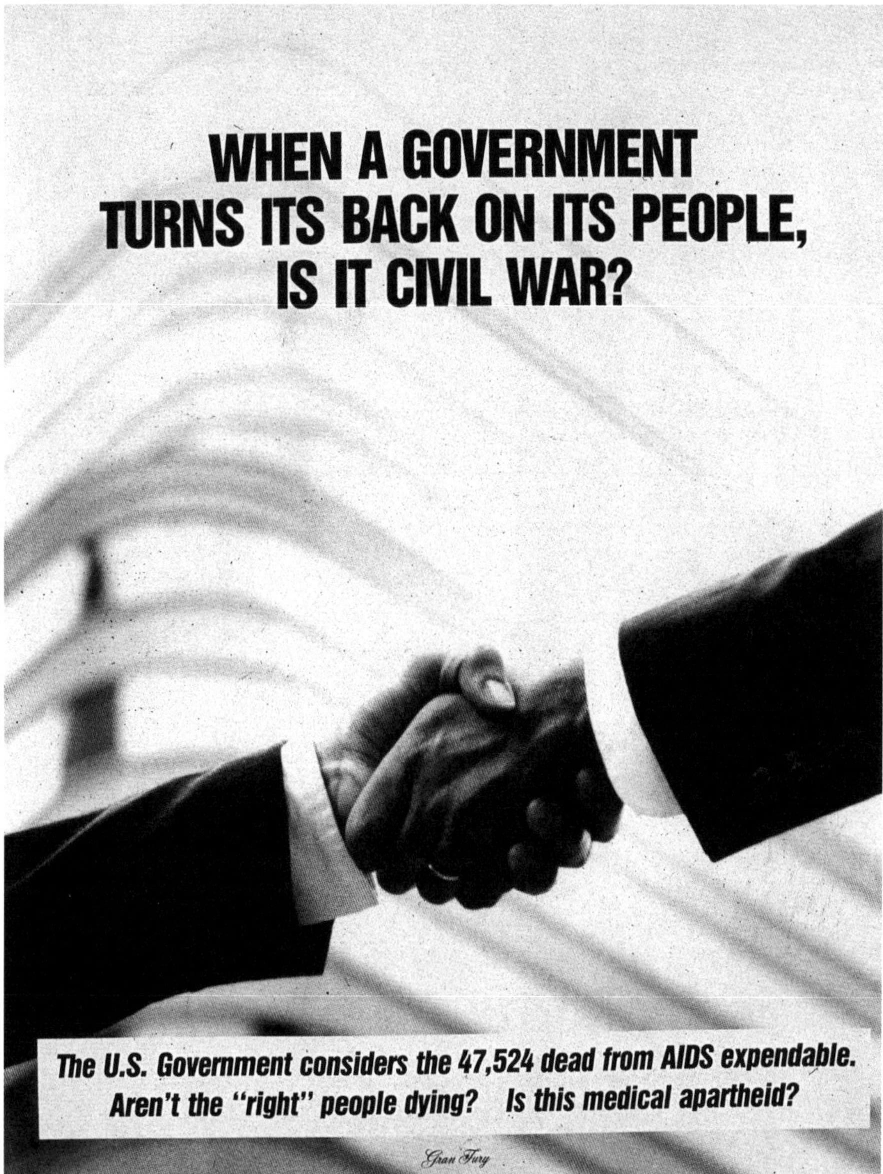

39

39

*When a Government
Turns Its Back on Its
People*, 1988
Offset lithography
on paper
Commissioned work
for the *Full Blown
Image AIDS: An Art
Exhibition about
Living and Dying*,
neue Gesellschaft
für bildende Kunst,
Berlin, Germany

40

Berlin Subway with
*When a Government
Turns Its Back on Its
People* billboard, 1988
Commissioned work
for the *Full Blown
Image AIDS: An Art
Exhibition about
Living and Dying*,
neue Gesellschaft
für bildende Kunst,
Berlin, Germany

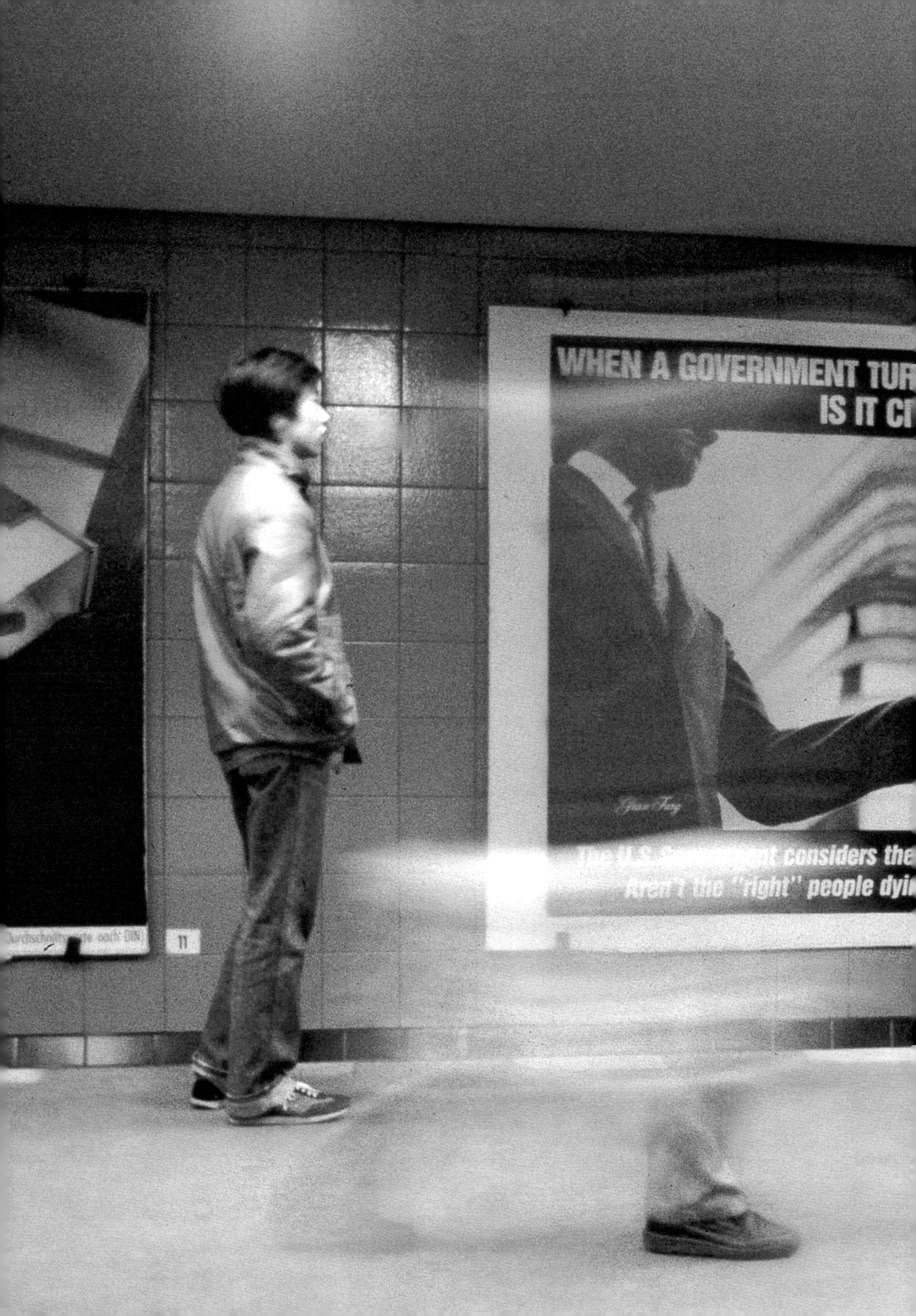

WHEN A GOVERNMENT TUR
IS IT CI
The U.S. Government considers the
Aren't the "right" people dyin

S BACK ON ITS PEOPLE,
AR?
dead from AIDS expendable
his medical apartheid?
Der Geschmack
Voll-Würzig. Männ

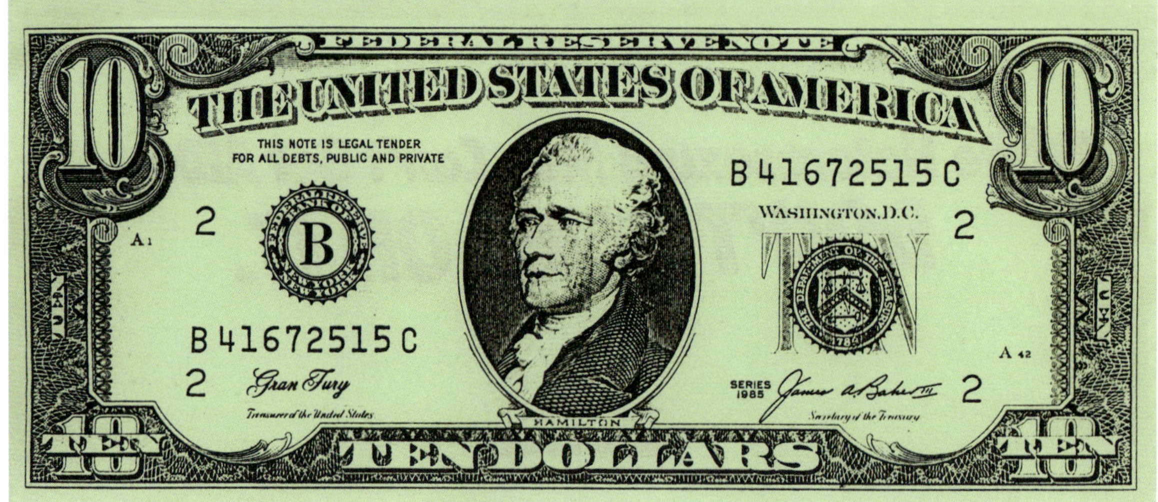

41

White Heterosexual Men Can't Get AIDS...
DON'T BANK ON IT.

Fight Back. Fight AIDS.

42

41, 42

*Wall Street Money
(10 dollar bill)*, 1988
ACT UP; Wall Street
Demonstration,
New York, United States
Photocopy on paper,
9 × 21.5 cm

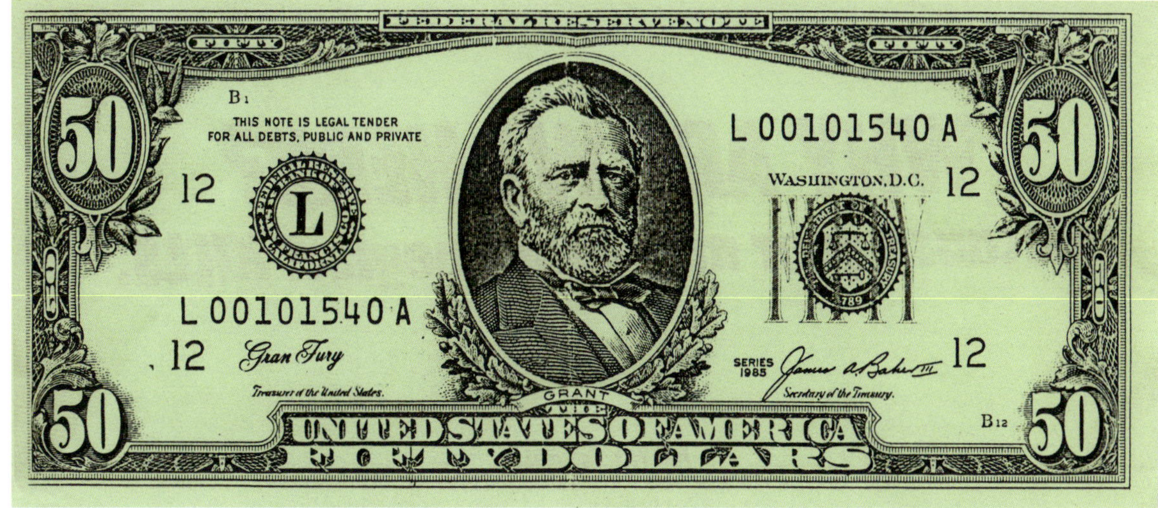

43

WHY ARE WE HERE?
Because your malignant neglect KILLS.

Fight Back. Fight AIDS.

44

43, 44
*Wall Street Money
(50 dollar bill)*, 1988
ACT UP; Wall Street
Demonstration,
New York, United States
Photocopy on paper,
9 × 21.5 cm

FUCK YOU!
FUCK YOUR PROFITEERING
DON'T BANK ON IT

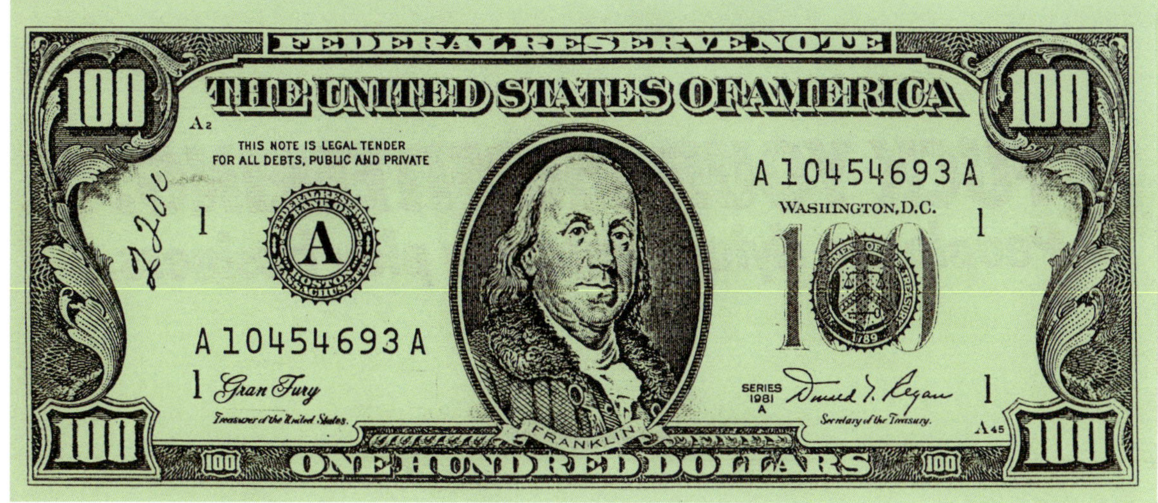

46

FUCK YOUR PROFITEERING.
People are dying while you play business.

Fight Back. Fight AIDS.

47

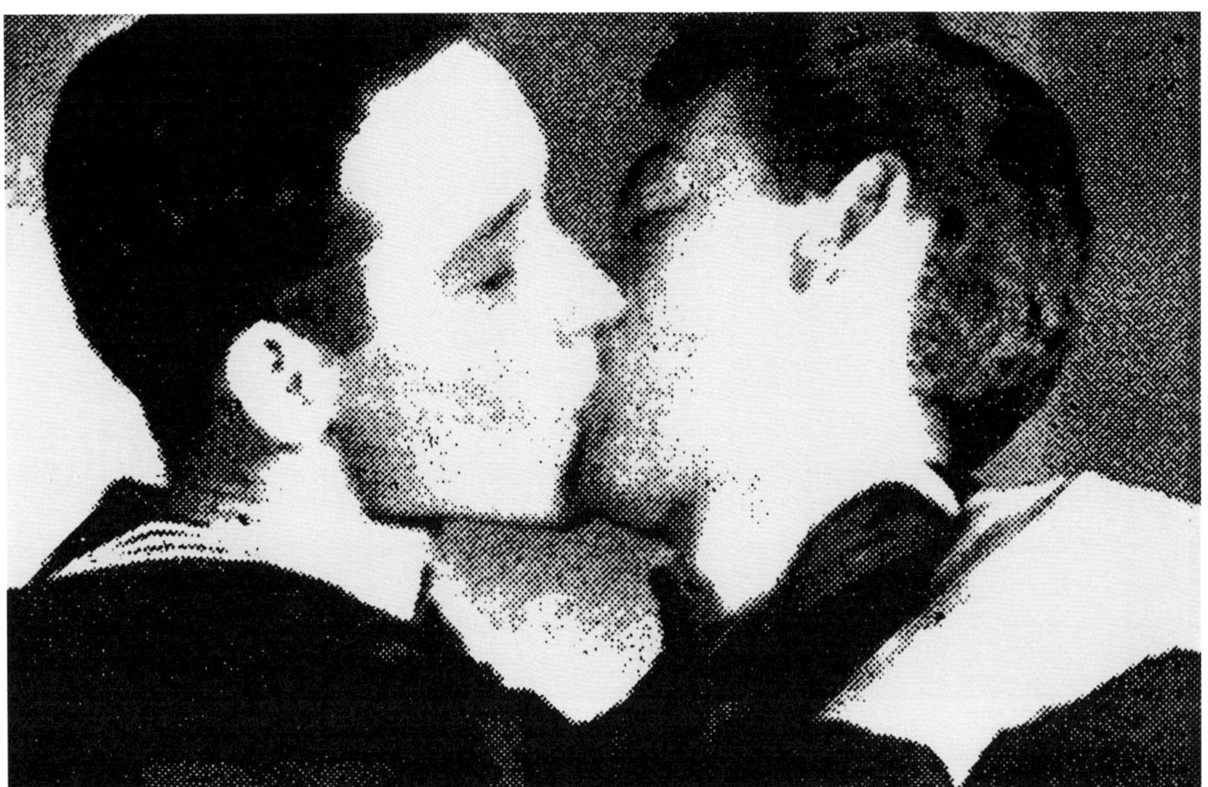

READ MY LIPS

KISS IN

Friday, April 29:
9:00 pm   March from Christopher & West Sts.
10:00 pm   Rally at Sheridan Square
10:30 pm   Kiss In at 6th Avenue & 8th St.
11:30 pm   Tracks—ACT UP/ACT NOW Fundraiser

FIGHT HOMOPHOBIA: FIGHT AIDS

SPRING AIDS ACTION '88: Nine days of nationwide AIDS related actions & protests.

Gran Fury

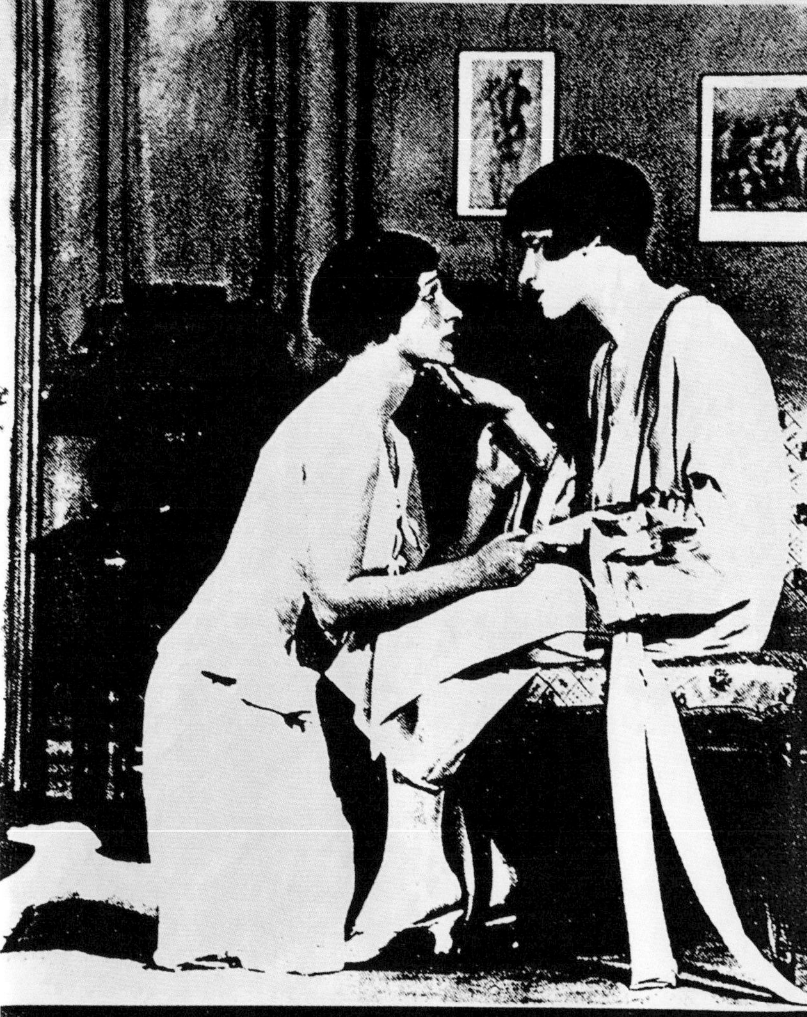

49

48
Read My Lips
(Men's ver.)
ACT UP, Spring AIDS
Action, 1988
Photocopy on paper,
42.5 × 27.5 cm

49
Read My Lips
(Women's, 1 ver.)
ACT UP, Spring AIDS
Action, 1988
Photocopy on paper,
42.5 × 27.5 cm

65

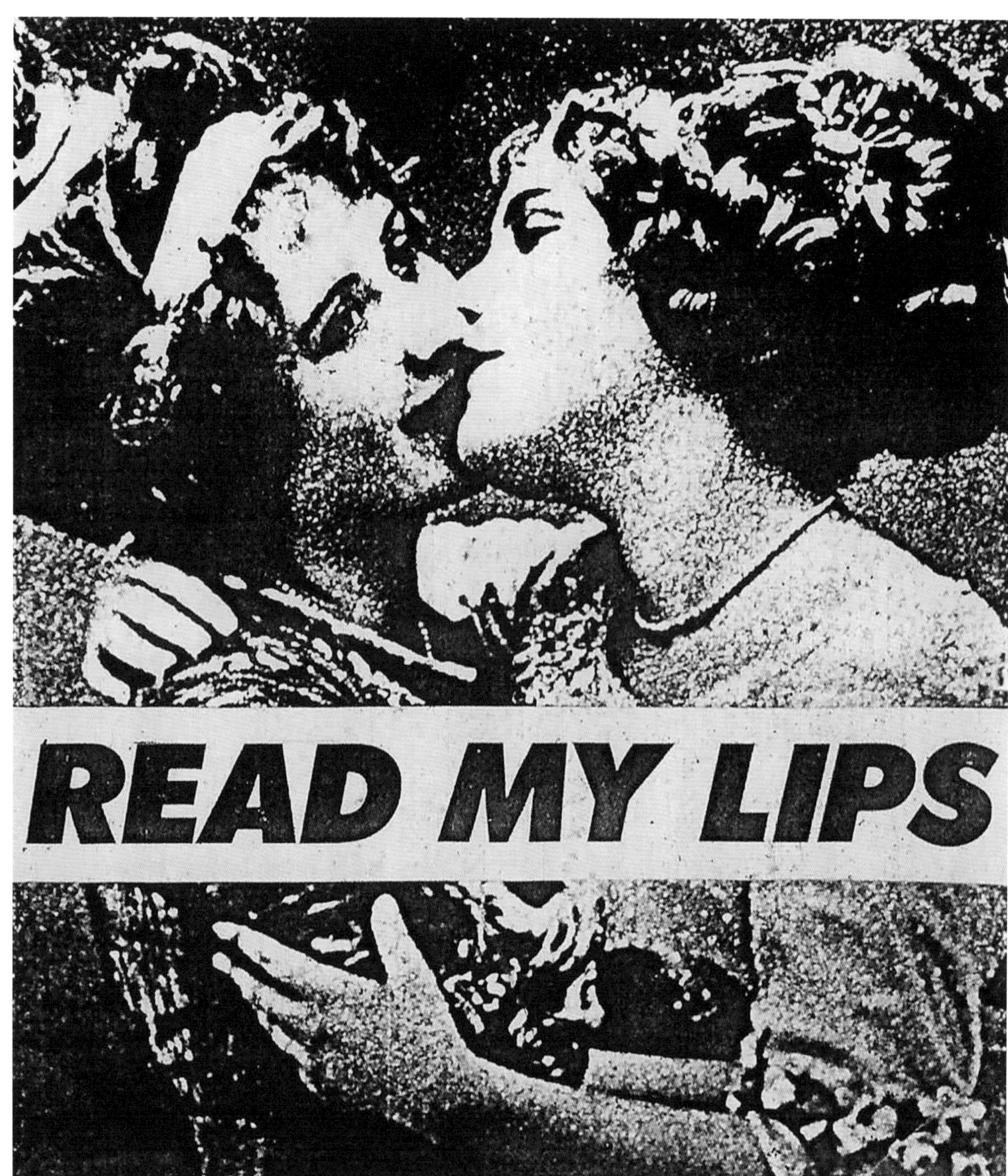

50

50

Read My Lips
(Women's, 2 ver.)
ACT UP, Spring AIDS
Action, 1988
Photocopy on paper,
42.5 × 27.5 cm

READ MY LIPS

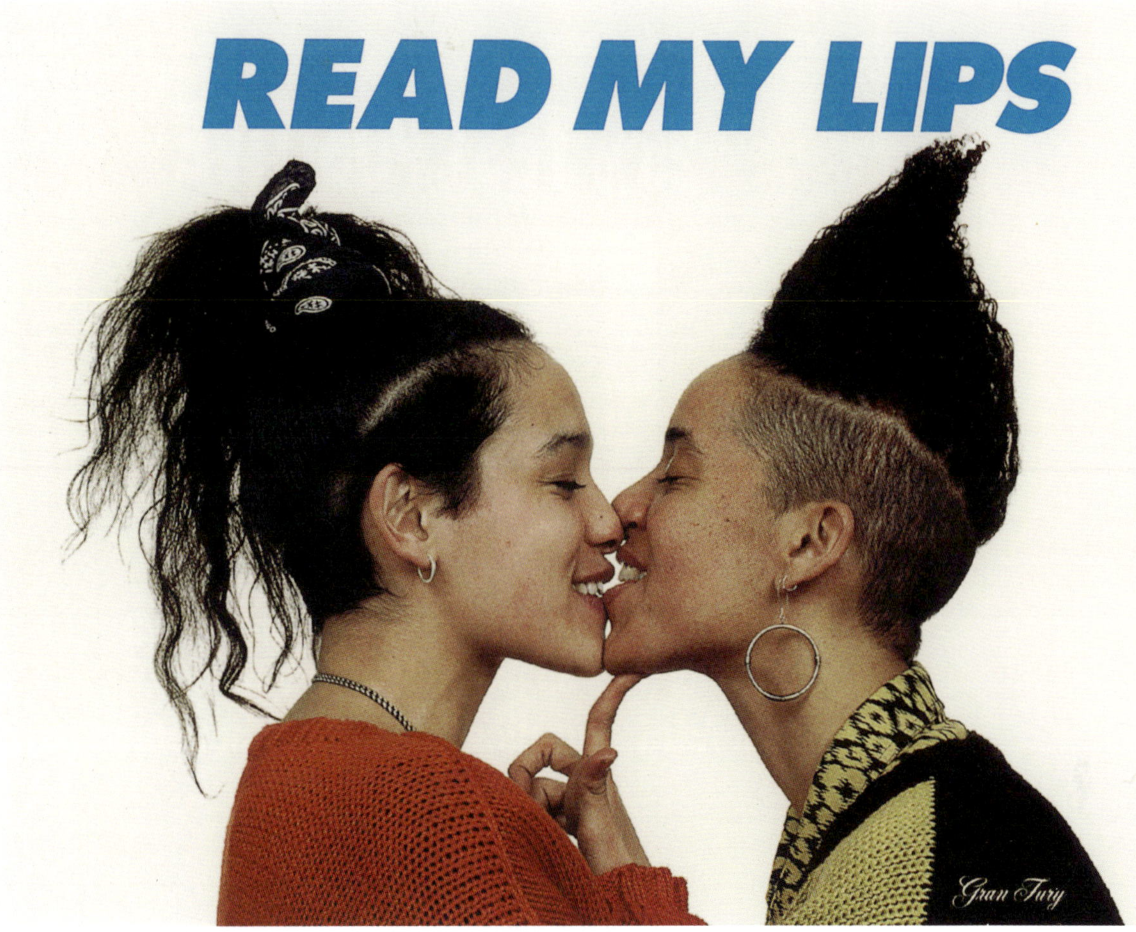

51

51
Read My Lips
(Women's, 3 ver.),
1989/2012
For ACT UP
Offset print on
postcard, 10.5 × 15 cm

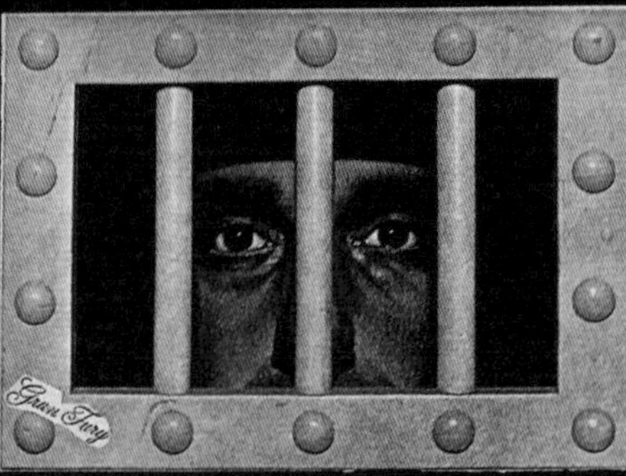

52

AIDS Behind Bars
ACT UP, Spring AIDS Action, 1988
Photocopy on paper, 41.5 × 26.5 cm

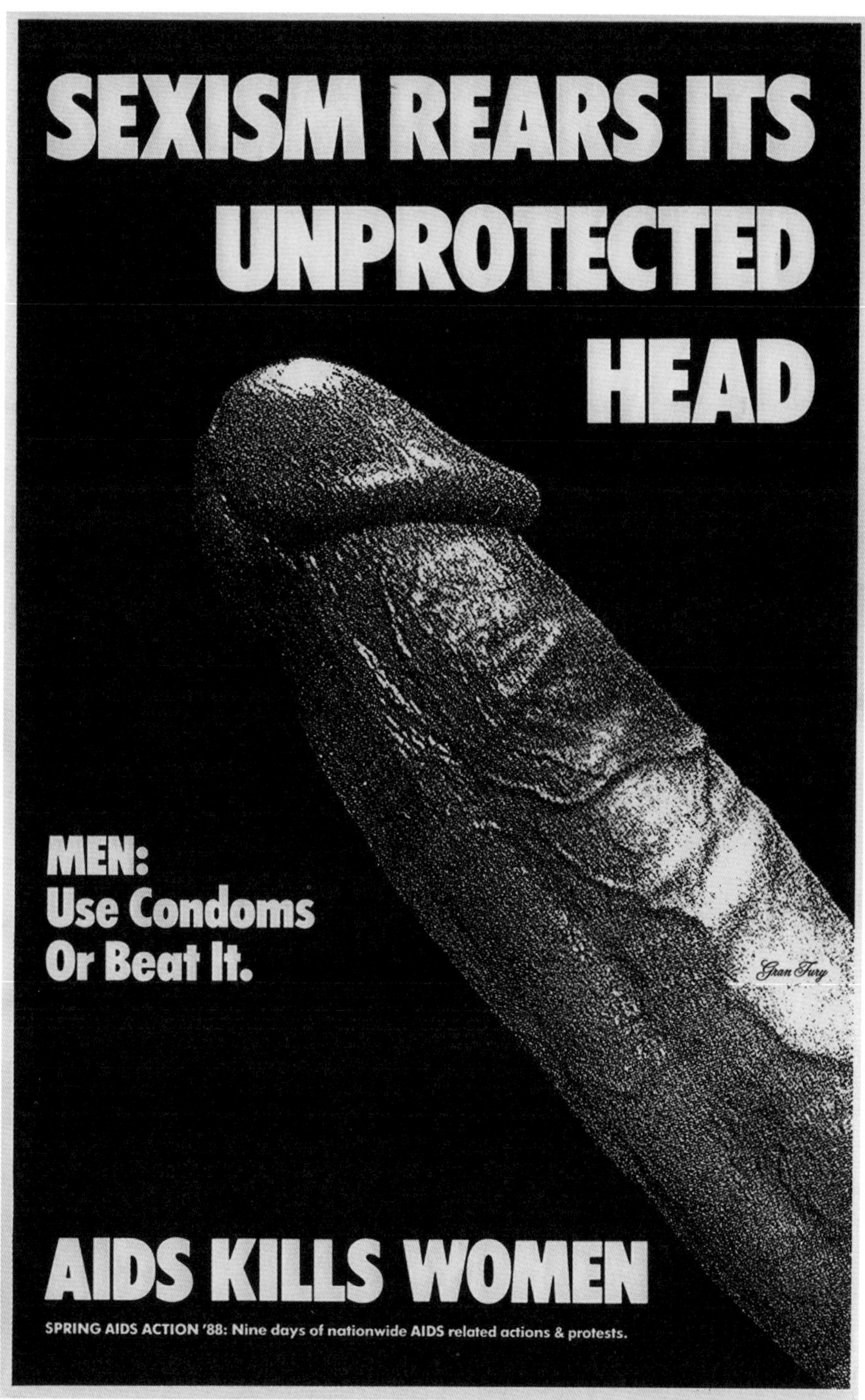

53

53

*Sexism Rears Its
Unprotected Head*
ACT UP, Spring AIDS
Action, 1988
Photocopy on paper,
41.5 × 26.5 cm

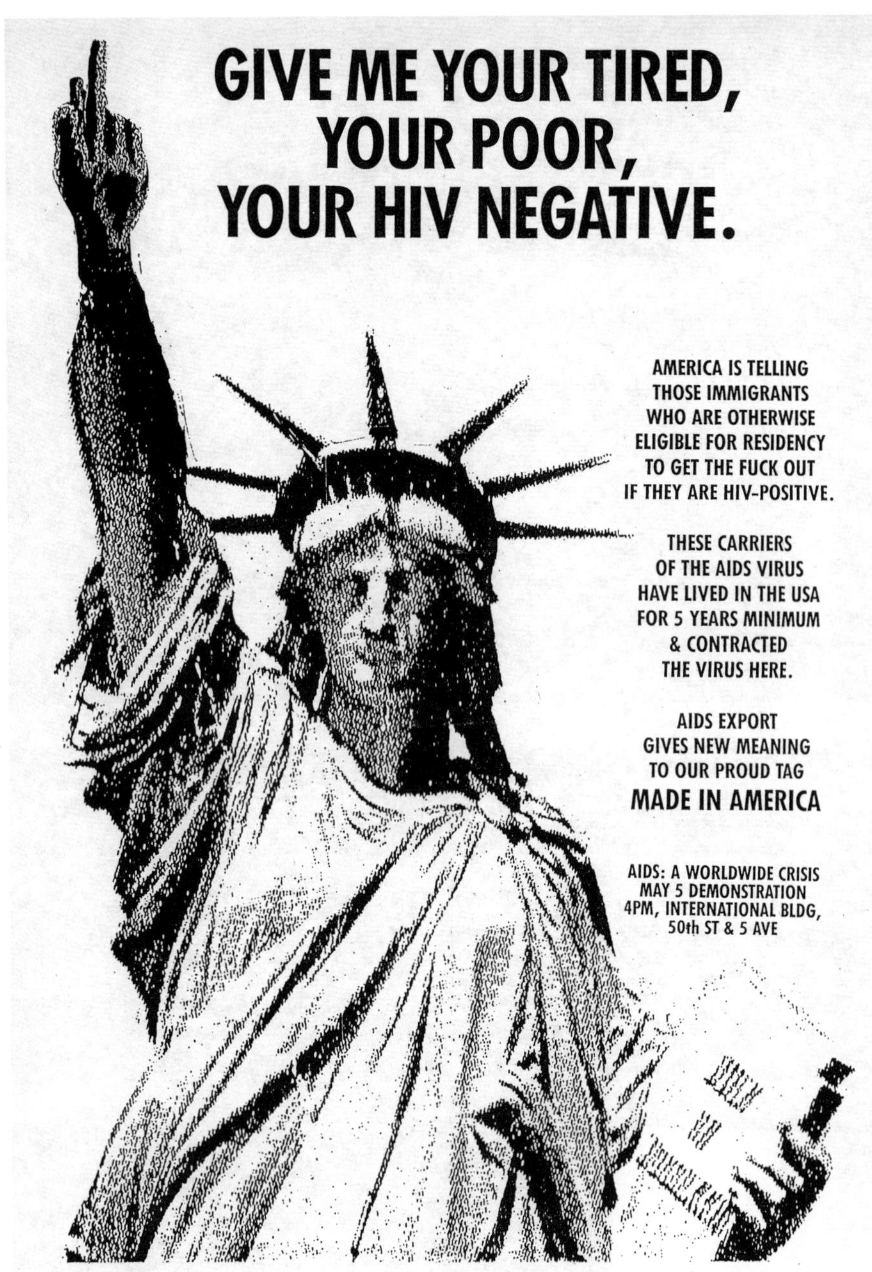

54
Give Me Your Tired, Your Poor, Your HIV Negative
ACT UP, Spring AIDS Action, 1988
Photocopy on paper, 41.5 × 26.5 cm
Division of Political History, National Museum of American History, Smithsonian Institution, Washington D.C., United States

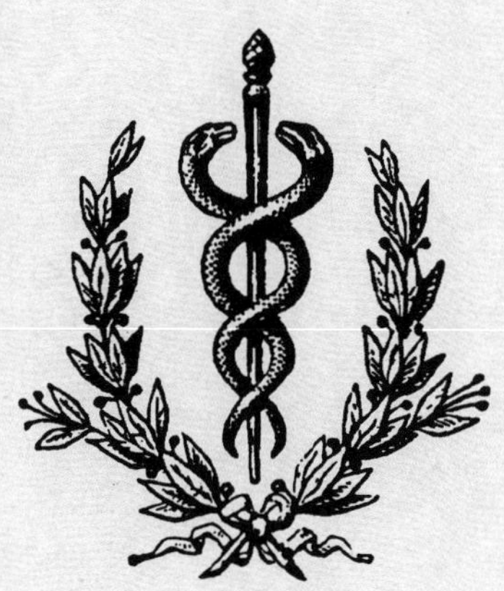

55

55
*All People With AIDS
Are Innocent*
ACT UP, Spring AIDS
Action, 1988
Photocopy on paper,
41.5 × 26.5 cm
Division of Political
History, National
Museum of American
History, Smithsonian
Institution,
Washington D.C.,
United States

56
Banner *All People
With AIDS Are Innocent*,
in front of the social
service agency Henry
Street Settlement,
New York, United
States, 1988
Gran Fury Collection,
Manuscripts and
Archives Division,
The New York Public
Library, United States

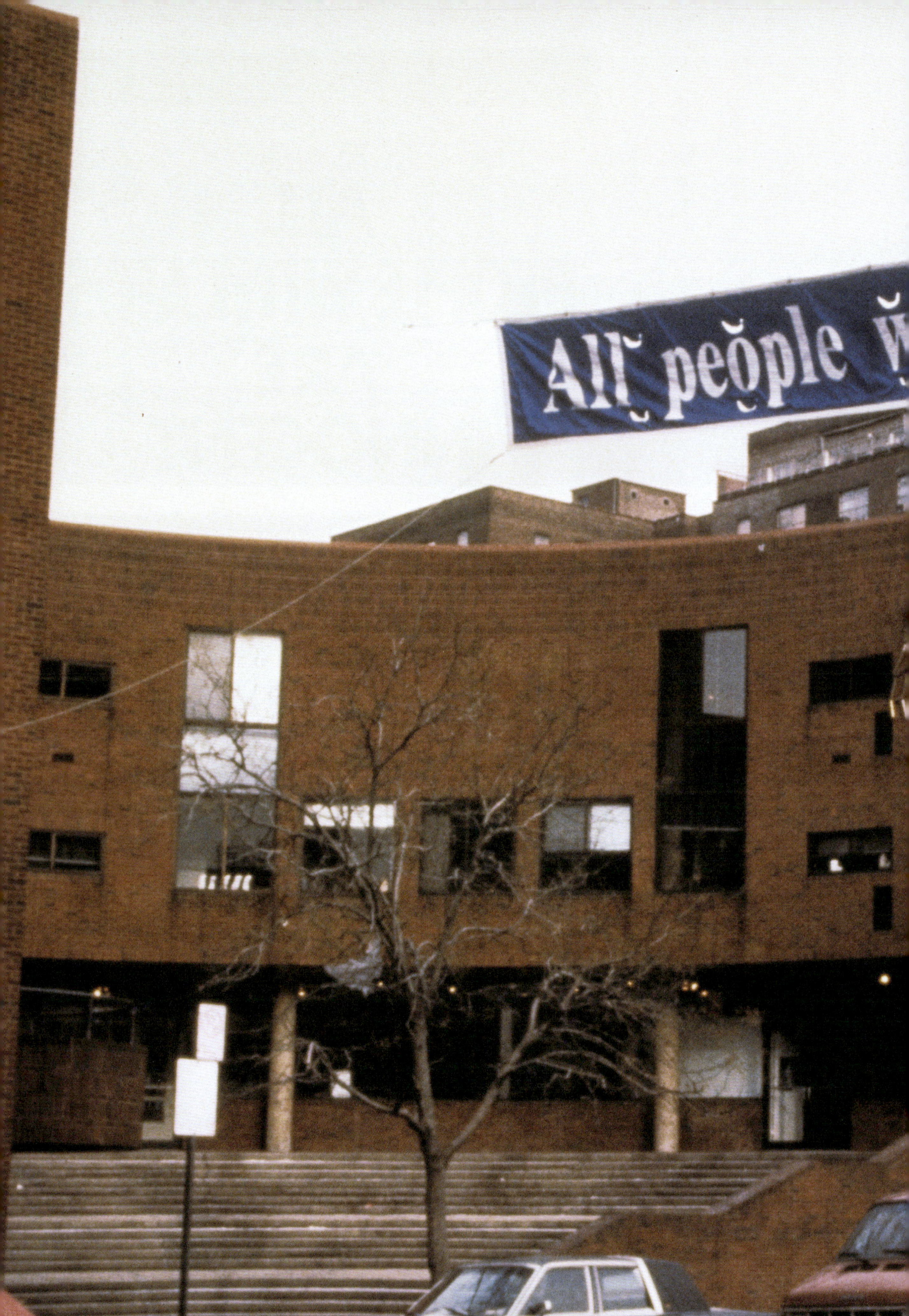
All people w

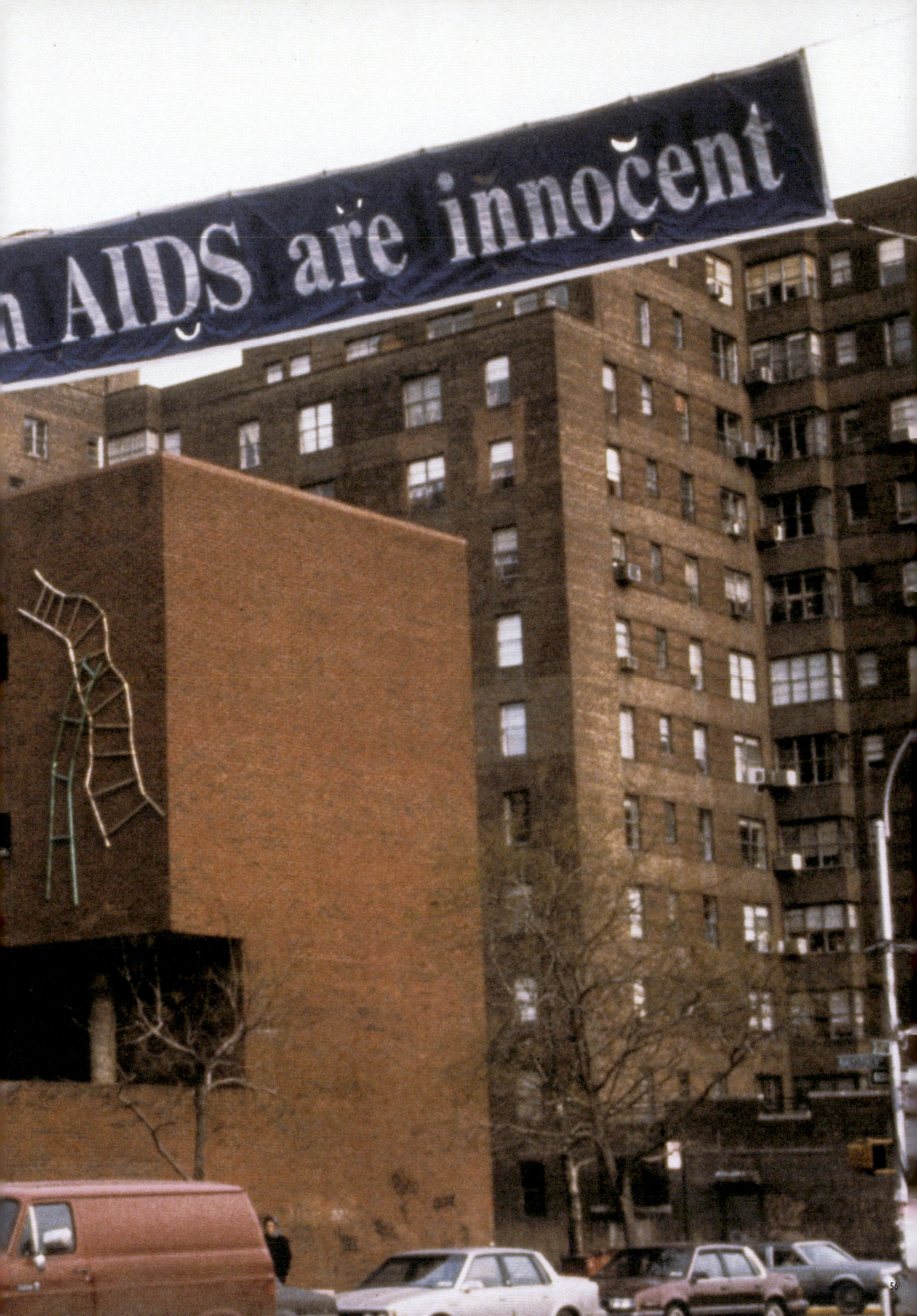
h AIDS are innocent

57
Art Is Not Enough, 1988
Offset print on paper,
54.5 × 34.5 cm
Poster for a series of
events at The Kitchen,
in 1988, New York,
United States

WITH 42,000 DEAD
ART
IS NOT ENOUGH
TAKE
COLLECTIVE
DIRECT
ACTION
TO END
THE AIDS
CRISIS
The Kitchen
December   512 West 19th Street   New York, NY 10011   January
Karen Finley   11/30–12/3   Wolfgang Stahle   1/3–28
Two In Twenty   12/6–23   Robert Longo   1/7
Stephen Petronio   12/8–18   Blueblack Collective 1/13–14
                                    Spin Doctors   1/18–2/18
Reservations 255-5793
Gran Fury

______

58
*Art Is Not Enough
[Over 700,000 Cases of
AIDS Worldwide]*, 1990
Offset print on paper,
29.5 × 21 cm
Gran Fury Collection,
Manuscripts and
Archives Division,
The New York Public
Library, United States

OVER 700,000 CASES OF AIDS WORLDWIDE
PEOPLE ARE TAKING DIRECT ACTION

In Washington, D.C., demonstrations by AIDS activists at the Food and Drug Administration resulted in the speedier release of experimental medicines for HIV related illnesses, and a reevaluation of the drug approval and distribution process.

In Yaoundé, Cameroon, prostitutes performing under the name 'Les Amis de Rose et Douglas" present their play "Marriage Avec Le Condom" in bars and social clubs to help women negotiate safer sex practices with their partners.

In Sao Paulo, Brazil, transvestite Brenda Lee has established the Casa de Apoio to provide care and shelter to HIV+ transvestites.

In West Germany, where 30% of all IV drug users test HIV+, Deutsche AIDS-Hilfe distributes over 600,000 clean needles annually in 90 cities to slow the spread of HIV infection.

In Mexico City, the grass roots organization Superbarrio stages media events and poster campaigns using the popular culture of professional wrestling to teach AIDS prevention and condom use.

In London and New York, demonstrations by ACT UP (the AIDS Coalition to Unleash Power) protesting the high cost of AZT resulted in a 20% reduction of its price by the manufacturer Burroughs Wellcome.

In Bangkok, Thailand, where HIV infection among prostitutes has increased tenfold in one year, choreographer Natee Teerarejjanapongs has organized safe sex strip shows in tourist bars to educate prostitutes and their clients about condoms.

In Amsterdam, while the United States hosts the Sixth International Conference on AIDS (June 21 to 24, 1990), activists will use computer and satellite broadcasts to facilitate the free flow of information across international borders and to protest U.S. policies which restrict the entry of foreigners with HIV infection.

ART IS NOT ENOUGH
TAKE DIRECT ACTION TO END THE AIDS CRISIS

Gran Fury

Funding for this project was provided by Hali Briendel, Eric Anderson, Earl Millard, and the Penny McCall Foundation. Photograph of Pope: Dennis Brack/Black Star

WITH 47,524 DEAD, ART IS NOT ENOUGH

Our culture gives artists permission to name oppression, a permission denied those oppressed.

Outside the pages of this catalogue, permission is being seized by many communities to save their own lives.

WE URGE YOU TO TAKE COLLECTIVE DIRECT ACTION TO END THE AIDS CRISIS

Gran Fury

59

Art Is Not Enough
Poster for the exhibition catalog
AIDS: The Artists' Response, at the Ohio State University, 1989
Offset print on paper

DURING THIS PROGRAM AT LEAST 6 PEOPLE WITH AIDS WILL DIE.

We cordially invite you to:

🕭 Turn grief into action. 🕭 Arm yourself with facts.

🕭 Demand access to health care and experimental drugs, explicit AIDS education, and legal protection for everyone.

Gran Fury

60

During This Program At Least 6 People With AIDS Will Die, program insert in The Bessies, New York Dance and Performance Awards, 1988
Offset print on paper, 10.5 × 17 cm

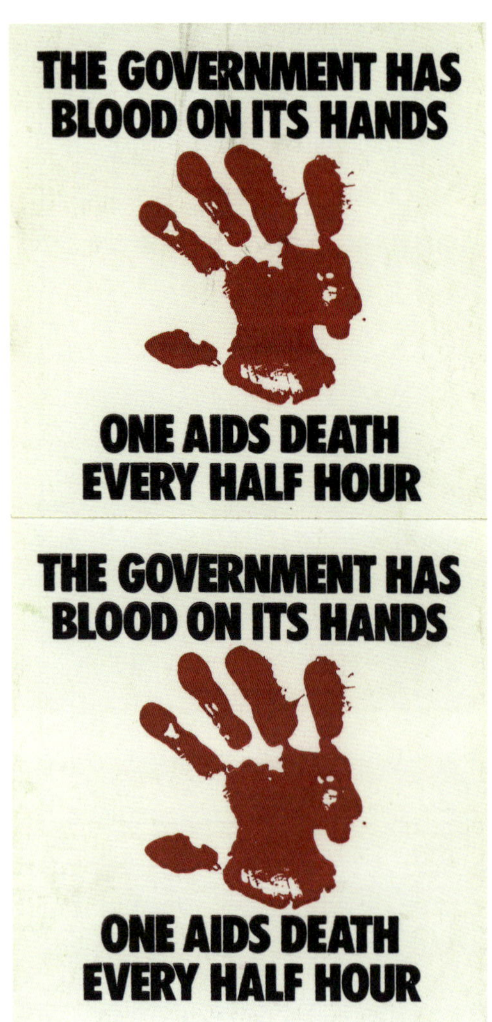

61

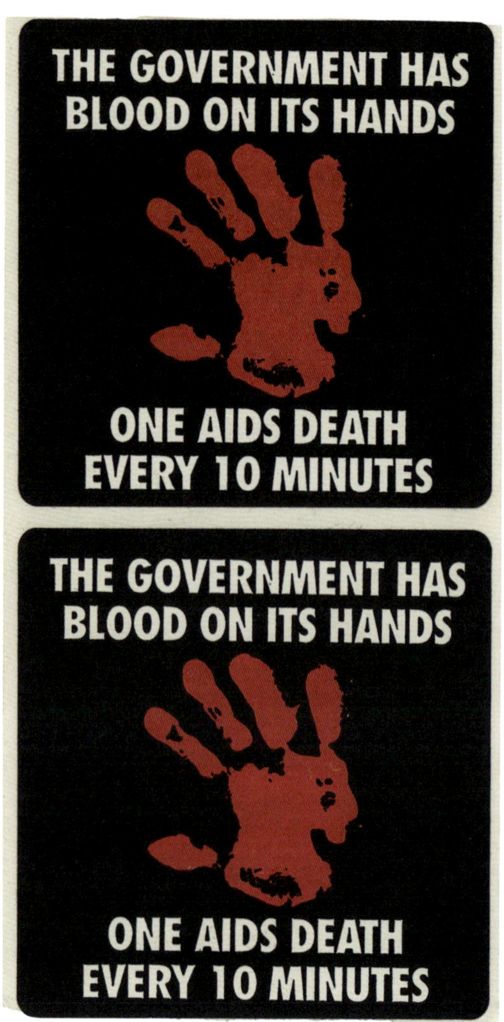

62

61, 62
The Government Has Blood on Its Hands, 1988
ACT UP, N.Y. City
Dept. of Health
Demonstration
Offset print on sticker, 7.5 × 7.5 cm
Gran Fury Collection, Manuscripts and Archives Division, The New York Public Library, United States

63
Bloody Handprint on Mailbox, 1988
Gran Fury Collection, Manuscripts and Archives Division, The New York Public Library, United States

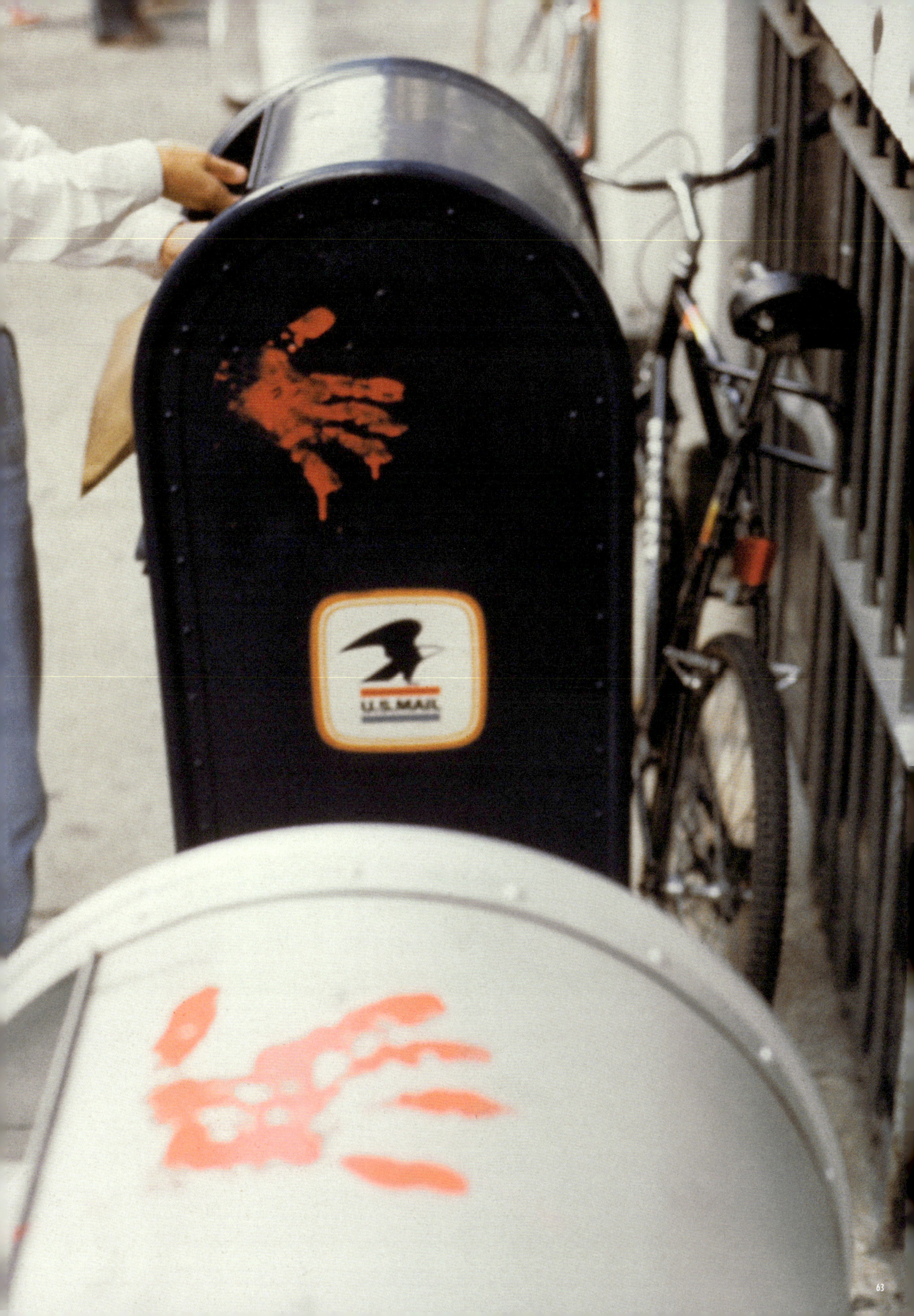

U.S. MAIL

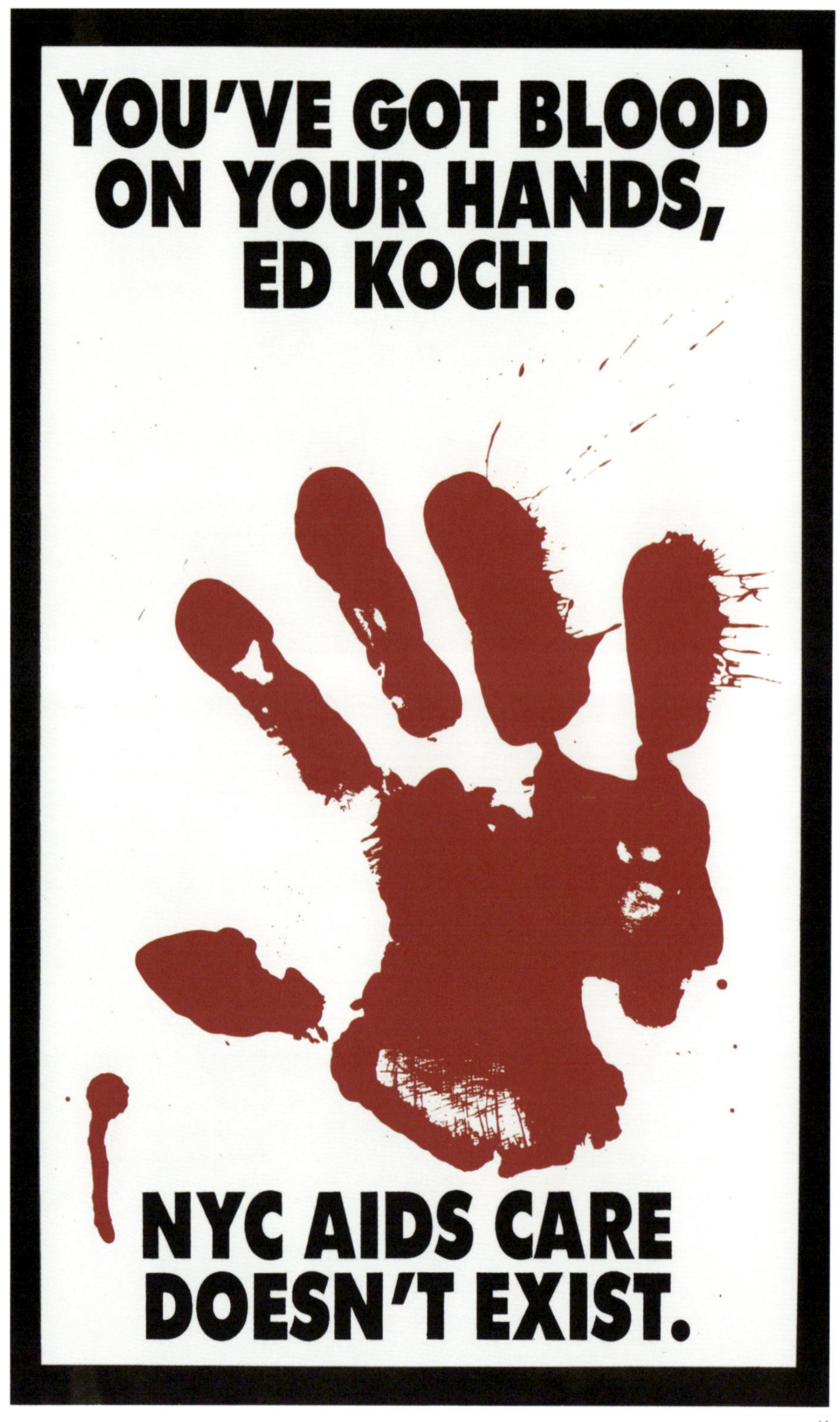

64
*The Government Has
Blood on Its Hands
(3 versions)*, 1988
ACT UP, N.Y. City Dept. of
Health Demonstration,
United States
Offset print on paper,
80.5 × 54.5 cm
Gran Fury Collection,
Manuscripts and Archives
Division, The New York
Public Library, United States

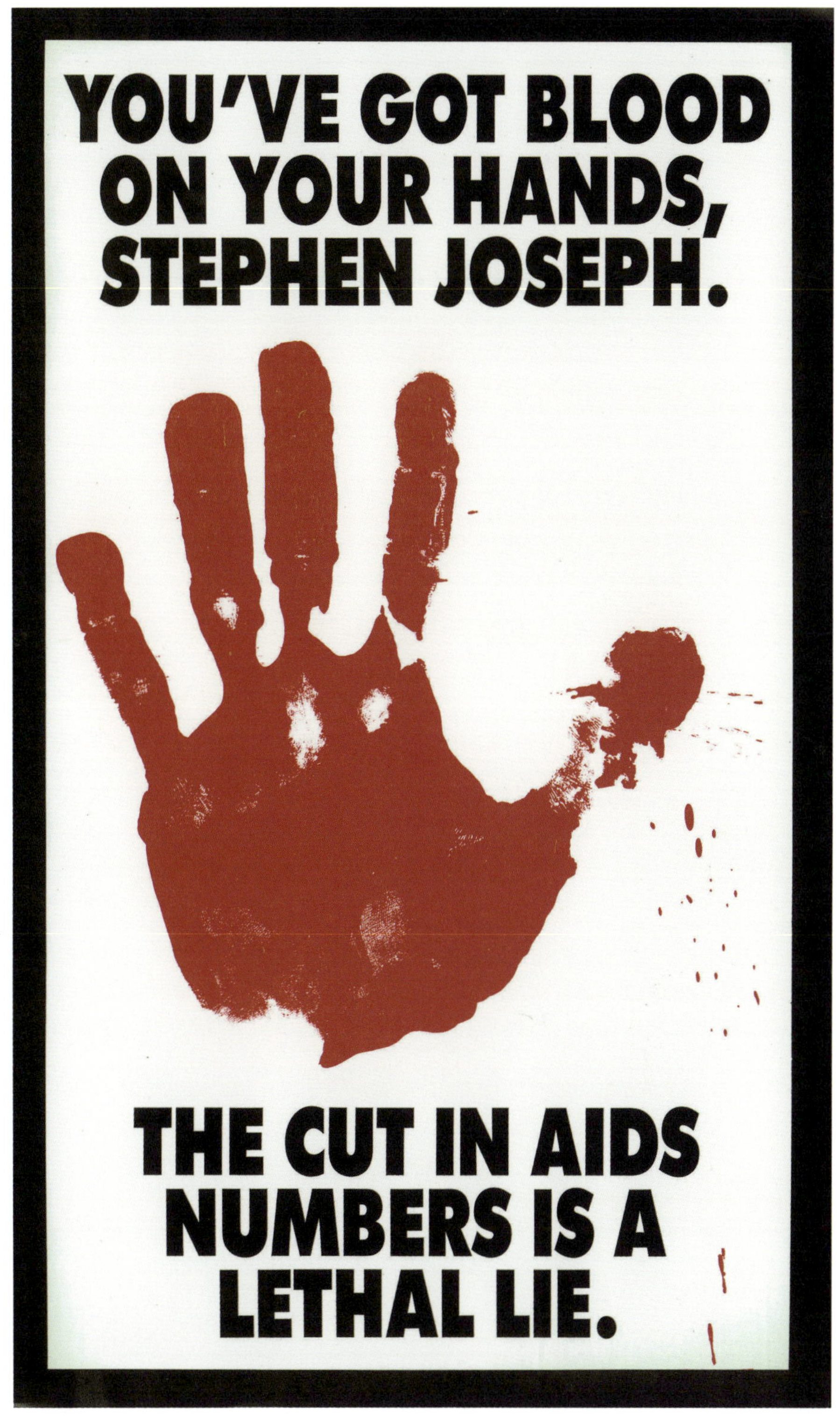

65

*The Government Has
Blood on Its Hands
(3 versions)*, 1988
ACT UP, N.Y. City Dept. of
Health Demonstration,
United States
Offset print on paper,
80.5 × 54.5 cm

66
*The Government Has
Blood on Its Hands
(3 versions)*, 1988
ACT UP, N.Y. City Dept. of
Health Demonstration,
United States
Offset print on paper,
80.5 × 54.5 cm

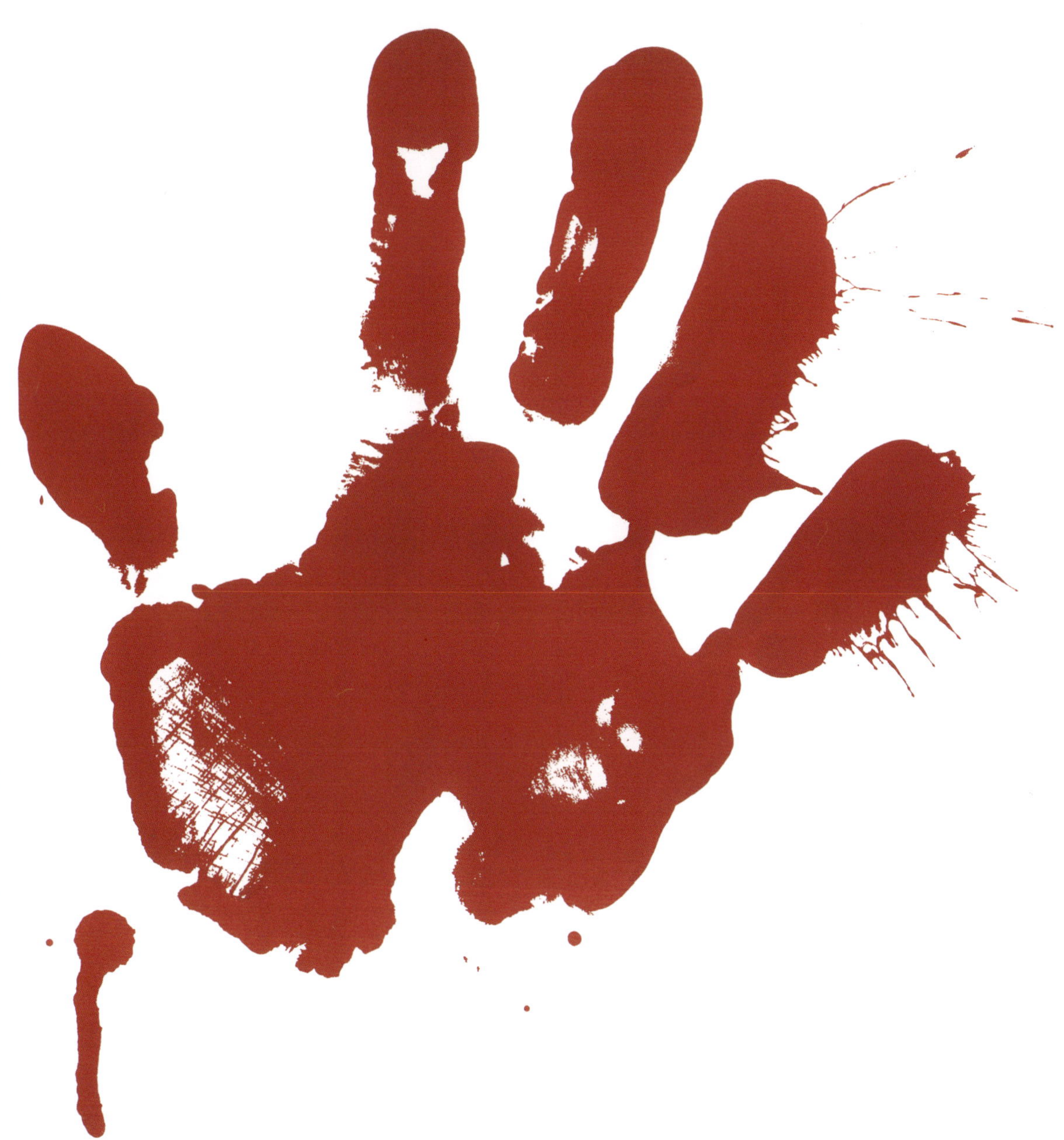

THE GOVERNMENT HAS
BLOOD ON ITS HANDS
ONE AIDS DEATH
EVERY HALF HOUR

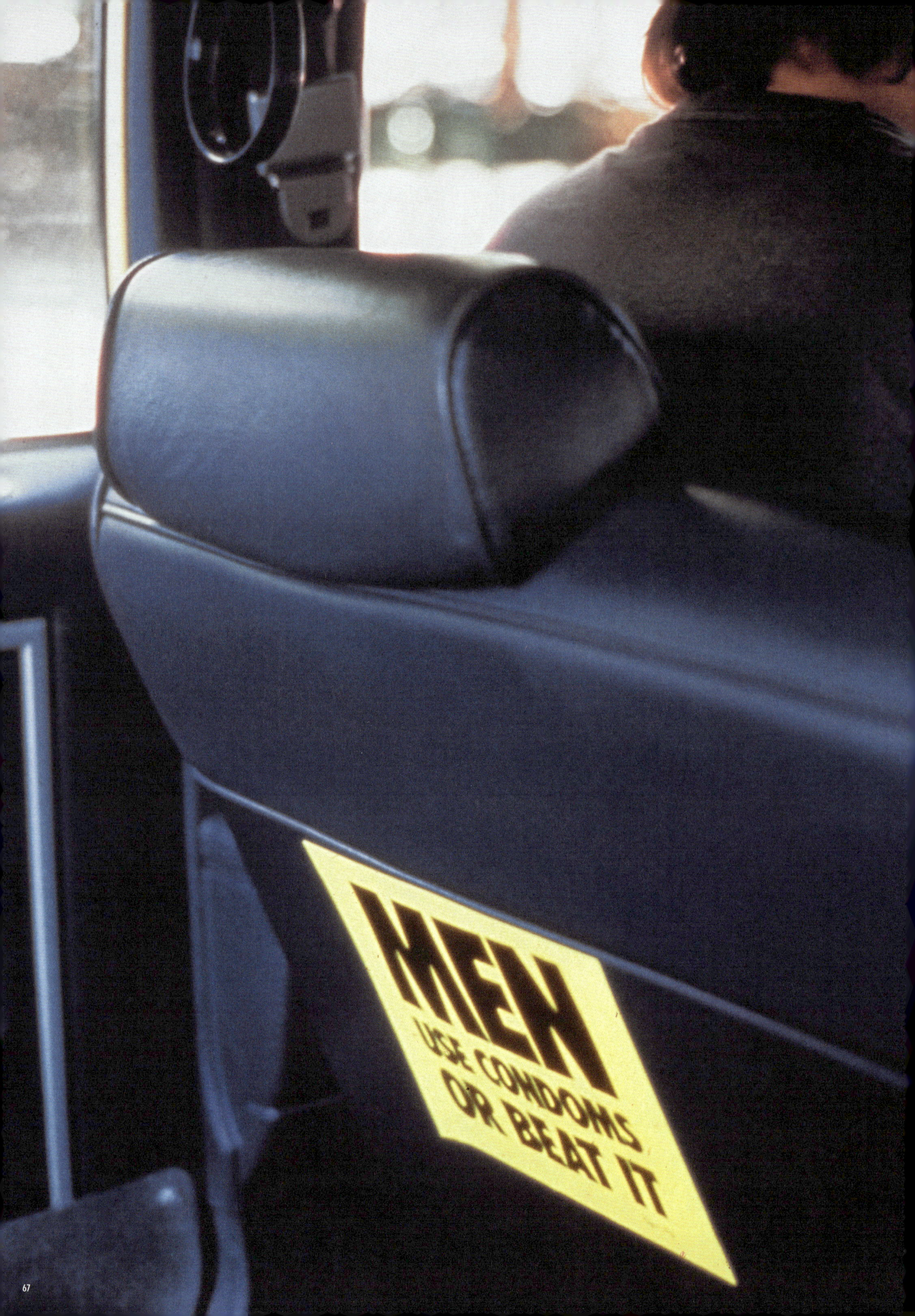
MEN
USE CONDOMS
OR BEAT IT

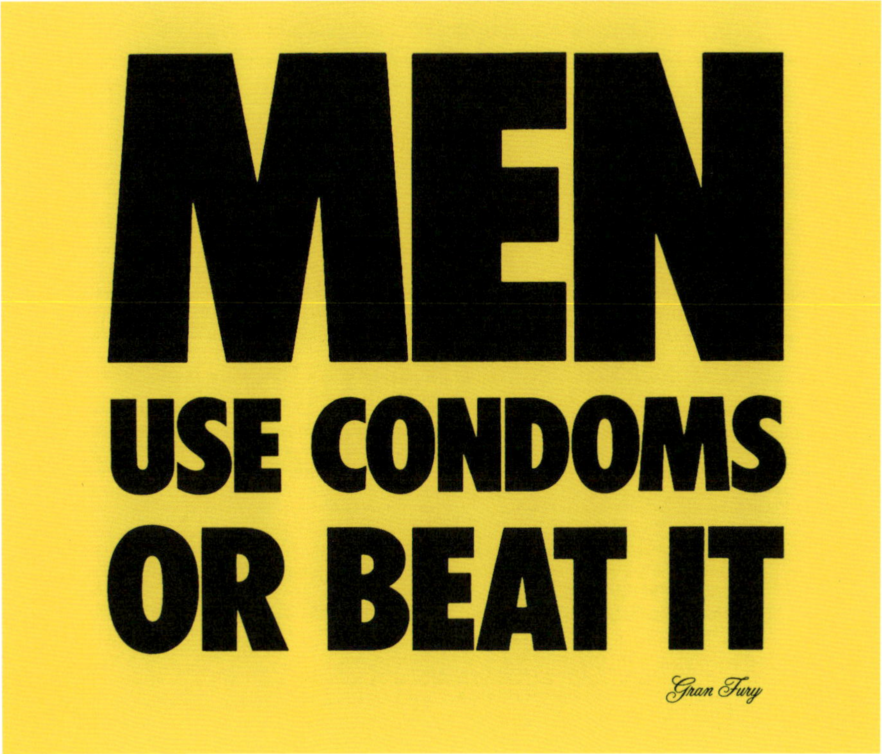

68

67

Men Use Condoms or Beat It, sticker in taxi, 1988
Gran Fury Collection, Manuscripts and Archives Division, The New York Public Library, United States

68

Men Use Condoms or Beat It, 1988
Silkscreen on sticker, 18 × 22 cm

69

Men Use Condoms or Beat It sticker on brick wall, 1988
Gran Fury Collection, Manuscripts and Archives Division, The New York Public Library, United States

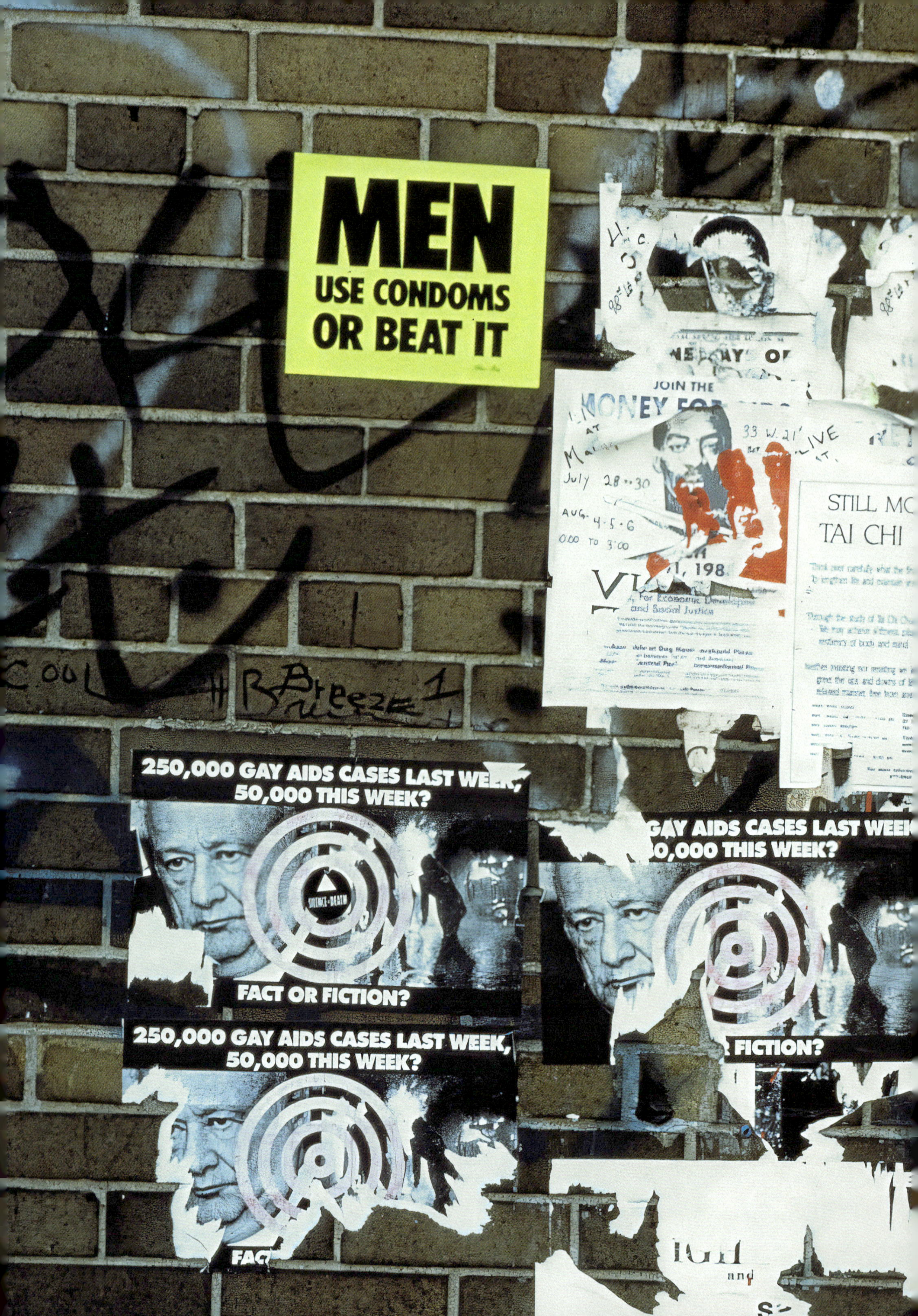

MEN
USE CONDOMS
OR BEAT IT
JOIN THE
MONEY FOR
33 W. 21
July 28-30
AUG. 4-5-6
0:00 to 3:00
1, 198
For Economic Development
and Social Justice
STILL MO
TAI CHI
COOL
#BBreeze 1
250,000 GAY AIDS CASES LAST WEEK,
50,000 THIS WEEK?
SILENCE = DEATH
FACT OR FICTION?
250,000 GAY AIDS CASES LAST WEEK,
50,000 THIS WEEK?
FACT
GAY AIDS CASES LAST WEEK
0,000 THIS WEEK?
FICTION?
and

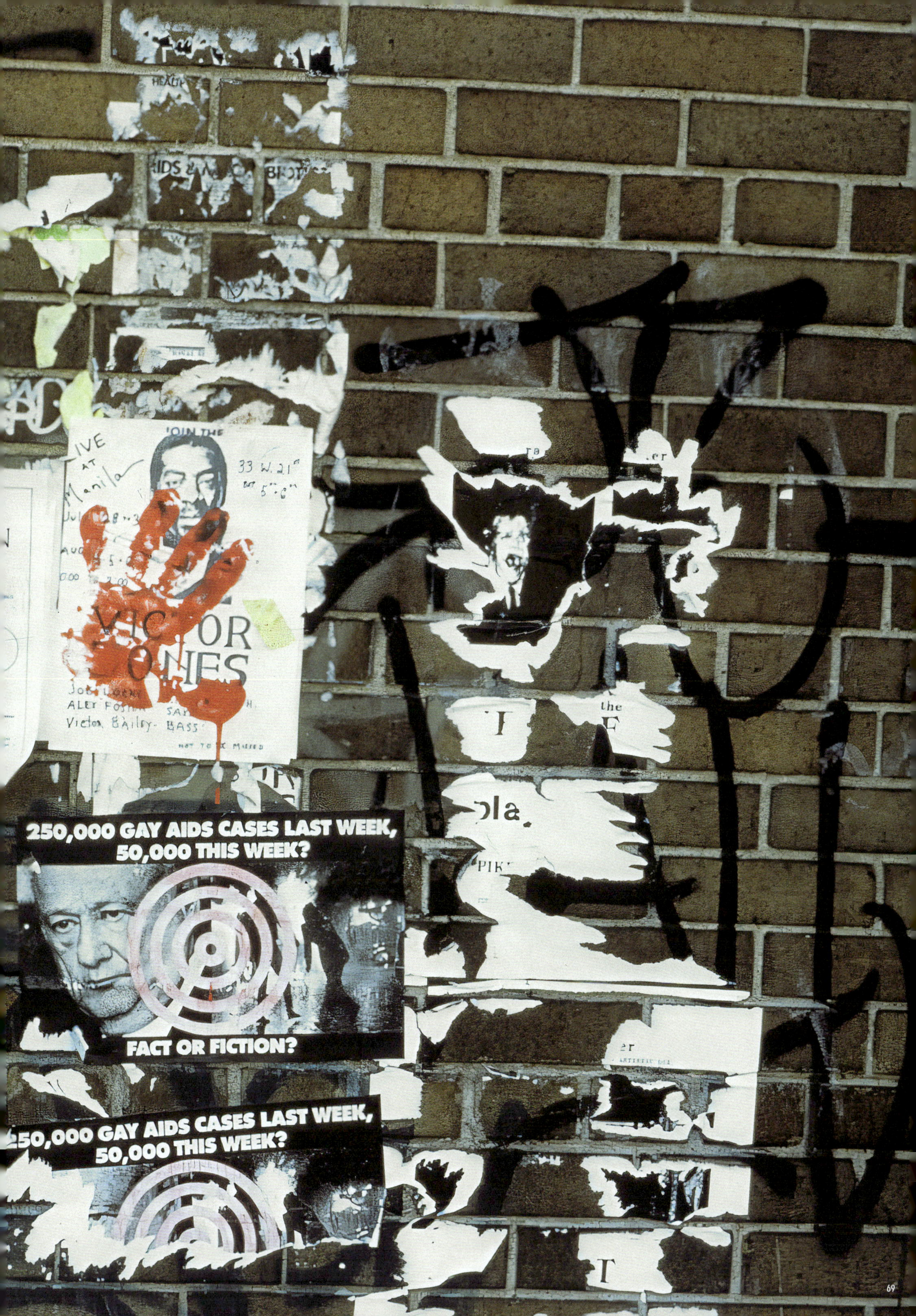
VICTOR
ONES
250,000 GAY AIDS CASES LAST WEEK,
50,000 THIS WEEK?
FACT OR FICTION?
250,000 GAY AIDS CASES LAST WEEK,
50,000 THIS WEEK?

70–72
The New York Crimes,
1989
ACT UP, Target City Hall
Demonstration,
United States
Offset print on
newsprint, 58 × 38 cm

The New York Crimes

Early Edition

New York: Today, high pressure systems likely as storms build and waves break. Highs and lows. Some clouds form completely clearing. Details at City Hall.

NOT TO BE CONFUSED WITH THE NEW YORK TIMES · NEW YORK, TUESDAY, MARCH 28, 1989 · FREE

AIDS and Money:

Healthcare or Wealthcare?

Decisions Made Disregard the Sick

Profiteering from healthcare is not news in this country, but AIDS, which stands at the crossroads of medicine, morality and free enterprise, throws the trauma of human greed into sharp focus. The relationship between money and government programs to end the AIDS crisis needs very close scrutiny.

EXAMPLE: AIDS is not yet big enough to be honored by the full attention of the financial community. According to a spokesperson for Hoffman-LaRouche Inc., "Sure one million AIDS cases is an exciting market, but it's not asthma." Profit incentives come first, even in matters of life and death. Investors play Beat the Clock, wondering if they will win the big bucks in the race between the development of new drugs and the "short" life expectancy of the people who need them.

EXAMPLE: The complex and rigid FDA protocols for approval of new AIDS drugs works within the confines of an Old Boy Network. AZT, a drug originally invented by the NIH, was sped through the process, while many applications by less connected researchers have been returned for misplaced commas. The FDA offers no assistance to outsiders for permeating their inscrutable systems. Consequently, smaller pharmaceuticals cannot satisfy the impenetrable pre-requisites, stockholders lose faith, and bankruptcy looms. Promising AIDS therapies are lost in the process.

EXAMPLE: Federal spending for AIDS education programs should have only one objective: to halt the spread of AIDS. However, in an attempt to suit ALL Americans (they are, after all, paying for it), the content of the campaigns is watered down in subcommittees, extracted is all the *specific* information which is necessary and useful to the affected communities — how to have safe sex and clean needles. The result: AIDS continues to spread, money is wasted, and the individuals that need the information most are walled out.

EXAMPLE: AIDS is consistently compared to other illnesses. Cancer experts state that considering the death toll, the amount of money spent on AIDS is proportionate to the amount spent on cancer. Cancer is not communicable. Nor are cancer patients victimized by discrimination, which can lead to the loss of housing and employment. Some also contend that AIDS is the result of "lifestyle", so it should be the burden of those who are stricken. That is exactly what people said about cancer thirty years ago.

EXAMPLE: Government short cuts, like the call for widespread mandatory testing, fit comfortably with the conservative agenda because they are finite: a seemingly concrete result for the money spent. Mandatory testing is pointless, arbitrary segregationism. The many remaining issues, from housing to hospitalization to the depletions of the national work force, are ignored. In its myopia, it temporarily lulls the "safe" into feeling safer, and avoids the inescapable long range costs.

So, the next time you pass a noisy demonstration calling for more money to fight AIDS, consider people with AIDS, who are being tossed around like political footballs while the powers that be bicker over who will reap the profits from their illness and who will foot the bill for their deaths.

THOUSANDS OF NEW YORKERS MAY BE DYING IN THE STREETS

STATE'S HIGHEST COURT FINDS CITY LEGALLY RESONSIBLE

NEW YORK, Mar. 27 — Recently released estimates show that thousands of New Yorkers may die in the streets in the next five years, victims of the Koch administration's callow indifference to homeless people with AIDS.

In another recent development, the New York State Supreme Court reviewed a case that centered around the city's responsibility to provide appropriate housing for a homeless man with AIDS related complex. In the case, *Phillips v. Grinker*, the court found that the city's Human Resource Administration has a legal responsibility to provide the plaintiff with a separate room rather than a shelter bed, where he would be continually exposed to potentially fatal infections.

Experts claim that City Hall's recently unveiled plan to provide 840 beds over the next three years for homeless people with AIDS (PWA's) fall drastically — if not criminally — short of what will be needed. Current figures released by the Coalition for the Homeless put the number of PWA's presently living on the street at 5,000. The Coalition, which unlike the city has attempted to verify the size of the homeless PWA population, predicts that by 1991 there will be upwards of 15,000 people with AIDS or HIV infection without homes. If the city meets its own deadlines, the projected facilities — eight sites scattered throughout the Bronx, Brooklyn and Manhattan — will bring to just over 1,000 the total number of beds available. This would still leave over 90 percent of the homeless PWA population living in the streets and shelters: over 14,000 people.

Little Cause for Hope

Ignoring the fact that the city has no plans for the design, development or operation of the facilities — casting doubt on its sincerity of purpose — there is little cause for hope that the city will be able to attain its own pathetically modest goals. The city has so far failed in its two-year-old promise to build a 12-bed annex to Bailey House, a 44-bed facility currently the city's only residence for homeless PWA's.

Other factors exist which make it even more unlikely that the city's plans will ever reach fruition. As with the homeless

Continued on next page

WOMEN AND AIDS: OUR GOVERNMENT'S WILLFUL NEGLECT

The AIDS crisis throws the inequities between women and men into sharp relief. When women are dependent on men financially, they are inevitably dependent on them for healthcare. When women are not dependent on men financially, men still control the medical system which provides their care. Women have only recently and partially been included in AIDS studies, the majority of which have been based only on the model of male bodies. These inequities have made it difficult or impossible for women to recieve experimental therapies and adequate health care. Women living with AIDS are among the many individuals tied up in the red tape of governmental bureaucracy. Many have died waiting.

AIDS is the leading cause of death for women between the ages of 25-35 in New York City. Of these cases, 51% are Black, 32% are Latino. While women comprise 8% of the national cases, they total 12% of the cases in New York City, and 28% in Newark. 29% of these cases are the result of heterosexual contact, 51% are IV drug users or the sexual partners of IV drug users.

Women are routinely denied access to experimental drug trials. These trials are often the only means of treatment for HIV infected persons. When women are not locked out explicitly by the design of the clinical trials, they are the victims of de facto discrimination: poverty and the lack

Continued on next page

N.Y. HOSPITALS IN RUINS; CITY HALL TO BLAME

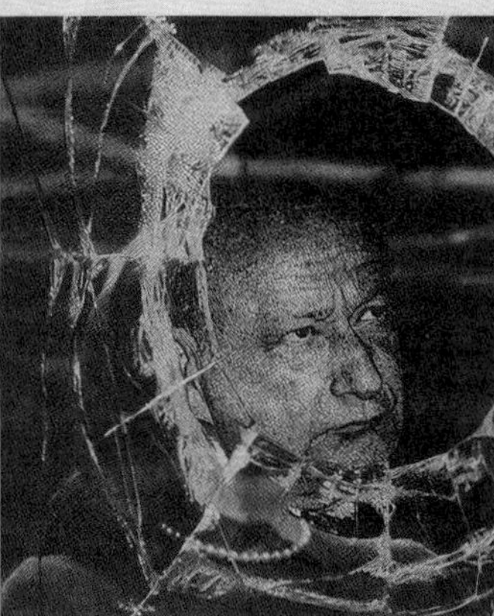

Mayor Koch examines the ruins of New York City after years of his neglect. Critics blame the demise of the hospital system and the lack of AIDS services on his administration.

KOCH FUCKS UP AGAIN

NEW YORK, March 27 — Healthcare in New York City is the issue no mayoral candidate dares to address. As the collapse of the city hospital system appears imminent, more New Yorkers will be affected by the AIDS epidemic than are infected by the human immunodeficiency virus or HIV, the virus believed to cause AIDS.

The city healthcare system, already in severe crisis after more than a decade of inadequate funding, staffing and patient management, must assume a disproportionate share of the burden of AIDS, which in this city is increasingly a poor person's disease. Preventive and community medicine for the city poor is virtually nonexistent and the overflow from city hospitals is already threatening to flood the emergency rooms of New York City's voluntary and private hospitals.

The city's "Strategic Plan for AIDS" states that New Yorkers infected with HIV should be treated at local AIDS Assessment Centers. These centers would provide their infected clients with a range of "primary care" services which include monitoring the immune system, treatment for current medical problems, and preventive therapy against HIV-related opportunistic infections.

"Either inadequate care or none," says a Brooklyn doctor

There are now only two AIDS Assessment Centers in the city. Healthcare workers complain that this is not nearly enough to meet current need, a need they say grows daily. One of the Centers, the Community Health Project in the Greenwich Village section of Manhattan, has a six-month waiting list for new clients. The other, Woodhull Clinic in the Bushwick Health Center in Brooklyn, which was treating over 700 people with HIV infection per month in 1988, has stopped taking new patients indefinitely. "This glut means that most people with HIV-infection and no health insurance are either receiving no care or going to emergency rooms and receiving inadequate care — or even the wrong care if they're misdiagnosed," said one doctor from the Woodhull Clinic.

The emergency rooms of the public hospitals are asked to provide healthcare to many poor people because primary care facilities in poor communities are overcrowded, inadequate or do not exist, and these emergency rooms are overtaxed in other ways. Although public hospitals have only 16 percent of the acute-care hospital beds in the city, they are hospitalized for more than 37 percent of the people who are hospitalized for AIDS-related conditions in New York City. The resulting shortage of beds means that it is common for patients, with and without AIDS, to wait several days in city emergency rooms until a bed is available.

Empty Beds and No Sheets

"It would be wrong to think the healthcare crisis results simply from a shortage of facilities," said a leader of a local healthcare workers' union: "there's a shortage of staff as well." The public hospitals' freeze on hiring personnel not directly involved in patient care means that the rest of the staff, including nurses and even some doctors, are performing tasks that are essential to a hospital's functioning but unrelated to direct patient care. This, plus the low salaries and the cap on the amount of overtime public hospital personnel can work, all make the prospect of working at a public hospital unattractive. Rumors of these working conditions have exacerbated in New York

Continued on next page

INSIDE

Cocaine IV Drug Use Undercounted
Research reveals the projected HIV sero-prevalence amongst IV Drug Users only counts the 250,000 heroin users, ignoring the 600,000 IV cocaine users.

Homeless Teenagers and AIDS
Covenant House, the only New York residence for homeless adolescents, councils abstinence to its clients. Meanwhile homeless teenagers 'often barter sex for food, shelter or money. Covenant House reports 35% of its new clients are HIV positive.

Koch City Plans: AIDS Deaths Help Gentrification
Economic redevelopment could actually benefit from the selective decimation of certain city communities by the AIDS virus. Koch's mania for redevelopment, realtors' greed and popular homophobia and racism cultivated by his administration, cut a swathe of death throughout the non-heterosexual neighborhoods of western Manhattan, the Lower East Side, south central Queens, central Brooklyn and virtually half of the Bronx.

Inmates with AIDS: Inadvertent Political Prisoners

NEW YORK, Mar. 27 — A prison is responsible for the health care of its inmates, a responsibility commanded by the Constitution and the Supreme Court. There are currently estimated to be 10,000-20,000 HIV-positive New Yorkers who spent some part of 1988 living as inmates at Rikers Island Prison. Most are distinguished by having a virus which is the leading cause of death among both male and female inmates there. Has NYC failed these people in fulfilling that responsibility?

Jose Vasquez thinks so. When he had his first bout with pneumonia in July 1987, he was sent to the Bellevue Hospital prison ward, where a battery of tests were performed, including tests for HIV antibodies and tuberculosis. When his test came back seropositive for HIV, he was returned to Rikers' "AIDS Dorm" where he was housed in the dorm's open ward with 40 other inmates.

Even after he recovered from his pneumonia, and his oral thrush and diarrhea were brought under control, he was not permitted to return to the normal life of an inmate in "general population." Prison policy requires that any inmate who has had one HIV-related infection remain in the AIDS Dorm as long as he is held on Rikers. Consequently, Mr. Vasquez's compromised immune system was exposed to all the various infections his wardmates were fighting off.

What he and the other ward residents did not know was that he had active tuberculosis. When Bellevue received the results of his TB test, Mr. Vasquez had already been returned to Rikers. Eight months later, the TB diagnosis arrived at Rikers. For Jose Vasquez, that only made matters worse. In a classic case of closing the barn door after the horse had escaped, he was placed in an isolation cell while being treated for his TB. The cell's toilet was clogged with feces, pigeons wandered in and out of broken windows leaving droppings next to his bed, and there was inadequate heat to combat the March cold. He was kept there for two weeks. While there, he was taken off his AZT because he developed a toxic reaction. This is a common problem among people with AIDS with multiple health problems related to their former drug use and lack of health care. Since AZT is the only drug available to HIV-infected inmates, his immune system continued to deteriorate.

Adequate medical care and non-segregated housing are only two of the issues raised by inmates recently interviewed at Rikers.

Unsafe sex and IV drug use occur on Rikers, but sex and drugs are illegal activities in jail, subjecting prisoners to further punishment. Condoms must be obtained through an infirmary appointment, requiring a kind of advance planning uncharacteristic of sexual behavior among any social group anywhere anytime.

Intravenous drug use was the route of HIV transmission for most of the infected inmates. While most are detoxed or must go "cold turkey" while at Rikers, no effort is made to bridge their adjustment upon release. Inmate representatives have repeatedly demanded the creation of halfway houses and social services designed to take advantage of one of the few positive aspects of the prison experience — it could save IV drug users' lives. The opportunies are lost when inmates return, homeless and cut off from social services to the streets of New York.

On the other hand, the recent arrest of nine Corrections Officers accused of smuggling drugs into the prison system highlights the ostrich-like response of the prison authorities to existing inmate drug use. Corrections officers are the source of the drugs and the handful of needles available — which are used and re-used by the inmates — increasing the likelihood of HIV transmission. The culprit is not only prison guard greed, but lack of adequate education for the inmates. "They give us a couple brochures and a lecture when we come in, but who you gonna trust when the same people have just thrown you in this hell-hole?" said one inmate. Inmate-initiated peer counselling programs — in their infancy stages in the state correctional system — have not been able to catch hold at Rikers, partly due to population transience. But much more can be done, the interviewed inmates agree.

For Jose Vasquez it has been too little too late: "I pled guilty to attempted robbery, but I didn't know it would be a life sentence," he said. New York State Commission on Correction statistics illustrate Mr. Vasquez's observation: prisoners diagnosed with AIDS live only half as long as people with similar backgrounds and demographic profiles who are not incarcerated.

Scientists discover real reason behind the high incidence of HIV infection in New York

---

What About People of Color? Race Effects Survival

Studies confirm what people of color have known for a long time: race is a major factor in surviving AIDS. It affects the amount and availability of AIDS information obtainable, and the quality of medical care people receive as well as the financial assistance available to them. It affects societal perceptions of a chronic long term condition.

The face of AIDS has never been totally a white, gay one in this country. The face of this illness is now also the face of a young Latino man or a young African-American woman. The demographics of this illness continue to permutate, as seen by the trail AIDS has cut through the minority communities of this country. As of September 30th, 1987, all reported cases of intravenous drug users with AIDS were people of color. People of color comprise 83 percent of the cases of heterosexual transmission. Latino and African-American gay men are never counted. Of 260 AIDS cases reported to the Minnesota Department of Health, 12 percent of them are people of color. People of color comprise 3.5 percent of Minnesota's population.

Historically, people of color have had limited access to quality healthcare. Consequently, responses to this limited access have developed. In a report published by Harvard medical researchers, we learn that blacks are less likely to have medical insurance than whites. Blacks use emergency rooms and clinics more. They have more difficulty in getting to doctors, hospitals and clinics than whites. Thirty-seven percent of the blacks in this study had not visited a doctor in a year. Of the blacks, 90 percent had not had an annual blood pressure check.

PWA's of color have consistently been denied access to experimental drug trials. A drug trial involving sickle cell anemia, a disease known to occur almost exclusively in blacks, excluded blacks from its roster.

Nationally, the incidence of AIDS in women of color has risen sharply. Vaginal sex is the primary means of heterosexual transmission. The risk of getting infected after having unprotected sex with the same partner varies from 10 to 45 percent. Negotiation of safer sex techniques for women of color involves battling traditional and religious belief systems; they risk a higher incidence of physical violence and loss of financial support. Among people of color, men with AIDS are known to outsurvive women with the disease almost unheard of. Children of color make up 78 percent of the pediatric AIDS cases for children younger than six. Abandoned children of color are the unwilling participants of unethical experimental drug trials, such as the trial at Kings County Medical Center in which children are strapped to hospital beds for a number of hours and are given a harmful placebo. [Ed. note: The sterile placebo affords the infant no good, and the needle can only be a portal for infection.]

For people of color, the issue is not better healthcare for those with AIDS, but better healthcare for all, regardless of their sex or sexual preference, skin color or economic situation. In treating the physical illnesses of AIDS, we treat symptoms of the greater diseases: the terminal conditions of sexism and racism, classism and homophobia.

N.Y. Health Commissioner Blinds Self to Crisis in Gay Community

Twice in the course of his testimony in criminal court last month, New York City Health Commissioner Stephen Joseph found it impossible to include the gay community of New York City on his list of city communities most severely affected by AIDS.

Joseph was on the stand for one and one-half days in the criminal trial of 11 members of the AIDS activist group, ACT UP.

Joseph as Oedipus?

On the stand the Commissioner's first failure to include gays among those most affected by AIDS was in answer to a direct question asking which communities have been hardest hit by the epidemic. "That's easy," beamed the witness, "the black and hispanic communities." While acknowledging the high toll that AIDS has taken in New York City's communities of color, many present in the court later expressed shock at the incompleteness of the Health Commissioner's answer. Several cited the high numbers of gay men who have died of the disease, and the growing numbers of gay men who are living with the disease in spite of the city's indifference and ineptitude in handling the health crisis. Others noted it was the gay community that developed models for AIDS education and AIDS care at a time when the city was spending next to nothing to halt the epidemic or alleviate the suffering. They feared that the Commissioner's refusal to recognize the crisis in the community might foreshadow cuts in funding for services to the community.

A Pattern Emerges

During cross-examination one of the defendants, acting as his own counsel, asked Joseph if he had not forgotten to include the gay community on his list of AIDS-affected communities. The Commissioner unequivocally declined the invitation to expand his original list. The courtroom full of AIDS activists, many of them gay, audibly gasped; it was clear to them that the city's Health Commissioner had intentionally written them off.

Asked to explain the Commissioner's manifest lapse, one longtime observer saw a pattern extending back to the release of the revised estimates: "Joseph couldn't acknowledge the suffering and the contributions of the city's gay community throughout this crisis. It would counter the new party line which says the crisis among gays is over, and the city won't have to fund services for them. There's little hope of relief for the community during the tenure of this shockingly insensitive Commissioner of Health."

Insults and Silence

In August of last year, the defendants entered Joseph's office at 125 Worth Street and demanded an explanation for the Health Department's recent cut in the estimates of infected gay and bisexual male New Yorkers from 250,000 to 50,000. (Many AIDS experts believe the Commissioner released the numbers to counter criticism from New York State that the city was systematically and catastrophically underestimating future AIDS service needs.) "What are you doing?" cried one of the defendants when he confronted the Commissioner in his office: "Your numbers don't add up!" Except for sporadic insults hurled at the activists who continued to pose their questions and express their concerns, Joseph remained silent throughout the half-hour encounter as, one by one, the ACT UP members were arrested and removed.

The next day the Commissioner decided to invite his ACT UP critics to his office for a discussion of the numbers anyway. Yet he decided to press charges against the 11 activists for asking their questions at an inconvenient time.

NEW YORK'S NEEDLE EXCHANGE PROGRAM: DESIGNED TO FAIL

NEW YORK, Mar. 27 — The needle exchange program in New York City, designed as a "pilot program" to reduce the spead of AIDS among intravenous drug users, is a morass of doubletalk; it is healthcare compromised by politics. Was it designed to fail? And by pitting the conservative black leadership of the city, who opposed the program, against the gay AIDS community, whose endorsement of the program he claims he secured, was Commissioner of Health and Human Services Stephen Joseph consciously seeking to divide these two potential allies, whose common interest in ending the AIDS crisis threatens the business-as-usual attitudes of city government?

By its own account, the city's response to the AIDS crisis has been woefully inadequate. Faced with a health crisis of immense proportions, and lacking the political will to marshal the necessary resources, NYC has spent nine long years attempting to avoid reality. In the poorest sections of the city, where IV drug use is endemic, this death-defying denial has taken on grim consequence: CONSERVATIVE estimates now indicate that 60 percent of the city's quarter million citizens who use IV drugs are now HIV positive. Also at risk for AIDS are their sexual partners and offspring.

Unable to deny the facts any longer, what did the Health Commissioner do? Did he move to force the State into expanding drug treatment programs and making treatment available on demand? Did he press to decriminalize the possession of syringes, and allow for over-the-counter sales? Did he support the creation of widespread clean needle and safer sex education campaigns, written in language that the affected communities could understand and respect? Did he endorse proposals to send mobile units - vans staffed with physicians and peer counsellors - into the impacted neighborhoods to reach the affected? All of these tactics have been successfully employed by needle exchange programs like those in Tacoma, Wa. and Liverpool, England.

The Commissioner chose to ignore these proven approaches. Instead, Dr. Joseph created his "pilot program."

Of course, only 200 addicts may participate. All must be willing to travel to lower Manhattan, to the city Health Department across the street from police headquarters. All must have a picture I.D. It's not enough to show up and ask for help either; all must be able to prove that they have already applied for treatement elsewhere. Even then, only one-half of those enrolled will actually be allowed to exchange a used needle for an unused sterile one; the other half will simply have their behavior (and their blood for the presence of HIV) monitored. Is it any suprise that in the first two weeks of operation only 12 people were enrolled?

There is a grim and inescapable logic to the Commissioner's behavior. A population rent asunder by drugs represents little political threat. If a fatal disease can further weaken and destroy, so much the better. Of course, in this enlightened age we must make the appearance of trying to solve problems, so we create pilot programs, replete with administrative procedures, bureaucratic bottlenecks and ample new busywork for City employees. And if in doing so, we create competition and dissention among our foes, better still.

Dr. Joseph stated that he considers his program to be "a sign post to open levels of thinking and inquiry." Inquiry leads us to the conclusion that his program is a failure. Thinking about it, we wonder if he does not prefer it this way.

Thousands Dying

Continued from previous page

population in general, the city continues to refuse to consider using city-owned buildings to provide housing, proposing instead to purchase privately-owned property. By failing to consult with community-based organizations before announcing the selected sites, the city has insured that the issue will remain embroiled in the political fires of competing interests. Already, two of the planned sites have caused heated controversy: the first because the current owners have invested in extensive renovations for use as a union-based outpatient medical care facility, the second because it has already been proposed as a community center and home for seniors.

Because the city provides no AIDS assessment or counseling services for homeless people, has not formulated any AIDS risk reduction guidelines, provides no early interventions or treatments targeted toward the HIV-positive population, and offers no assistance to those seeking possibly lifesaving medications such as AZT or aerosolized pentamidine, it is highly unlikely that the rate of illness and infection will slow any time soon. Eventually the city may be spurred to action if it is faced with the possibility of being held criminally negligent, or worse, in the deaths of thousands of people.

The plight of New Yorkers who are sick and dying in the streets may finally move the populace into forcing the city to find the political will to seriously address the problem. Until a time of such resolve, an unacceptable situation can only grow worse.

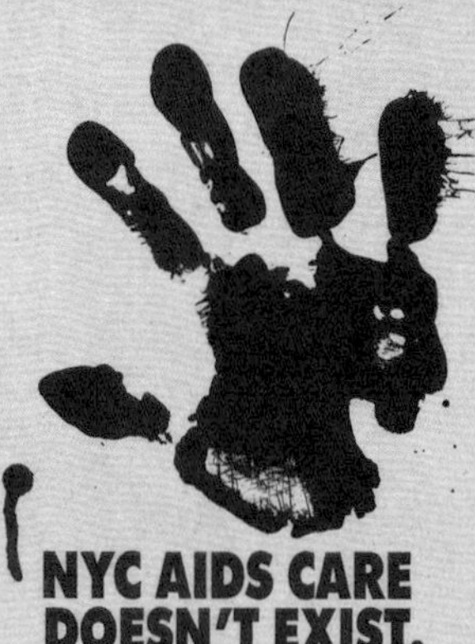

City Judge, State and Federal Officials Refute City AIDS Estimates

Bruce Lembert

Federal and state health officials today harshly criticized the data, assumptions and results of New York City Health Commissioner Stephen B. Joseph's revised estimate of New Yorkers infected with HIV, the virus which causes AIDS. And in a stunning, related victory for New York AIDS activists, city criminal judge Laura E. Dreger today acquitted 11 members of ACT UP, the AIDS Coalition to Unleash Power, of charges of criminal trespass at the Department of Health last year after Dr. Joseph released his new estimate.

In an Atlanta press conference, Dr. James W. Curron of the Centers for Disease Control (CDC) harshly criticized the adequacy of New York City's AIDS surveillance program. "By their own admission", Curron said, "The City undercounted HIV-related deaths among IV drug users by 130%." Drug users account for a majority of new city AIDS cases. "New York City surveillance data is a joke," Curron continued. "As a result, our picture of the extent of HIV infection in the nation's hardest-hit area is incomplete." While Dr. Joseph estimated 149,000 to 226,000 New Yorkers are HIV-infected, the CDC estimate is 230,000 to 345,000.

In Albany, State Health Commissioner Dr. David Axelrad also attacked the City estimates. "New York City cut its estimates to fit lowered funding projections," said Dr. Axelrad, "while they use higher estimates in private conferences with state personnel in order to request more state funds. Dr. Joseph's revision was irresponsible at best, hypocritical at worst."

In 1986, the City Department of Health had estimated 400,000 New Yorkers were infected with HIV. In July 1988, Commissioner Joseph released revised estimates which slashed that figure in half, to 200,000. Estimates of infected men who have sex with men decreased 80%, and estimates of infected IV drug users decreased by half. Yet actual AIDS caseload figures show rates of infection are increasing among gay men of color and especially among IV drug users. The new City estimates were supported by a report issued in February 1989, by an "independent" outside committee appointed by Dr. Joseph. "The 'independent national' committee was a figleaf devised by Dr. Joseph to rectify an estimate based on zero filework and deeply flawed epidemiological assumptions," commented Dr. Axelrad.

Meanwhile at 100 Centre Street, City criminal judge Laura E. Dreger acquitted 11 members of ACT UP for criminal trespass. On August 3, 1988, the activists, concerned with the fiscal implications of the lowered estimates, confronted Dr. Joseph in his office at 125 Worth Street. Dr. Joseph swore and threatened the protesters, then had them arrested. In her opinion, Judge Dreger wrote "the defendents believed, and the evidence indicates they were correct, that the new city estimates were based on actual fieldwork and false assumptions about similarities between AIDS in New York and in San Francisco." The judge attempted to avoid setting a precedent that would enable future protesters to interrupt city officials by dismissing the charges "in the furtherance of justice" rather than acquitting them on the necessity defence they had advanced in court.

ACT UP member William Monaghan, one of the 11 acquitted defendents, said of the victory, "we put Stephen Joseph on trial for lying to the citizens of New York, and we won. More New Yorkers should become involved in changing the city's course on AIDS."

Mayor Koch, contacted thorough his press office, refused comment. Dr. Jospeh said "I have nothing to say. I stand by the results ratified by the independent national committee."

20,000 New Yorkers have been diagnosed with AIDS (Acquired Immune Deficiency Syndrome) and 12,000 of these have died. More than half of new cases are in IV-drug users, most of whom are African-American and Latino.

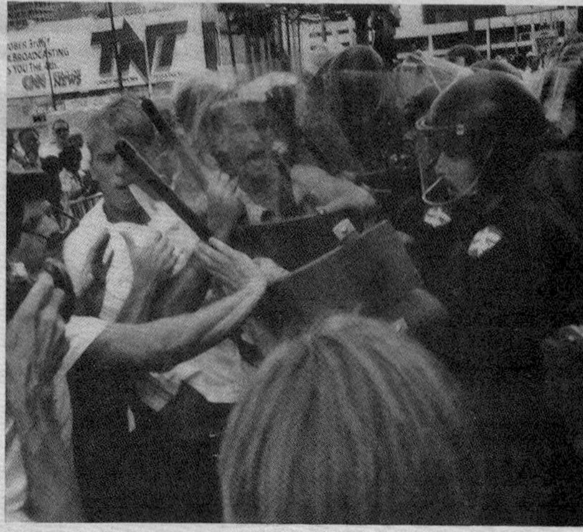

Letters

To the Editor:

As a native New Yorker, and one formerly proud of the services provided by our City's hospitals, I write to express my outrage over the poor standard of care endured by too many AIDS patients. One recent incident will serve to show how inadequate and indeed morally reprehensible the City's response to the AIDS crisis has been. Furthermore, these disgraceful and actually life-threatening lapses in both care and ethics threaten primarily—though not exclusively—the less advantaged (i.e. those without a private, hospital-associated physician).

The incident I would like to address occurred recently at one of the better-known East Side Manhattan hospitals, one in fact reputed to be a reliable provider of care for People With AIDS (PWAs).

A friend of mine, a Person With AIDS, was suffering from a form of pneumonia which he had correctly presumed to be PCP (Pheumocystis carinii pneumonia), an all too common infection striking People With AIDS. Upon arriving at the hospital's emergency room, extremely weak, gasping for breath, near collapse, and all alone, he was told he would have to wait three days for a bed. Yes—*three days* for a bed, when he was suffering from what thus far has been the leading cause of death for PWAs. However, he was subsequently told he could be admitted immediately if (and only if) he agreed to participate in a medical trial involving the use of aerosol pentamidine as treatment for his PCP. It was not explained to him that aerosol pentamidine is used as a prophylactic—*not* as treatment for full-blown cases of POP, the indicated mode of treatment for PCP being *intravenous* pentamidine or bactrim, another drug. As a result of becoming a guinea pig under conditions it would have been difficult for so ill a person to refuse, this patient nearly died. As a doctor later told him, and with no apparent concern, "We nearly lost you." Only at the last moment, after aerosol pentamidine had predictably failed and the patient was near death, was he given the correct medication (bactrim); the drug which should have been the initial choice, not the final.

That direly ill patients are being railroaded into dubious trials, after being threatened with the alternative of a three day wait in an overcrowded, unprepared hospital, is not the sort of thing one expects to hear about in a civilized society. One shudders to think how many similar tragedies are being played out in our hospitals each and every day.

We have had many years to brace ourselves properly for this epidemic. It is an indelible black mark on our City leaders' records (and consciences, should they possess such) that so little has been done—and that so little continues to be done. Only an unfeeling, uncaring, and incompetent government could state, upon unveiling its budget for AIDS care for the coming year, that it was entirely inadequate.

How many more New Yorkers will suffer degredation, disgraceful care, and death before our elected officials acknowledge the right of all citizens to speedy, responsible, and decent health care? What does the lack of this basic right say about our society's current state? And what does it say about New York's future? Indeed, a recent Rockefeller Brothers funded study, the Citizens' Commission on AIDS, warned that, due to the costs of the epidemic and the shortage of hospital beds, "New York's standing as the center of finance and business is at stake"—not to mention, of course, our standing as a caring, humane City.

If the above incident happened but once it would in itself be a disgrace. That it is continuing to occur, in whatever form, in whichever hospital, in ever-increasing numbers, is a human nightmare that must be addressed—and redressed—immediately.

THOMAS MCKEAN
New York, N.Y., March 28, 1989

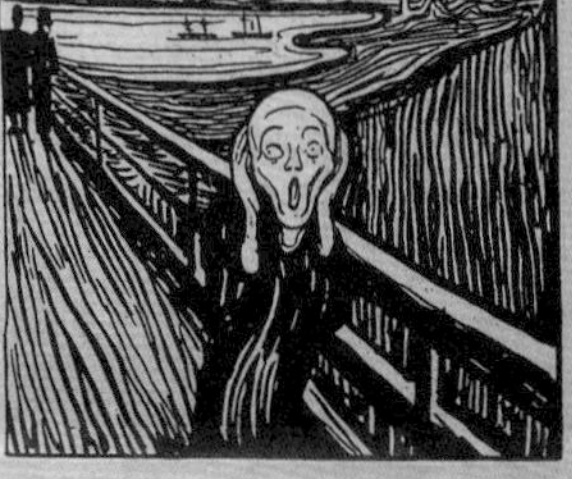

KOCH FUCKS UP

Continued from front page

City a nursing shortage that is nationwide. "It's crazy," said the union leader. "At the same time you find people waiting for beds in the emergency room, you'll find empty beds in the hospital, just waiting for someone to put clean sheets on them. Until there's more staff we can handle no more patients."

City Hall to Blame

When questioned about the implications of funding allocations at the public hospitals, past and present officials at the Health & Hospitals Corporation, the public interest corporation that operates the system of city-owned hospitals and healthcare facilities, point out the constraints under which the corporation operates. "Remember," said a former official of Bellevue, flagship hospital of New York City's system of public hospitals, "that it's the mayor, the City Council and the Board of Estimate that fix our budget. Remember that the city holds all the money the corporation makes through Medicaid payments and insurance companies, and only disburses it when it's convenient for the city." Three-quarters of the corporation's budget comes from Medicaid and private insurance; the rest, directly from the city. Because the city holds the corporation's money, a two-percent across-the-board city budget cut results in an eight-percent reduction in the amount of the corporation's budget that the city funds.

The former Bellevue official shook her head sadly: "If a hospital overspends one year, its budget for the next year is slashed, with no regard for how it will affect sick people. I quit my position rather than be a party to letting 230 staff people go, knowing the serious hardship it would cause the hospital population. Right now it's the mayor who makes the funding decisions and until the people with power in this city challenge those decisions, they'll be made with one eye on next year's budget and the other on this year's election, with no concern for the long-term wellbeing of the people of this city."

WOMEN AND AIDS:

Continued from front page

of a support system denies them access to even the information about these trials. All of these factors decrease a woman's life expectancy. The average woman with AIDS lives 6 months after diagnosis. The average white male lives up to 39 months. In addition, many women with AIDS live beneath the poverty level: they are often caring for a man and children with AIDs. Drug use and malnutrition complicate and intensify immunosuppression. The lack of a primary care physician or health insurance means these women are further distanced from an armed fight against these illnesses.

In 1989, the median income for women working full time in the paid labor force was $16,843. Men earned $25,894. However, since not all men and women work full time, the median income for ALL workers (part and full time) stands at: men $17,114, women $7,610. AZT, the only federally approved treatment for AIDS, costs up to $10,000 per year.

In 1984, roughly 60% of children in households maintained by women lacked private health insurance coverage as compared with 19% of children in married couple households.

One out of every 26 babies in the Bronx is born antibody positive. The chances of a seropositive woman giving birth to a seropositive baby is estimated at 20-50%. Statistically, this implies that at least one woman in every 26 giving birth in the Bronx is seropositive, and in fact implies that considerably more carry HIV. The public interest in AIDS babies, the "innocent victims" of AIDS, creates an emotional bias, rendering the mothers invisible. BABIES CANNOT BE BORN WITHOUT WOMEN! Recent debates over the possible overturning of Roe -v- Wade, or at the least a restricted access to abortion in many states, serve to underline the fact that the white men running this country will continue to control our bodies whether we like it or not.

At the beginning of the AIDS epidemic, the CDC counted 101 cases of self identified lesbians with AIDs. The CDC still refuses to add lesbian and bisexual women to its sexual identity categories for transmissability. Yet 9% of the cases of women with AIDS fall into the "no known cause" category, as compared with 3% of men. How can we be sure that lesbians do not fall into this 9%? Cunnilingus as a means of transmission is not being discussed, let alone reported, even though there are 3 documented cases of woman to woman sexual transmission. The lack of statistics or studies on lesbian sexuality provide abundant evidence of the CDC's built-in homophobic methodology.

The majority of AIDS education campaigns have been geared toward the white middle class woman, when in fact, it is the poor, largely Black and Latino women's communities that needs information the most. Even so, women need more than just safe sex information. They need self-empowerment, self esteem and autonomy. In the time-honored tradition of American politics, there is disdain and a willfull ignorance about the facts of women's lives. Until women are given decent wages and decent services — health care, childcare, education and housing — AIDS will continue to be the leading killer of women in New York City.

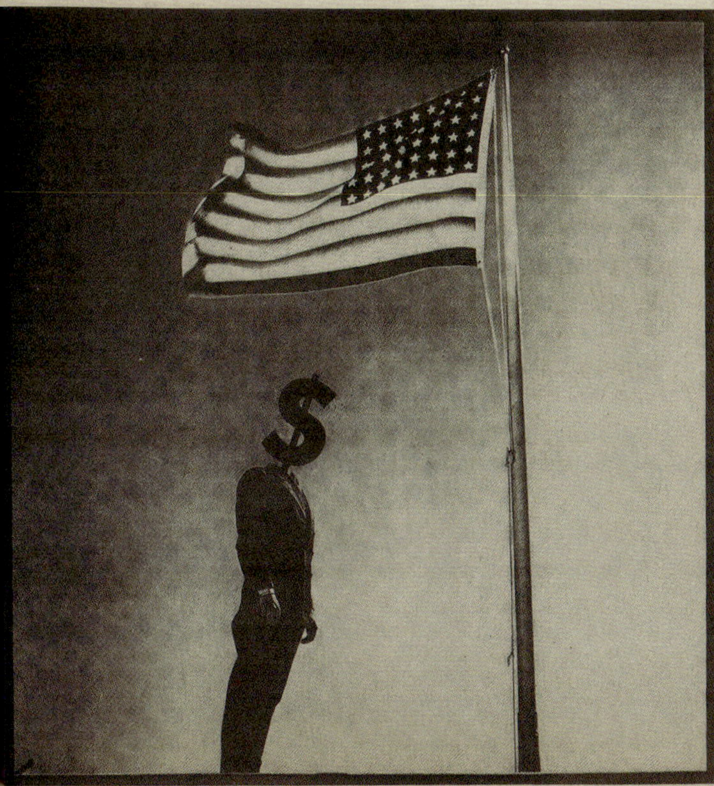

Mario Fiddles While New York Burns

At first glance, New York State's Medical Care Facilities Finance Agency appears to have created a funding program to develop an adequate housing and care network for people with AIDS (PWA). Its Long Term Health Care Revenue Bond Program will issue bonds to finance intermediate healthcare facilities for PWA's who do not require hospitalization but are not able to care for themselves. In order to qualify for the program, a healthcare provider must have 501 C3 non-profit tax status, a certificate of need study for the proposed project, and the Department of Health's approval. Once these conditions are met, the state will issue bonds to raise money to finance an approved project for a healthcare facility. Theoretically, the bond program could loan tens of millions of dollars in the coming years for the development of healthcare facilities.

Closer inspection shows that the program, in spite of the good intentions behind it, "isn't enough" in the words of our hyperapologist Governor Mario Cuomo. The bond program merely reacts to the shortage of care facilities. The burden of development rests in the hands of healthcare providers and imaginary coalitions which probably will not materialize in response to this program. Requiring bond applicants to obtain a costly certificate of need study and DOH approval before the guarantee of funding is hardly an incentive for development. Even if an applicant is successful in getting a project approved, because bonds are issued to cover development costs only after a project is approved, valuable time will be lost before funds can be made available. The state lags far behind in providing care facilities for AIDS patients right now. This bond program doesn't stand a chance of redressing the imbalance.

New York State's response to the deteriorating condition of its bridges in 1988 provides an example of how this crisis in care might be handled differently. When faced with the need for major bridge renovations, the Department of Transportation placed a referendum on the ballot to allow voters to decide whether or not to raise 2 billion dollars in taxes. Voters approved the referendum and thereby established a capital fund to finance the renovations. Such a pro-active approach could be used to address PWA hospital needs. An established capital fund would provide a clear incentive for developers and healthcare providers to create new facilities, and would allow for expediting development. Furthermore, such a fund would allow for seed money to help applicants cover the costly expenses of preparing their proposals. If this level of commitment were demonstrated by the state (recent polling indicates voters would support such a referendum), developers and healthcare providers would be more likely to follow the lead. The current bond program fails to lay a foundation for realistically addressing PWA healthcare needs. "A thousand points of light" won't support the nuts and bolts of healthcare development. But aggressive pro-active development program for PWA care facilities just might build bridges to support everyone affected by this crisis.

Now You See It: Now You Don't

AIDS AND MEDIA

Although backtracking would later reveal at least 95 people living with AIDS by mid 1981, "Gay Related Immuno-Deficiency" (GRID) — the bigoted misnomer which preceded "AIDS" — was not officially named or recognized by the government, medical community or media until June 5, 1981. From this date until January 1, 1983 — 19 months later — *The New York Times* ran a mere 7 articles on this "mysterious new plague." The accidental deaths due to Tylenol tampering — a total of 52 people in three months of late 1982 — merited 54 articles in the *Times* alone (more than one article per person), with four front page stories. In these same three months, at least 300 people with AIDS died in America.

As a nation, America depends upon the media to serve up palatable slices of an alleged "global village" in tightly edited spots or tucked neatly into columns of type. Media creates visibility, which, in effect, re-creates events and generates public attention. All broadcast news is constructed and controlled by the medium of television itself. Before AIDS, mentions of lesbians and gay men in mainstream media were virtually nonexistent. With no small irony, suddenly these same people and many other "unmentionables" have become visible on dominant media respecting the hierarchy of a world run by white men they often only appear as stigmatized, helpless, dying victims. A simplistic and reductive ladder is built with the innocent (white) baby and innocent (white) hemophiliac perched atop a descending order of unfortunate mothers, depraved queers and unrepentant junkies.

Both broadcast and print media have insistently and intentionally abused the language and terminology of this crisis: from creating a (non-existent) "general population" which excludes at least half the nation, to idiotically referring to HIV as the "AIDS virus," erasing the complexities of HIV-related illness. The words "risk group" reveals television and print media's punitive hysteria which denies the possibility of safer sex and drug use practices and insists instead on a well labled villain. We are all in a high risk group.

Coverage of the AIDS pandemic vacillates wildly in mainstream media. Rock Hudson's death began a fever pitch of coverage generated by the usual lure of gossip and destroyed glamor. Peaking in early 1988 with Masters and Johnsons' incoherent ramblings about heterosexual transmission from kissing, stories about AIDS began to disappear, reaching a two year low in late 1988. As the "general population" became convinced of its invulnerability, the media suppressed the unappealing stories of thousands of homeless and low income people living with AIDS or the dilemmas of women of color as they attempt to control their own bodies.

In the dominant media, stories must be considered both important and interesting. Newspersons rely upon vague intuitive standards for what makes news stories important and interesting; these standards are cultural and political. These values are not natural or given but rather reflect specific training, information and methods and serve to make the news formulaic and repetitive as occurrences are fit into existing modes.

There is a differential access to the media, determined largely by one's ability to be an "authoritative source," perceived to speak definitively on a given subject. Such seemingly insignificant formal aspects such as image quality, sound quality, context and hierarchy (arrangement) of images, style (narrative/documentary) or even titling an individual on the screen serve to frame and represent those who speak even before the first word is spoken.

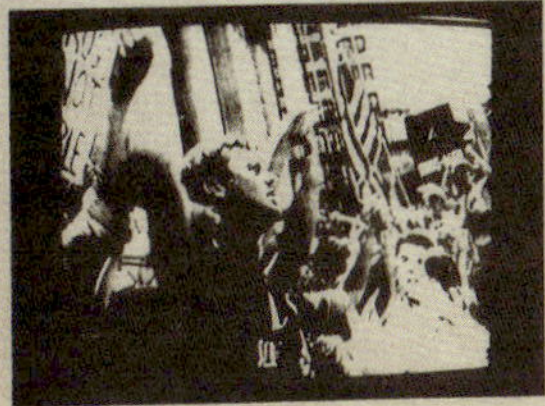

AIDS activist media can and does raise public awareness and mobilize action, replacing the vicious fiction with life-saving information neglected by the experts. Our media should create healthy suspicion.

Seven years and 300 days after the official recognition of AIDS, at least 50,000 people have lost their lives.

Read this issue carefully.

ESSAY

Re: Visions of AIDS

It's a fact that the AIDS crisis is not over. It's a fact that it will continue to damage the communities hardest hit thus far. It's a fact that more and more people will be diagnosed with AIDS and HIV infection. It's a fact that the healthcare systems in this city, in this country, are not prepared to provide help to all who needs it.

The AIDS epidemic has amplified the inadequacies of healthcare and human services in New York City. There has been much talk of the "imminent collapse" of the New York City healthcare system in the face of AIDS. It has already collapsed. The AIDS epidemic has distressed whatever is left of the healthcare system to the point where its inequalities can no longer be covered up. The lack of beds, housing, medicine and treatments, the shortage of nurses, doctors and staff cannot be ignored.

The groups of people affected by AIDS will no longer stand for the discrimination they face when seeking treatments and services that are rightfully theirs. Healthcare is a right. Recognizing this, people are taking direct action demanding affordable quality healthcare for everyone.

But the newspapers tell a different story. The dominant view in the dominant press is that AIDS is moving out of the gay community into the African-American and Latino communities; that the gay community is merely coping with the sadness and death; that the African-American and Latino communities are helpless. Because all of this is an orchestrated attempt to minimize protest against the government and prevent all of the groups affected by AIDS from coalescing into a formidable progressive political force, each of these views must be contested.

There are no shifts among the groups affected by AIDS. There are no "changing faces of AIDS." There are only changes of perception within the press.

The first cases of AIDS appeared among a small number of gay men in New York and San Francisco. However, things are often not the same as they appear. AIDS probably existed in developing countries 10 to 15 years prior to these first "appearances" among gay men in the United States. Globally, the majority of cases of AIDS has occurred among people of color. In the United States, AIDS was present among a number of groups in this country before it first became *visible* when some people able to afford health care become ill with infections that alerted the medical establishment to AIDS. How many wrongly diagnosed deaths have occurred during this crisis? How many times have fatal opportunistic infections been mistaken as the causes of death among people who were *invisible* to the medical establishment because they could not afford health care? The supposed changes among the different groups affected by AIDS actually reflect changes in visibility.

They also reflect subtle changes in attitude. No one can pretend that AIDS is a "gay disease" any longer. This has been the case for a number of months; however, the press must account for its behavior in the beginning of the epidemic. The press framed AIDS as a "gay disease." Little was done to help the lesbian and gay community. The attitude of the Reagan administration was moralizing and punitive. Threats of quarantine were entertained on the front pages of newspapers. Government funding was withdrawn from organizations attempting to educate gay men about safer sex. When AIDS had a gay face, no one cared except lesbians and gays.

The lesbian and gay community has responded militantly to the public apathy and government inaction regarding AIDS. It has had to defend its civil liberties, educate its members, and demand its rights to healthcare. Service organizations and advocacy groups have been established. There has been a resurgence of activism. Lesbians and gays have not only coped during the AIDS epidemic. They have taken responsibility for their own well being.

The widespread preoccupation with AIDS as a "gay disease," especially within the press, validated denial about the affect of the AIDS epidemic among people of color for years — years that could have been better spent mobilizing efforts to stop AIDS. Despite the media's efforts to pin AIDS on one community or another, community activists have responded to the epidemic within their communities.

It is rarely recognized that African-American and Latino community activists have been doing work around AIDS since the beginning of the epidemic and that activists who have established organizations and groups to fight AIDS in these communities have faced enormous obstacles. There were no health and human services available to these communities before the AIDS epidemic; these services are still not available. Plus, the lack of resources has prevented organizations from reaching all the people who need to be addressed, in ways that are culturally relevant. People in these communities continue to struggle against government indifference and widespread apathy to the conditions of their existence.

Regardless of the press, the AIDS epidemic has engendered a new community comprised of groups of people affected by AIDS. In response to government inaction, the groups of people affected by AIDS have been mobilized to save their communities from within. The proliferation of these efforts constitutes a new force for social change. Together, the groups of people hardest hit by AIDS will change the unjust healthcare system in New York City and in the United States.

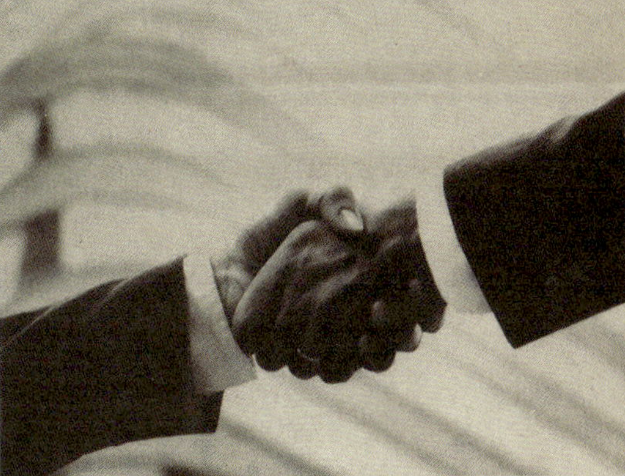

The U.S. Government considers the 47,524 dead from AIDS expendable. Aren't the "right" people dying? Is this medical apartheid?

One million [People with AIDS] isn't a market that's exciting. Sure it's growing, but it's not asthma.
—Patrick Gage
Hoffman-La Roche, Inc
THIS IS TO ENRAGE YOU.

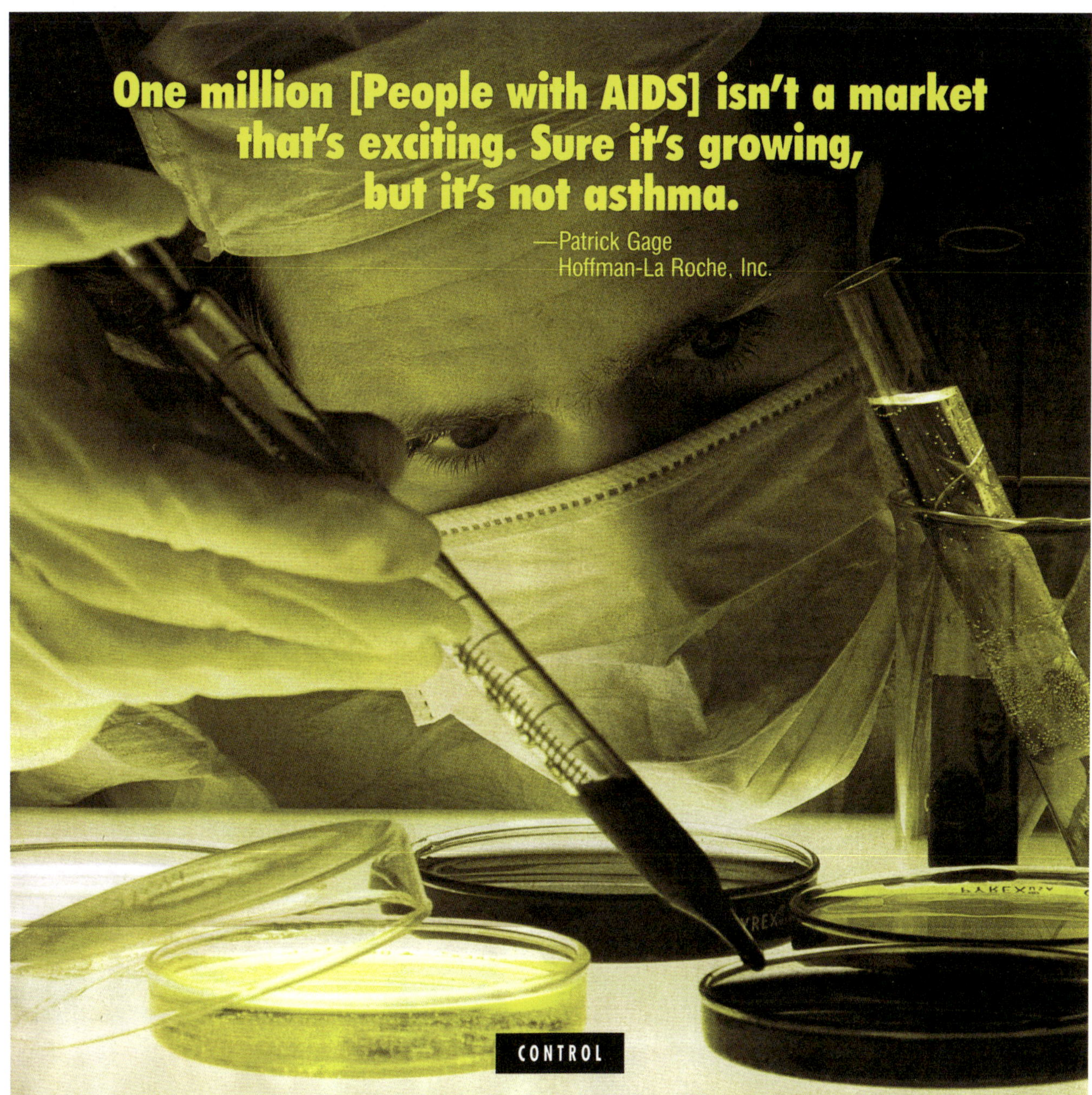

73

73
Control
Artforum, Oct. 1989
Offset print on paper,
26.5 × 26.5 cm

74
Control
Artforum, Oct. 1989
Offset print on paper,
26.5 × 26.5 cm

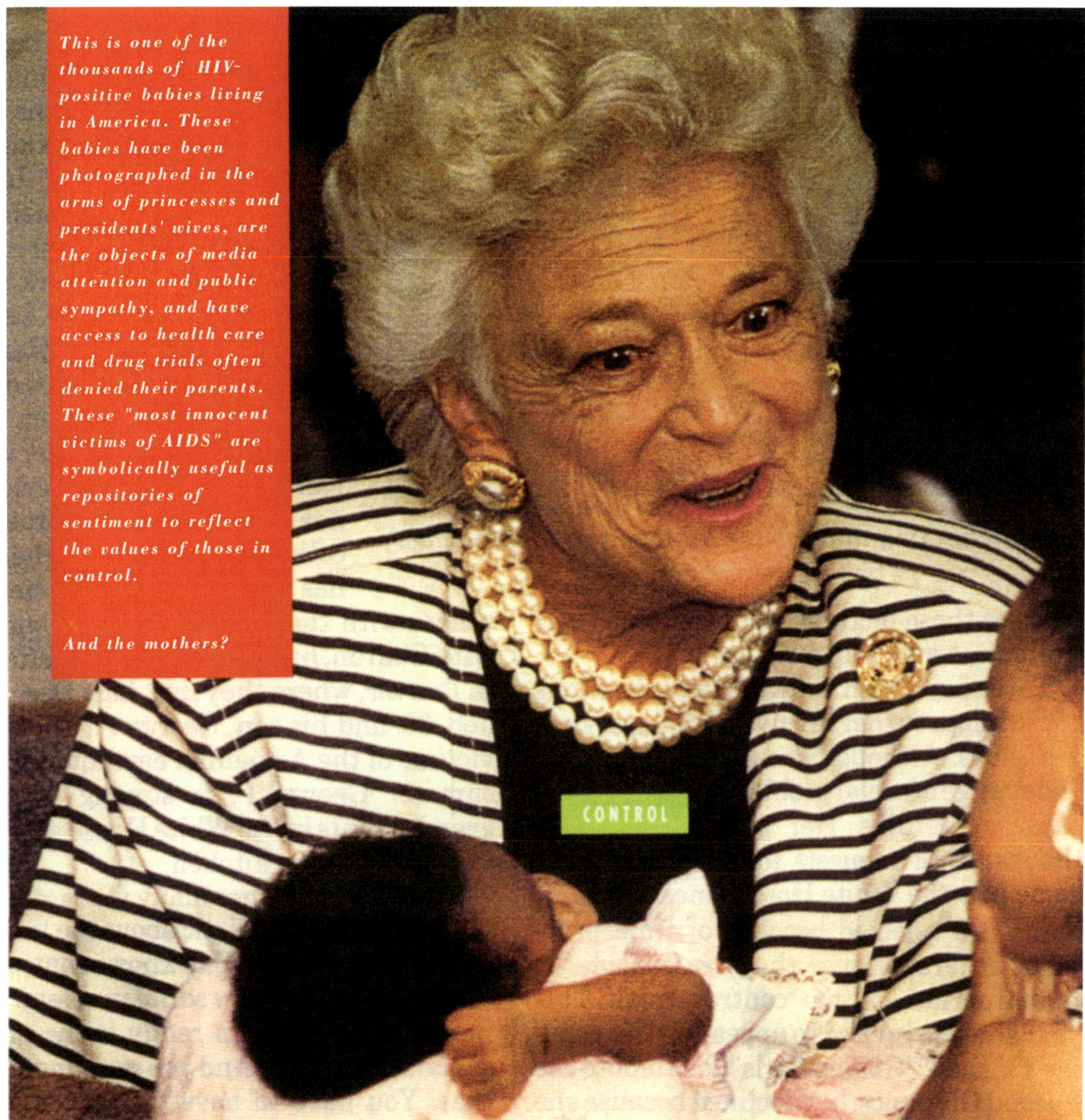

This is one of the thousands of HIV-positive babies living in America. These babies have been photographed in the arms of princesses and presidents' wives, are the objects of media attention and public sympathy, and have access to health care and drug trials often denied their parents. These "most innocent victims of AIDS" are symbolically useful as repositories of sentiment to reflect the values of those in control.

And the mothers?

CONTROL

74

The New York Times

Founded in 1851

ADOLPH S. OCHS, *Publisher 1896–1935*
ARTHUR HAYS SULZBERGER, *Publisher 1935–1961*
ORVIL E. DRYFOOS, *Publisher 1961–1963*

ARTHUR OCHS SULZBERGER, *Publisher*
ARTHUR OCHS SULZBERGER JR., *Deputy Publisher*

•

MAX FRANKEL, *Executive Editor*
ARTHUR GELB, *Managing Editor*
WARREN HOGE, *Assistant Managing Editor*
JOHN M. LEE, *Assistant Managing Editor*
ALLAN M. SIEGAL, *Assistant Managing Editor*

•

JACK ROSENTHAL, *Editorial Page Editor*
LESLIE H. GELB, *Deputy Editorial Page Editor*

•

LANCE R. PRIMIS, *President*
J. A. RIGGS JR., *Exec. V.P., Manufacturing*
HOWARD BISHOW, *Sr. V.P., Operations*
RUSSELL T. LEWIS, *Sr. V.P., Production*
ERICH G. LINKER JR., *Sr. V.P., Advertising*
JOHN M. O'BRIEN, *Sr. V.P., Finance & Human Resources*
ELISE J. ROSS, *Sr. V.P., Systems*
WILLIAM L. POLLAK, *V.P., Circulation*

Why Make AIDS Worse Than It Is?

The AIDS epidemic is far from over. But the toll of new cases, which has been rising for years, may at last be about to level off and then decline. Gloomier numbers released this week by the General Accounting Office mask the possibility that the epidemic's worst rages may be abating.

The G.A.O. study argues that AIDS cases are now under-reported, the true toll being a third higher. Thus total cases by the end of 1991 could reach 300,000 to 480,000, higher than the 285,000 cases projected by the Federal Centers for Disease Control. Representative Henry Waxman, who commissioned the study, cites the new figures to urge more money for AIDS research and health care.

Mr. Waxman draws attention to the new figures in a just cause. But more important for [CONTROL] shape of the epidemic is the number of [CONTROL] tions. In certain major groups, these se[CONTROL] leveling off. If so, the epidemic will peak, and maybe sooner than many forecasters expect. The reason is that the disease is still very largely confined to specific risk groups. Once all susceptible members are infected, the numbers of new victims will decline.

There are already signs of that. The rate of new infections among homosexual men in New York and San Francisco has dropped sharply since 1983, and among white gay men in New York it is now less than 1 percent. Among New York addicts, the proportion infected seems to have stabilized at 50 to 60 percent since 1984. New addicts are still being infected, but in numbers that are offset by those who die of the disease.

Since infection precedes overt disease by five years or so, a decline in infection will be followed five years later by a drop in new cases. Thus cases among gay men in New York should level off soon, though the C.D.C.'s new and wider definition of AIDS may mask any plateau for some months.

The AIDS virus can be heterosexually transmitted to the regular partners of bisexual men and addicts, but is generally not spreading beyond these groups. The evidence comes from interviewing first-time blood donors and people attending sexual disease clinics. In almost all cases, those infected with the virus turn out to be gay, addicted or the sexual partners of those who are.

A disquieting exception to this trend has appeared recently in the South Bronx, where 15 percent of infected people at a sexual disease clinic had no known risk factor. But many had used crack. With the sale of drugs for sex in crack houses, there has been an outbreak of diseases like syphilis, which may foster spread of the AIDS virus through sores that break the skin. Heavy use of crack in a community with many infected drug users could sustain the epidemic among its heterosexuals.

•

[Th]e national caseload of AIDS is the sum of many separate epidemics that started at different times in different cities. If drug abusers in other cities become infected at the same 50 percent rate as in New York, the virus has many new victims awaiting it. But in Los Angeles and Seattle, for instance, the proportion of addicts infected has stayed at about 15 percent. Unless the crack epidemic spreads or some new population becomes susceptible, it's reasonable to hope that the AIDS plague will at least level off in the next few years.

Advocates for people with AIDS sometimes accept good news badly; steadily rising tolls are such a powerful argument for new resources. When New York City Health Commissioner Stephen Joseph last year halved the estimated number of infected New Yorkers, from 400,000 to 200,000, he met with more rage than relief.

The epidemic is terrifying enough without playing politics with the numbers. The more directly prevention can be targeted at those most at risk — notably black and Hispanic gay men, intravenous drug addicts, crack users and their communities — the sooner the deadly tide will be turned.

75

75, 76
Control
Artforum, Oct. 1989
Offset print on paper,
26.5 × 26.5 cm

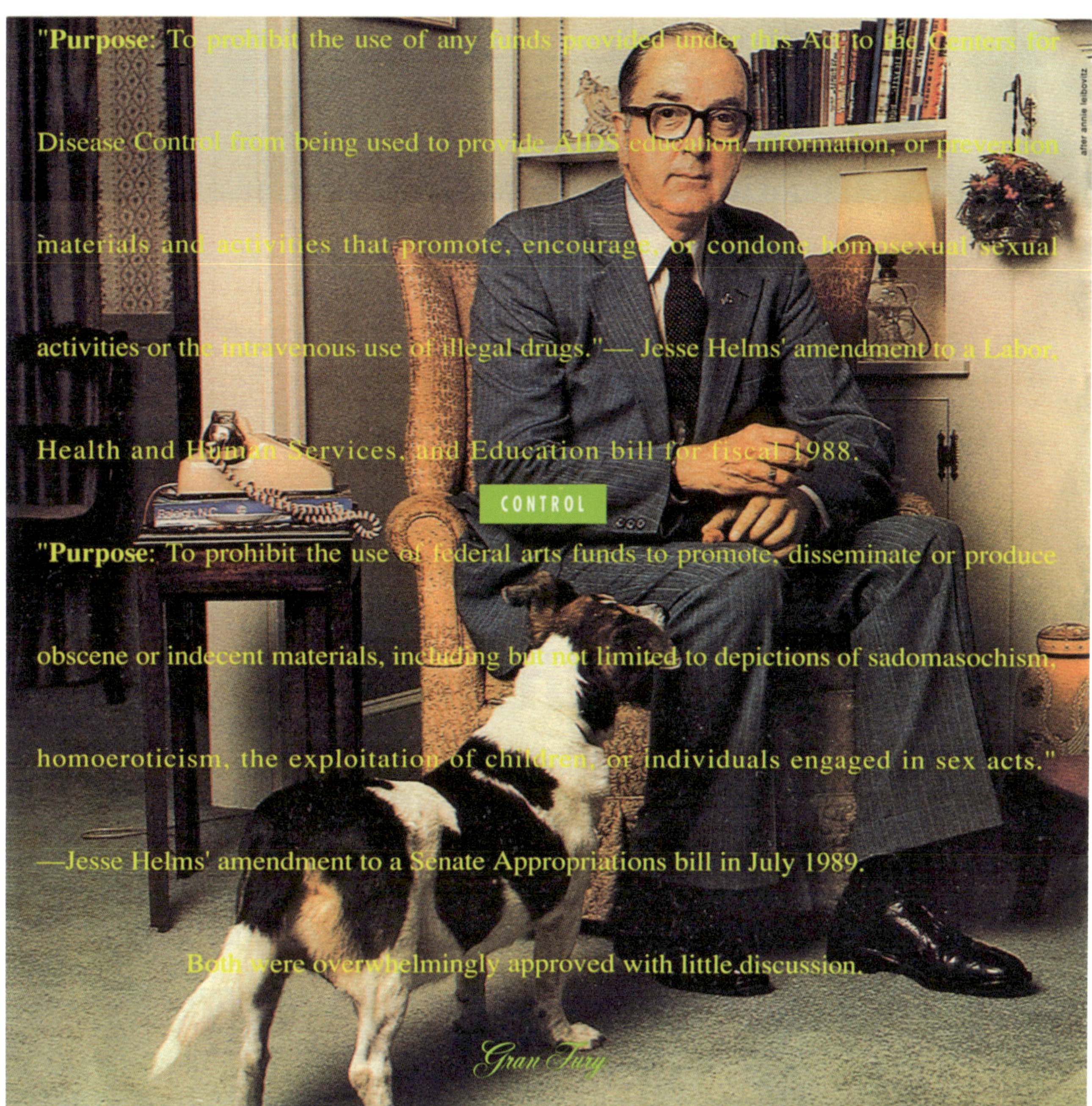
after annie leibovitz

"Purpose: To prohibit the use of any funds provided under this Act to the Centers for Disease Control from being used to provide AIDS education, information, or prevention materials and activities that promote, encourage, or condone homosexual sexual activities or the intravenous use of illegal drugs."— Jesse Helms' amendment to a Labor, Health and Human Services, and Education bill for fiscal 1988.

CONTROL

"Purpose: To prohibit the use of federal arts funds to promote, disseminate or produce obscene or indecent materials, including but not limited to depictions of sadomasochism, homoeroticism, the exploitation of children, or individuals engaged in sex acts."

—Jesse Helms' amendment to a Senate Appropriations bill in July 1989.

Both were overwhelmingly approved with little discussion.

Gran Fury

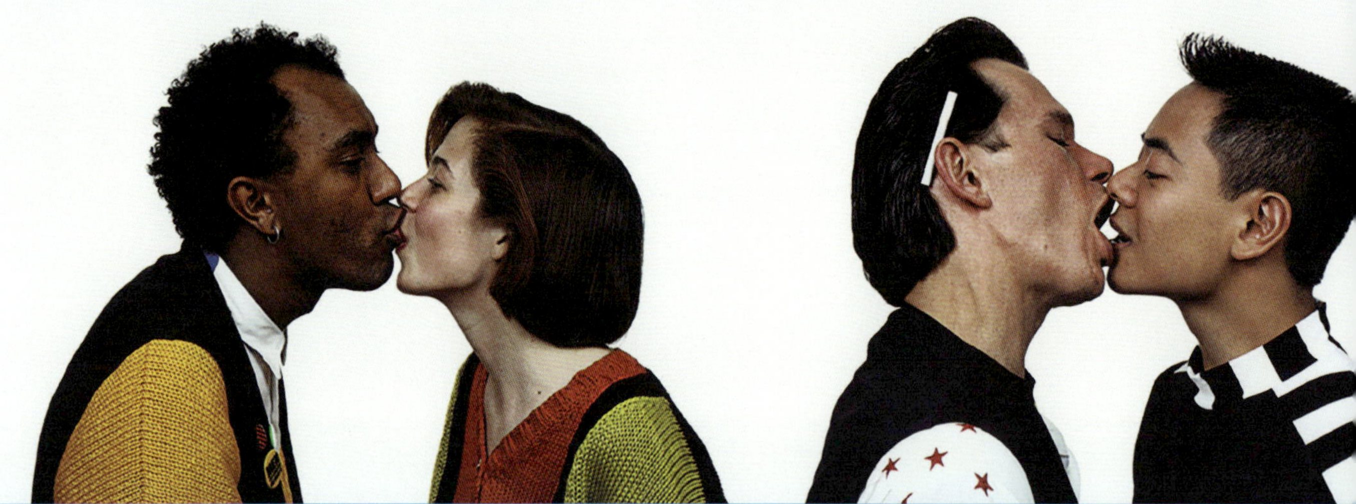

77

Kissing Doesn't Kill (ver. 1), 1989–90
Four color bus poster,
76 × 355.5 cm
Commissioned work
for the project Art
Against AIDS: On the
Road, San Francisco,
United States

78, 79

Kissing Doesn't Kill (ver. 1) billboard on bus,
1989–90
Four color bus poster,
76 × 355.5 cm
Commissioned work
for the project Art
Against AIDS: On the
Road, San Francisco,
United States

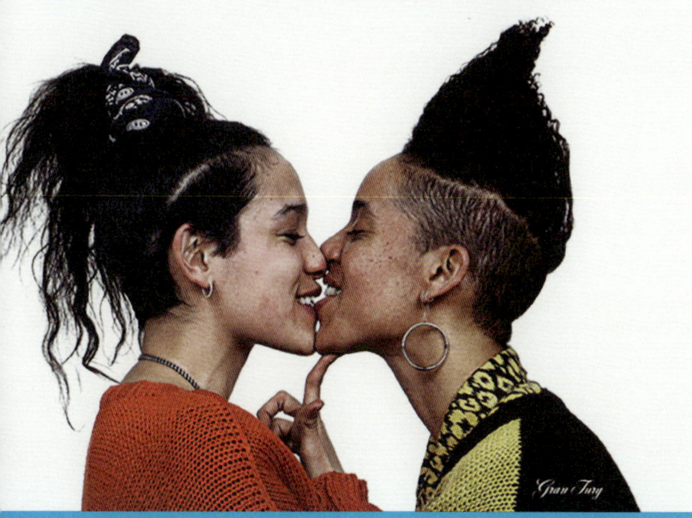
NDIFFERENCE DO.
Gran Fury
MAKE AIDS A POLITICAL CRISIS.

77

KISSING DOESN'T KILL: GREED AND INDIFFERENCE DO.
GRAN FURY
for Art
Against
AIDS...
On The R

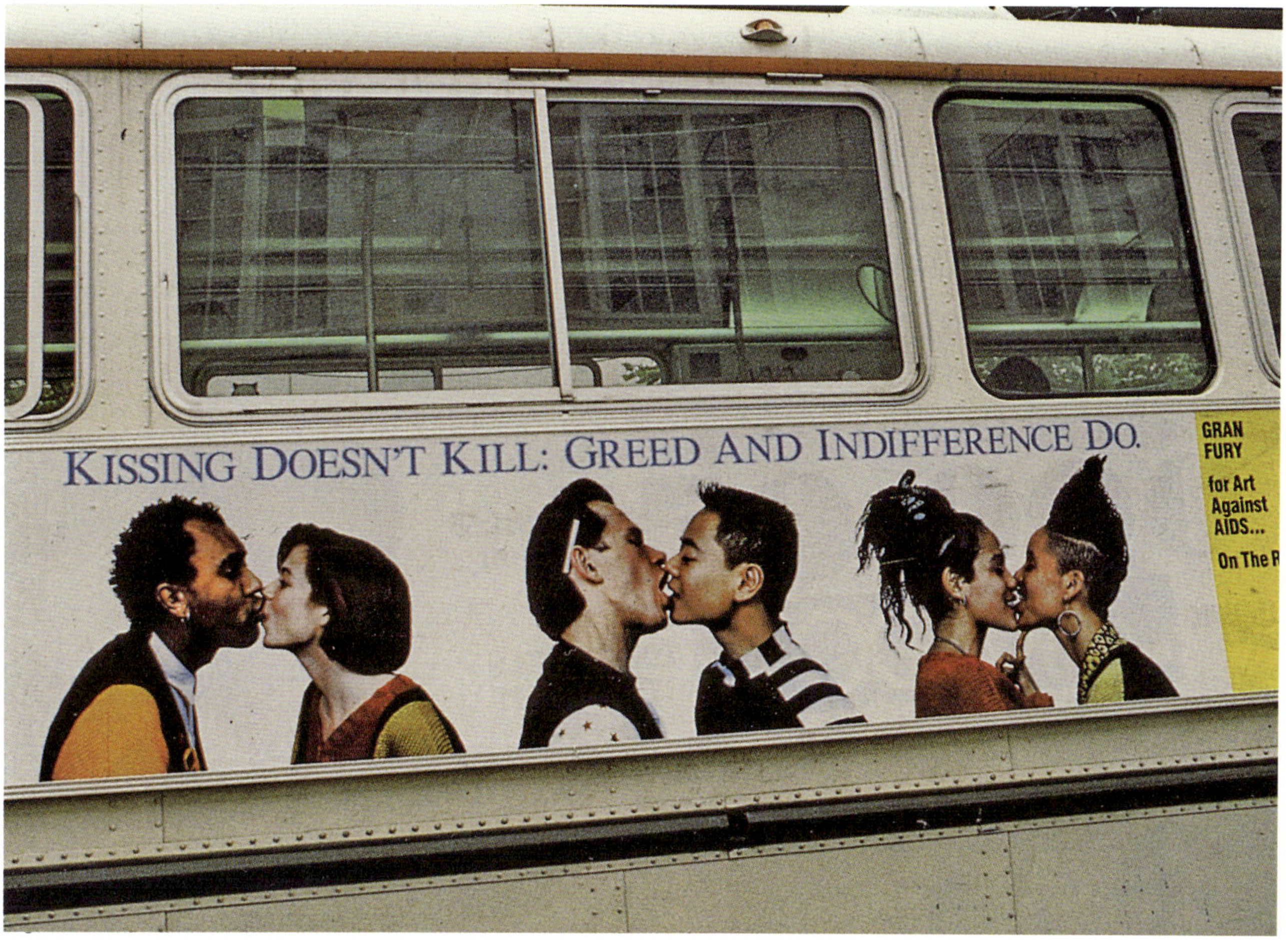

78

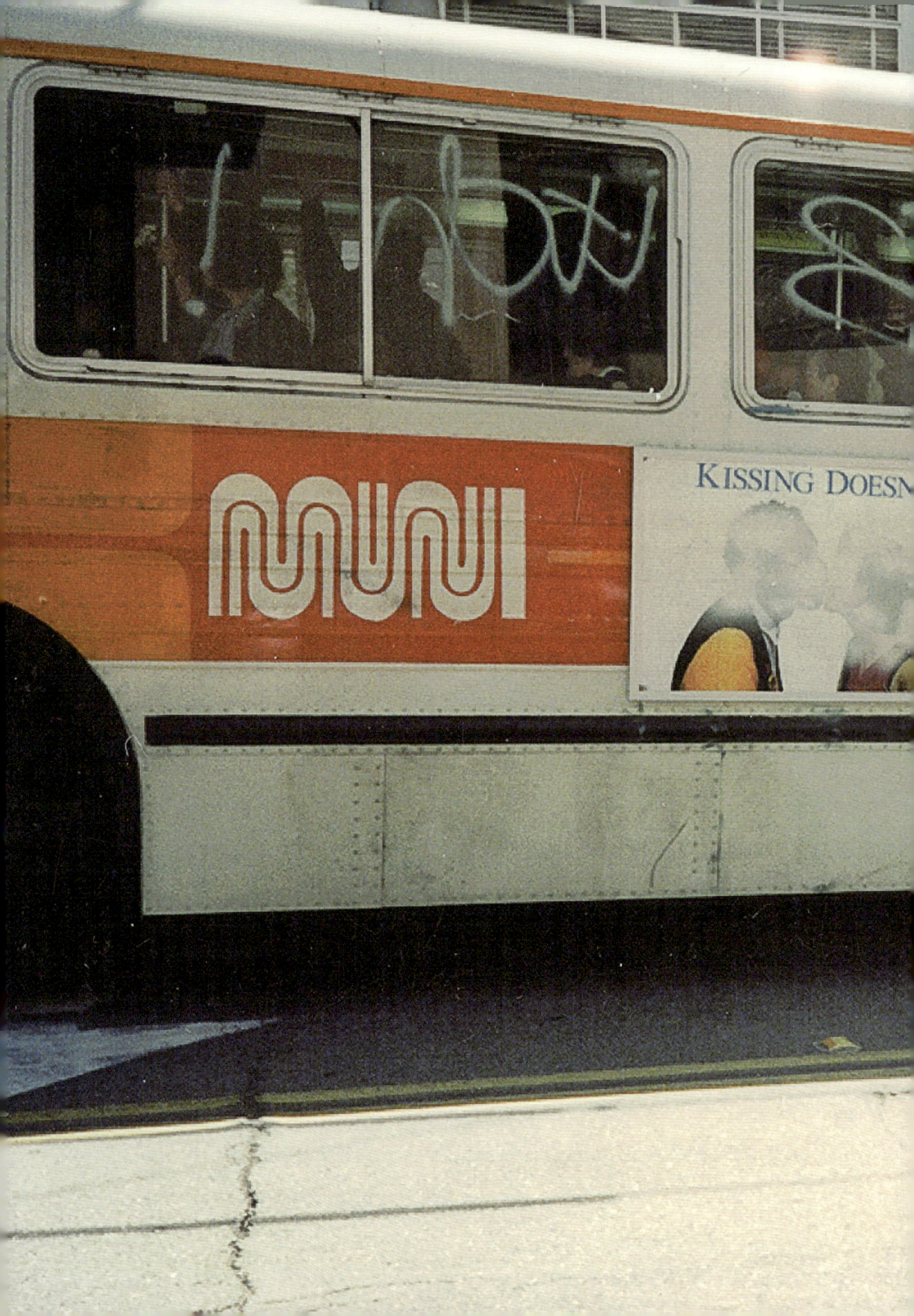
muni
KISSING DOESN

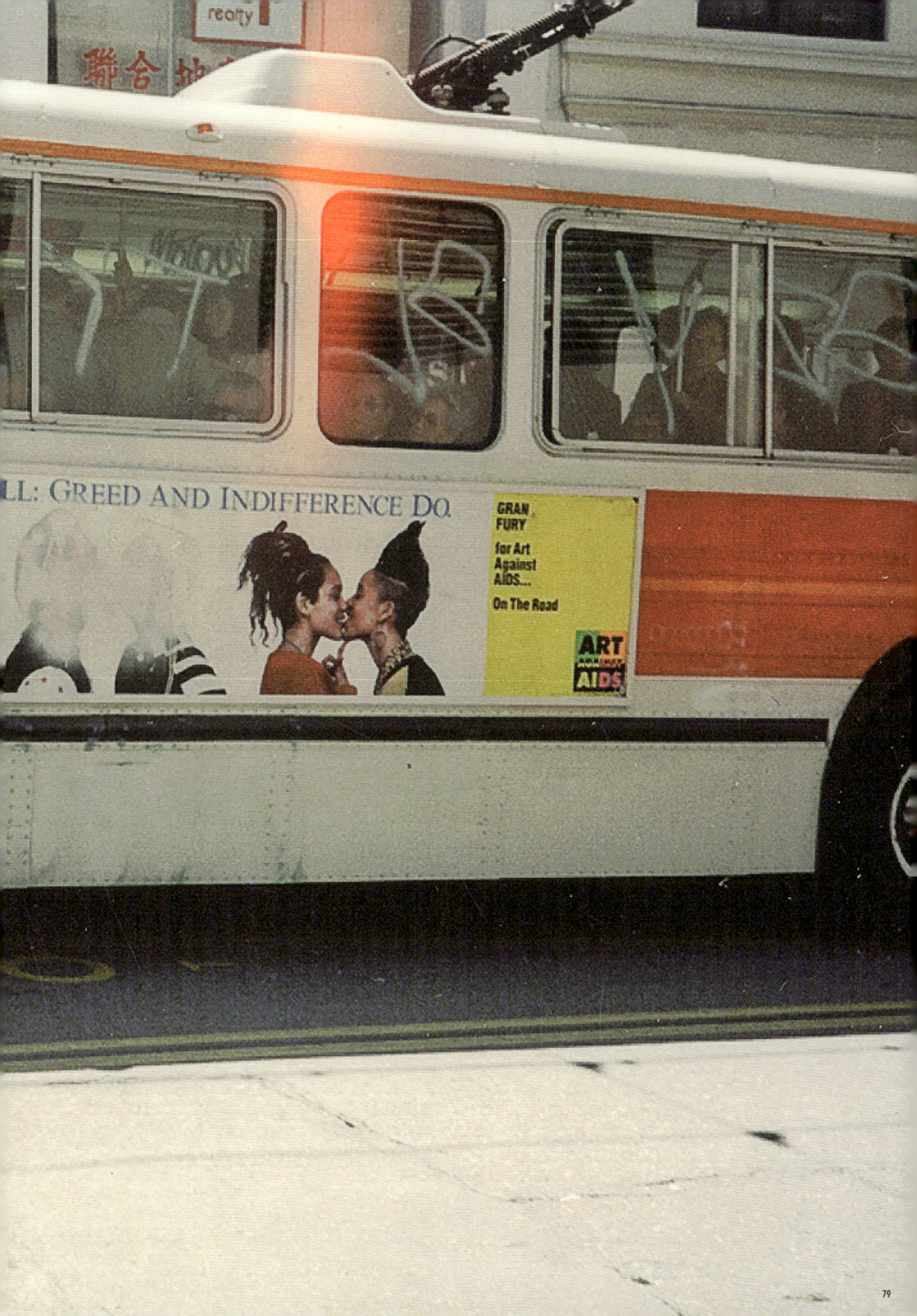
LL: GREED AND INDIFFERENCE DO.
GRAN FURY
for Art Against AIDS...
On The Road
ART AGAINST AIDS

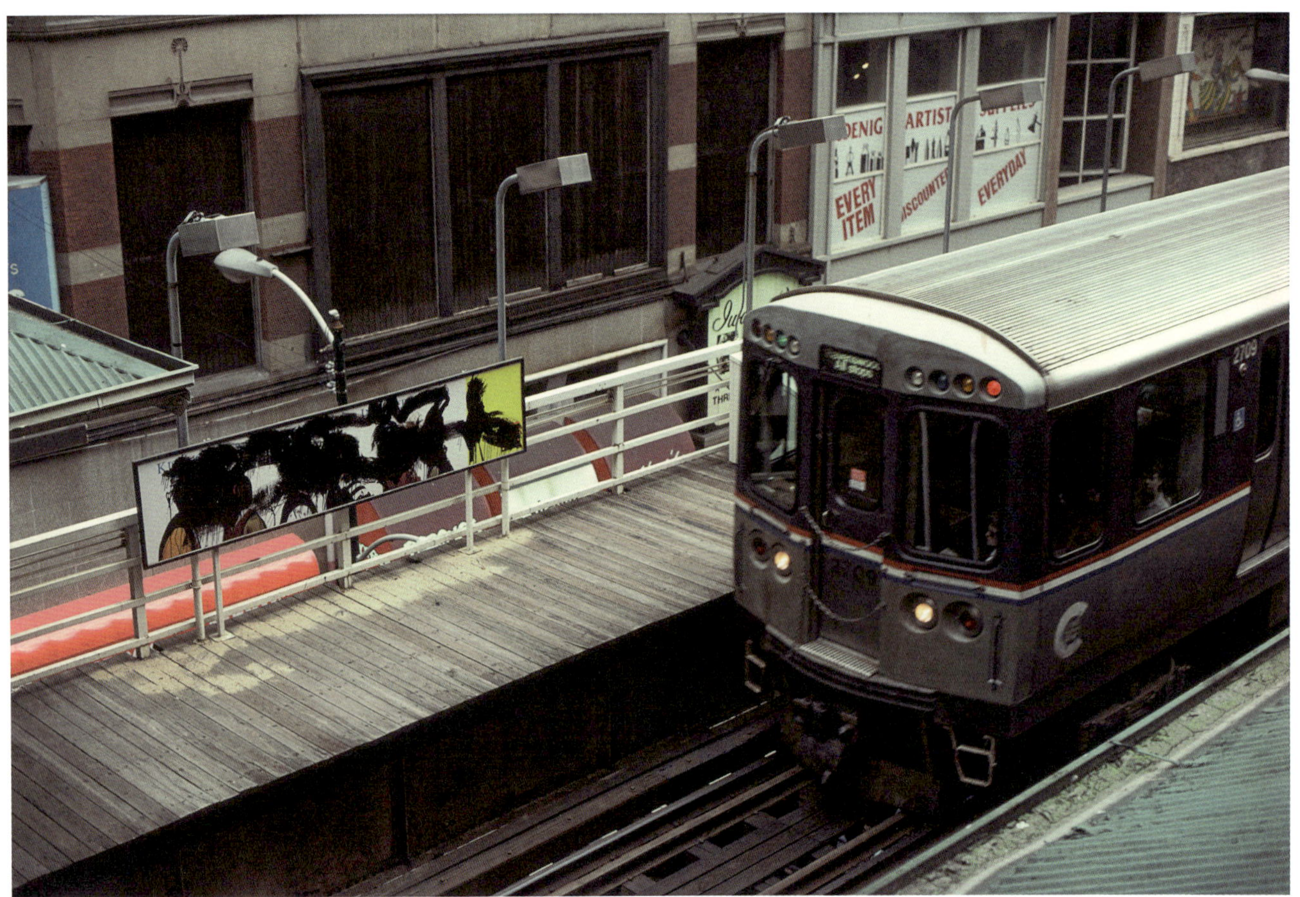

80

80
Bill Stamets
Photograph of *Kissing
Doesn't Kill (ver.1)*
on train station, 1990
Commissioned work
for the project
Art Against AIDS: On
the Road, Chicago,
United States

104

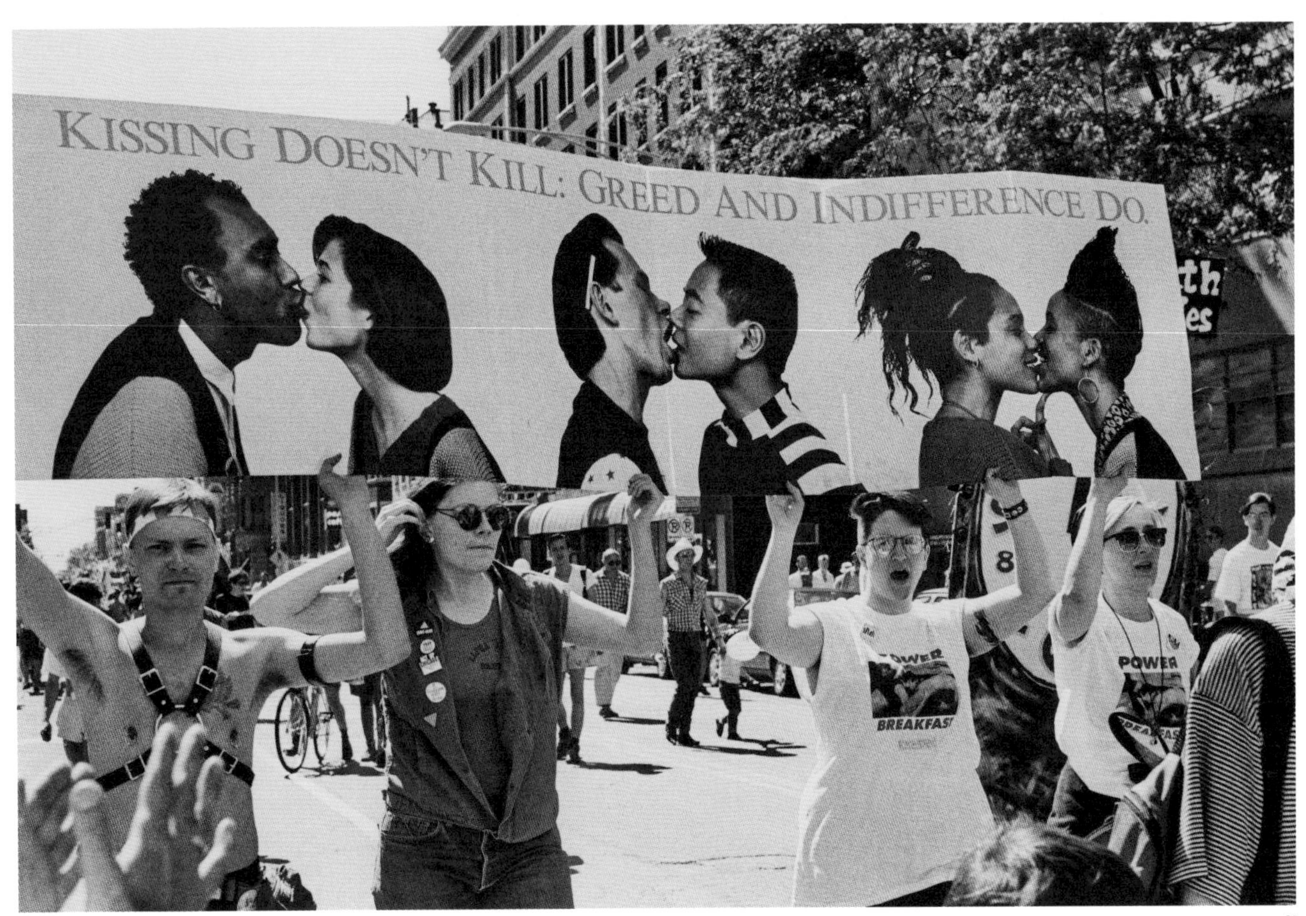

81

81
Lisa Howe-Ebright
ACT UP members carrying
Kissing Doesn't Kill (ver.1)
at Chicago Gay Pride
Parade, United States,
June 24, 1990
Lisa Ebright Photography,
Windy City Times,
Chicago, Illinois, United
States

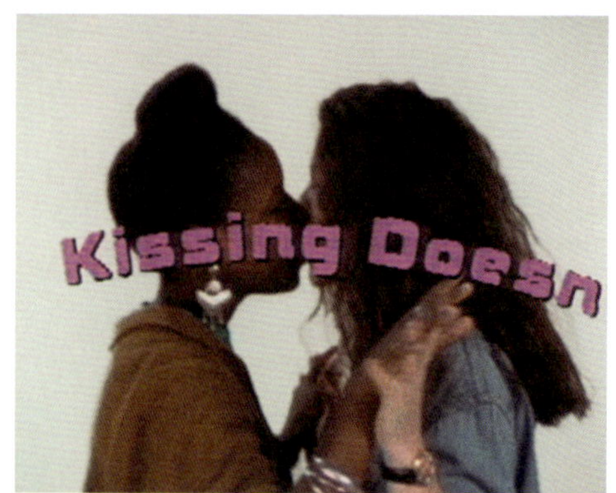

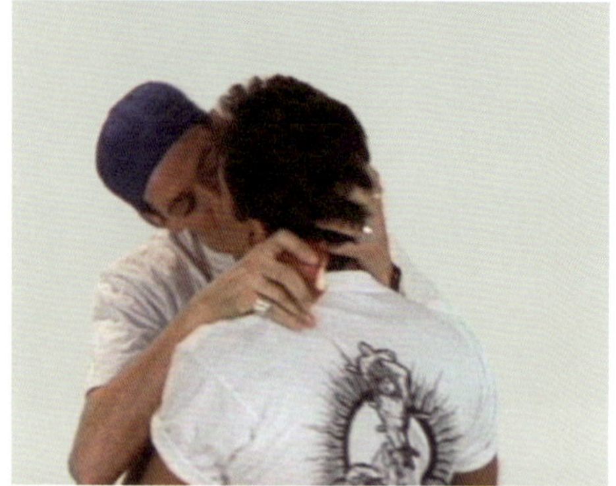

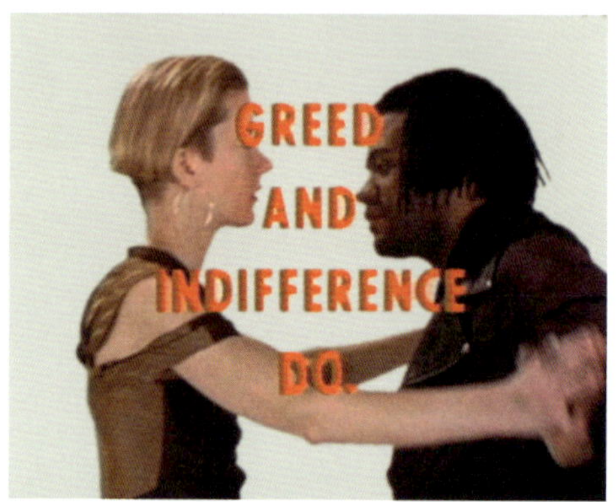

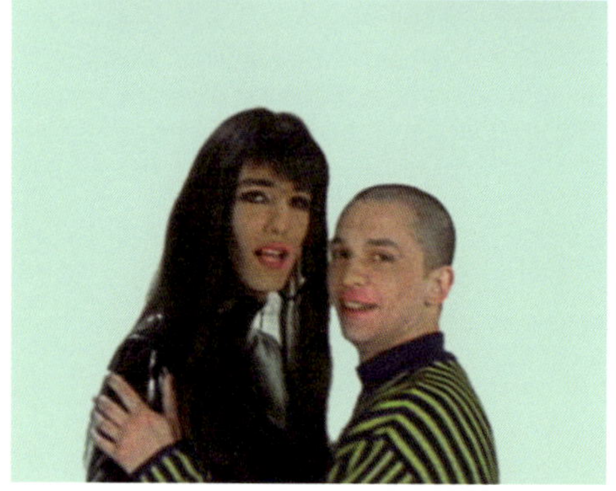

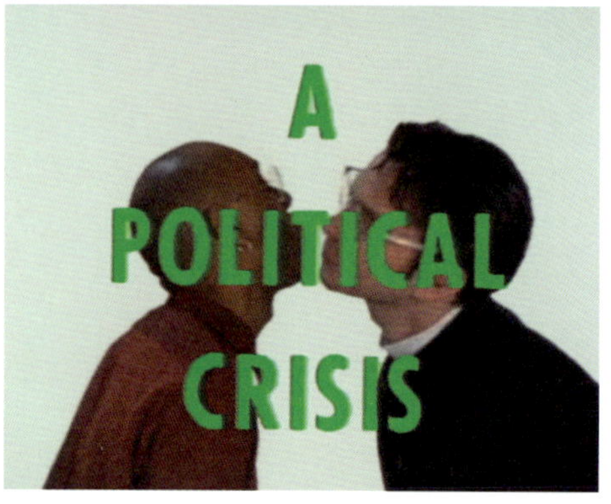

82-86

82–86
Stills from *Kissing
Doesn't Kill*, 1990
Video, 30" each

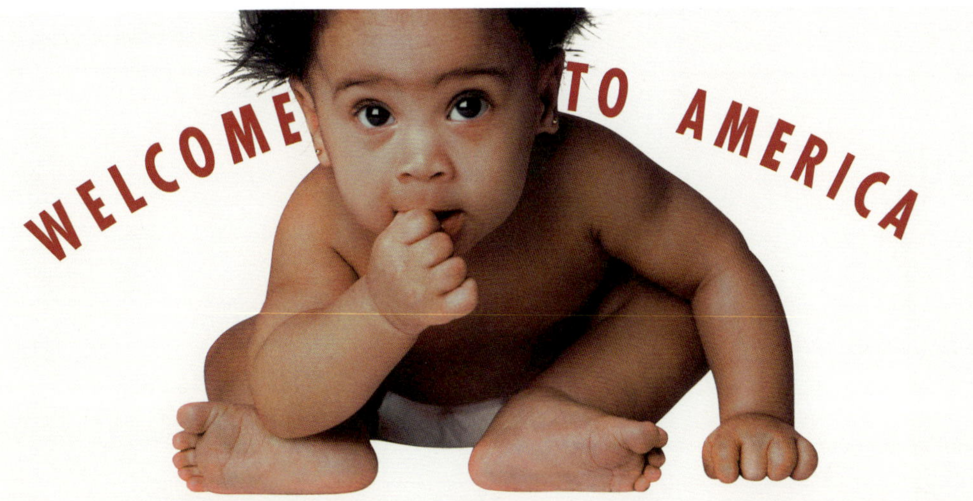

87
Welcome to America,
1989
Offset print on
paper set in billboard,
320 × 701.5 cm
Image World: Artand
Media Culture
The Whitney Museum
of American Art, New
York, United States

88
Welcome to America
billboard in SoHo
at the corner of
Broadway and
Houston, 1989
Sponsored by The
Whitney Museum of
American Art, New
York, United States

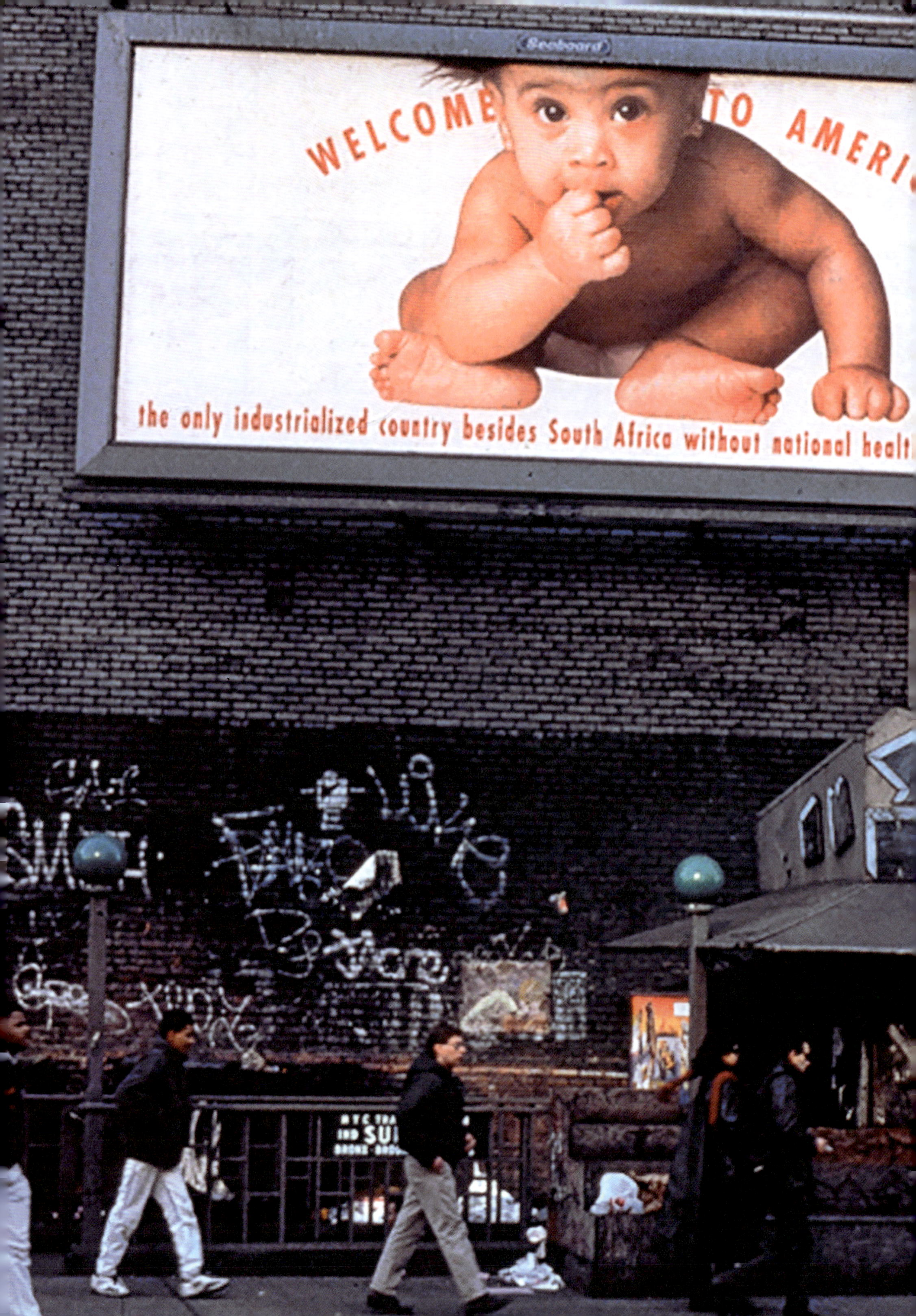
WELCOME TO AMERICA
the only industrialized country besides South Africa without national healt

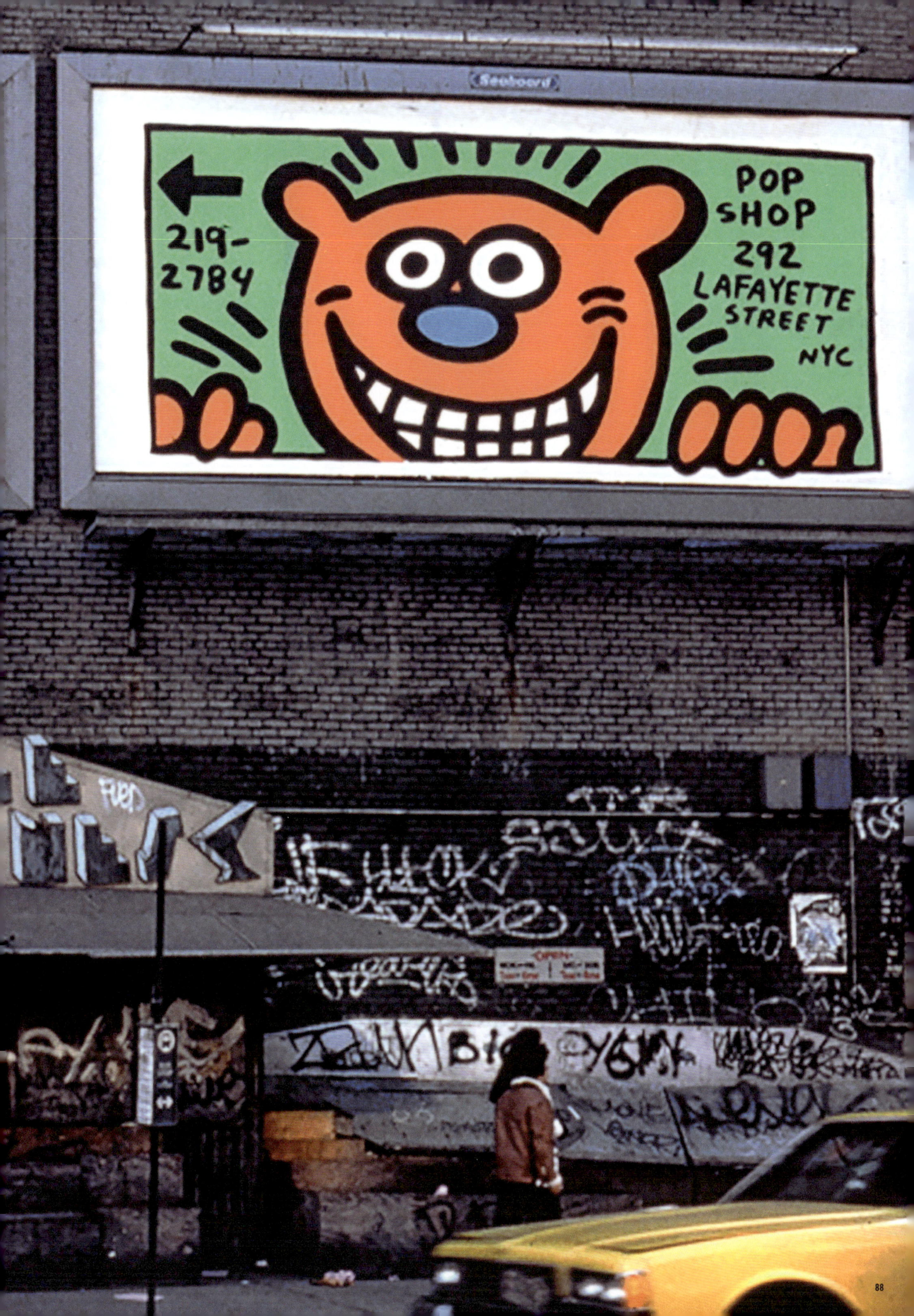

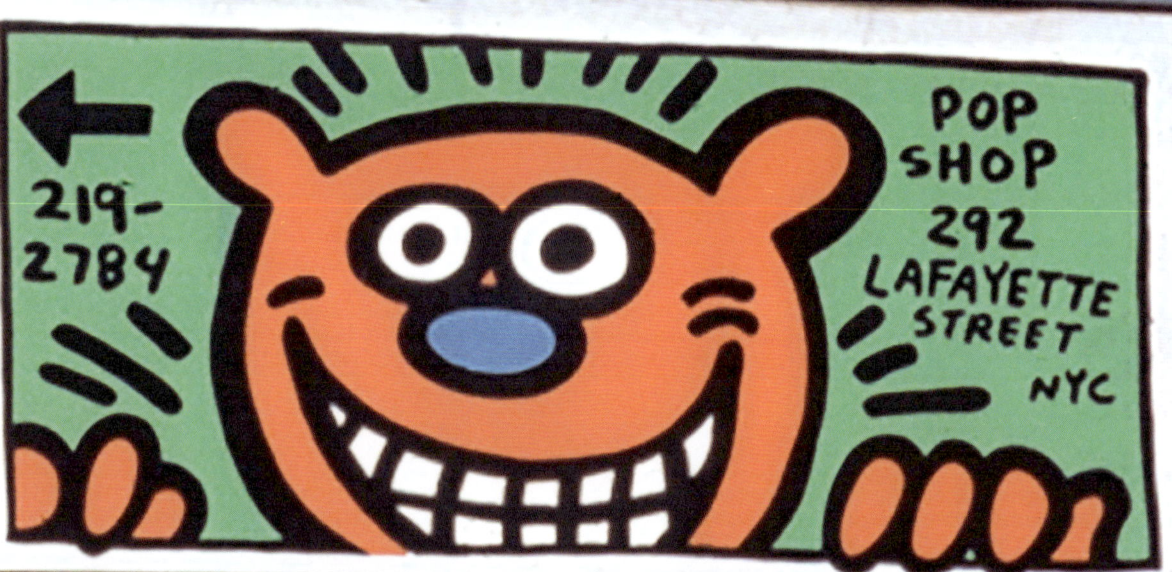
219-
2784
POP
SHOP
292
LAFAYETTE
STREET
NYC

89
*Wipe Out, Bomb
Magazine* cover, no. 34,
Winter 1991

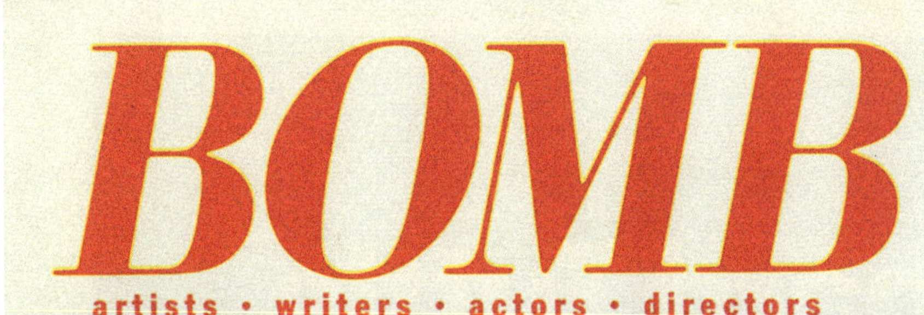
BOMB
artists • writers • actors • directors
WINTER 1991 $4.00
JESSICA HAGEDORN
PHIL HARTMAN
ROMULUS LINNEY
LARI PITTMAN
WHIT STILLMAN
2 BLACK 2 STRONG

The medical fact of AIDS is made more critical by the fear and hatred of drug addicts, gays and lesbians, women, people of color, and the poor.

These prejudices must be wiped out before the AIDS crisis can be solved.

Everyone must have equal access to healthcare, education and housing.

AIDS ISN'T OVER FOR ANYBODY UNTIL IT'S OVER FOR EVERYBODY.

A PROJECT BY Gran Fury FOR THE DECADE SHOW: FRAMEWORKS OF IDENTITY IN THE 1980s.
MAY 17–AUG 19, 1990

Gran Fury

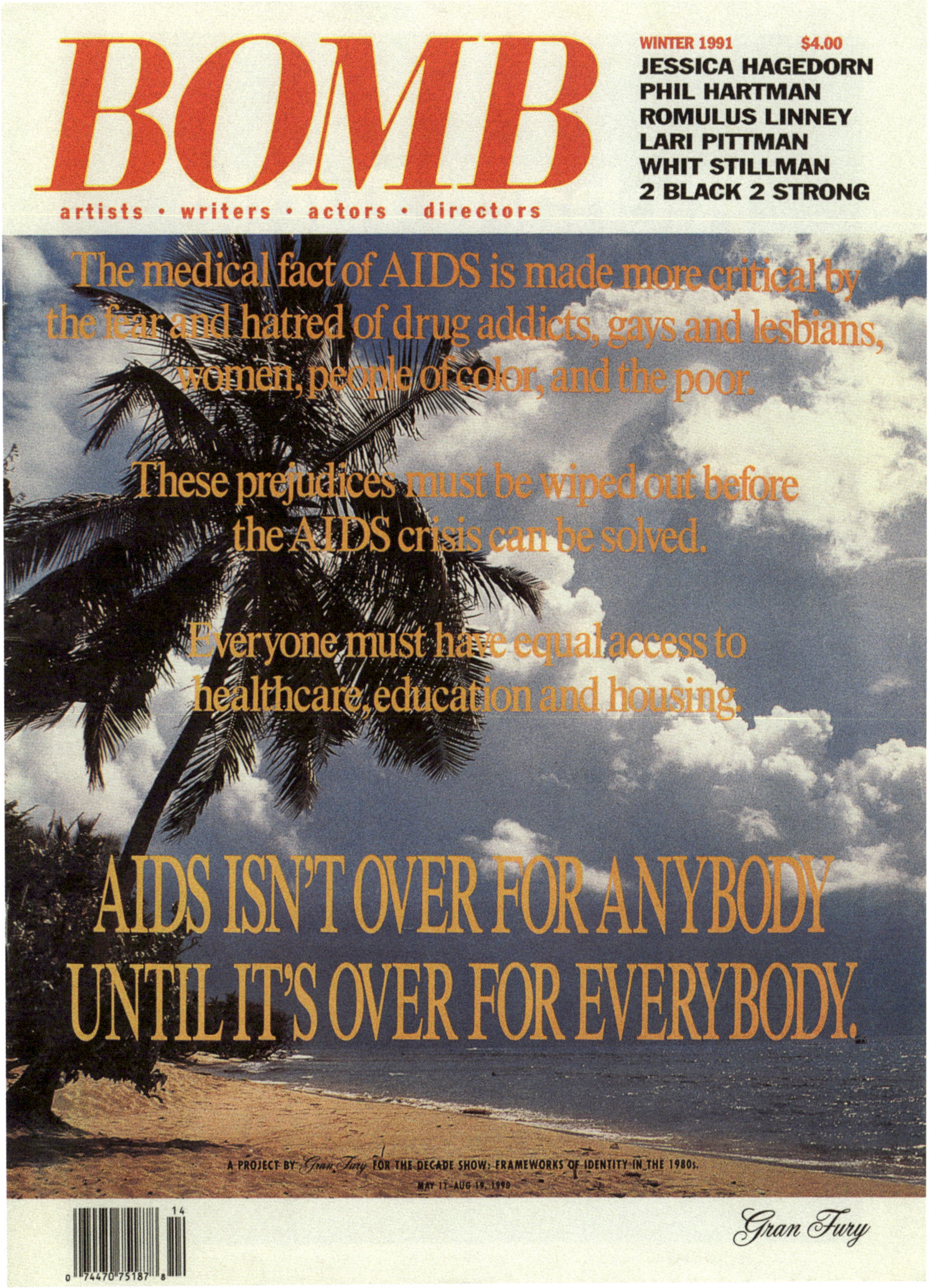

89

The Catholic Church has long taught men and women to loathe their bodies and to fear their sexual natures. This particular vision of good and evil continues to bring suffering and even death. By holding medicine hostage to Catholic morality and withholding information which allows people to protect themselves and each other from acquiring the Human Immunodeficiency Virus, the Church seeks

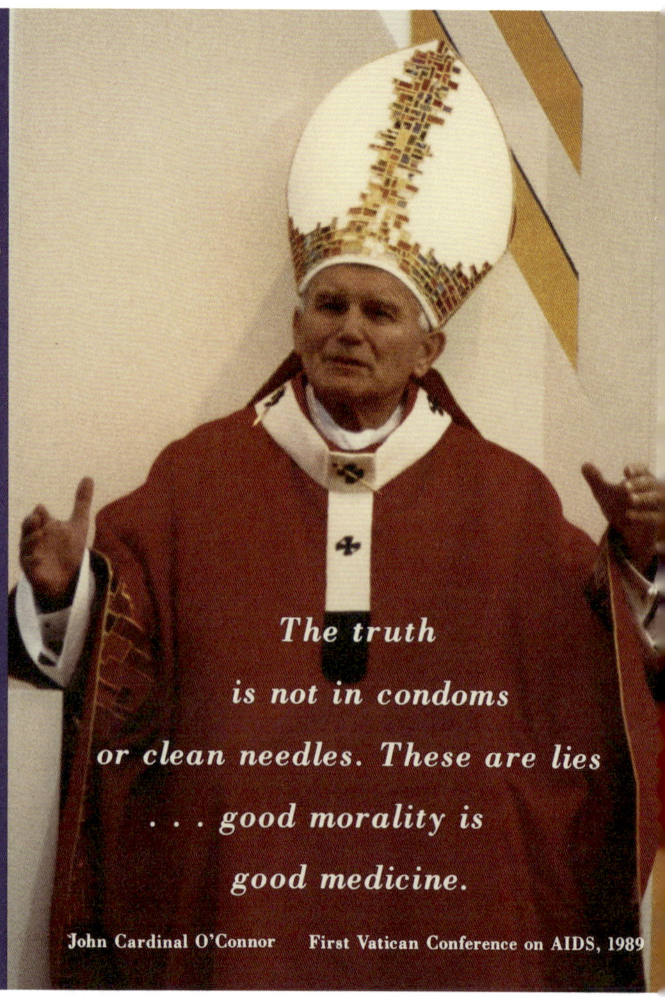

112

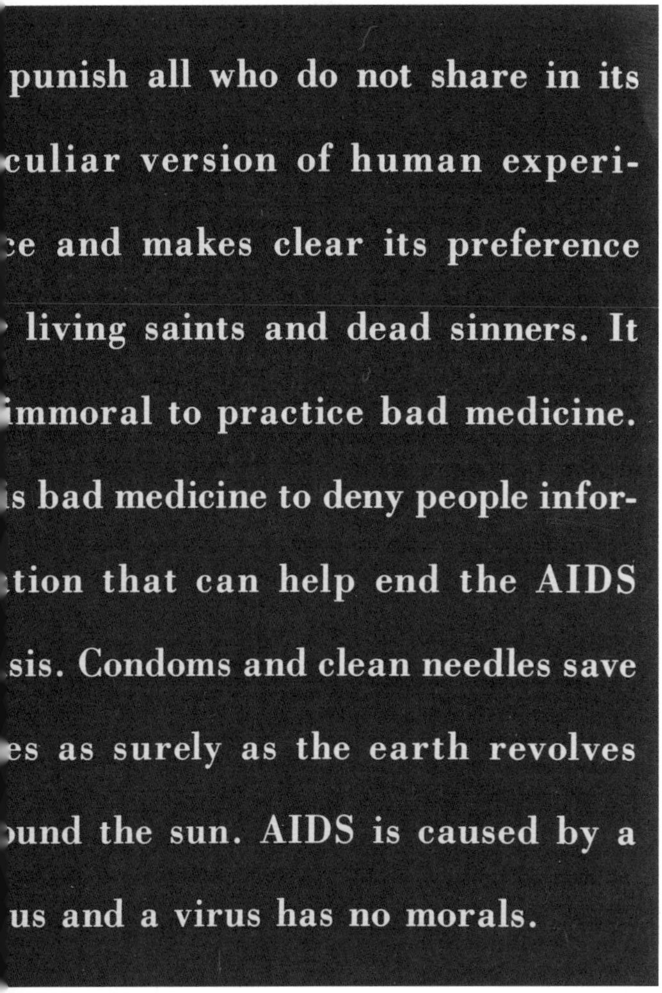

punish all who do not share in its
culiar version of human experi-
e and makes clear its preference
living saints and dead sinners. It
mmoral to practice bad medicine.
s bad medicine to deny people infor-
tion that can help end the AIDS
sis. Condoms and clean needles save
es as surely as the earth revolves
und the sun. AIDS is caused by a
us and a virus has no morals.

90

90
The Pope and the Penis
"Aperto 90," 44th
Biennale di Venezia,
Italy, 1990
Offset print set in
billboard, 305 × 762 cm
Gran Fury Collection,
Manuscripts and
Archives Division,
The New York Public
Library, United States

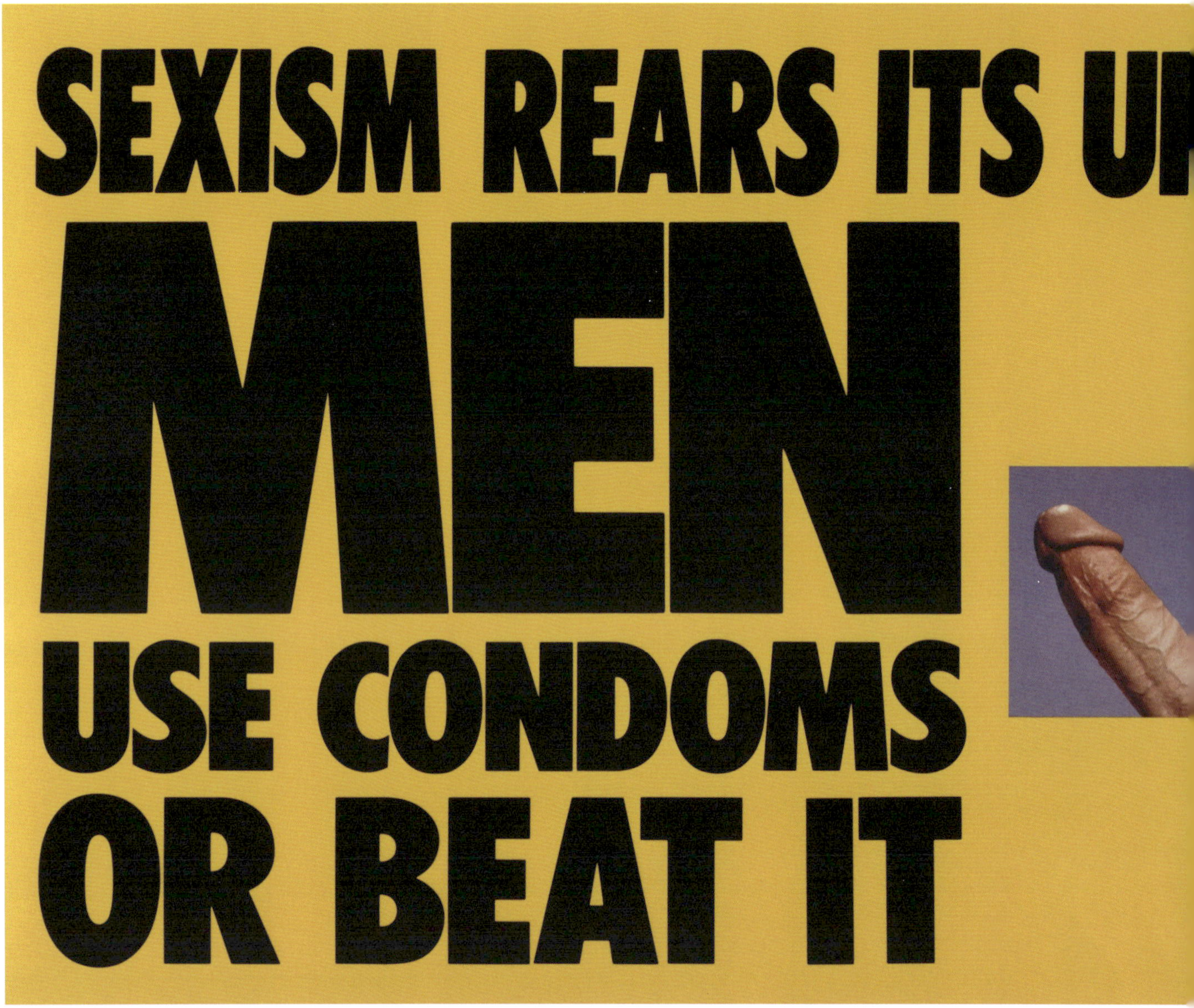

SEXISM REARS ITS UP
MEN
USE CONDOMS
OR BEAT IT

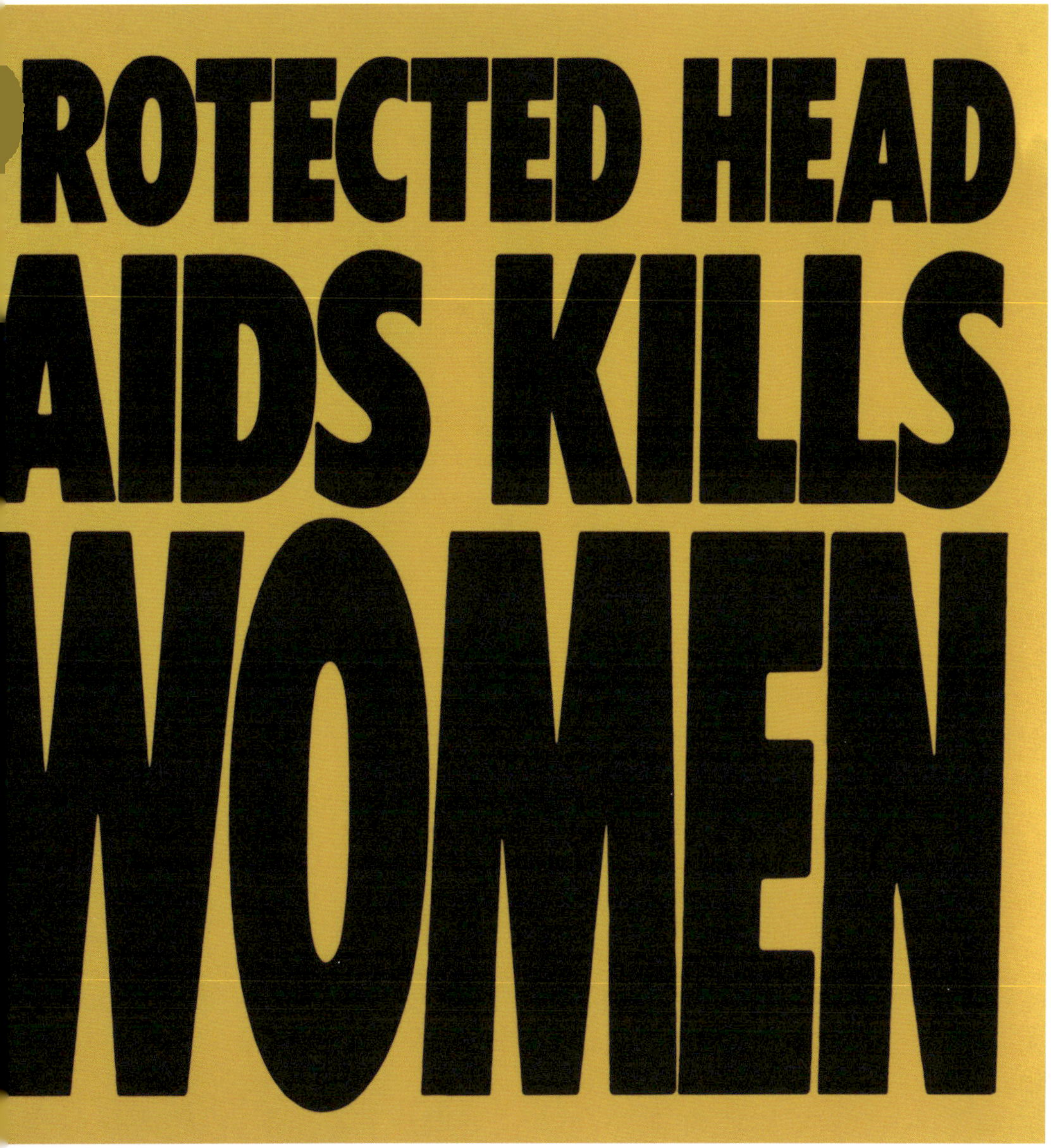

91

91
The Pope and the Penis
"Aperto 90," 44th
Biennale di Venezia,
Italy, 1990
Offset print set in
billboard, 305 × 762 cm
Gran Fury Collection,
Manuscripts and
Archives Division,
The New York Public
Library, United States

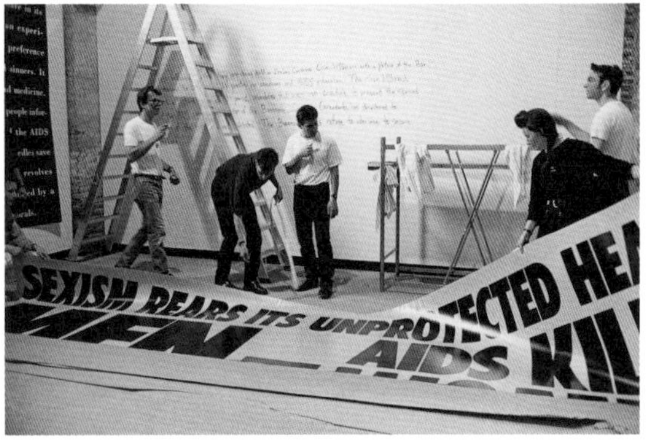

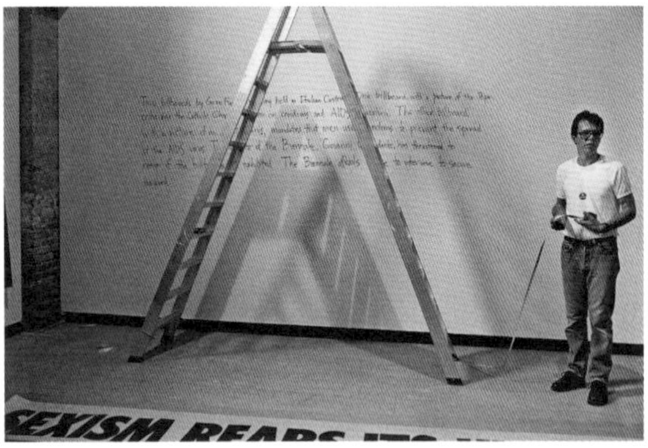

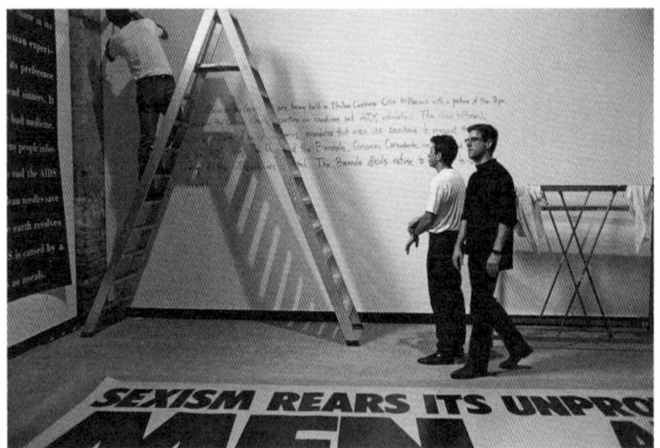

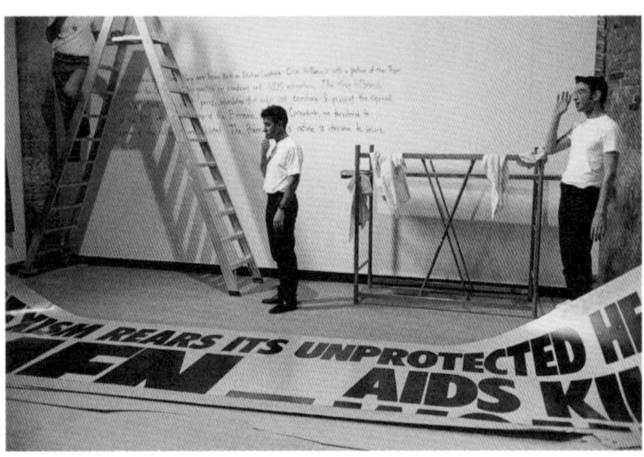

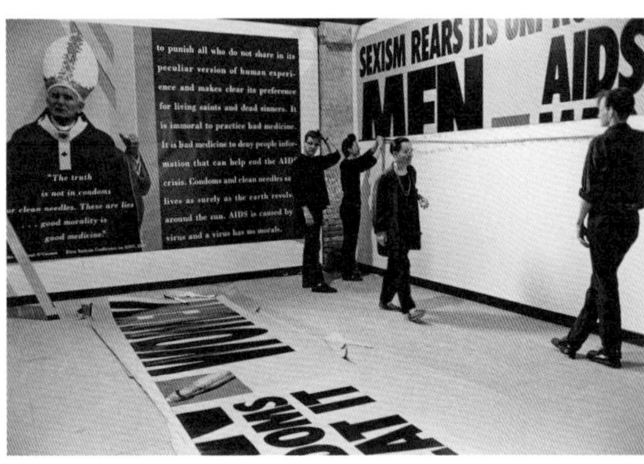

92-97
Bruno Jakob
Installation photographs of *The Pope and the Penis* at the 44th Biennale di Venezia, Italy, 1990
Gran Fury Collection, Manuscripts and Archives Division, The New York Public Library, United States

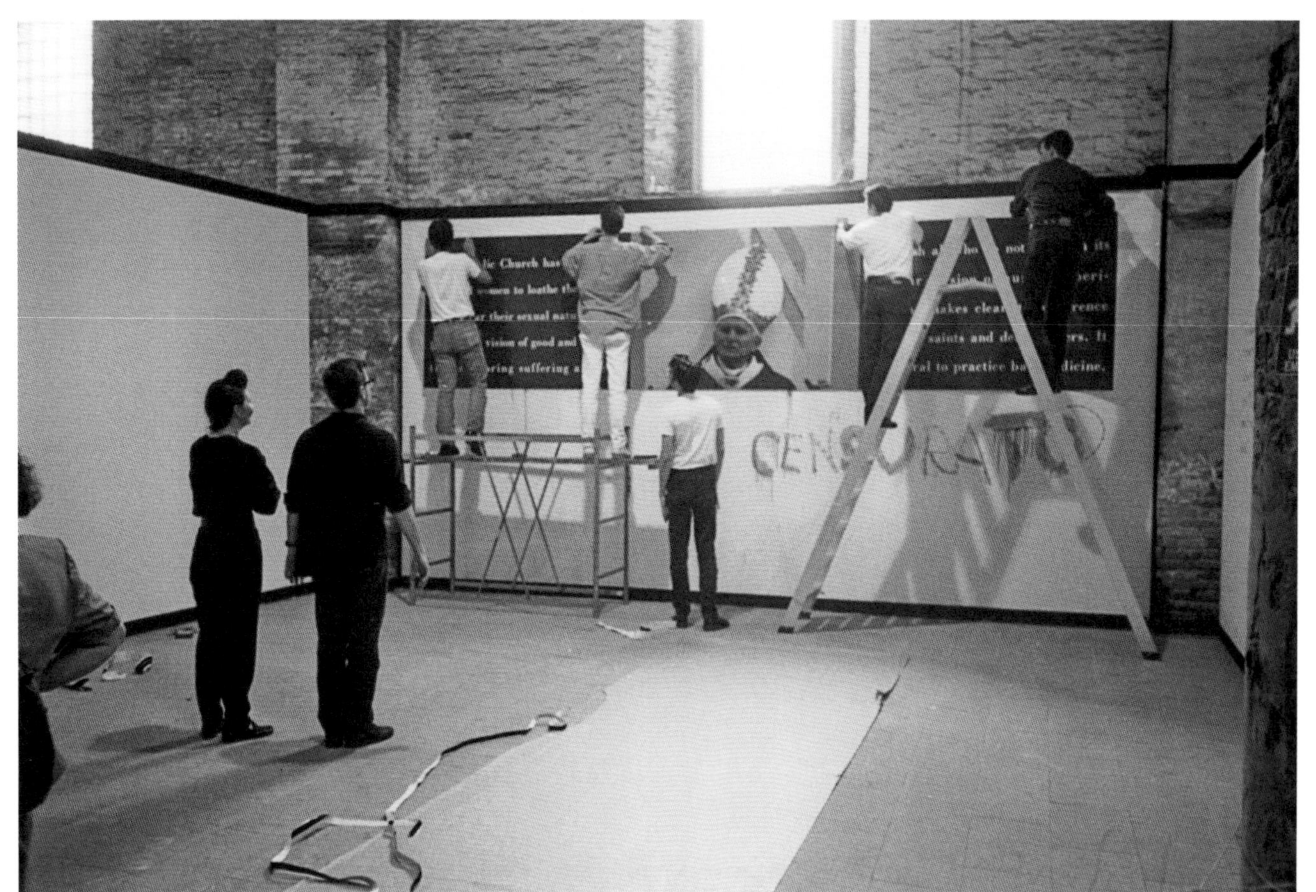

97

IL PAPA E L'AIDS SCANDALO IN BIENNALE

LA VISITA DEL DALAI LAMA

la Nuova

Venezia

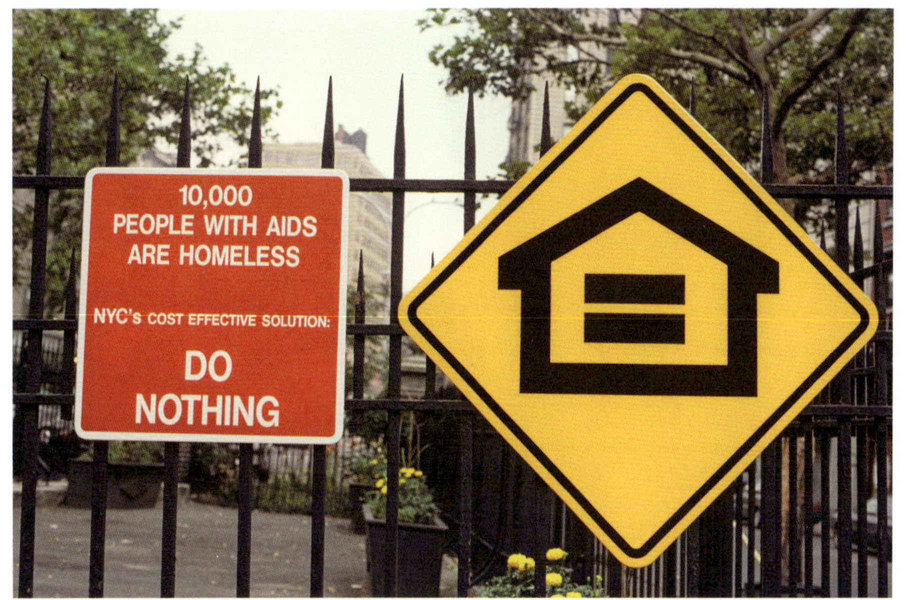

99

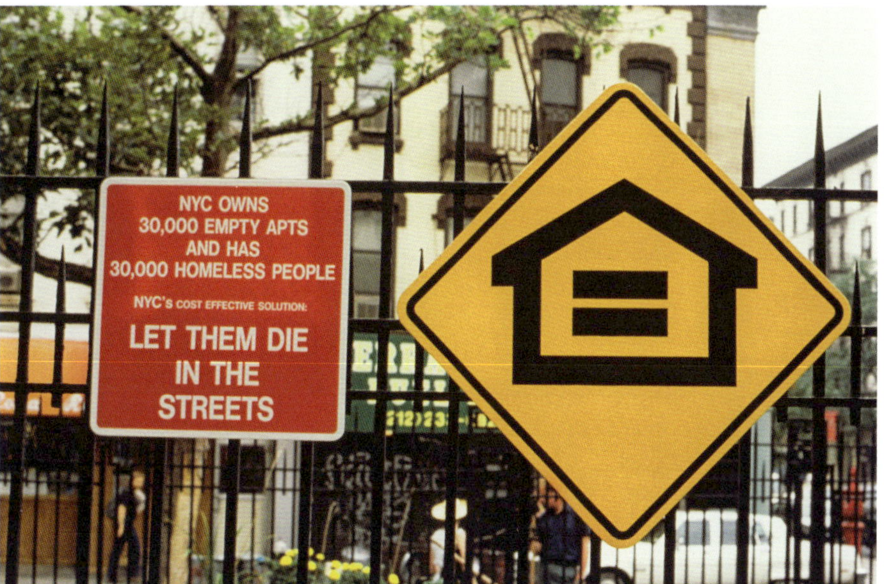

100

99, 100

Let Them Die in the Streets, 1990
Lieutenant Joseph Petrocino Park, Lower Manhattan Community Council, New York, United States
Signs, porcelain enamel on steel, 25.5 × 45.5 cm (each)
Gran Fury Collection, Manuscripts and Archives Division, The New York Public Library, United States

98

Reproduction of *La Nuova Venezia* cover with the "Biennale scandal" about the installation of *The Pope and the Pennis*, 1990

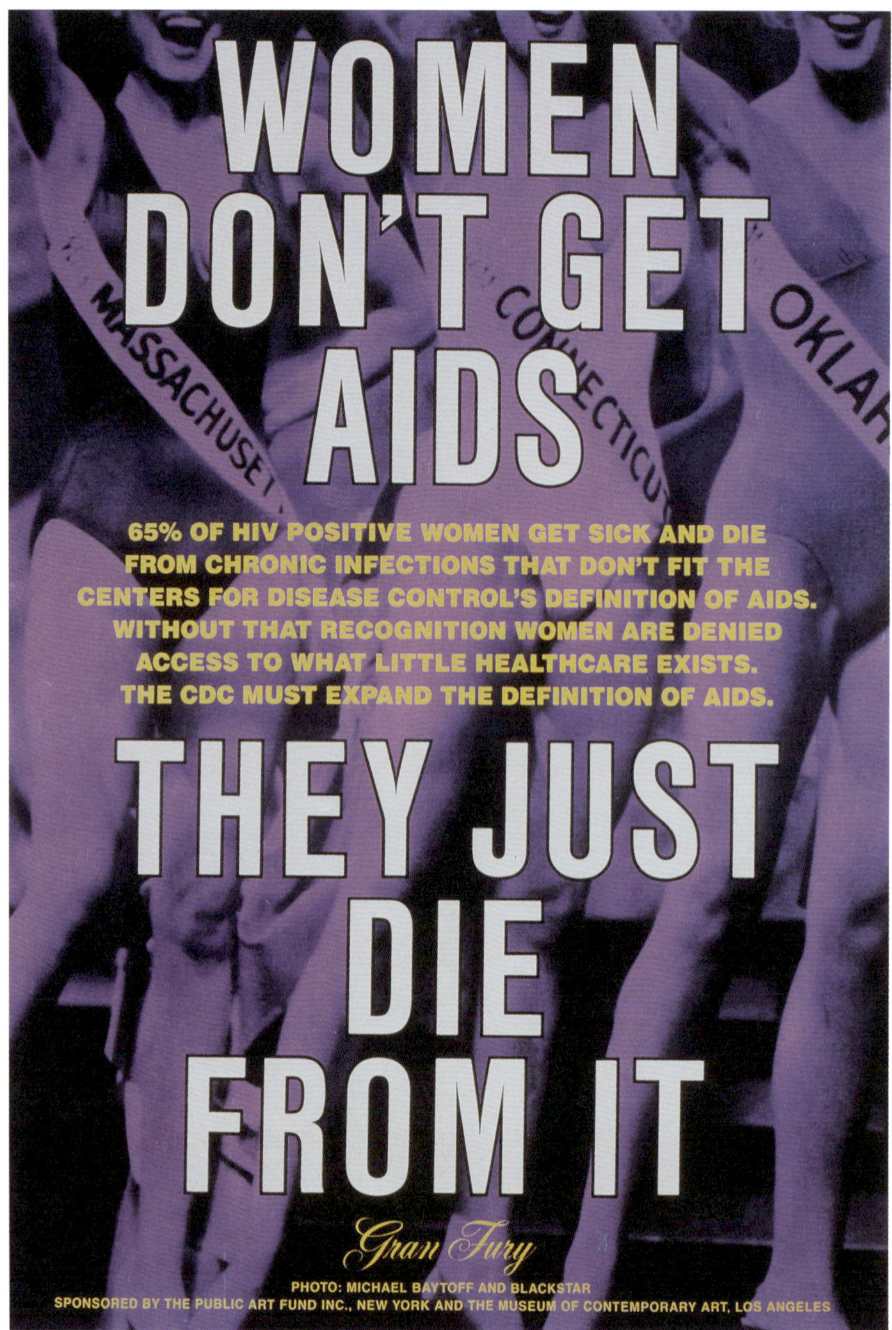

101

101

Women Don't Get AIDS,
1991
Ink on acetate,
178 × 119.5 cm
Public Art Fund, New
York, and The Museum
of Contemporary Art
Los Angeles, United
States

102

Paula Goldman
Installation view of
Women Don't Get AIDS,
in Los Angeles, United
States, 1991
The Museum of
Contemporary Art, Los
Angeles, United States

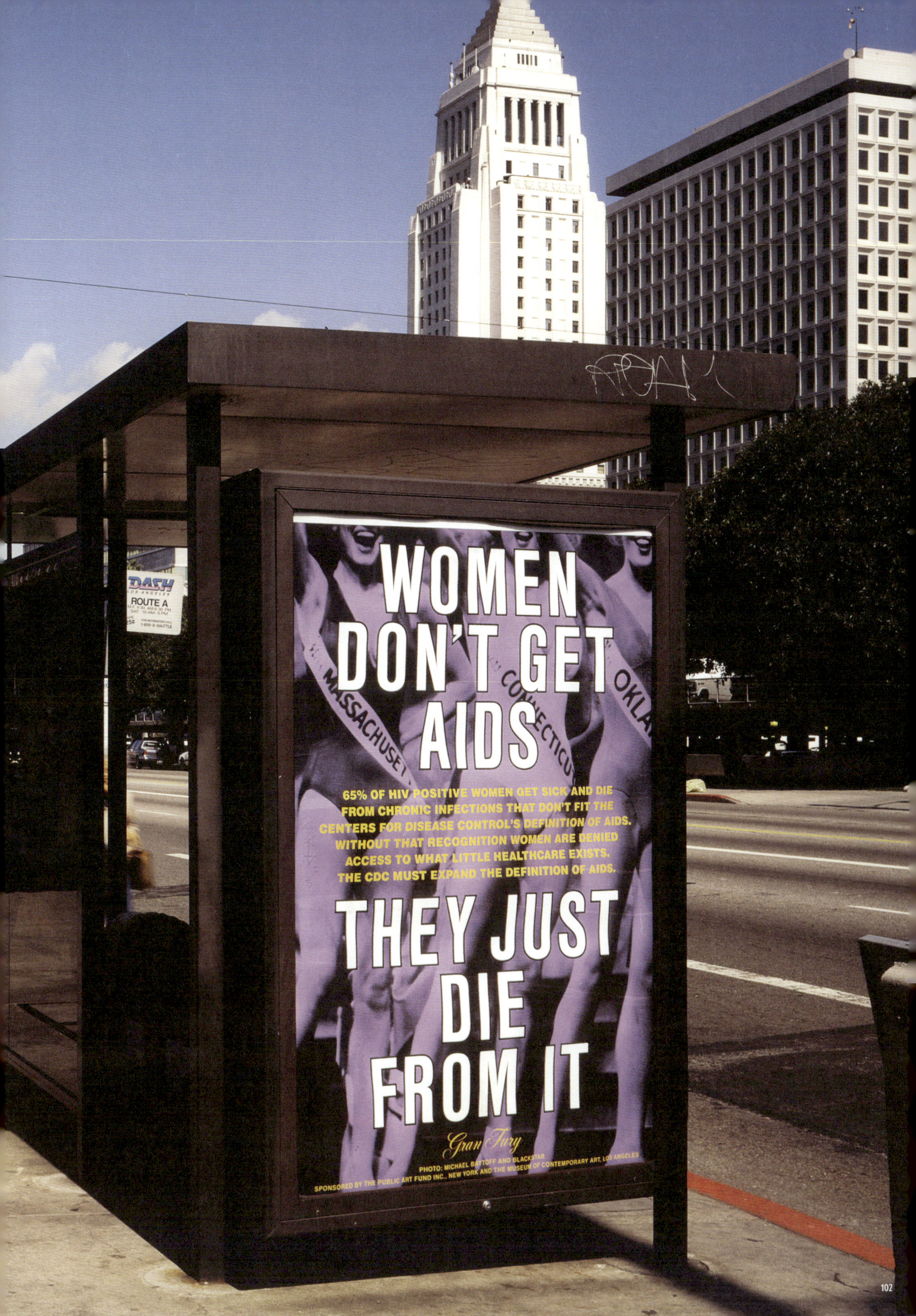

WOMEN
DON'T GET
AIDS
65% OF HIV POSITIVE WOMEN GET SICK AND DIE
FROM CHRONIC INFECTIONS THAT DON'T FIT THE
CENTERS FOR DISEASE CONTROL'S DEFINITION OF AIDS.
WITHOUT THAT RECOGNITION WOMEN ARE DENIED
ACCESS TO WHAT LITTLE HEALTHCARE EXISTS.
THE CDC MUST EXPAND THE DEFINITION OF AIDS.
THEY JUST
DIE
FROM IT
Gran Fury
PHOTO: MICHAEL BAYTOFF AND BLACKSTAR
SPONSORED BY THE PUBLIC ART FUND INC., NEW YORK AND THE MUSEUM OF CONTEMPORARY ART, LOS ANGELES
MASSACHUSETTS
CONNECTICUT
OKLAHOMA

LOVE FOR SALE
Free Condoms Inside

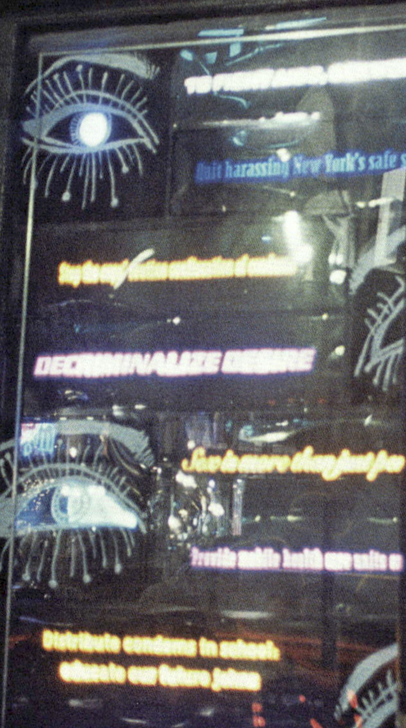
Quit harassing New York's safe sex workers
DECRIMINALIZE DESIRE
Distribute condoms in schools; educate our future johns
Make it legal to tote a needle

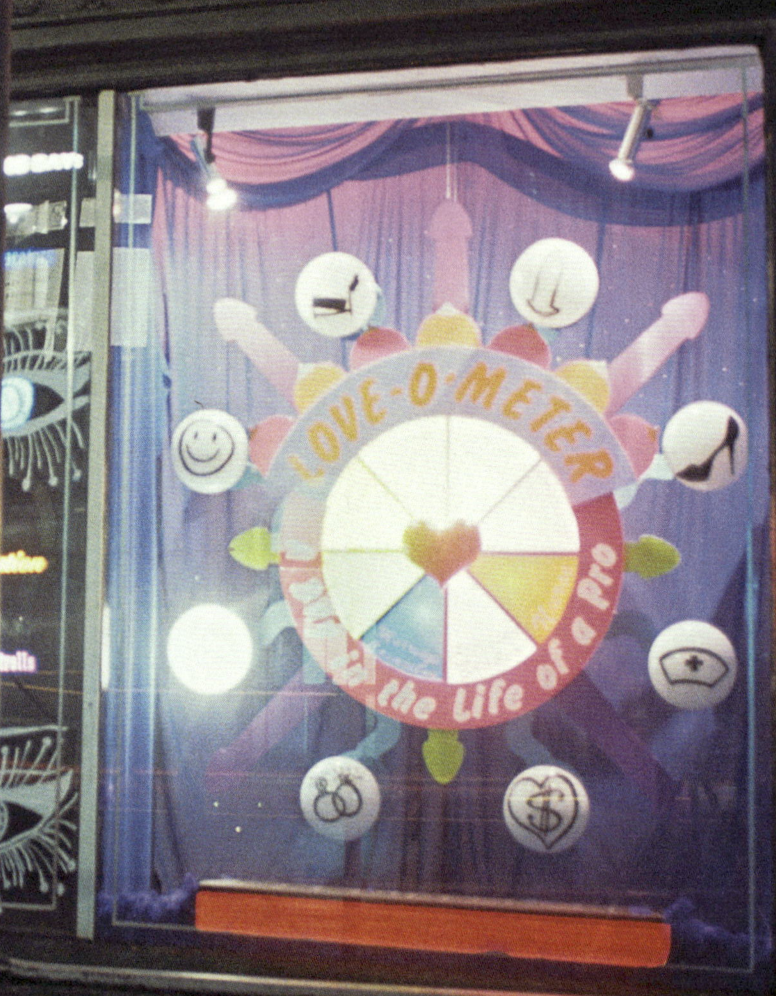
LOVE-O-METER
the Life of a Pro

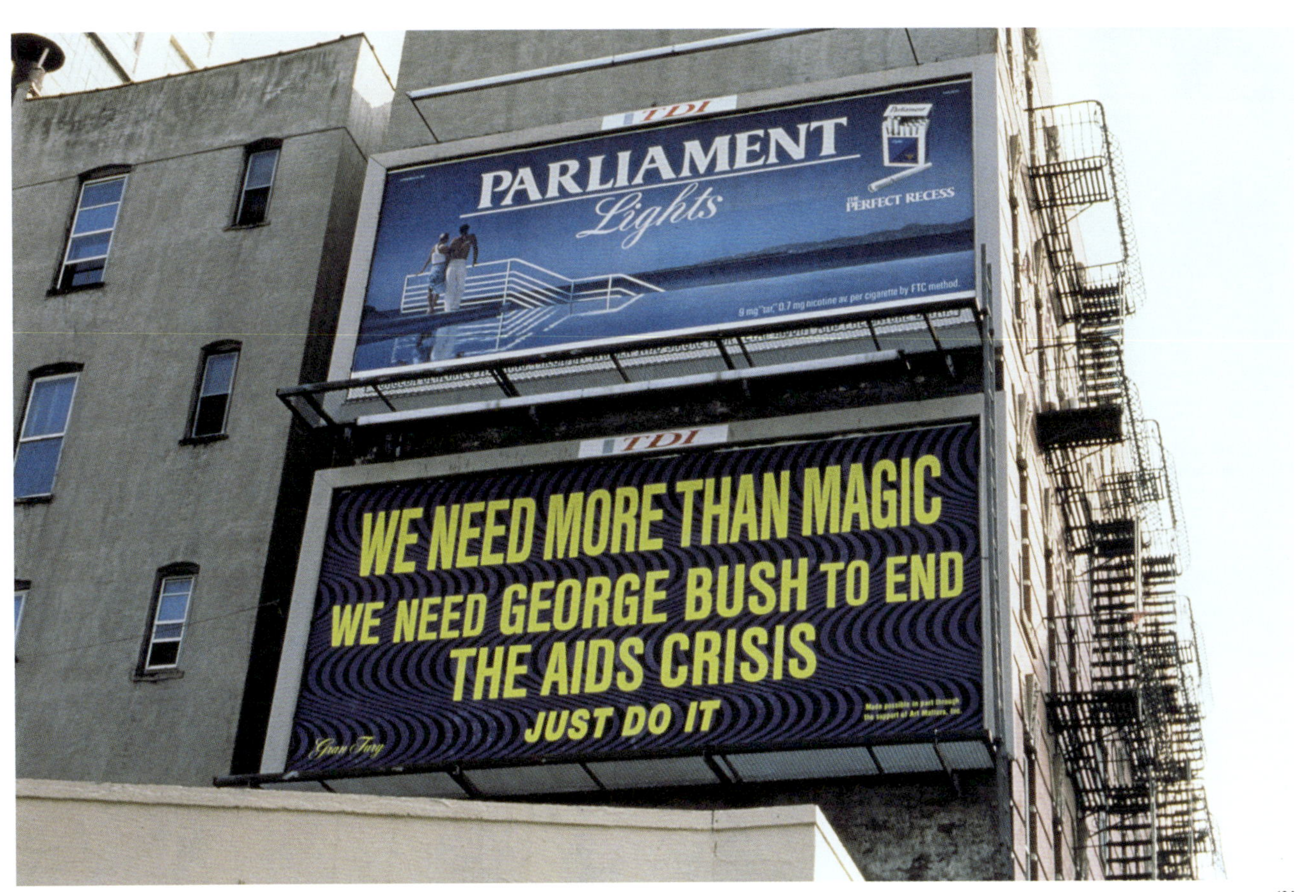

104

103
Gran Fury and
Prostitutes of
New York (PONY)
*Love For Sale... Free
Condoms Inside*, 1991
The New Museum
for Contemporary
Art, New York,
United States,
Mixed media,
window installation
Gran Fury Collection,
Manuscripts and
Archives Division,
The New York Public
Library, United States

104
Just Do It, 1991
(Partial support from
Art Matters)
Offset print on
paper set in billboard,
366 × 731.5 cm
Gran Fury Collection,
Manuscripts and
Archives Division,
The New York Public
Library, United States

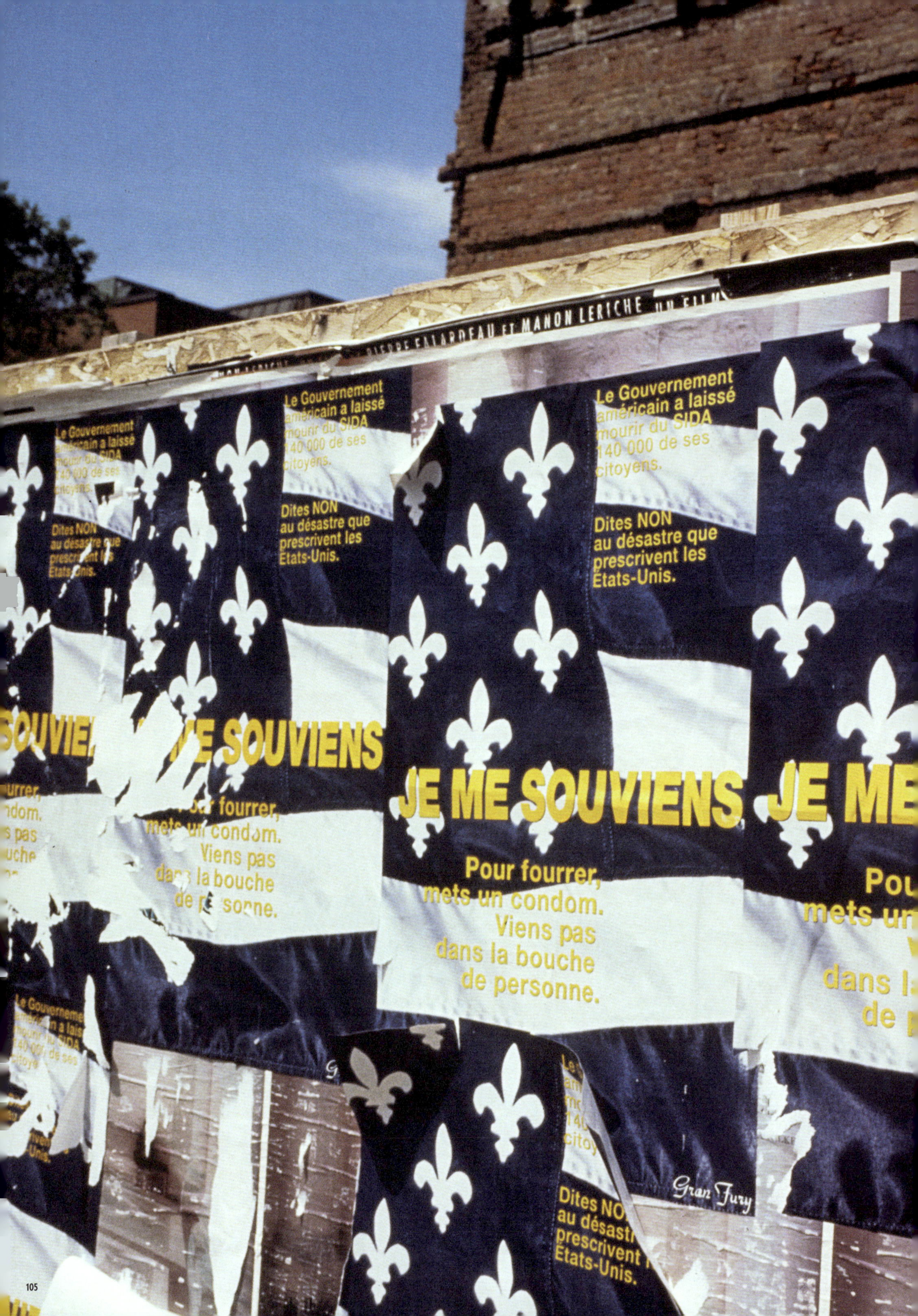
Le Gouvernement
américain a laissé
mourir du SIDA
140 000 de ses
citoyens.

Dites NON
au désastre que
prescrivent les
Etats-Unis.

JE ME SOUVIENS

Pour fourrer,
mets un condom.
Viens pas
dans la bouche
de personne.

Gran Fury

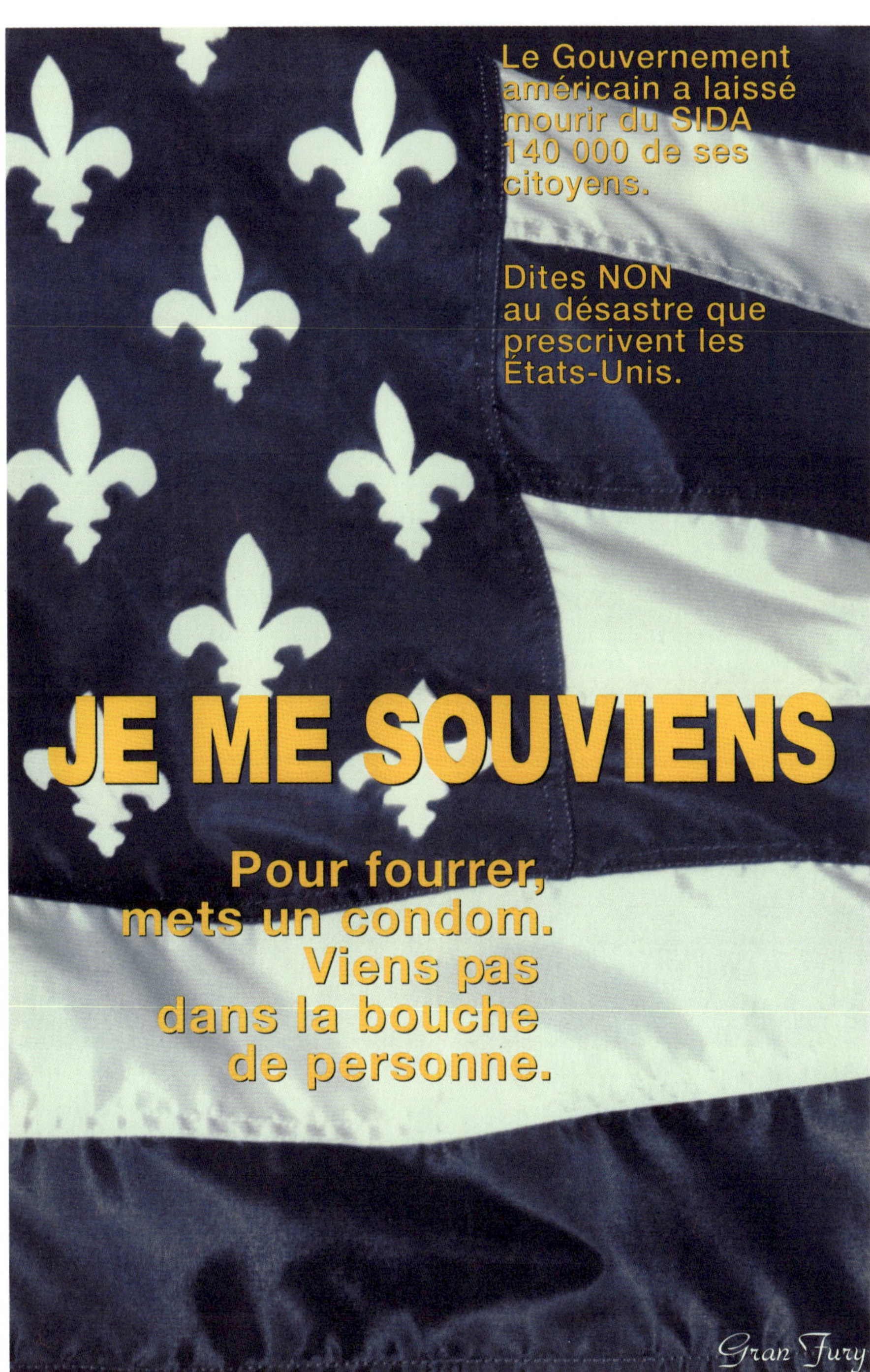

106

105

Je Me Souviens
[I Remember] poster
on wall, 1992
Musée d'art
contemporain de
Montréal, Canada,
Gran Fury Collection,
Manuscripts and
Archives Division,
The New York Public
Library, United States

106

Je Me Souviens
[I Remember], 1992
Offset print on paper,
87.5 × 58 cm
Musée d'art
contemporain de
Montréal, Canada

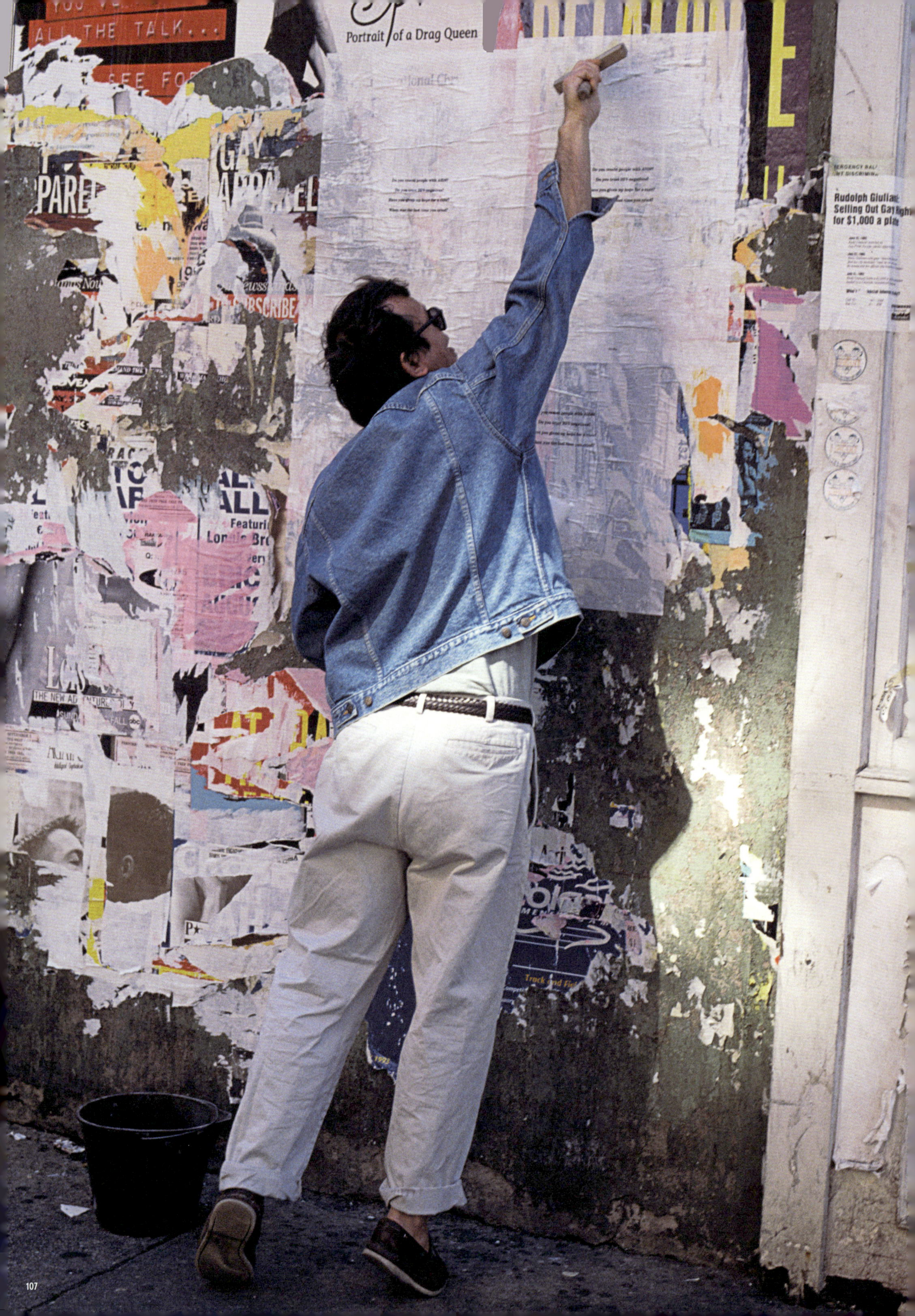

Portrait of a Drag Queen
GAY
APPAREL
Rudolph Giuliani
Selling Out Gay Rights
for $1,000 a plate

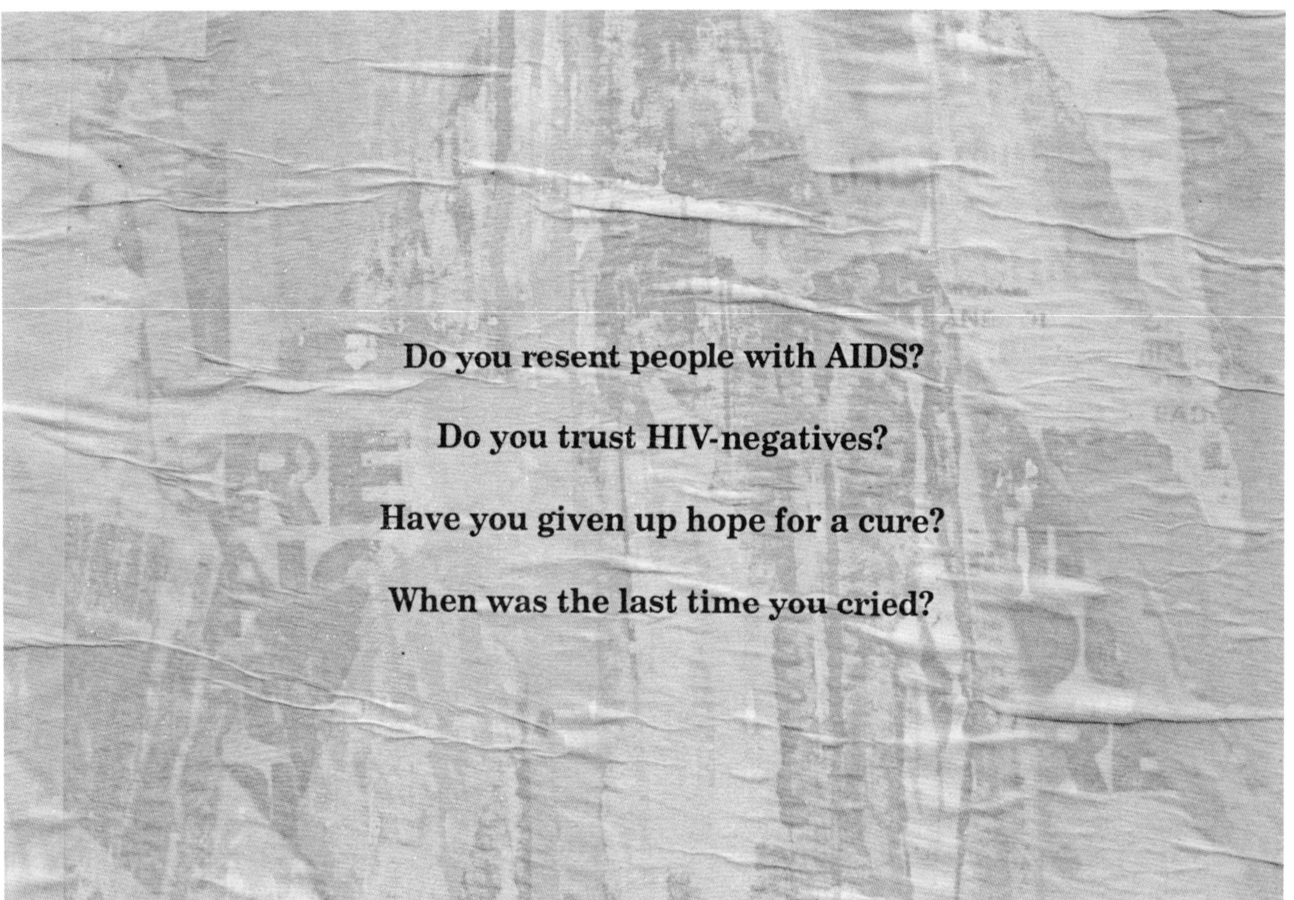

108

107
Mark Simpson
wheatpasting *Four
Questions* poster, 1993

108
Four Questions, 1993
Offset print on paper,
61 × 51 cm

109
Four Questions, 1993
Offset print on paper,
61 × 45 cm
Gran Fury Collection,
Manuscripts and
Archives Division,
The New York Public
Library, United States

Do you resent people with AIDS?

Do you trust HIV negatives?

Have you given up hope for a cure?

When was the last time you cried?

Gran Fury

GRAN FURY TALKS TO DAVID DEITCHER

——

Source: GRAN FURY. *Gran Fury: Read My Lips.* New York: 80WSE Press, 2011.
Originally published in FERGUSON, Russel; OLANDER, William; TUCKER, Marcia; FISS, Karen (Eds.).
Discourses: Conversations In Postmodern Art And Culture. New York/Cambridge/London:
New Museum of Contemporary Art/MIT Press, 1992.

DAVID DEITCHER How did you come together as a group?

MARK SIMPSON It started when The New Museum [of Contemporary Art] offered ACT UP [AIDS Coalition to Unleash Power] the opportunity to use the window, and a group of people got together and did that [img. 103].[1] When that project was over, the group met again. We wanted to do more and Gran Fury came out of that.

TOM KALIN Upward of fifty people worked on the window. There were big workshop sessions, like the one where the slabs of concrete were made by cutting rubber stencils. All the labor-intensive work was being done in someone's studio with fifteen or twenty people there at a time. Various people came in for specific tasks. I came in myself because I knew how to do mural photography. Other people came with their own abilities—the person who made the neon and so on. After the window happened people didn't meet as a group for a month. Then we had a potluck dinner. Various people, many of whom are here now, called each other up and started to meet and to talk about making the posters.

MS The people who joined together said that they wanted to work together as a group again—Gran Fury hadn't been chosen yet as a name.

DD Are there people who join and then go away, and then come back again? And if they do go away, are they welcome back?

MS Yes. Some people come only once in a while, and others come regularly.

DD There are other members of ACT UP who do visual work, like the Silence = Death Project. What relationship does Gran Fury have to them?

DONALD MOFFET There's some overlap.

AVRAM FINKELSTEIN I'm the only one here from that project.

DD But there were others involved in the design of that initial poster, right?

AF Yes, but they only overlapped with this collective by lending the use of the *SILENCE = DEATH* [img. 125] image to The New Museum window. They preceded us by almost a year.

DD Are there others still involved with the Silence = Death Project, including yourself, who also do other activities?

AF That's right.

DD Consisting of what?

AF That's not something I'm really comfortable answering because that collective works differently.

DD I'm curious because, as someone who walks around lower Manhattan a lot I see so much work that I can variously attribute to Gran Fury, the Silence = Death Project, or ACT UP. For instance, prior to the recent demonstration at City Hall there was a proliferation of funny, scathing fact-based posters pasted to walls. Were they your work?

AF No, Ken Woodard[2] designed those posters.

TK I think it's important to disentangle who did what. But who really knows who Little Elvis[3] is?—the people who made those stickers saying, "The AIDS Crisis Is Not Over" [img. 110]. And so, in terms of a history, it's really obscure and will probably stay that way.

DD Can Gran Fury support its activities?

MICHAEL NESLINE Financially? No.

TK But we're beginning to get grants.

ROBERT VAZQUEZ We're deep in debt and we've just been winging it, or getting small contributions.

DD So the work that has been done—with the exception I guess of the New Museum piece—was work that you had to support yourselves with your "paying" jobs?

MS Including the New Museum piece. They gave us $200 and we spent $2000.

AF ACT UP gave us the rest. A lot of it is begged, borrowed, and stolen. That's just the way ad hoc groups function.

110
Little Elvis
THE AIDS CRISIS IS NOT OVER, 1987
Bumper sticker,
9 × 28 cm

DD How would you describe the function of Gran Fury?

MN I'd say that all of us are interested in creating art work—or propaganda—that addresses the AIDS crisis and that will be seen by different parts of the public and affect their understanding of this crisis. It would provoke them, cause a reaction, make them think, and hopefully educate them. Our projects should have the effect that a demonstration by ACT UP has.

RV I believe that the work is meant to stimulate thought and to bring a whole new vocabulary—a whole new way of looking—to bear on the AIDS health crisis, by presenting imagery that is different from the mainstream stuff that people are subjected to by the mass media. We want people to question what is out there. One of the ways that Gran Fury does this is by using imagery that's already in circulation. The project that comes to mind most recently is the Art Against AIDS project, which we are calling the Benetton ad[4] because it looks very trendy [imgs. 77-80].[5]

TK I think what we do is make interruptions in public information and dominant media concerning AIDS, and what we've done has made use of a variety of tactics. There's been stuff that's responded to the sex-negative advertising that's been put out by the Department of Health in New York that promotes abstinence and is unrealistic or presents information that tries to enrage people or to provoke them into demonstrating. When ACT UP was given a Bessie Award,[6] we bought a half-page ad in the program to interrupt that space—to put a decoy into it. For a moment people took it for granted, just like *The New York Crimes* project [imgs. 70-72].[7] People might think that it's true, and it might slip in and do its damage.

DD So you insinuate yourselves into spaces and situations by appropriating particular formats. That's a bit like the tactics that Situationists used in Europe during the late 1950s and 1960s. How self-conscious are you about the relationship that your works have to commercial art (Benetton, for example) as well as contemporary and historical art forms?

TK Name them.

DD Well, I could begin with John Heartfield[8] [1891–1968] [img. 111] and Dada,[9] but I suppose I'm really thinking about Hans Haacke, Barbara Kruger [img. 113], Jenny Holzer [img. 114], or Situationism.[10]

LORING MCALPIN It's all up for grabs.

TK Like "Futura Extra Bold"—Barbara's[11] type of choice. We don't sit around and say, "Let's do a piece like so-and-so." It happens as work is being done because it's in our lives. Some of us make art outside of this context—outside of this collective project—and some of us don't. It's just one part of the flow of information that people who live here in New York are accustomed to.

MS Besides, all those people appropriate what they do...

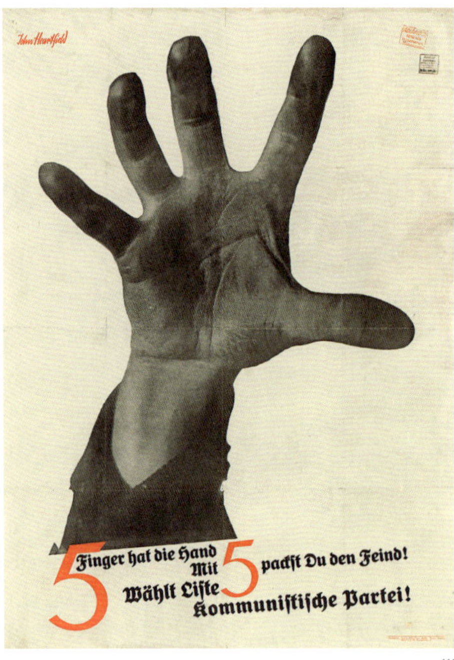

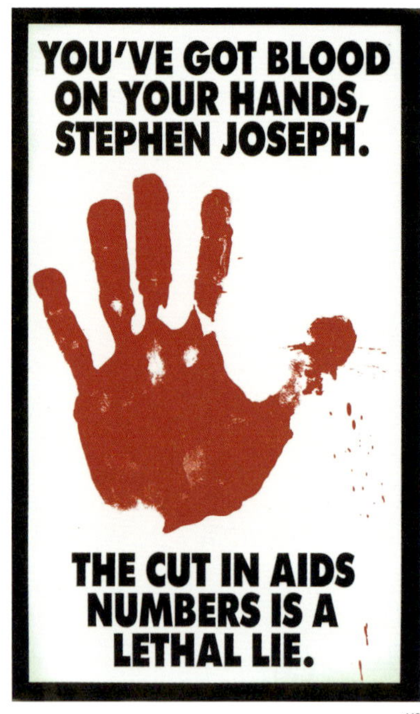

111

112

RV It's not as if appropriation is unique to what we do. Madison Avenue appropriates "fine art" constantly.

RICHARD ELOVICH You're probably hearing that there's a concern, an awareness of where different things come from, but I think that that's kept in perspective. I think we're aware of where things are coming from, but we have priorities.

DD Because there are larger issues involved?

RE Yes. And sometimes this flares up in discussion. I think that the one consensus is that there are priorities.

DD Another "appropriation" of yours—*The New York Crimes*—astonished a lot of *Times* readers who went to their local newspaper dispensing machines and found your work passing—with complete success—as the front section of their daily paper. Tell me how that came about.

MN Avram had this idea of doing a parody of *The New York Times*, and we all thought that was a really cool idea. So we approached different committees at ACT UP to submit articles about various issues, and those articles were laboriously edited and rewritten and re-edited and then it was laid out.[12]

DD Any response from *The Times*?

TK No. We should have been more aggressive about it.

MN Mathilde Krim [1926-2018] at amfAR [American Foundation for AIDS Research] got a phone call from Hoffman-La Roche.[13] They were extremely distraught and nervous, because of the back cover[14] [img. 115].

They assured Mathilde Krim that the gentleman who was quoted is a really good guy. They were very upset about it, and they wanted to know what could they possibly do so that they wouldn't be firebombed or something. Mathilde apparently wasn't sure what to think. She spoke to David Corkery[15] and he said well, hey, the guy said it, and he's fair game. If they want to do something, then why don't they spend more money on AIDS or contribute money to some appropriate cause.

RV Mathilde Krim is not a member of Gran Fury. [Laughter]

DD When you said you've responded to the sex-negative materials that the Department of Health has been disseminating, what projects were you referring to?

TK Well, one thing that we're doing right now is the San Francisco bus project, it's jointly sponsored by Creative Time in New York and Art Against AIDS nationally. It's a photograph showing a series of six heads: one lesbian couple, a gay male couple, and a heterosexual couple of mixed color, all kissing just like in the Benetton ads.

RV Another strategy we employed last year that we haven't talked about is the *AIDS: 1 in 61* [1988] poster [img. 33], which was a case where we took advantage of two things that the media were putting out at the time. One was that heterosexual women didn't have to worry about HIV transmission through sex. The other was that one out of sixty-one babies being born in New York were HIV-positive. When we got together to do that piece, we had no idea that it would end up being a "racism" poster. We were able to articulate something that no one else—or very few people—were really aware of at that time, by drawing two statements together to articulate something as it hadn't been before.

TK I think it's also important to talk about the translation of that poster because I remember that the voice of the Spanish translation was a very different voice. It was much more like a call to action, and it was empowering. The English was much more like a savvy, accusatory thing.

LM It's something that we did struggle with for a while because at a certain point we wanted to start reaching out to other communities. It was a problem simply realizing that there was a lot of work that needed to be done for those communities and that we had to think before stepping in to do it. How could we understand what their issues really were?

RV At the same time that this was happening with Gran Fury, the issue of race started coming up more and more at ACT UP's weekly meetings as more and more people of color walked into the organization. So for a lot of people it was a new way of thinking—realizing that there were different people within the AIDS community that were not necessarily white homosexual men, and that you had to reach these people. The next question was: how do you reach them in the most culturally sensitive way? I very much respect Gran Fury for that *1 in 61* poster because it was clear and it wasn't condescending. It spoke about the issues, and the

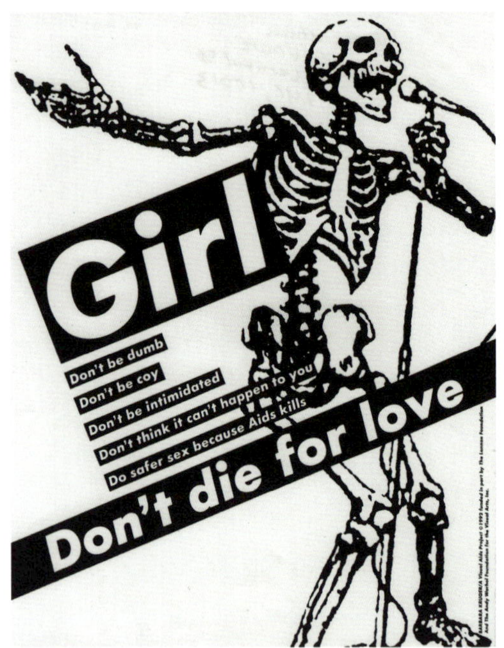

113

114

reaction that I got from Latino people who read it was that it was a kind of rallying call. They said, it's good that someone is saying this and that this crisis is being acknowledged.

TK As a group I think we're realizing that, when you hammer out this copy word for word, month after month, and then you translate it into Spanish and, well, it makes no sense. The syntax of it isn't culturally specific, culturally relevant. It's all about trying to squeeze the right meaning into the wrong shape. I think, for me at least, this points up the fact that if we want to do additional projects that will reach a specific non-white and/or non-English-speaking community, instead of trying to have our ideas channeled, we have to go to the community and try to work with something that already exists in terms of concern and voice.

DD What other posters would you think of in relation to this issue?

DM There's one that states, "When a government turns its back on its people, is that civil war?" [img. 38]. That's a billboard project that developed shortly after *1 in 61*.

MN We spent a good summer hashing over the wording and the image.[16]

AF Maybe it had its best life as subway billboards in Germany which is what that odd format was designed for, because we were in this exhibition in Berlin.

MS That's what it was made for. And so there were sixteen up total: eight each for two weeks—seven in German, one in English.

LM We had problems in New York just getting it up because we had arranged to have it on Sale Point[17] billboard spaces last fall, but when

113
Barbara Kruger
Untitled (Girl, Don't die for love), 1992
Black and white print on paper, 71 × 54.5 cm
Courtesy of the artist, Sprüth Magers and Mildred Lane Kemper Art Museum, Gift of Visual AIDS, 2004, St. Louis, Missouri, United States

114
Jenny Holzer
MANY ILLNESSES CAN BE CONSIDERED A DEADLY WEAPON. WHY IS HIV THE ONLY ONE TREATED THAT WAY?, 2016

they saw the copy they said, you can't put that up beside our other advertising. That delayed the project another few months until we finally just went out and sniped it.[18]

DD So you've tried to do work on billboards in the city but they weren't accepted?

AF Yes. That's where the appropriation techniques backfire because you can't get the space. Also there's a tendency, I fear—harkening back to the Silence = Death project—that when you appropriate a sort of yuppie technique or an appeal to a non-politicized audience, that people tend to embrace the commerciality of it, embrace only the look of it, and it loses its edge. In that way appropriation loses its bite and sometimes I worry about it as a long-term strategy.

DD It seems ironic that Gran Fury has actually revitalized a strategy that— at least within the context of art world business-as-usual—has become a cliché of academic postmodernism, a non-issue. Among the "happening" artists, dealers, and critics nobody talks about appropriation anymore, but in a discussion of activist work like yours it's still meaningful. Perhaps that's what happens when you return appropriation to its functional, political roots in Dada.

DM We haven't exhausted it. There were other interesting things we learned from the billboard project besides what we've mentioned. Once it went up, something I think we suspected was confirmed: It's not a very effective billboard because it has way too many words on it. It's okay in a subway where the viewer is doing nothing but standing, but it doesn't work as a billboard for the streets of New York because its function there would have to be something you can read as you approach it and pass it by, and this one is too long to do that.

DD Yes, but there are sites where it can work. You've put one up on the side of a building at Church and White Street which is a great location because it can be seen from several vantage points. It's very near city government offices; for instance, the Courts on Broadway, and the Department of Social Services which is one block away. Obviously, the context is important to the success or failure of any piece.

TK Now I'm thinking about "With 47,524 Dead, Art Is Not Enough" [img. 59]. That statement we made for a specific context and now we're being flogged for it.

DD I wasn't aware that it was originally made for a calendar for the Kitchen.[19] I came upon it later, in the window of Printed Matter, and it did make me wonder. For example, are there cultural responses to the AIDS crisis that are illegitimate?

AF I don't think we are saying that any type of cultural response is illegitimate or irrelevant. What we are saying is that what, in terms of Western culture, is regarded as a "cultural" response completely

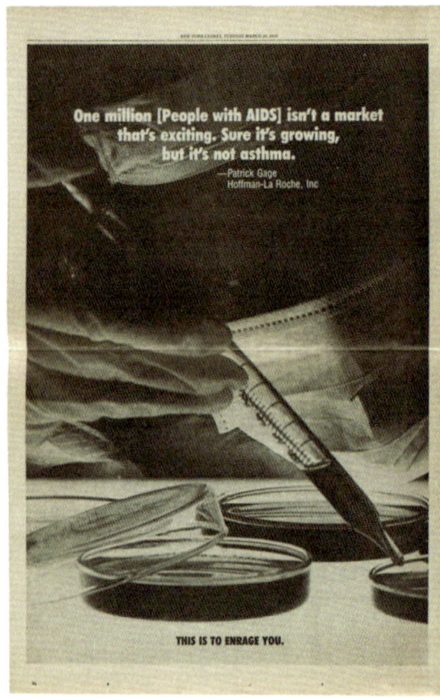

115

115
Gran Fury
The New York Crimes,
1989
ACT UP; Target City
Hall Demonstration,
United States
Offset print on
newsprint, 58 × 38 cm

disregards alternative responses. When we came up with *Art Is Not Enough* many issues arose that we'd discussed on and off: the appropriateness of being invited into gallery spaces, what that means to the kind of work we do, where it's appropriate and where it isn't.

MS That was stuff that came up later. The original piece was planned for the Kitchen. The people we were targeting with that information were artists and their audience. We were saying, "Art is not enough; do something more." When we did it, we were thinking, art is not enough; fundraising is not enough; memorials are not enough. You know, it was a call to people to get off their asses and do something more.

TK In a sense you're both right, but it makes me anxious to carry this discussion forward. What Avram was saying is true: when you have sixteen words you can't say that direct collective action is culturally specific and depends on what you do. Not everybody has the ability or the freedom to go to daytime demonstrations, for instance. I think the problem may stem from a limitation within the format and language of advertising. When you polish everything down to this burnished sixteen-word sentence it doesn't say all the other things that you may be trying to refer to.

AF I still consider this project successful, even though it's largely misunderstood. It's created a debate in the art world that previously didn't exist, at least with reference to AIDS.

TK I don't agree with that. I don't want to contribute to a polarized view of this situation between artmaking and activism, or artmaking and direct political action. I guess I'm thinking about this raging debate that centered on the organization of a show called *Against Nature*, which featured art by gay men.[20] The question was, is it okay to be making work that is lyrical, or camp, or humorous? Or should art work be terse, direct and didactic? I just think that those polarizations are simplistic and unhelpful for the most part. But I also think there's merit in a lot of discussion and I think that's one of the ways in which Gran Fury gains its strength.

DM I am unwilling to back off from *Art Is Not Enough* because it does say a lot. The art world is no more or less implicated in this mess than any other professional field in this country; it just so happens that this is where we are. In the midst of this crisis the statement still makes sense to me.

AMY HEARD Especially in something like the Ohio State catalogue[21] where you opened it up and smack dab in the middle there's this huge thing—"With 47,524 Dead, Art Is Not Enough. Our Culture Gives Artists Permission to Name Oppression, a Permission Denied Those Oppressed. Outside the Pages of This Catalogue, Permission Is Being Seized by Many Communities to Save Their Own Lives. We Urge You to Take Collective Direct Action to End the AIDS Crisis." People were giving us the eye and were a little bit mad—who are you to tell us what to do? But it's important that they have to confront this issue, just like *The New York*

Crimes forced the Wall Street banker on his way to work to think about the sort of inequities within this society and the government's response to AIDS. I think that's why I stand by it, because we have to think about what it means.

RE I feel more ambivalent about *Art Is Not Enough* because I think that when we originally composed the slogan there was a context for it. We were suggesting that memorials are not enough, and that quilts[22] are not enough. Now it has become an "art" argument. I sat through a performance last week of Tim Miller[23] in which he basically threw a tantrum. It was so manipulative in terms of using activism for a kind of self-serving purpose. Miller staked a position by attacking Dennis Cooper's work and saying, there's no room for any kind of obsessiveness or darkness in work now, because everything has to be about getting those hospital beds. I felt much more positively about the use of *Art Is Not Enough* in *The Village Voice*[24] [img. 116]. I'll give an example of how highly charged the situation has become. An artist, David Wojnarowicz [1954–1992], went to a presentation on AIDS issues at the School of Visual Arts, and he was in a rage because he felt like he was fighting his way out of a paper bag. He wasn't quite sure where things were going—what it was all about. His work deals explicitly with AIDS issues and he's living with AIDS. He felt that the presentation we gave suggested that there was something wrong with showing his work in galleries. He felt he'd struggled and kept at it and finally now he was able to make some kind of living by exhibiting his work in galleries. He gets his butt kicked by the FDA, by various government agencies, only to find that it's being kicked by AIDS activists. I don't want to function in that way. I came out of art school in the mid-seventies, going to galleries and seeing [Dan] Flavin [1933-1996] and [Joseph] Kosuth, and I know what it's like for covert rules to be operating.

AH I don't think we want to be prescriptive about it. I think it's more of a provocative thing.

TK One of the things I liked about the piece was the fact that we implicate ourselves when we say it. After all, we're using art to say that art is not enough.

RE I think it worked a little better in the *Voice* because it's a call to arms, as opposed to an indictment for not doing the right thing. The *Voice* piece used an image of a demonstration more explicitly than did the Kitchen poster. There was a demonstration image at the Kitchen too, but it was on the reverse side. By putting the slogan and the image together, and by the timing of it, I think it functions more as a call to arms than an art argument.

MN I think there is an art argument to be made. I'm not so naïve about the artworld as to perceive it as one monolithic thing, but there is a major part of the artworld which takes in the latest issue and chews it up as fodder. I don't think that the AIDS crisis should be allowed to be exploited in that way by artists. And if we serve as a goad to prevent that from happening, then that's all for the best to me.

DD I want to continue to discuss this issue, but from a slightly different perspective. What is to be gained—or lost—for you as a group of activists by using the museum/gallery/artworld setting?

MN As a nonartist who is a member of an art collective, the thing that is most interesting to me about being part of the artworld is the power that is granted to artists. Mark put it eloquently in the past when he remarked that an artist is one of the few people in our society who can say, "I want to do my piece in the middle of the airport," and actually be permitted to do it. ACT UP cannot have a demonstration in an airport, and that is why it's valuable to me to participate in this artistic endeavor. I'm perfectly willing to exploit the power of the artworld if it will allow us to do what we want to do where we want to do it. But I absolutely cringe at the idea that because AIDS is this year's hot artworld topic, that next year AIDS will be *passé*. If that means that Gran Fury is *passé*, that's fine, but AIDS is not an issue that can be disposed of because it's last year's issue. If *Art Is Not Enough* addresses that, more power to it.

TK I agree with a lot of what you're saying. Some artworld responses—and the ways that world describes the relationship between art and AIDS—can be horrifying. I'm thinking about the catalog essay for the Art Against AIDS auction,[25] or more recently, this "Blow the Whistle on AIDS" campaign which is my particular pet peeve and has attracted the participation of every major museum in the country. It consisted of selling a silver-plated designer whistle for $250 for the regular edition, and $500 for the limited edition, so that you can "blow the whistle on AIDS." Only forty percent of the money is being given to amfAR—which itself is questionable as a conduit to people who really need money like the Community Research Initiative,[26] or countless small community-based agencies that are dealing with people of color—and yet this is what the artworld considers to be a healthy response to AIDS. Rosalind Solomon or Nicholas Nixon's[27] horrifying photographs of people with AIDS are other troublesome reactions often construed as positive artworld responses. We don't need more Nicholas Nixon images. We don't need "Blow the Whistle…"

DM I think we used to thumb our noses a bit at the power and the performance of that complete art system, with its journals and magazines, but that power is real.

DD What kind of power?

DM The power of distributing the word, of telling people what some people are doing. The press has been crucial to us in a lot of ways, whether or not we want to acknowledge that, or respond to it, or just say it's okay.

DD At first you said, if I can quote you, "We had to get out of Soho—get out of the art world."

DM But that's just what we did in our first project: the *1 in 61* piece was not only culturally explosive for us, but territorially we went to the Bronx; we went everywhere. I think it's a question of strategy. To date, the

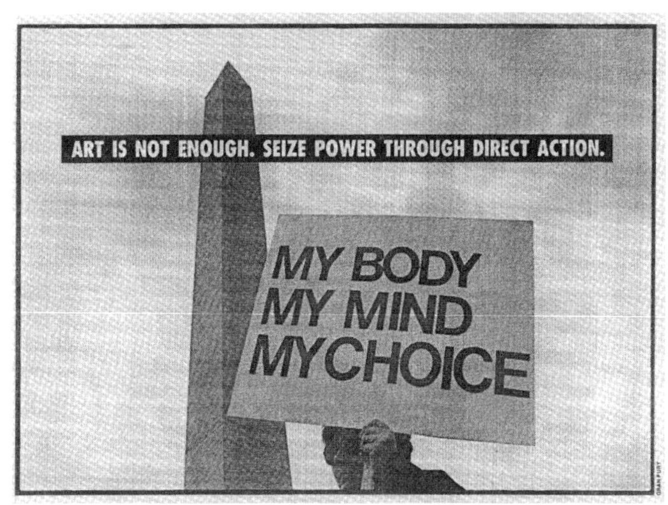

116

only time the work of Gran Fury has ever appeared in a gallery was this painting, *Riot* [1988] [img. 37], which intentionally reflected on a specific project by General Idea [img. 5]. I don't think it's a question of anyone in the group being proscriptive about operating in the museum or gallery context. I don't think that as an artists' collective we're unlike other individual artists and collectives who are involved in institutional critique. It's just that we happen to be doing it rather narrowly, in relation to issues specific to AIDS.

MS One of the reasons we accepted the New Museum project was because it made a window on Broadway available and we wanted that opportunity to reach everyone who walked by it; not just people who go to the galleries. Since then we've considered doing projects in galleries, and we probably will, because of the potential that they offer to reach people.

JOHN LINDELL There's a sacrifice involved in using the gallery/museum art system. We only get to talk to that world. We wanted to use billboards to speak to a broader audience but were censored by those who control billboard space because of the character of our work. We were also censored monetarily because we need thousands of dollars to rent those billboards. By choosing to use the gallery setting—it's a classic situation— we can say anything we want, but we say it to fewer people.

DD Then it must have been satisfying to do the window at the New Museum not just because of the site's unique relationship to the street but because of the nature of the New Museum as an institution.

MS Well, yes and no. Because the New Museum was the only place like that. Bill Olander [1950–1989], who initiated the project, was really the only person that could have done what he did. We're not going to the Whitney Museum.[28]

AF Originally that project was proposed to me by David Meieran,[29] a friend of Bill Olander's, who was contacted by him. My initial reaction

116
Gran Fury
Art Is not Enough.
Seize Power Through
Direct Action
Published in *The Village*
Voice, circa 1980s
Offset print on
newsprint

was, did they understand that we are not an art collective? When I spoke to Bill, I said that the answer was yes, that we would probably want to take that window space and make it into a demonstration. After all, that is what we do at ACT UP. I asked, would there be parameters, and he said no, you can do whatever you want so long as you know what that is, and it was on those terms that the project was accepted. After that we organized into this group.

TK I think you could really work yourself into a corner though, if you were to make a firm distinction between being a political collective and being an art collective. I insist on a politic that resides in a lot of different places. In addition to direct action it resides in education, in making images or making informational fact sheets, or whatever.

NOTES

1 *Let the Record Show…* appeared in the window of The New Museum of Contemporary Art from November 20, 1986–January 24, 1987. See Douglas Crimp, "AIDS: Cultural Analysis/Cultural Activism." In: *AIDS: Cultural Analysis/ Cultural Activism* (Cambridge, Massachusetts: MIT Press, 1988), 3.

2 Ken Woodard was a member of ACT UP.

3 Elvis Presley's nickname for his penis. Little Elvis was founded by ACT UP member Rick Sugden.

4 Clothing manufacturer Benetton created a campaign photographed by Oliviero Toscani that included images of multi-racial couples.

5 Art Against Aids is an organization that raises funds for AMFAR, the American Foundation for AIDS Research. In 1988 it commissioned Gran Fury to design a project that would run on the outsides of buses in San Francisco.

6 Off-Broadway theater awards.

7 On April 28, 1989, ACT UP staged a demonstration with civil disobedience at New York City Hall. Gran Fury produced a "fake" *New York Times* to coincide with those actions. Six thousand copies of *The New York Crimes* masquerading as the first section of the newspaper "of record," were wrapped around the latter, and placed in newspaper dispensing machines throughout Manhattan.

8 In the essay "This is to enrage you: Gran Fury and the graphics of AIDS activism" Richard Meyer observes that the "bloody hand" disseminated by Gran Fury and printed in the *The Government Has Blood on Its Hands* (1988) poster "directly recalled John Heartfield's *A Hand Has 5 Fingers. With 5 You Can Repel the Enemy! Vote List 5*. Heartfield's graphic was created for the German elections of 1928, a year in which the number five carried a double significance, marking both the date of the election and the row on the ballot where Communist party candidates were listed. Rather than merely simulating Heartfield's design, Gran Fury revised and updated it. Where Heartfield's image featured the sullied hand of a worker, reaching up and out as if to stop us in our tracks, Gran Fury's graphic depicted a handprint, a trace of a body that is no longer present, presumably because it has died from government neglect." In Nina Felshin: (ed.), *But is it Art? The Spirit of Art as Activism* (Seattle, WA: Bay Press, 1995), 70. [Editor's Note]

9 Dada, or Dadaism, was an avant-garde art movement that took place in Europe after the First World War.

10 Situationism, or the Situationist International, was an avant-garde artistic and political movement that took place in Europe during the second half of the twentieth century.

11 Refers to Barbara Kruger, American conceptual artist that worked appropriating and relocating images from magazines and advertisements, including texts in Future Bold or Helvetica Ultra Compressed types.

12 *The New York Crimes* included a number of illuminating and equally incriminating articles, among them, "AIDS and Money: Healthcare or Wealthcare?," "Thousands of New Yorkers May be Dying in the Streets: State's Highest Court Finds City Legally Responsible," "Women and AIDS: Our Government's Willful Neglect," "N.Y. Hospitals in Ruins; City Hall to Blame," "Inmates with AIDS: Inadvertent Political Prisoners."

13 A pharmaceutical company.

14 On the back cover of *The New York Crimes*, Gran Fury printed a full-page mock advertisement for Hoffman-La Roche, Inc. that showed a surgical-masked scientist measuring liquids out of a pipette into pyrex discs. Across the top of this image they superimposed a block of text containing the following comments of Patrick Gage, an employee with that firm: "One Million [People with AIDS] isn't a market that's exciting. Sure, it's growing, but it's not asthma." Across the bottom of the image was the statement, "THIS IS TO ENRAGE YOU."

15 AMFAR employee and ACT UP member.

16 It also says: "The U.S. Government considers the 47,524 dead from AIDS expendable. Aren't the 'right' people dying? Is this medical apartheid?"

17 Sale Point was a billboard rental company serving the New York area.

18 "Sniping" refers to the practice of illegally wheatpasting posters in public spaces.

19 On one side of the December/ January 1988–89 calendar for the Kitchen was a photograph of demonstrators, and on the other was the statement, "With 42,000 Dead, Art Is Not Enough."

20 *Against Nature* was curated by Dennis Cooper and Richard Hawkins, and was exhibited at Los Angeles Contemporary Exhibitions from January 5–February 12, 1988.

21 Jan Zita Grover organized the exhibition, *AIDS: The Artists' Response*, for the Hoyt L. Sherman Gallery at Ohio State University in Columbus (February 24–April 16, 1989).

22 The AIDS Memorial Quilt project collected together hundreds of quilts made to memorialize those who died of AIDS.

23 Tim Miller is a performance artist and one of the so-called "NEA Four".

24 It appeared as the centerpiece of the "Voice Centerfold" (*Village Voice*, April 18, 1989), where it functioned to advertise a night of performances at P.S. 122 to benefit ACT UP. In this case, the statement was superimposed on a photograph of the march on Washington for abortion rights that took place on April 9.

25 The auction, held at Christie's, New York, to benefit amfAR in 1987, was accompanied by a catalog with an essay by Robert Rosenblum. In it he described art's capacity to give pleasure to the senses, fortify the spirit, and raise money for AIDS research, but denied that it has the "slightest power to save a life." See Rober Rosenblum, "Life Versus Death: The Art World in Crisis." In: *Art Against AIDS* (New York: amfAR, 1987), 32. For a critique of this position see Douglas Crimp, "AIDS: Cultural Analysis/ Cultural Activism." In *AIDS: Cultural Analysis/Cultural Activism* (Cambridge, Massachusetts: MIT Press, 1988), 3–16.

26 The Community Research Initiative was founded by Michael Callen (1955–1993) and Joseph Sonnabend (1933–2001) in 1987 to provide community based drug trials and promote treatment literacy for PWAs.

27 Rosalind Solomon and Nicholas Nixon are photographers who both exhibited photographs of people very visibly sick with AIDS. ACT UP protested a Museum of Modern Art (MOMA) show of Nixon's work.

28 Shortly after this interview was conducted, Gran Fury was invited to participate in the exhibition *Image World: Art and Media Culture* at the Whitney Museum. The show's organizers turned over the wall facing the front window of the museum to Gran Fury, where they exhibited *Kissing Doesn't Kill, Greed and Indifference Do*. The museum also rented billboard space at two locations for another work by Gran Fury.

29 David Meieran was a member of ACT UP and the video collective Testing The Limits.

GRAN FURY TALKS TO DOUGLAS CRIMP

———

Originally published in CRIMP, Douglas. "Douglas Crimp talks to Gran Fury."
ArtForum 41, no. 8, Apr. 2003.

DOUGLAS CRIMP One of your members, Mark Simpson [1950–1996], is no longer with us. Perhaps we can officially dedicate our remarks here to his memory. When did Mark die?

TOM KALIN Mark died of AIDS on November 10, 1996.

DC Okay, let's begin with a work that seems appropriately sad. Ten years ago a few of you in Gran Fury made a poster with four questions [img. 108], the last of which was, "When was the last time you cried?" Was that the final work done under the auspices of the group?

LORING McALPIN Well, after that we did the flyer *Good Luck, Miss You*[1] [1995] for [the exhibit] *Temporarily Possessed* at the New Museum. That was meant as our farewell.

DC That was 1995. You did the four questions in '93. Do you remember the other three questions?

AVRAM FINKELSTEIN "Do you resent people with AIDS? Do you trust HIV-negatives? Have you given up hope for a cure?" The conversation leading to that work was largely driven by Mark Simpson. We were grappling with a problem we had at that later stage—trying to put very complex things into a very concise text. This work was a response to our frustration at being unable to articulate the complexity of the issues. We decided to just go bare bones and say how we felt, which had never been our primary focus.

TK I remember that Mark always had a yellow legal pad in his house on which he wrote all sorts of things. And those questions were among the things he wrote. They were about feeling alienated as someone living with AIDS and about feeling less well physically. That, and the fact that the visibility of the crisis and the AIDS activist demonstrations had faded away.

AF Up to this point, the only emotion we had directly articulated was anger. But it's funny that you should even mention this work, Douglas, because, unlike a lot of the other things we did, there was no response at all to that piece.

LM Well, we were addressing a different audience. It was really directed toward our own community. We were trying to acknowledge something

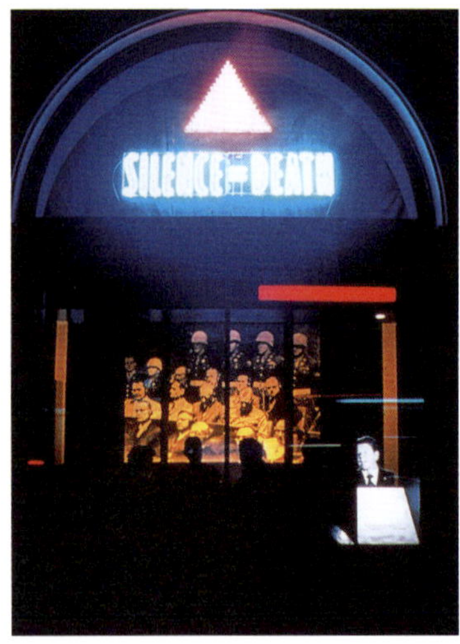

117

but not judge it, to ask, "What's happening now? Where did our anger go? What are we going to do?"

TK In my memory, you all went out with buckets of wheat paste, just like we did in 1988 with *AIDS: 1 in 61* [img. 33], the first work we did with the name Gran Fury.

DC How did Gran Fury come into being as a collective?

MICHAEL NESLINE It happened by degrees. Bill Olander [1950–1989], the curator at the New Museum, came to an ACT UP meeting with a proposal that ACT UP use the museum's window on Broadway for a visual demonstration. At the end of the meeting, everyone who was interested met in the back corner of the Lesbian and Gay Community Center.

DC The result was *Let the Record Show....* This was 1987 [imgs. 117]. How did such a complex work get formulated by such a large group?

TK I remember there was a kind of bullet-style accumulation of political points compiled from clippings people brought in from the *New York Times*. The main idea came from demos where we yelled "shame" at public figures who were doing nothing about AIDS. So we decided we'd single out public figures who had made outrageous statements about AIDS, show a photograph of each of them, and cast their words in concrete. And then these AIDS criminals somehow got connected to the Nuremberg trials. It probably went back to the *SILENCE = DEATH* poster [img. 122] with the pink triangle.

AF This is the way ACT UP functioned on every level. People would bring news items to the meetings. They would throw out snippets from articles, and whatever resonated became the issue we'd organize around. It was an organic process, and Gran Fury worked that way for a long time.

DONALD MOFFETT The form developed in the same collaborative way. The issues unfolded, and the form followed.

MARLENE McCARTY Absolutely. Someone would say, "I know how to make a photo mural." Somebody else would say, "I have access to a LED."

TK I remember volunteering to make the photo mural of the Nuremberg trials because I knew how to make murals by ironing paper to canvas with glue. I remember Don Ruddy at another meeting cutting rubber letters with an X-Acto blade to cast the sentences in concrete. The process was additive, like a collage. It just turned out to have a coherent appearance, which made it seem much more planned than it really was.

MN Well, Mark Simpson actually knew what was going on. He described to me what the window was going to look like before it existed.

117
ACT UP ad hoc
Let the Record Show...
(ver. 1), installation
view, 1987
Mixed media,
window installation
The New Museum
of Contemporary
Art, New York,
United States

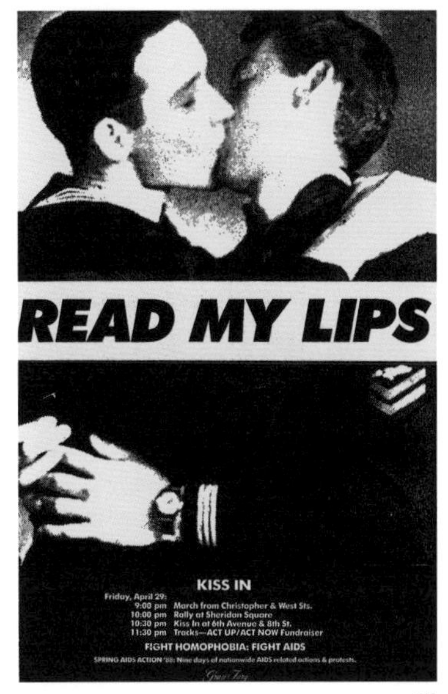

118

MM Each time we gathered to work on the window, a different constellation of people showed up. It wasn't until later that we decided to form a collective.

LM When we were disassembling the window, there was a discussion about what to do next.

TK We had a meeting and said, "Let's continue this." The poster *AIDS: 1 in 61* [1988] came out of that meeting. It was then that we took the name Gran Fury, which was the Plymouth model of choice for the New York Police Department. But that group was still larger than the one around this table: it included Don Ruddy, who later died of AIDS; Anthony Viti was involved in that discussion, I'm sure Todd Haynes was involved, Mark Harrington.

LM Steve Barker. The group was variable up until after we made the posters for "Nine Days of Protest" that included *Read My Lips* [1988] [img. 118].

DC How did a shifting group of people become a collective with a fixed membership?

JOHN LINDELL Since initially the meetings were open, anybody could come, but it became frustrating.

MM You couldn't move forward; you always had to backtrack and regroup.

JL There was a debate about whether we should be open or closed, and we finally decided to be closed.

TK We went from being wheat pasting hooligans to suddenly having real resources and opportunities and a platform from which to speak. This brought about a crisis of conscience in discussing how to articulate the group because the stakes had been raised.

DC What was your first high-stakes opportunity?

LM It was *Kissing Doesn't Kill* [1989–90] [imgs. 77-81], which was part of a public-art project called Art Against AIDS: On the Road. Within a year or so, our poster was on buses and subway platforms in San Francisco, Chicago, New York, and Washington, D.C. Up until then, we were still having a dialogue with the whole membership of ACT UP. When we presented this project, suddenly there were three hundred people commenting on it; we just realized that we couldn't work with that much feedback.

MN We decided we wanted to function independently, but we asked ACT UP for a percentage of the profits from sales of T-shirts with our images printed on them. Of course this didn't include the *SILENCE = DEATH* T-shirts, since that wasn't a Gran Fury design, but it

118
Gran Fury
Read My Lips
(*Men's ver.*), 1988
ACT UP, Spring
AIDS Action
Photocopy on paper,
42.5 × 27.5 cm

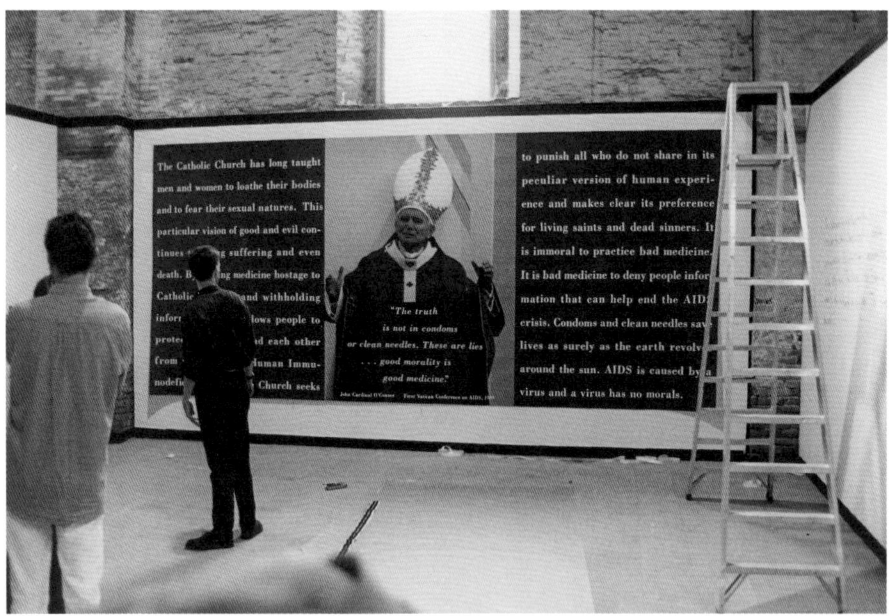

included *Read My Lips*, which sold a lot. They agreed, but we didn't get the money from them on a regular basis.

TK Well, there was a little bad blood.

ROBERT VAZQUEZ-PACHECO I remember that well, because I was at-large representative from the floor of ACT UP, and I would hear discussions about Gran Fury: "Every other committee of ACT UP is open; why is it that with Gran Fury we don't know who they are and their membership is closed?" It was counterintuitive for the ACT UP membership to have a closed group.

DC In other words, Gran Fury began as an ad hoc committee of ACT UP members, then broke away from the larger organization, just as, later, members of the ACT UP Treatment and Data Committee split off from the larger group to form TAG,[2] the Treatment Action Group, and the P.W.A. [Public Works Administration] Housing Committee evolved into Housing Works. My memory is that other artists and graphic designers in ACT UP became resentful of the status Gran Fury had attained in the art world. And in the end it is certainly unjust that ACT UP's graphic style is very often credited to Gran Fury alone, when in fact many others who were never members of Gran Fury contributed to the invention of that style.

MN Just as a footnote to what you're saying, Douglas, one of the things that really made a big difference in the legitimization of Gran Fury is the article that you published in the AIDS issue of *October*.[3] You made the argument for why what we were doing was legitimate in the context of art.

TK Our work is also indebted to the appropriation work of the early '80s that you wrote about. But it's true, the *October* article eventually led to things like the Biennale di Venezia [img. 119], to a kind of institutional

119
Bruno Jakob
Installation
photographs of
The Pope and the Penis
at the 44th Biennale di
Venezia, Italy, 1990
Gran Fury Collection,
Manuscripts and
Archives Division,
The New York Public
Library, United States

exposure that probably wouldn't have happened otherwise. We went from T-shirts and posters to billboards and international exhibitions.

MM The aftermath of that has been really weird. I'm still active in the art world. I teach in the United States and Europe, and I'm constantly asked how we put together our art collective. It always blows my mind, because we came together with such a sense of urgency, with goals that had nothing to do with wanting to make art or to change the way people look at art.

DC Probably very few people understand what it is to make art collaboratively within the compass of an activist movement. They seem to believe that Gran Fury was a group of artists who contributed to AIDS activism or to ACT UP, but in fact it's the other way around. All of us were members of ACT UP, and that's why we were able to accomplish what we did. More importantly, it's why we did what we did in the first place.

LM We began at an unusual historical moment. AIDS was turning into a huge catastrophe, and there was no adequate public response. So there was a space for some kind of voice to raise questions. None of us had any doubts that we had to be there.

AF But as soon as we realized we had a voice, we started to mock ourselves. Every so often we would be cackling, "Oh, that's so Gran Fury."

LM We simply realized the extent to which we were using institutional power.

TK I don't think we were being ironic. It was just a question of the tensions that arose from having a larger platform and still trying to speak effectively about urgent concerns.

DM What goes unsaid is that the institutional support was instrumental for us, because from the very beginning, we decided we weren't going to say, "We can't do this because there's no money." We started out really small with things that we could afford on our own, and then the money started coming in for real, and it facilitated a continuation of our work, so this can't just be a discussion about the ironies of what we were doing.

TK I only meant to address this bigger point. The collective proceeded from activist concerns, and the fact that we were in sync with the art world and able to use those resources was great. But at a certain point, we began to have the opportunity to address issues further away from what we knew best. For instance, in Montreal, with the piece for the opening of the new building for the Museum of Contemporary Art, *Je Me souviens* [1992] [imgs. 105, 106], I remember discussions about what it meant to make a piece in French talking about French-Canadian identity.

LM We also had a long discussion about whether we should be in the Biennale di Venezia at all. We had wanted to hang banners in the street, remember? And they said, "No, you can't do that." And there was a moment when we wondered whether it was enough for us to just be inside an art institution, but we decided it was a public enough venue to merit doing it.

AF It was also an opportunity to talk about condom use in the belly of the beast, to confront the Catholic Church on its home territory.

MM I want to go to bat for Venice. We cannot forget how much press came out of that piece, which was far more public than a billboard would have been. That work got AIDS on the cover of *Express*.

RV But we're being disingenuous when we say that we planned to send a huge photograph of an erection to Venice [img. 91], intended as a provocation to the Pope [img. 90], and worried that no one would notice. We knew very well what we were doing.

MN The director of the Biennale tried to dismiss the controversy by saying, "Oh, the penis. That's just kitsch." In the meantime Cicciolina was back there being fucked by Jeff Koons.[4]

TK It was funny, we made Jeff Koons look just decorative and irrelevant next to something authentic that rippled through the art world—a situation that then got quickly reversed, sadly.

DC Here's perhaps the inevitable question: after achieving such success, why did you stop?

JL We stopped because there were questions that we wanted to address that we couldn't find a means to address. Toward the end we talked about doing something about the fact that after nearly ten years of AIDS awareness the infection rates for gay men were still going up. We found that our way of working was inadequate to the situation, and we couldn't change our way of working.

MN We tried to invent new strategies. We tried to collaborate with the Guerrilla Girls [img. 120] and with PONY [img. 103], but those collaborations didn't prove to be successful.

RV I left the collective a while before it disbanded. One reason was that I was working in communities of color, and I remember a discussion about the bus-shelter poster we did that showed white women [img. 121]. I argued that if you use white women, only white women will pay attention to it. But we went with the picture of the white women, and I thought, "I need to move on now," because my politics had changed.

MN It's interesting that you mention that project, Robert, because if somebody asked me what was the final project Gran Fury did, I would have said *Women Don't Get AIDS. They Just Die From It.* [1991], which was the last snappy one-liner we came up with. And as disappointed

GUERRILLA GIRLS DEMAND A RETURN TO TRADITIONAL VALUES ON ABORTION.

Before the mid-19th century, abortion in the first few months of pregnancy was legal. Even the Catholic Church did not forbid it until 1869.*

*Carl. N. Flanders, Abortion, Library in a Book, 1991

A PUBLIC SERVICE MESSAGE FROM **GUERRILLA GIRLS** CONSCIENCE OF THE ART WORLD

120

as we were by that project, the fact is that the issue we were trying to address—the failure of the CDC's AIDS definition to include the diseases women were getting—changed after we did that poster; the definition of AIDS expanded to include many more illnesses specific to women. I'm not saying we can take credit for the change, but our poster was part of the activist work that pressured the CDC to change the definition.

TK Our disbanding also corresponds to the growing efficacy of groups like TAG and the introduction of protease inhibitors. The horrible irony is that literally the day Mark Simpson died, I came home after taking care of his body and there was the *New York Times* magazine with Andrew Sullivan's cover story about the end of AIDS. Mark had tried protease inhibitors, but he had a staph infection, and they didn't work. And now supposedly people don't die of AIDS anymore, so Mark's death sadly came at the moment of the final dosing of that earlier chapter in AIDS treatment.

MM The attitude toward AIDS changed when it went from being a crisis situation to a chronic, manageable disease.

DC I think you're making a leap that is historically inaccurate. At the time that you did the final poster with the four questions, things were not getting better. It would be two long years before the introduction of protease inhibitors, and not only had things become extremely complex, but many of us were feeling terrible despair. The enthusiasm with which we had approached what we were doing in the early years of ACT UP couldn't be sustained, because death was taking too great a toll. Also, we had brought about a lot of change up to a certain point, but then stasis set in.

120
Guerrilla Girls
Guerrilla Girls Demand a Return to Traditional Values on Abortion, 1992
Offset print on paper, 43 × 56 cm
Museu de Arte de São Paulo Assis Chateaubriand, gift of the artists, 2017, MASP.10641

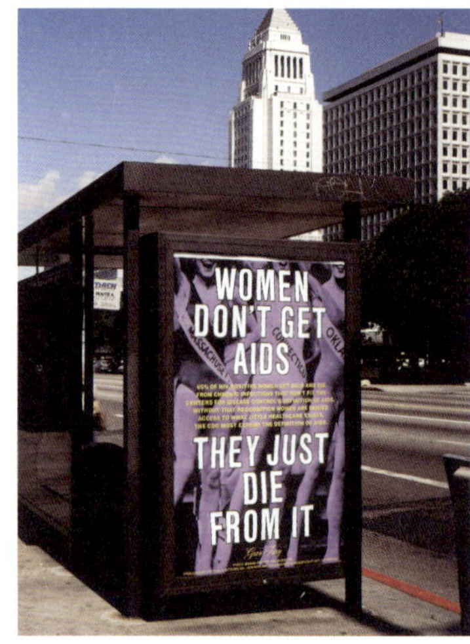

121

MN If you remember what the initial goals of ACT UP were—to publicize the crisis, to get drugs into bodies, and to end the AIDS crisis—we accomplished two of the three. The third still remains to be achieved.

JL I also want to make it dear that the dissolution of Gran Fury wasn't quick, and it wasn't happy in any way. Our decision to stop didn't come as a relief. It was the result of frustration with our inability to find a means to continue working.

LM I think what we accomplished was to drive a wedge into public discourse and open a space where AIDS could be talked about in all its dimensions. By the time we stopped, that was happening. Maybe our function was just to initiate that discussion—to expect us to last until the discussion is over is absurd.

DC On top of all the other horrifying events of the present—including the Bush administration's rush to war—AIDS here and now is still a crisis. And nobody talks about it.

MN That's not entirely true. Just this week the newspapers reported that the rate of new infections among young African-American males in the United States has inched up by a percentage point. The information is there, and that's a huge difference from the time that ACT UP started.

AF But the urgency is not there.

DM What I hear now is a rhetorical neglect coming out of the White House that is very similar to where we were fifteen years ago.

DC And many of the things that we accomplished as activists we would now have to fight for all over again. For example, ADAP funding is being cut all over the country. And when was the last time any of you saw prevention information in, say, a gay bar?

RV With the introduction of protease inhibitors we didn't see people die as quickly. But in fact people of color are dying just as quickly as before. With the introduction of protease inhibitors the focus of people doing AIDS policy work shifted to AIDS in Africa, and with their attention elsewhere, horrible policies like mandatory name reporting began to happen here.[5]

DC To return to the question of irony, today Gran Fury is remembered less among activists than within the art world. It's not for nothing that this is an interview for *Artforum* and not for a magazine about queer politics. I guess we probably have to admit that the resting place of Gran Fury is the museum.

MM But in fact the final resting place is not the museum, it's the Public Library.

121
Paula Goldman
Installation view of
*Women Just Don't Get
AIDS*, in Los Angeles,
United States, 1991
The Museum of
Contemporary Art, Los
Angeles, United States

DC I meant the museum metaphorically. But yes, let's be clear that the Gran Fury Collection is in the public domain and available in the Manuscripts and Archives Division of the New York Public Library.

DM That legacy is an educational resource for another generation. After all, we didn't come out of nowhere. We dragged the history of this kind of art into the '80s and the early '90s. And it will be reinvented again.

NOTES

1 Published in this volume.
2 Group that originated from ACT UP, founded with the aim to accelerate and motivate research efforts for AIDS treatment drugs. [Editor's Note]
3 Douglas Crimp, "Introduction." *October*, v. 43, winter 1987. [Editor's Note]

4 This is a reference to Jeff Koons' series of sculptures and paintings *Made in Heaven*, presented for the first time at the 1990 Biennale di Venezia. Available at https://jeffkoons.com/exhibitions/solo/made-in-heaven. Retrieved Nov. 22, 2023. [Editor's Note]
5 Name reporting policies for people living with HIV were a tool for epidemiological control that started in the U.S.A during the 80's. By 1983, it was mandatory in all states. LGBTQIA+ organizations, public health agents and HIV/AIDS activists opposed these policies because of their discriminatory potential. [Editor's Note]

REPRODUCTION
OF WORKS

—————

ACT UP, ACT UP ad hoc, Avram Finkelstein,
Catherine McGann, Donald Moffett,
Donna Binder, Ellen B. Neipris, Eugene Gordon,
Lola Flash, Silence = Death Project, T. L. Litt,
Tom McKitterick, Vincent Gagliostro

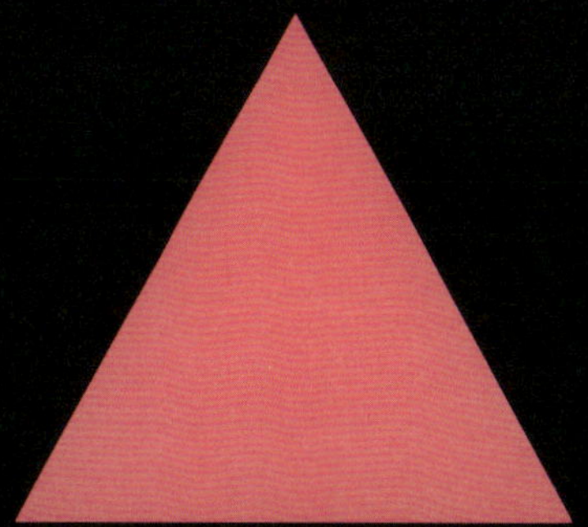
© 1987 AIDS Coalition To Unleash Power

SILENCE=DEATH

Why is Reagan silent about AIDS?   What is really going on at the Center for Disease Control, the Federal Drug Administration, and the Vatican?
Gays and lesbians are not expendable...Use your power...Vote...Boycott...Defend yourselves...Turn anger, fear, grief into action.

© 1987 AIDS Coalition To Unleash Power

122
Silence = Death Project
SILENCE = DEATH, 1987
Offset print on paper,
85 × 56 cm
Avram Finkelstein
Archive, New York,
United States

123
Silence = Death Project
AIDSGATE, 1987
Offset print on paper,
85 × 56 cm
Avram Finkelstein
Archive, New York,
United States

124
Donald Moffett
He Kills Me, 1987
Offset print on paper,
59.5 × 95.5 cm
Courtesy of the artist
and Marianne Boesky
Gallery, New York and
Aspen, United States

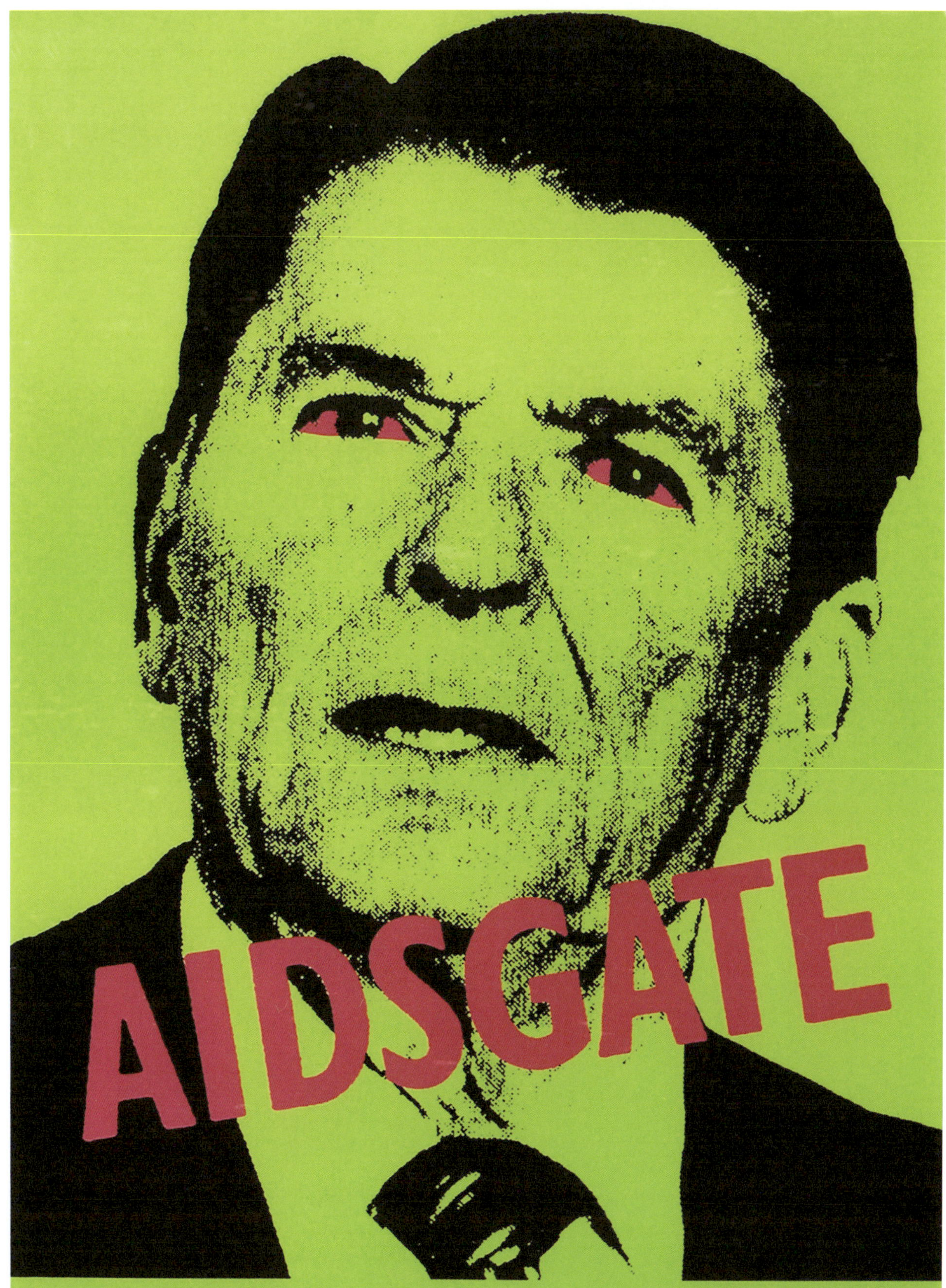

AIDSGATE
This Political Scandal Must Be Investigated!
54% of people with AIDS in NYC are Black or Hispanic... AIDS is the No. 1 killer of women between the ages of 24 and 29 in NYC...
By 1991, more people will have died of AIDS than in the entire Vietnam War... What is Reagan's real policy on AIDS?
Genocide of all Non-whites, Non-males, and Non-heterosexuals?...
SILENCE = DEATH

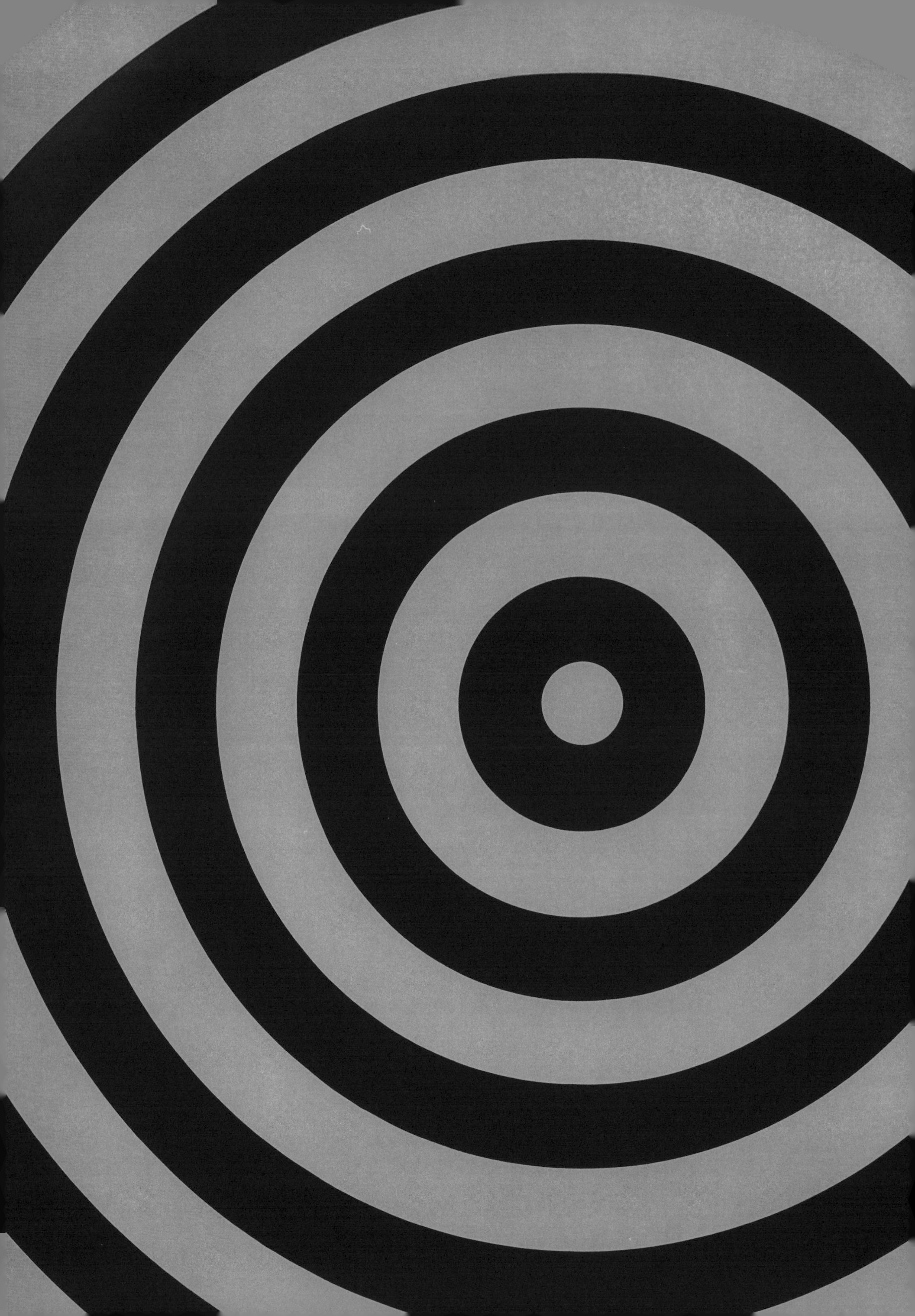

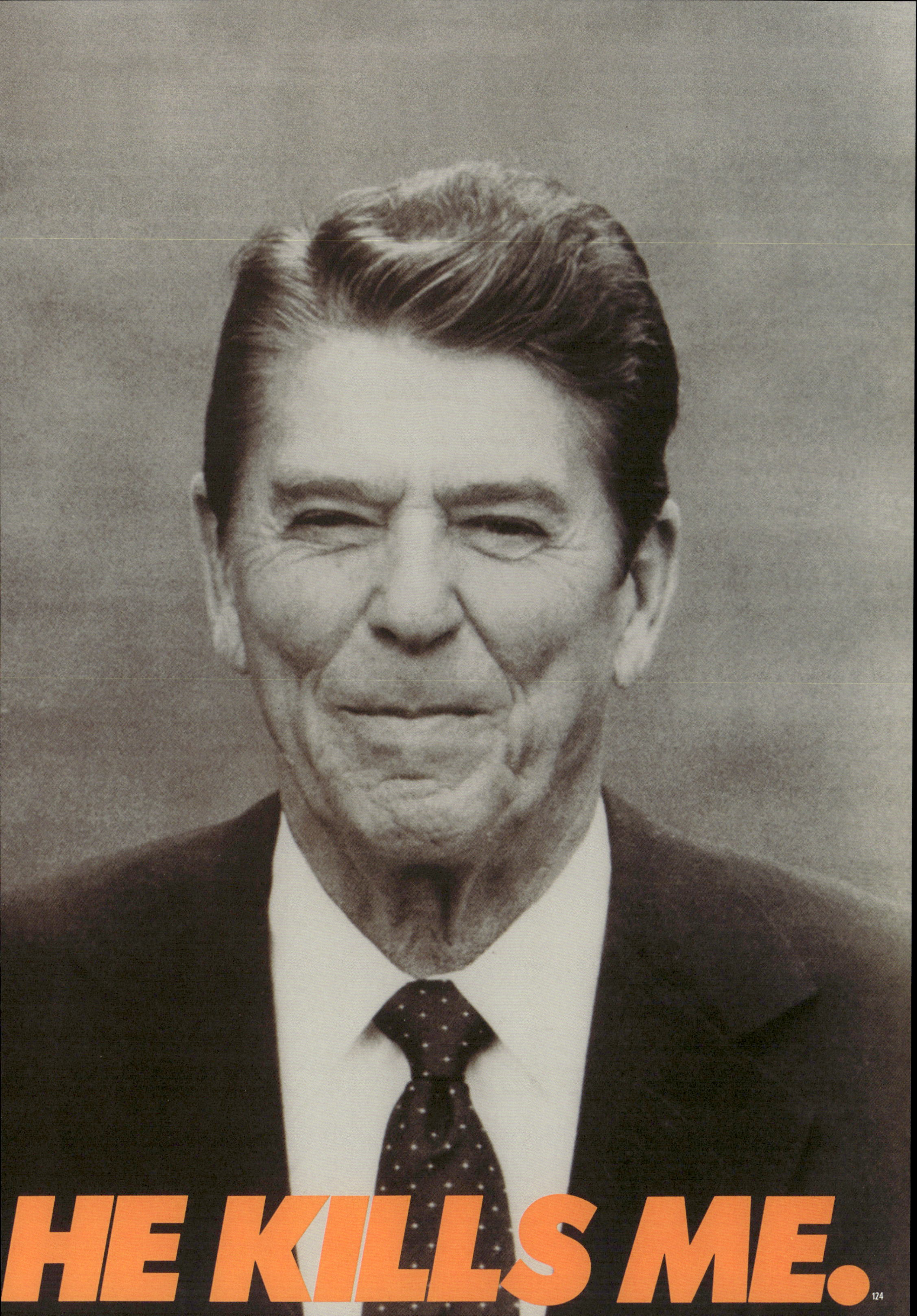
HE KILLS ME.
124

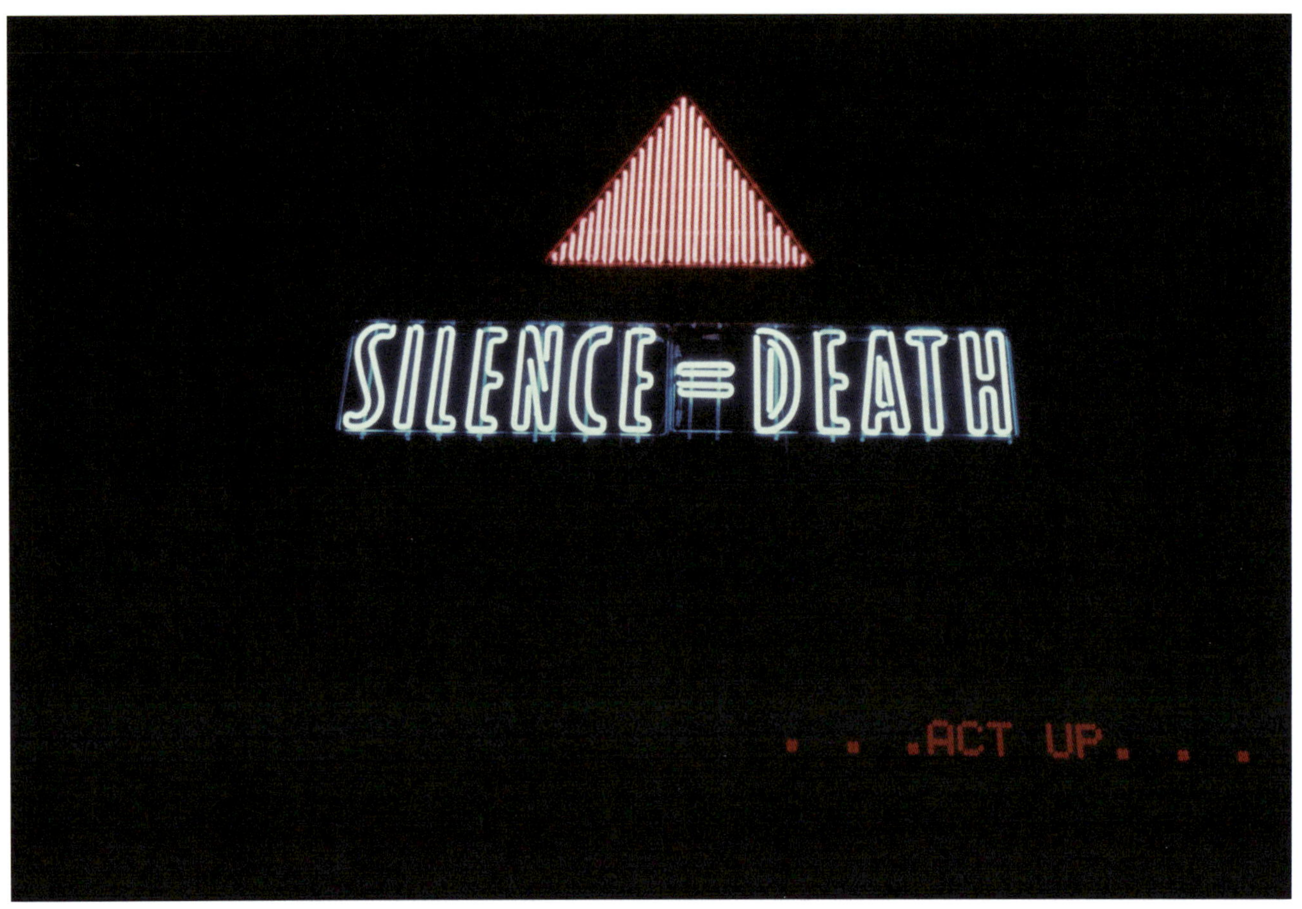

125

125, 126
ACT UP ad hoc
Let the Record Show…
(ver. 1) installation
view, 1987
The New Museum
of Contemporary
Art, New York,
United States
Mixed media,
window installation
Gran Fury Collection,
Manuscripts and
Archives Division,
The New York Public
Library, United States

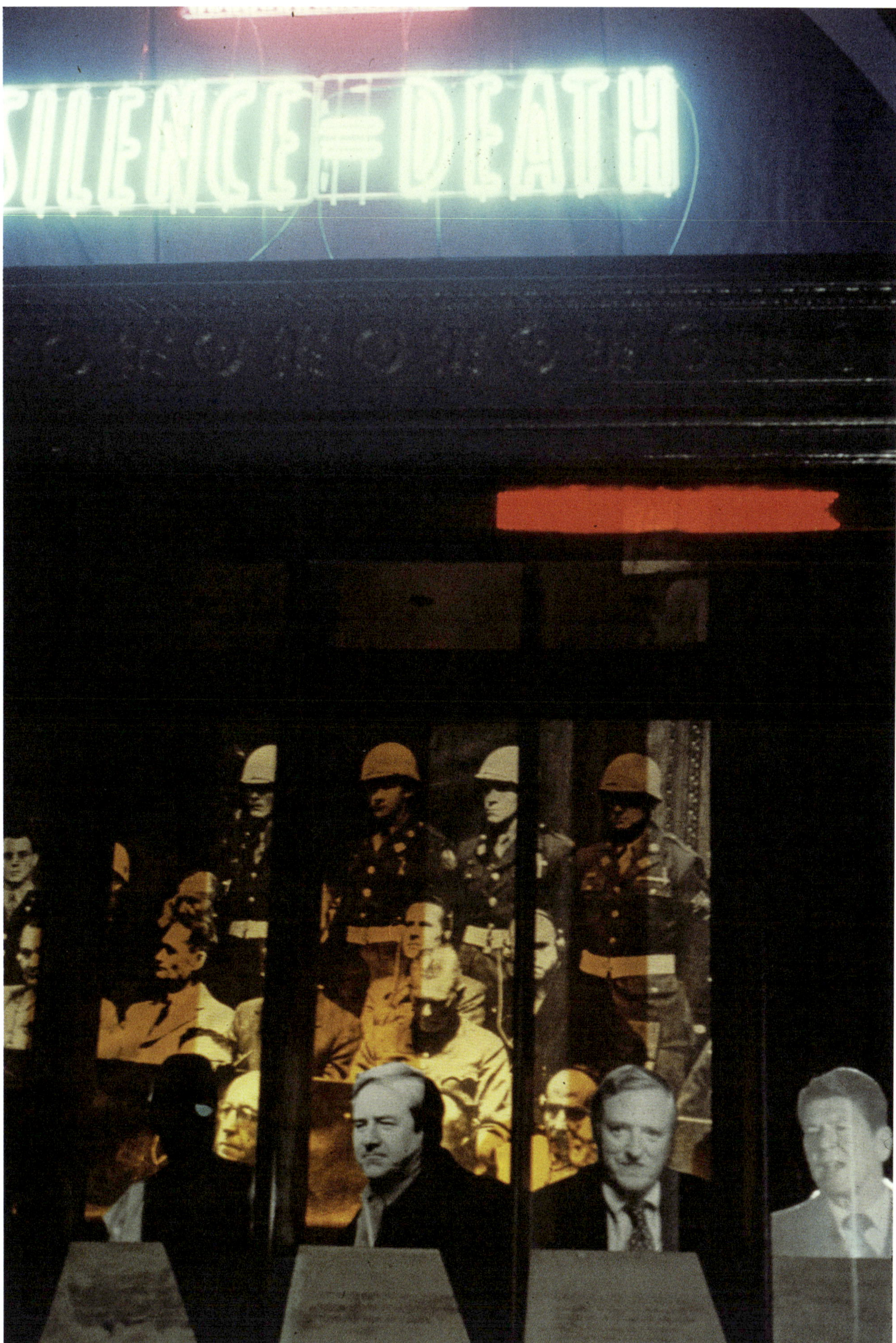

SILENCE=DEATH

127

127
ACT UP
Let the Record Show,
1987
Offset print on paper
29.5 × 21 cm

NATIONAL AIDS DEMONSTRATION

AT

THE WHITE HOUSE

June 1, 1987
12:30 ~~pm~~ pm — The White House
4:00 pm — International Conference on AIDS at the Washington Hilton

WE ARE ANGRY:

- At the Government's policy of malignant neglect
- At the irresponsible inaction of this president
- At the shameful indifference of our elected representatives
- At the criminal hoarding of appropriated funds by government agencies

They Waste Our Money, Our Time, Our Lives!

TAKE ONE DAY OFF FROM WORK...TURN RAGE INTO ACTION!

Chartered buses will be leaving the Community Center, 208 West 13th Street, at ~~7:00 AM~~ 6:00 AM and will return that evening. $20.00 round-trip.

Send check by May 26th to the address below or call (212) 460-5681.
Include name, address, and phone number.

SPONSORED BY THE AIDS COALITION TO UNLEASH POWER
and other concerned organizations in Washington, Los Angeles , and San Francisco.

A.C.T.U.P.   496A Hudson Street., Suite G4, New York, NY 10014

128

128
ACT UP
National AIDS Demonstration at The White House, Washington, D.C., United States, 1987
Offset print on paper, 29.5 × 21 cm

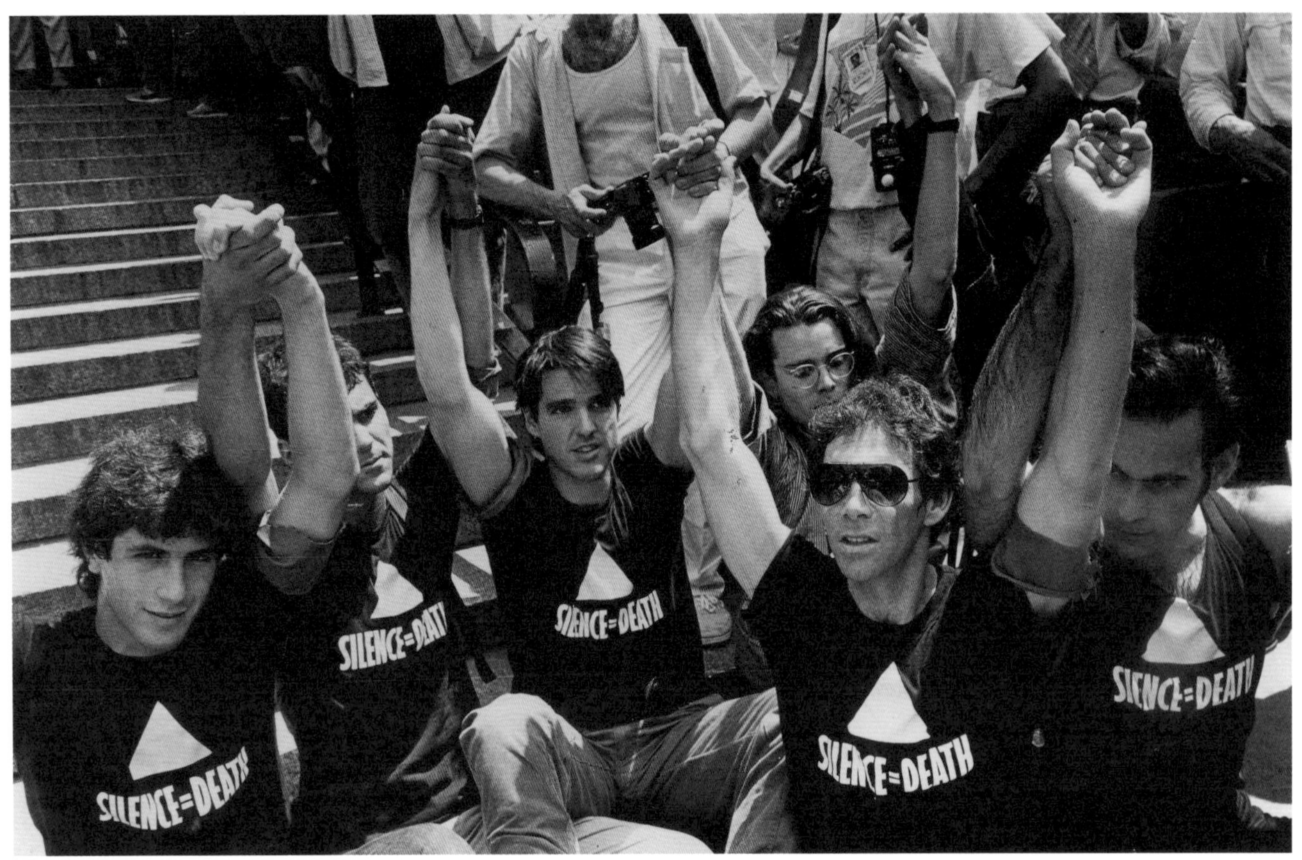

129
Donna Binder
ACT UP Demonstration
at Federal Plaza,
from left to right:
Steve Gendin, Mark
Aurigemma, Douglas
Montgomery, Charles
Stimson, Frank O'Dowd,
Avram Finkelstein,
New York, United
States, June 30, 1987
Collection of the
artist, New York,
United States

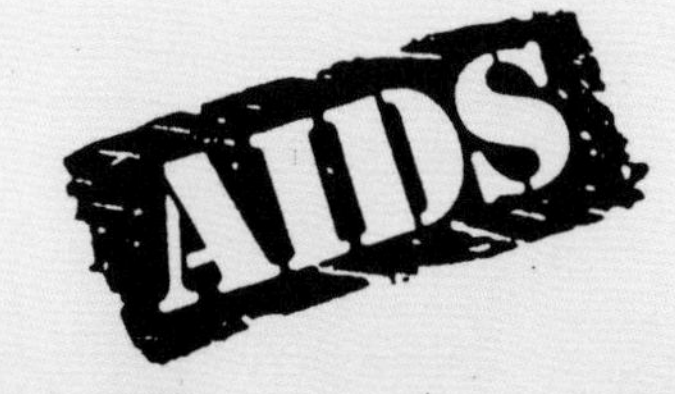

130
ACT UP
25,000 are Dead,
circa 1980s
Offset print on paper,
29.5 × 21 cm

131
Eugene Gordon
Members of ACT UP
hold up signs and
placards during the
New York Gay and
Lesbian Pride march,
United States,
June 26, 1988
New-York Historical
Society, Eugene
Gordon Photograph
Collection, United
States

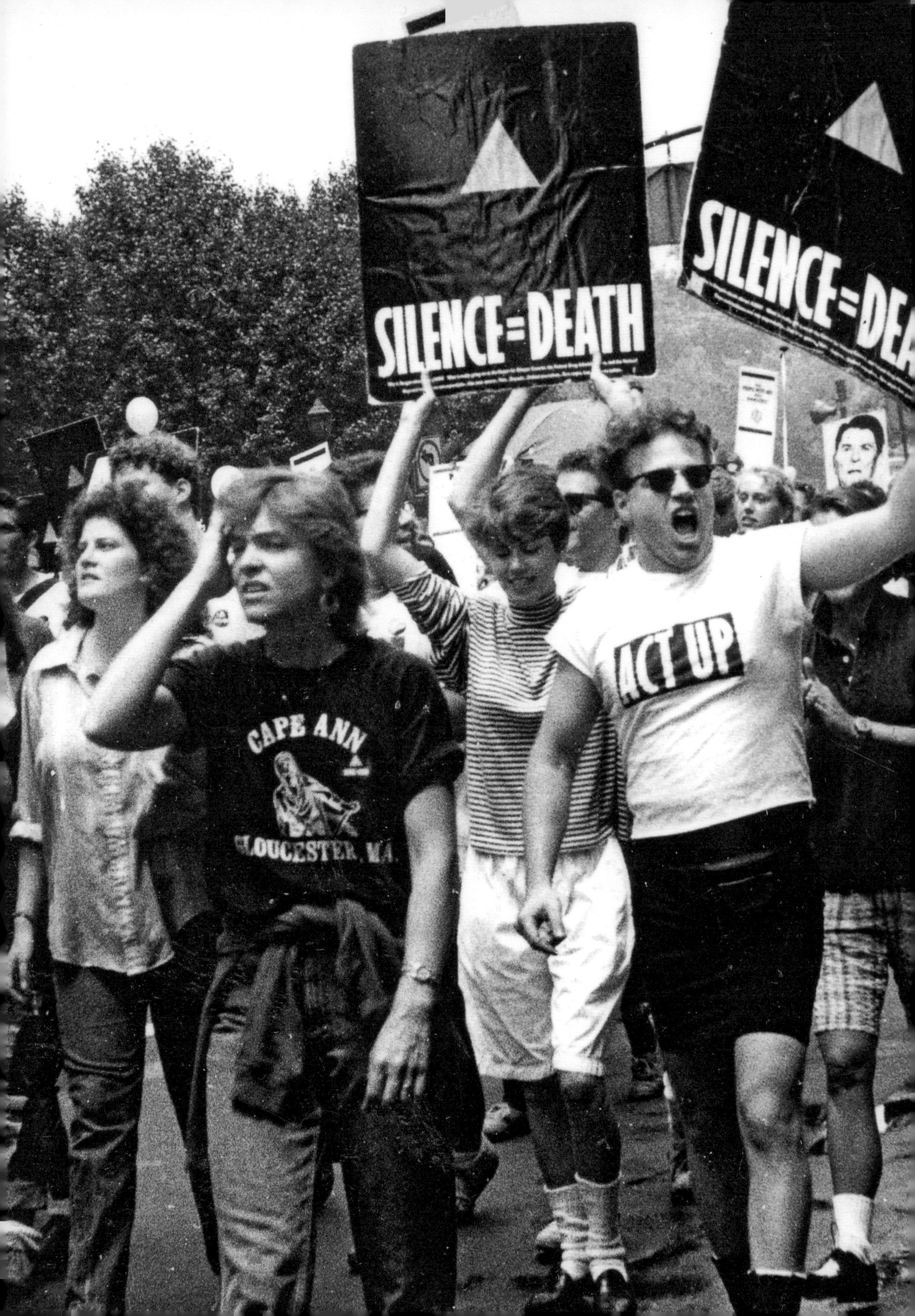

SILENCE=DEATH
SILENCE=DEA
CAPE ANN
GLOUCESTER, MA.
ACT UP

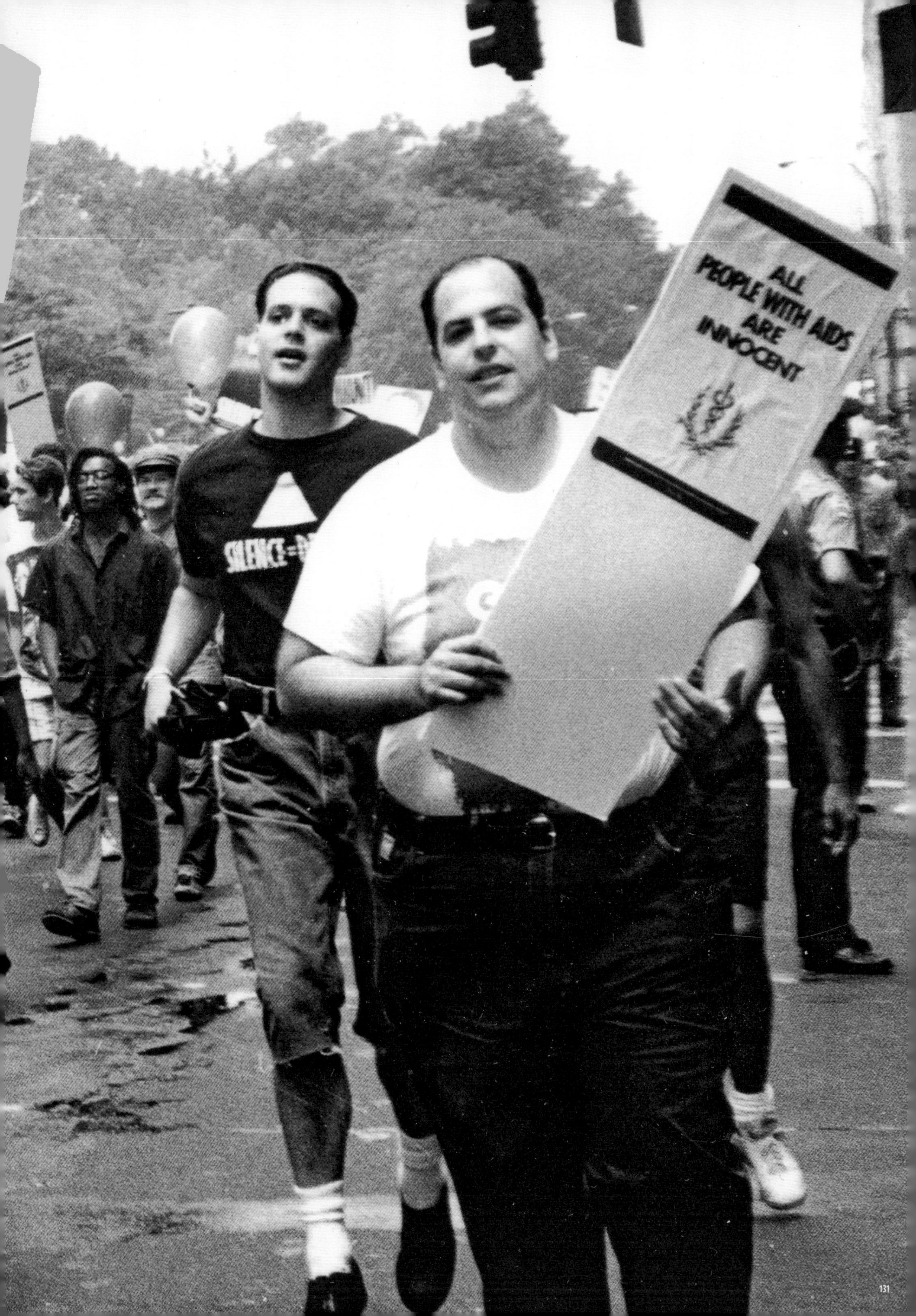

ALL
PEOPLE WITH AIDS
ARE
INNOCENT
SILENCE=DEATH

132

ACT UP
AIDS, Politics, & $$$$,
circa 1980s
Offset print on paper,
29.5 × 21 cm

AIDS, POLITICS, & $$$$

In July 1976, a strange new illness struck American Legionnaires at a convention in Philadelphia. Within ten days the Public Health Service had launched an investigation and within six months all the resources of this nation were marshalled to identify this new disease, treat it, and prevent it recurrence. Twenty-nine people had died.

In June 1981, the U.S. Government first recognized the AIDS epidemic. *Government research, however, did not begin until eighteen months later, after 1,800 cases were identified.* The President did not publicly utter the word "AIDS" until 1987. It took *six years and 20,000 deaths* for him to announce his first and only actions against it: to call for widespread antibody testing, and to appoint an advisory commission containing not a single AIDS expert. Nonetheless, even that commission's early recommendations for increased funding and a comprehensive national policy are falling on deaf ears. *This administration has publicly resisted every effort to protect the rights of people with AIDS, to educate the public against further spread, and to increase funding to fight this disease.*

ACT UP was formed in March 1987 to hold the government publicly accountable for its participation in this genocide. We believe the government failed to act swiftly and effectively against this disease because it was seen to be a disease of marginal minorities: gay men, IV-drug users, and people of color. *IN NO OTHER CIRCUMSTANCE WOULD THE PROJECTED DEATHS OF HUNDREDS OF THOUSANDS OF AMERICANS BE CONSIDERED "ACCEPTABLE LOSSES."*

One year ago we marched here, at the center of this nation's financial resources, to demand the commitment of those resources in an all-out effort to fight this disease. Yet instead of constructive action, today the government is allowing, and even encouraging, profiteering by drug companies at the expense of people with AIDS; the National Institutes of Health is floating racist proposals to test vaccines on a massive scale in Africa; and the Administration is shifting the emphasis *away* from research for a cure to a policy of containment, effecting the wholesale abandonment of an entire class of people afflicted with this disease. We are faced with no choice but to fight for our lives.

We recognize that every AIDS death is an act of racist and homophobic violence and we will no longer tolerate the criminal neglect of our government. We pledge to continue this fight, and through our arrests, bear witness to the genocide. We are here on behalf of the 25,000 Americans living with this disease, and out of respect for the 32,000 lost to it.

WE WILL NOT GO QUIETLY. *WE ARE NOT GOING AWAY.*

WE DEMAND:

- **A COMPASSIONATE COMPREHENSIVE NATIONAL POLICY ON AIDS!** We demand legislation to prohibit discrimination in employment, housing, insurance, and health care.

- **A NATIONAL EMERGENCY AIDS PROJECT** empowered to cut through red tape and direct national policy on AIDS!

- **INTENSIFIED DRUG TESTING, RESEARCH, AND TREATMENT EFFORTS,** with an emphasis on making a broader range of drug trials available to all people with AIDS, ARC, or who are HIV-positive.

- **A FULL-SCALE, CULTURALLY SENSITIVE NATIONAL EDUCATION PROGRAM** committed to reaching all individuals, particularly those in the highest-risk groups, with information and materials explicit enough to do the job.

NO MORE BUSINESS AS USUAL!

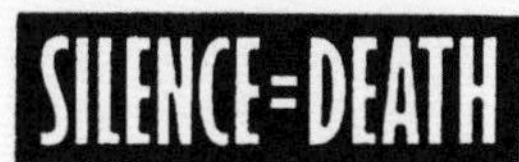

ACT UP
The AIDS Coalition To Unleash Power • (212) 533-8888

ACT-UP is a diverse, non-partisan group of individuals united in anger and committed to direct action to end the AIDS crisis.

133
Ellen B. Neipris
ACT UP member Gregg
Bordowitz carried
away by the police.
Wall Street II,
Mar. 24, 1988
Collection of the
artist, New York,
United States

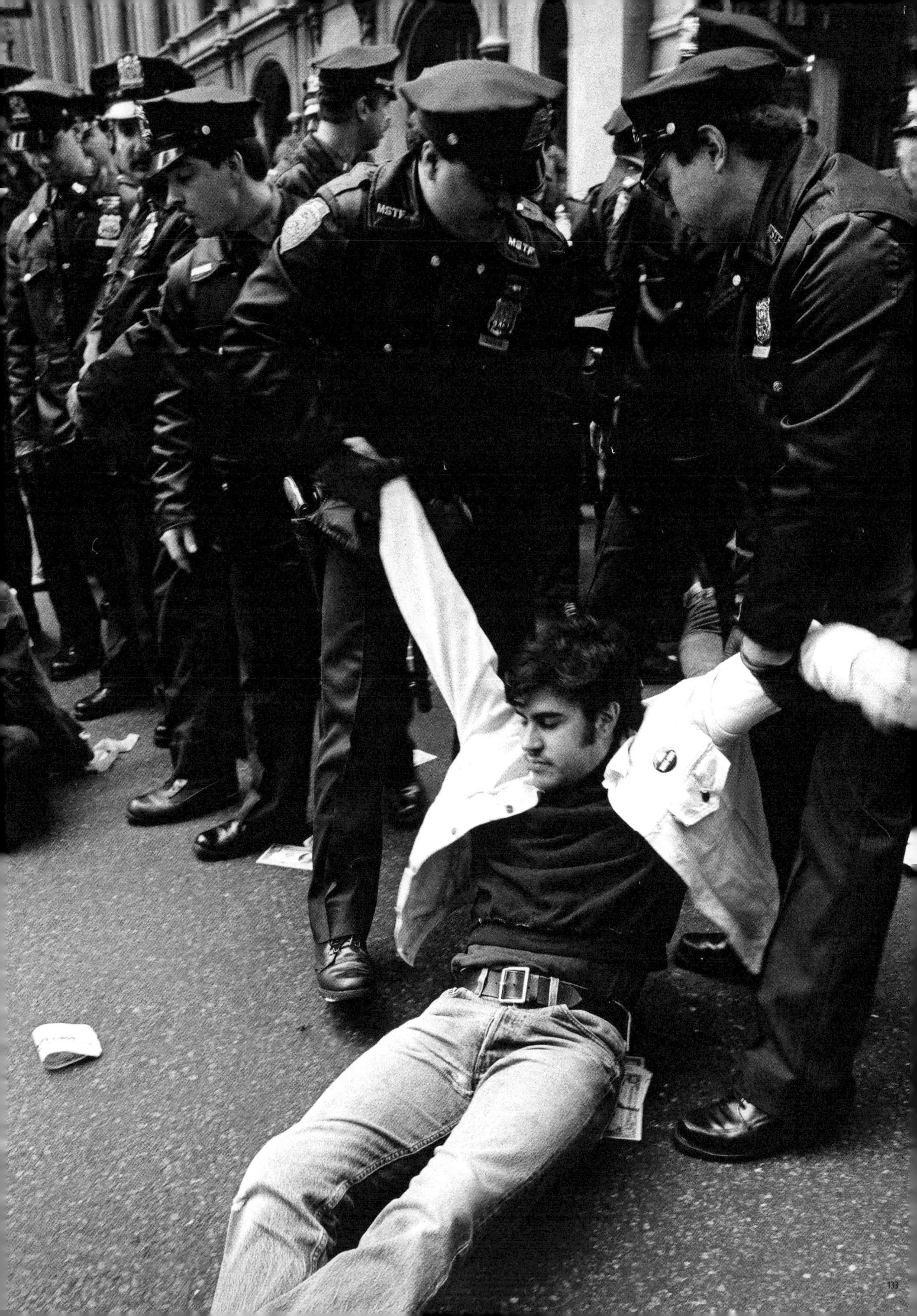

134

ACT UP

AIDS Is Not a Ball Game,
1988
Offset print on paper,
29.5 × 21 cm

AIDS IS NOT A BALL GAME.

MEN! DON'T ENDANGER THE WOMEN YOU LOVE!*

AIDS is the leading cause of death among women between the ages of 25 to 34 in NYC.

HERE'S THE SCORE:

SINGLE	Only *one* woman has been included in government sponsored tests for new drugs for AIDS.
DOUBLE	Women diagnosed with AIDS die *twice* as fast as men.
TRIPLE	The number of women with AIDS has *tripled* as a result of sexual contact with men in NYC since the 1984 World Series.
THE GRAND SLAM	MOST MEN STILL DON'T USE CONDOMS.

USE CONDOMS. NO GLOVE, NO LOVE!

*And if you can't be with the one you love, protect the one you're with.

SPRING AIDS ACTION '88—Nine Days of National AIDS Related Actions and Protests.

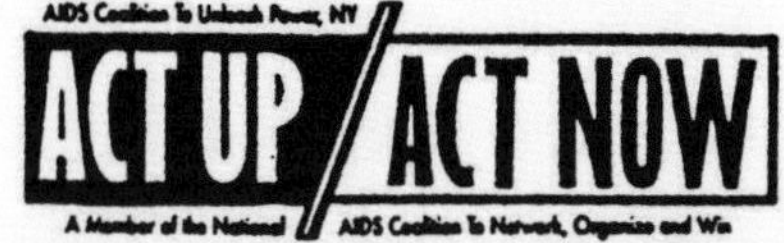

The AIDS Coalition To Unleash Power (212) 533-8888

ACT UP is a diverse, non-partisan group of individuals united in anger and committed to direct action to end the AIDS crisis.

135
ACT UP
*Missing 200,000
New Yorkers*, 1988
Offset print on paper,
29.5 × 21 cm

MISSING: 200,000 NEW YORKERS

On Tuesday, July 19, 1988, New York City Health Commissioner Stephen C. Joseph announced new estimates for the number of gay and bisexual men infected with HIV, cutting the previous estimate of 250,000 by 400%, to 50,000. This statistic is based on a ludicrous estimate that only 100,000 gay and bisexual men live in N.Y.C. Historically many groups—women, children, people of color and IV drug users—have been made invisible by the city's AIDS policies and services. This is unacceptable. Now the city wants to make gay and bisexual men invisible as well. This too is unacceptable.

STEPHEN JOSEPH SAYS YOU DON'T EXIST. PROVE HIM WRONG!

SHOW UP!

RALLY & DEMONSTRATION
THURSDAY, JULY 28
NYC HEALTH DEPT.
125 WORTH ST. AT FOLEY SQ.
(BROOKLYN BRIDGE/CITY HALL SUBWAY STATION)

ACT UP 4:00 – 6:30 PM **SILENCE=DEATH**

WE EXIST!
CITY HEALTH CARE DOESN'T!

que 6,000 hombres homosexuales y bisexuales han muerto del SIDA

que 300,000 hombres homosexuales y bisexuales en New York, 25% de ellos hombres de minorias, son estimados ser 'HIV' positivo

que segun la Comision de Salud de la ciudad de New York, sin una cura, 80% de estos moriran dentro de 15 años

que una ciudad con casi medio million de ciudadanos estimados 'HIV' positivos ha proveido solamente 2 clinicas para cuidarlos

que Ed Koch, el alcalde de la cuidad con la mayoria de casos del SIDA en el mundo, ha revocado todos recursos del grupo contra la discriminacion del SIDA

que no hebido un programa municipal dirigido a los hombres homosexuales de minoria y ni este ano tampoco. Koch a dicho que "No!"

que la administracion de drogas y comidas todavia niega a dar su consentimiento a 40 drogas que han resultan efectivos contra el SIDA

que personas con el SIDA han sido obligadas a obtener estas drogas en otros paises y que los EEUU ha rogado que paises afables no vendan estas drogas a los Americanos

que la enmienda del Senador Jesse Helms ha aplastado cualquiers recursos por materiales educacionales dirigidos a la comunidad homosexual

que la historia *muestre*

que las mujeres han sido excluidas efectivamente de todos tratamientos probando drogas experimentales y, en realidad, todas rebuscas acerca las mujeres y el SIDA casi no existen

que aunque la cuenta de lesbianas con la SIDA aumenta, el Centro de Regulacion de Enfermedades mantiene ninguna categoria por casos de infection y transmission lesbiana

que violencia contra homosexuales, in particular cuando el agresor menciona el SIDA, han triplicado desde 1984

que la Comision Federal del SIDA ha dicho que la falta de leyes federales vigentes contra la discriminacion a causado alboroto nacional

que el Cirujano General de los EEUU ha dicho que la demora homicida del gobierno en reconociendo y tratando con el SIDA es resultado directo de discriminacion oficial contra los homosexuales

ACT UP fue formado en Marzo de 1987 para declarar el gobierno culpable por el homicido que ha cometido. Creemos que el gobierno a negado a responder aprisa y efectivamente contra el SIDA porque el SIDA esta visto como una enfermedad de minorias desechadas; homosexuales, adictos de drogas inyectables y las minorias. Continuaramos a luchar contra indiferencia y estupidez oficial. Continuaramos siendo testigos a la negligencia criminal que ha devastado nuestra

¡TENEMOS QUE *LUCHAR!*

comunidad. Lograremos esto a traves de acciones directas porque creemos que ¡basta! de atendernos mismos tranquilamente. Participamos con orgullo en los Dias de "Gay and Lesbian Pride." Reconocemos que cada hombre homosexual y cada lesbiana quien han caido a el SIDA han muerto de violencia contra los homosexuales. Marchamos por los valientes quienes viven con este mal, y con respecto de los que han fallecido. ACT UP! FIGHT BACK! FIGHT AIDS!

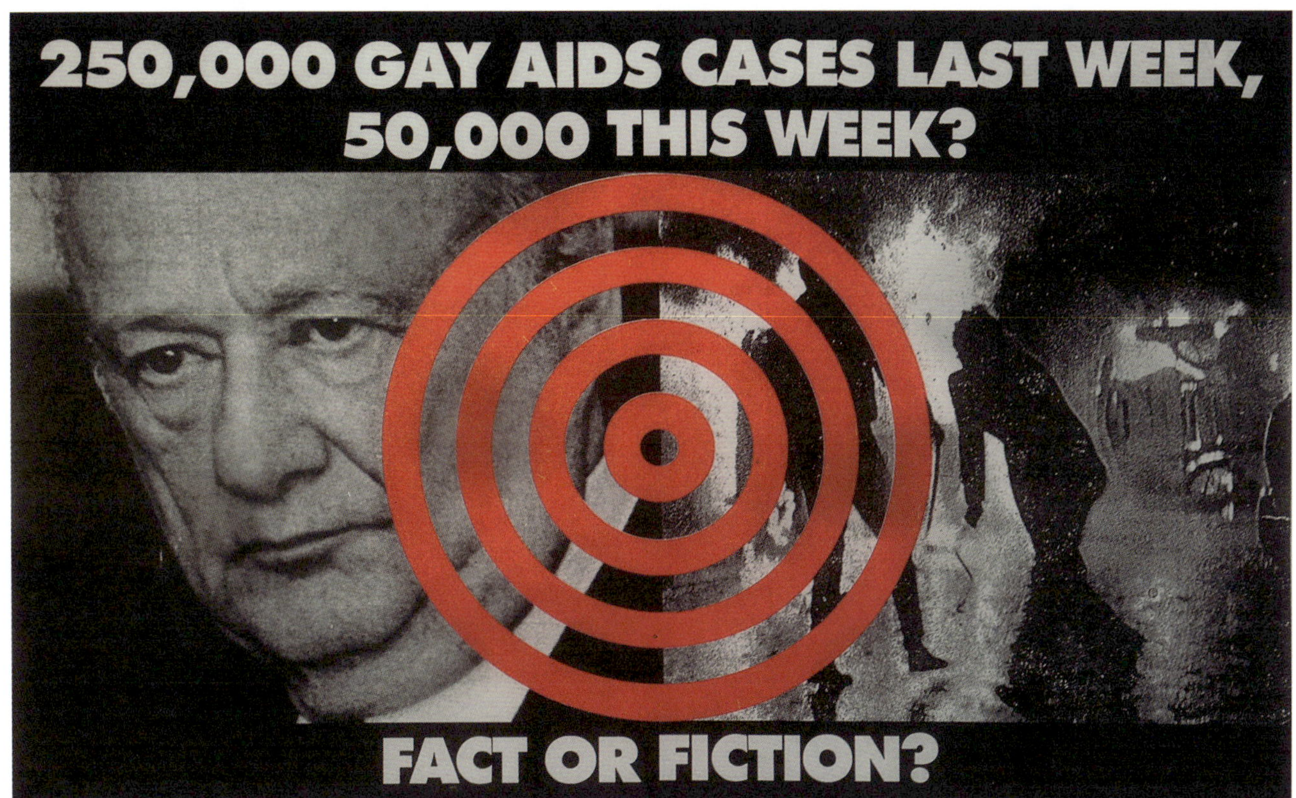

137

136

ACT UP
Que la historia muestre
[Let the Record Show],
circa 1980s
Offset print on paper,
29.5 × 21 cm

137
**Avram Finkelstein and
Donald Moffett**
Fact or Fiction, 1989
Offset print on paper,
22 × 34.5 cm
Avram Finkelstein
Archive, New York,
United States

138
Tom McKitterick
Seize Control of
the FDA, action at
the Food and Drug
Administration
Headquarters in
Rockville, Maryland,
United States,
Oct. 11, 1988
Collection of the
artist, New York,
United States

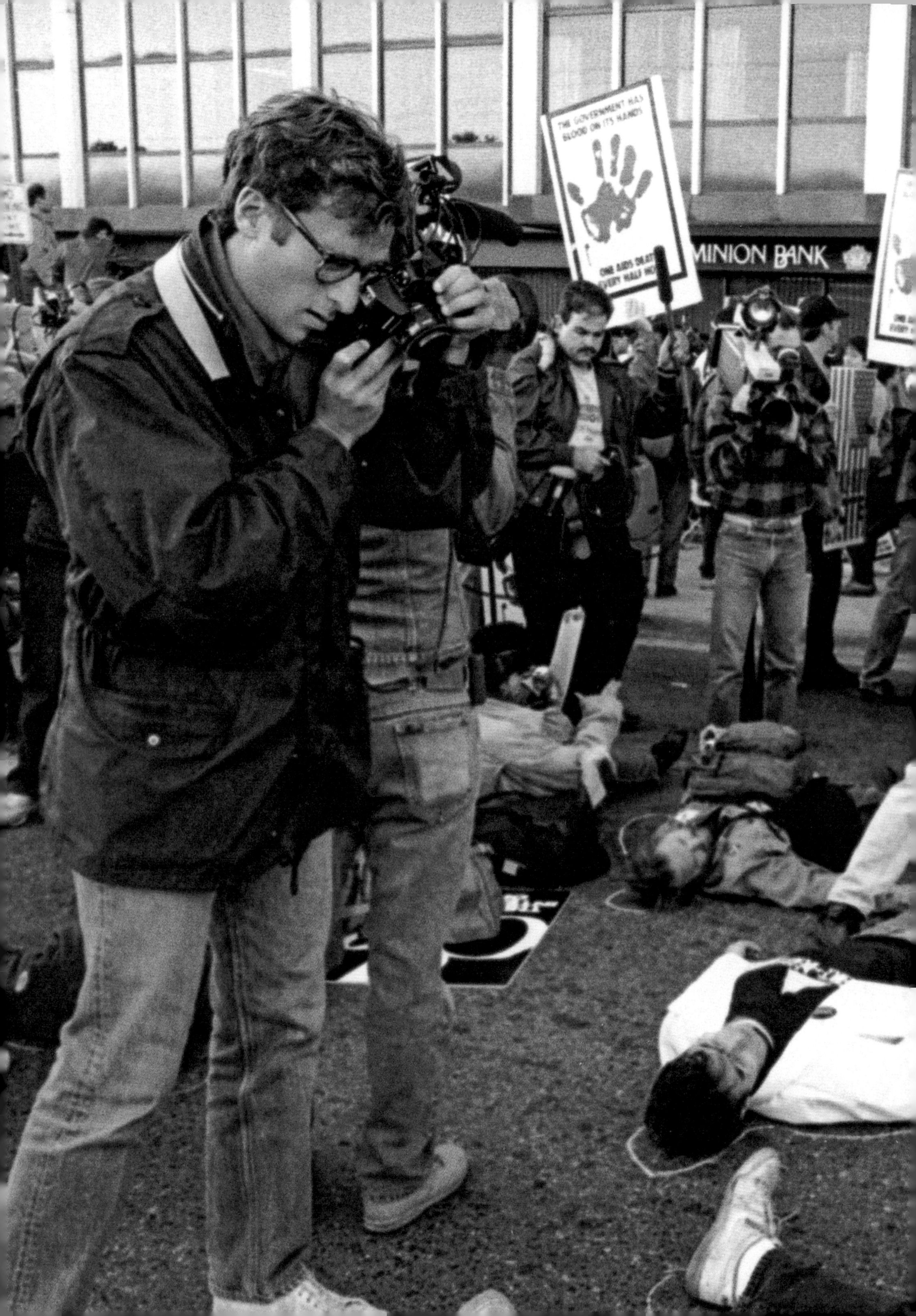

THE GOVERNMENT HAS
BLOOD ON ITS HANDS
ONE AIDS DEATH
EVERY HALF HOUR
MINION BANK

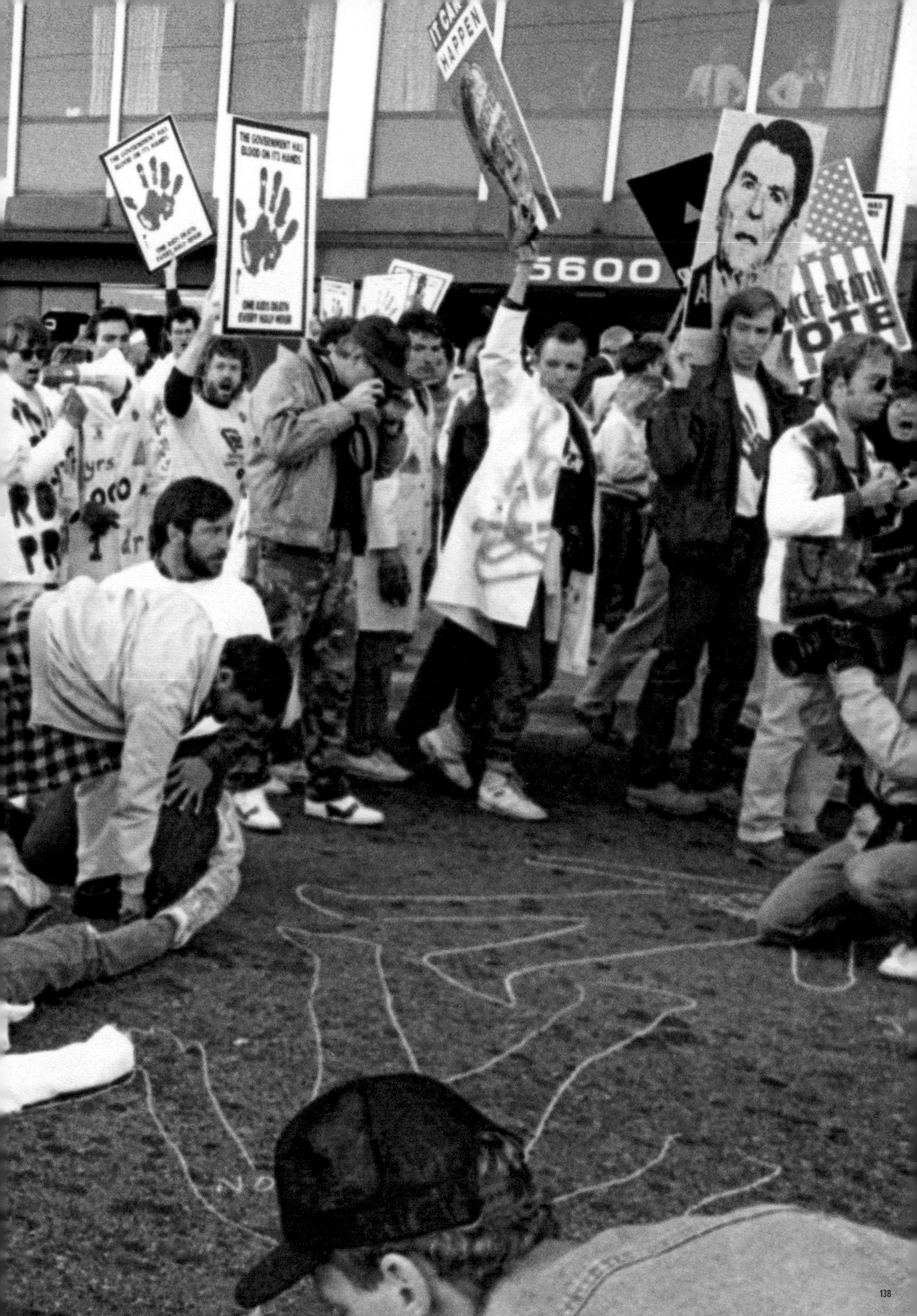

IT CAN
HAPPEN
THE GOVERNMENT HAS
BLOOD ON ITS HANDS
THE GOVERNMENT HAS
BLOOD ON ITS HANDS
5600
LIFE-OR-DEATH
VOTE

139
Catherine McGann
Seize Control of
the FDA, action
at the Food and
Drug Administration
Headquarters in
Rockville, Maryland,
United States,
Oct. 11, 1988
Collection of the artist,
Burbank, California,
United States

140
T. L. Litt
Seize Control of
the FDA, action
at the Food and
Drug Administration
Headquarters in
Rockville, Maryland,
United States,
Oct. 11, 1988
Collection of the
artist, Medford,
Massachusetts,
United States

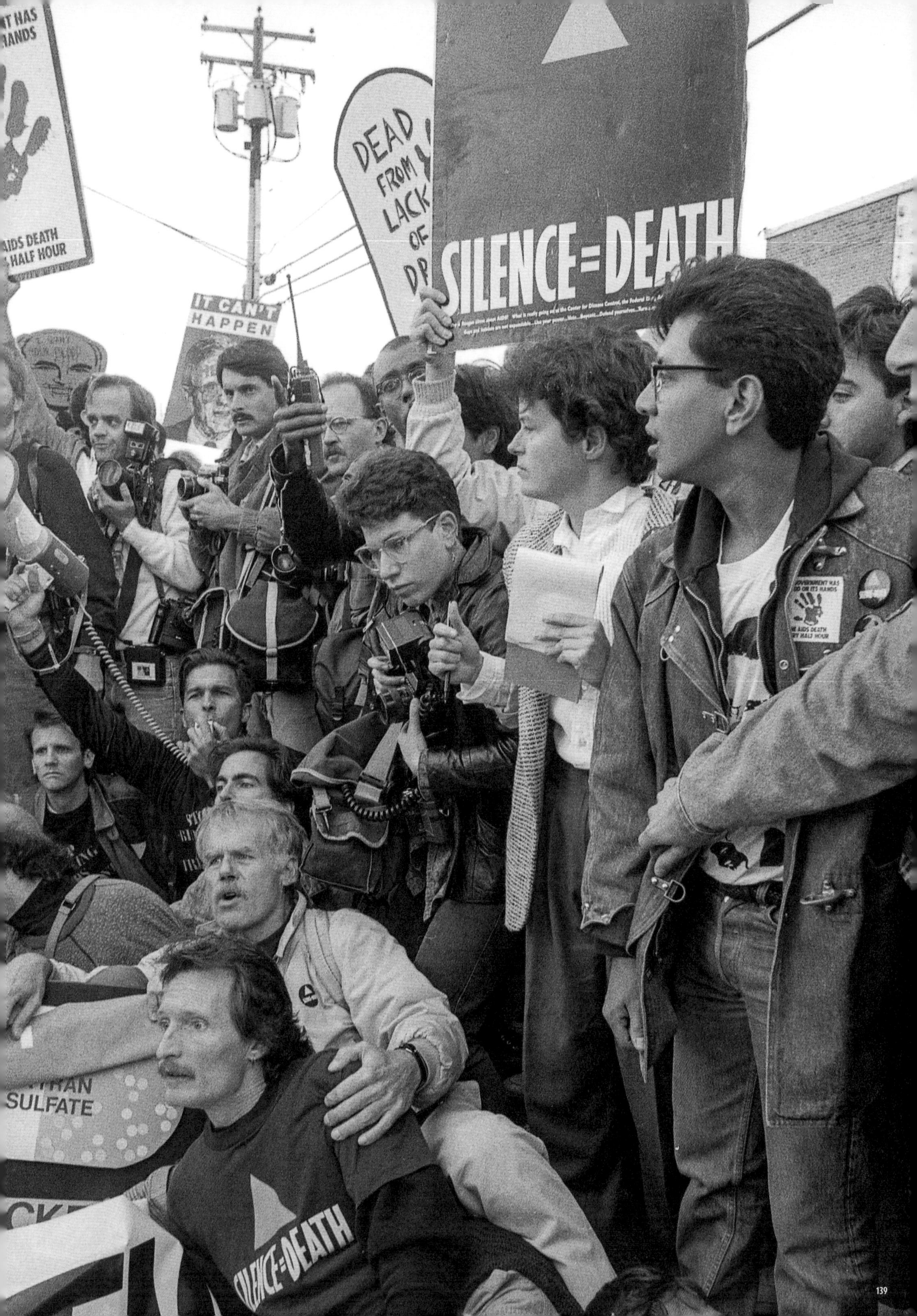

AIDS DEATH
HALF HOUR
DEAD FROM LACK OF DR
IT CAN'T HAPPEN
SILENCE=DEATH
THAN SULFATE
SILENCE=DEATH

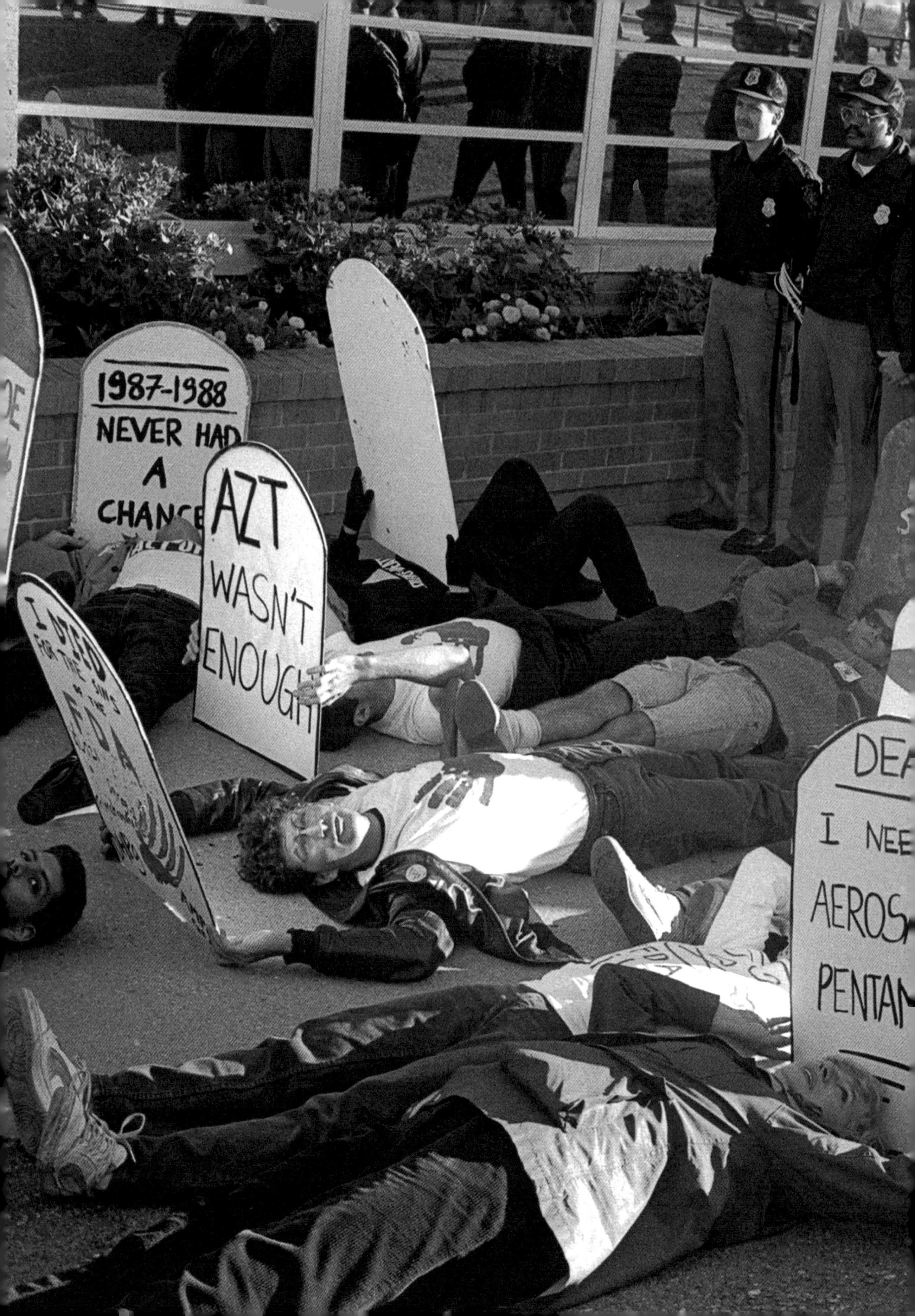

1987-1988
NEVER HAD A CHANCE
AZT WASN'T ENOUGH
I DIED FOR THE FDA
DEA
I NEE
AEROS
PENTAM

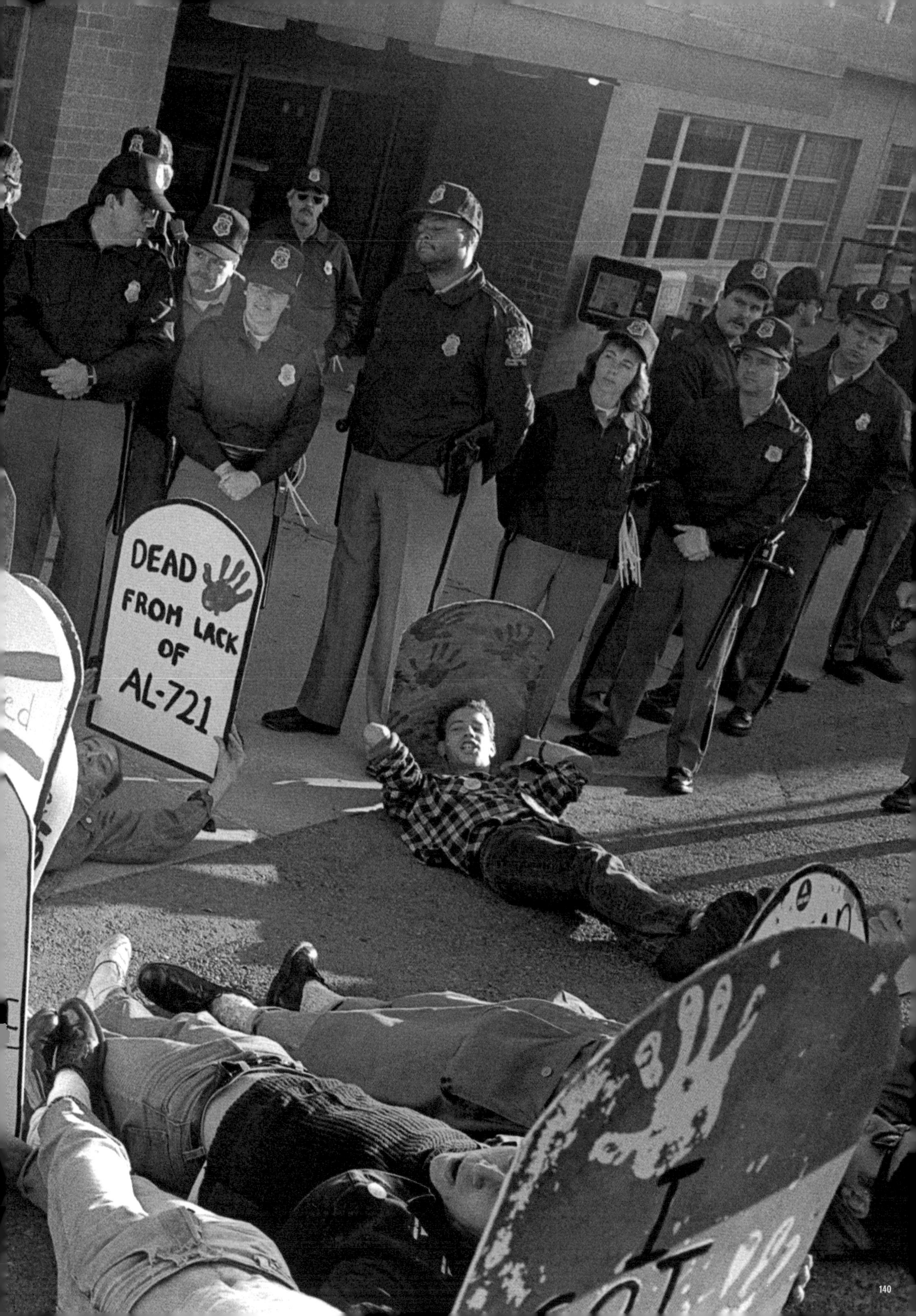
DEAD
FROM LACK
OF
AL-721

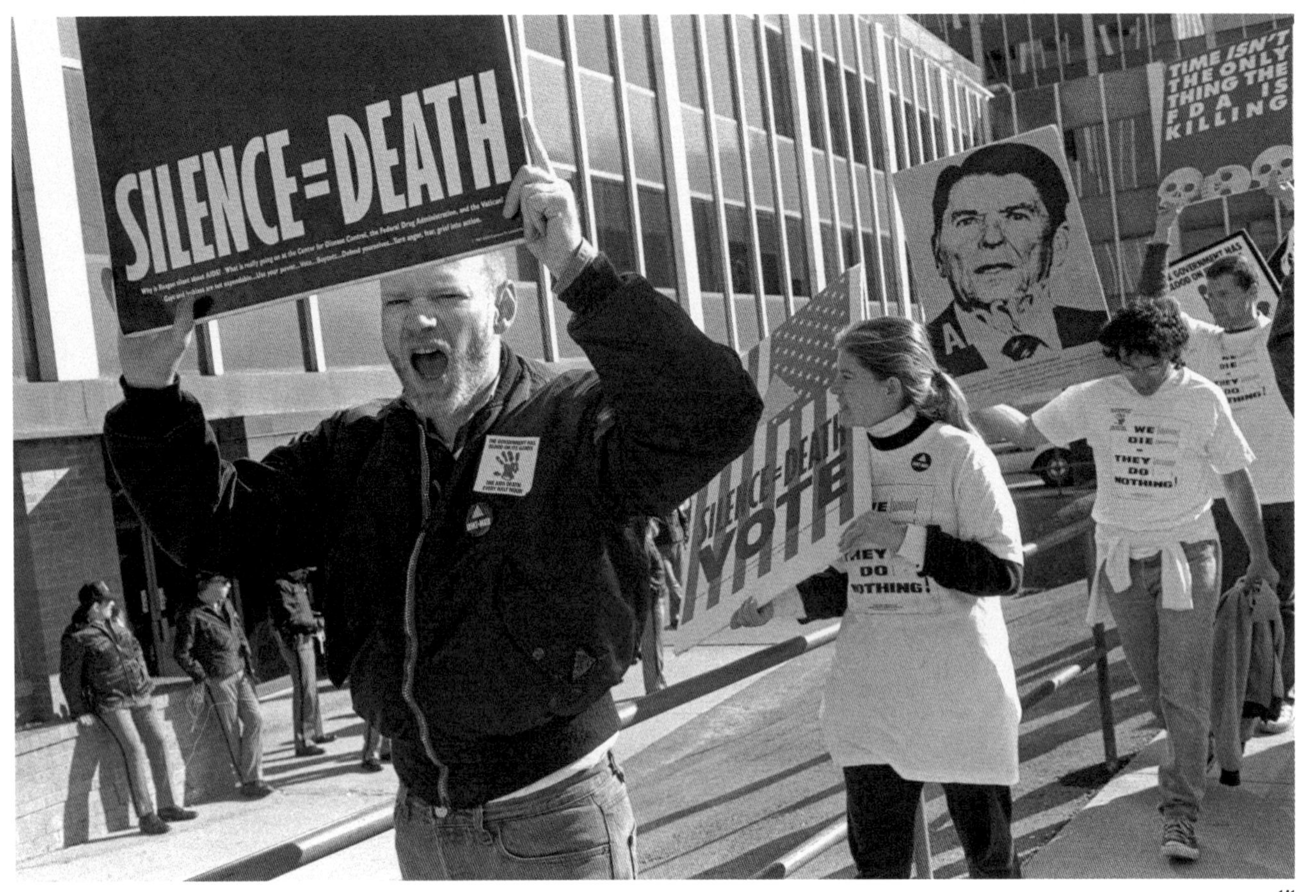

141

141–143
T. L. Litt
Seize Control of
the FDA, action at
the Food and Drug
Administration
Headquarters in
Rockville, Maryland,
United States,
Oct. 11, 1988
Collection of the
artist, Medford,
Massachusetts,
United States

184

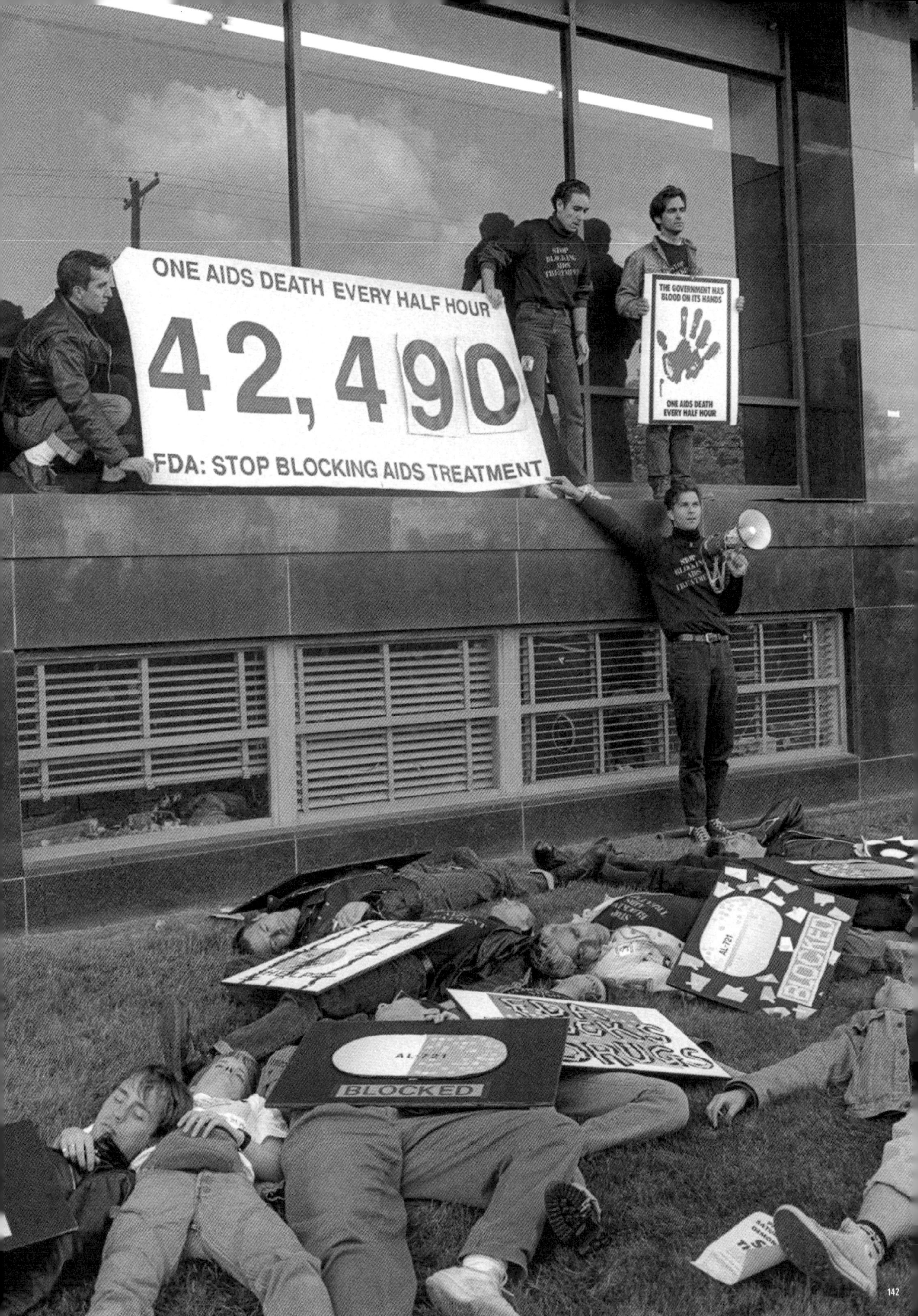

ONE AIDS DEATH EVERY HALF HOUR
42,490
FDA: STOP BLOCKING AIDS TREATMENT
THE GOVERNMENT HAS BLOOD ON ITS HANDS
ONE AIDS DEATH EVERY HALF HOUR
AL-721
BLOCKED
AL-721
BLOCKED
DRUGS

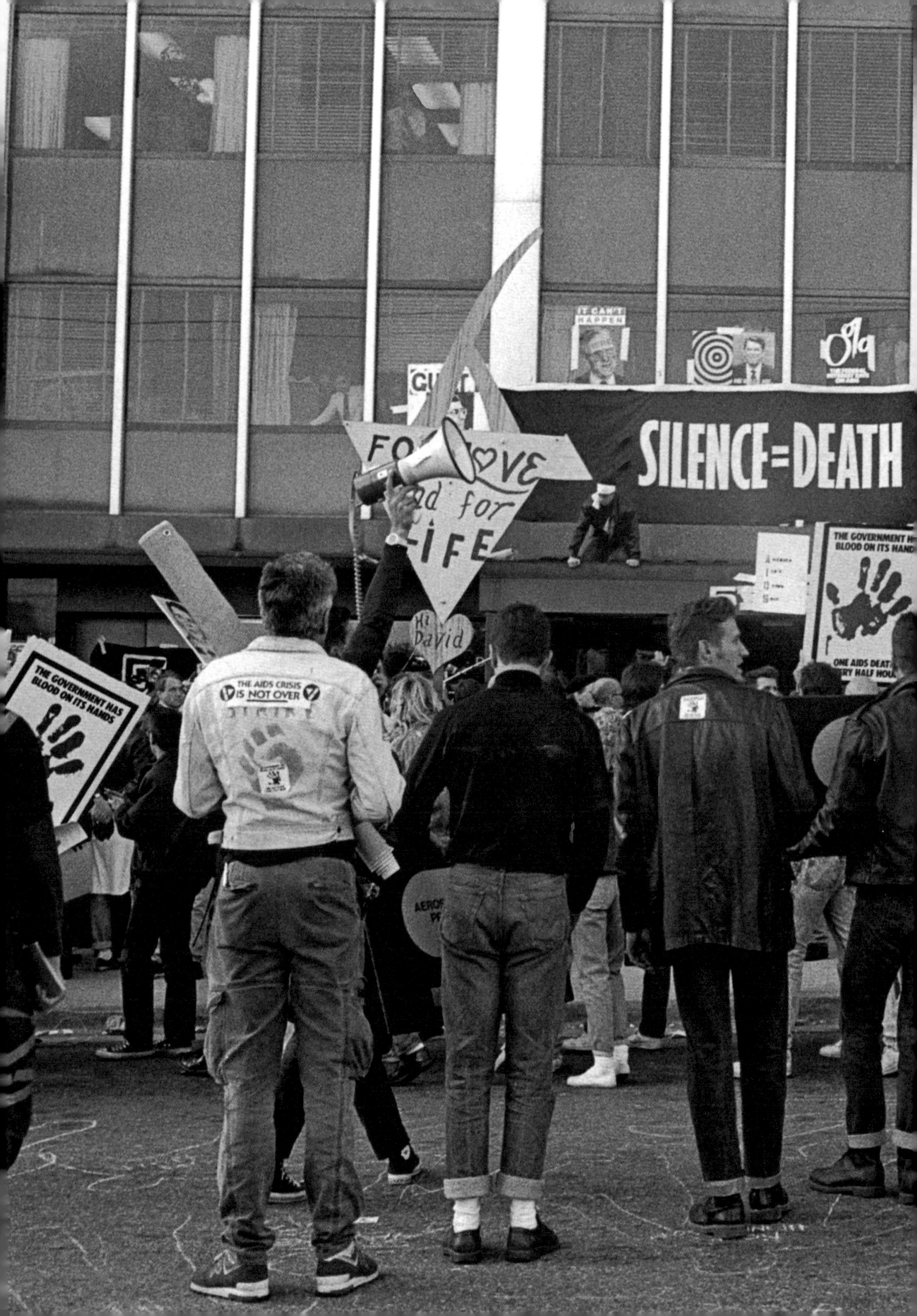
IT CAN'T
HAPPEN
SILENCE=DEATH
FO LOVE
d for
LIFE
Hi David
THE GOVERNMENT H
BLOOD ON ITS HAND
ONE AIDS DEAT
ERY HALF HOU
THE GOVERNMENT HAS
BLOOD ON ITS HANDS
THE AIDS CRISIS
IS NOT OVER

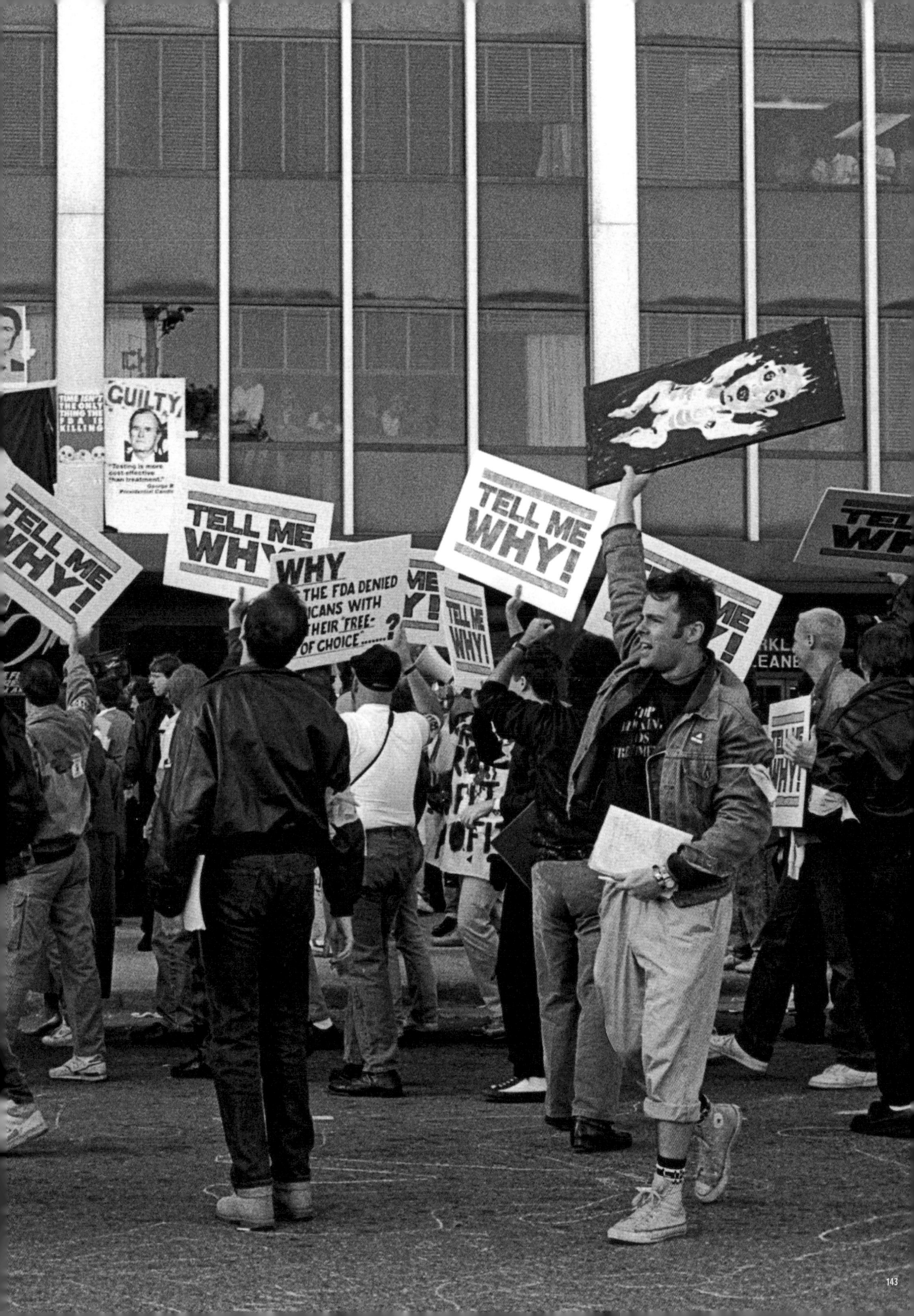
TIME ISN'T THE ONLY THING THE FDA IS KILLING
GUILTY
"Testing is more cost-effective than treatment."
George B
Presidential Candi
TELL ME WHY!
TELL ME WHY!
WHY
THE FDA DENIED
ICANS WITH
THEIR "TREE-
OF CHOICE ......?
TELL ME WHY!
ME WHY!
TELL ME WHY!
ME WHY!
TELL WHY!

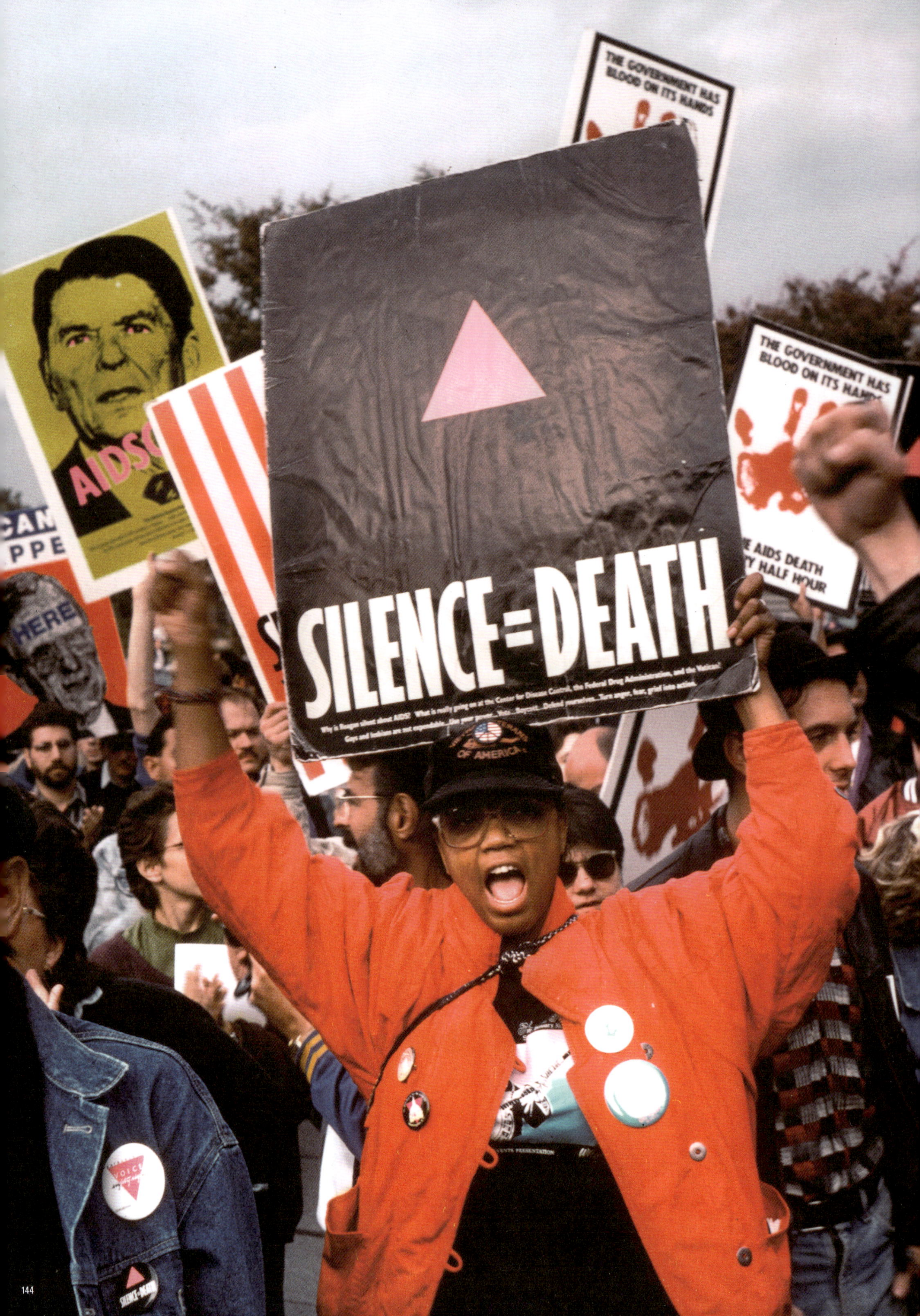
AIDS
THE GOVERNMENT HAS BLOOD ON ITS HANDS
THE GOVERNMENT HAS BLOOD ON ITS HANDS
ONE AIDS DEATH EVERY HALF HOUR
SILENCE = DEATH
OF AMERICA
SILENCE = DEATH

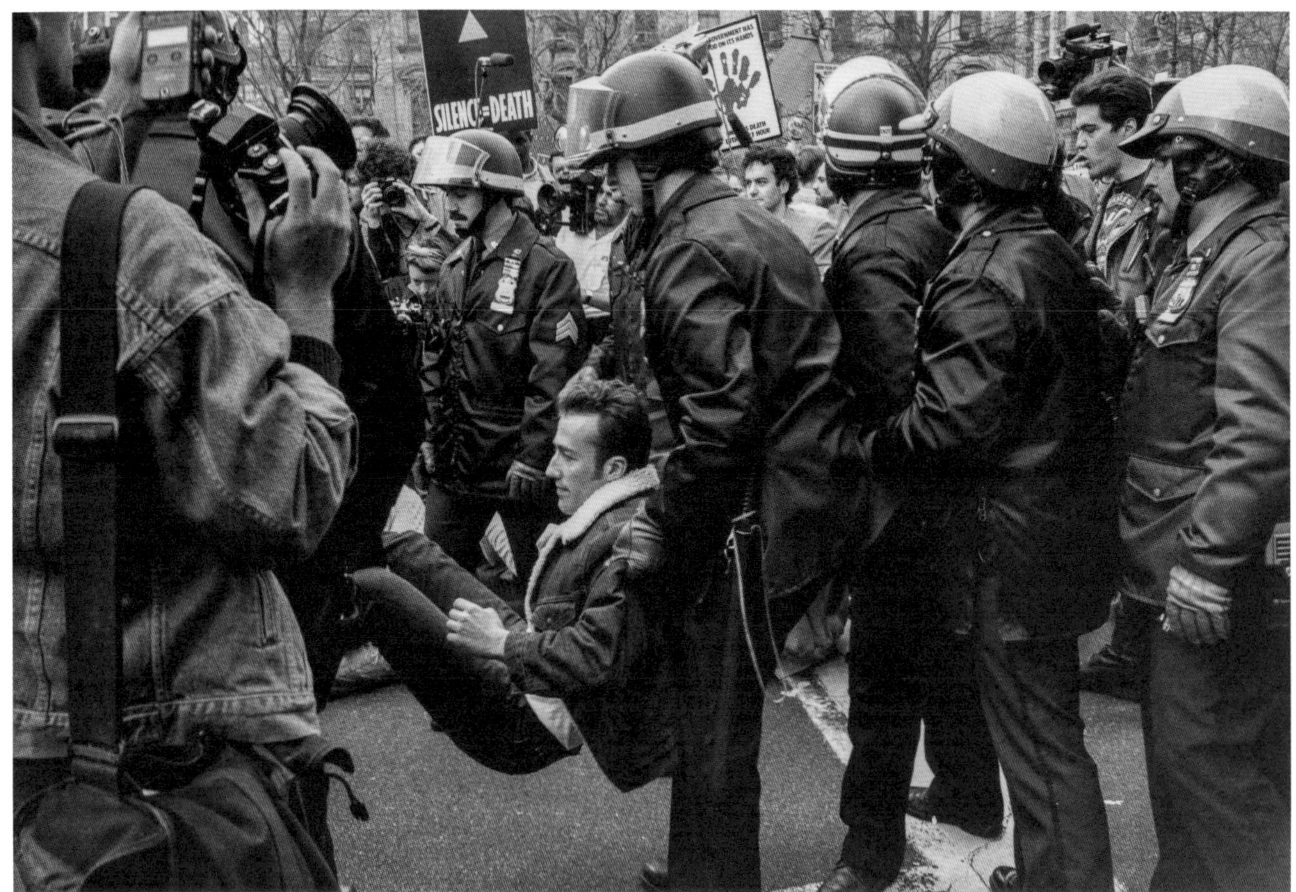

145

144
Ellen B. Neipris
Seize Control of
the FDA, action
at the Food and
Drug Administration
Headquarters in
Rockville, Maryland,
United States,
Oct. 11, 1988
Collection of the
artist, New York,
United States

145
Tom McKitterick
Joe Ferrari, ACT UP
member, is carried
away by the police,
Target City Hall,
New York against
mayor Ed Koch,
United States, 1989
Collection of the
artist, New York,
United States

146

ACT UP
*Stop Church
Interference in Our
Lives*, 1989
Offset print on paper,
29.5 × 21 cm

147

T. L. Litt
Stop The Church,
ACT UP and Women's
Health Action and
Mobilization (WHAM!),
Dec. 10, 1989
Collection of the
artist, Medford,
Massachusetts,
United States

STOP CHURCH INTERFERENCE IN OUR LIVES

Cardinal O'Connor has eagerly stepped into the political arena breaking the barrier separating Church and State! December 10th we bring our anger to his doorstep!

THE **7** DEADLY SINS OF CARDINAL O'CONNOR AND CHURCH POLITICIANS:

1. ASSAULT OF LESBIANS AND GAYS In the "Ratzinger Letter" on the pastoral "care of homosexuals" the church declares that people should not be surprised when a "morally offensive lifestyle is physically attacked." This position encourages the escalating violence against lesbians and gays.

2. BIAS Church governed "morality" and public policy have been militantly opposed to the repeal of anti-lesbian and gay discriminatory laws and criminal sodomy statutes. O'Connor openly fought the New York City Gay Rights Bill. The cardinals and bishops cannot impose their rules on our bodies and our lives.

3. IGNORANT DENIAL In Rome O'Connor addressed the Vatican Conference on AIDS stating "Good morality is good medicine." No form of church morality can comfort a homeless person with AIDS or get needed medical treatment to people who are sick. O'Connor's opinion fosters genocide.

4. ENDANGERING WOMEN'S LIVES O'Connor stated "I wish I could join Operation Rescue" while urging all "good" Catholics to escalate their attacks on abortion rights and women's health facilities. The National Conference of Catholic Bishops chose O'Connor to spearhead the church's anti-abortion political movement. O'Connor's response: "We have to be more aggressive. That's what my bones are telling me." To be "more aggressive" O'Connor proposes an order of nuns dedicated to full-time legal, medical and political opposition to abortion.

5. NO SAFE SEX EDUCATION O'Connor openly opposes education about sex, safer sex, contraception, condoms and AIDS in both parochial and public schools. The archdiocese has also opposed safe-sex education in AIDS health care facilities, even when these facilities have been donated by the city. By advocating abstinence as the only means of prevention, O'Connor denies reality, denies life-saving information and endangers all of our lives.

6. NO CONDOMS The National Conference of Catholic Bishops and O'Connor's opposition to condom use is a major component in the continued spread of AIDS and is *killing people*. HIV infection is now believed to be growing fastest among adolescents. Without immediate information about preventative methods, which includes condoms, people will continue to die.

7. NO CLEAN NEEDLES Sharing needles is the most frequent mode of transmission for new cases of HIV infection in New York. The National Conference of Catholic Bishops opposes needle exchange programs which supply clean needles to IV drug users, to prevent the spread of HIV infection, as a "quick fix solution." New York's drug treatment programs have a six-month waiting list; sterile syringes can protect a drug user from HIV infection.

For centuries the church leadership has tried to govern individual morality and to limit everyone's right to choose for themselves. These men (and they always are and have been men) must be told that they cannot impose their morality on people who do not share their doctrine. This violates freedom of religion. Church leadership must be recognized for what it is: A powerful, wealthy corporation lobbying to turn morality into medicine, and religion into political policy.

DEMAND TO MAKE YOUR OWN CHOICES

ACT UP (AIDS COALITION TO UNLEASH POWER) AND **WHAM** (WOMEN'S HEALTH ACTION AND MOBILIZATION) ARE COORDINATING THE LARGEST DEMONSTRATION AT THE CHURCH IN HISTORY.

JOIN US ON DECEMBER 10TH FOR A MASS DEMONSTRATION AND CIVIL DISOBEDIENCE

**MEET AT ST. PATRICK'S CATHEDRAL
SUNDAY, DECEMBER 10, 1989
9:30 A.M.**

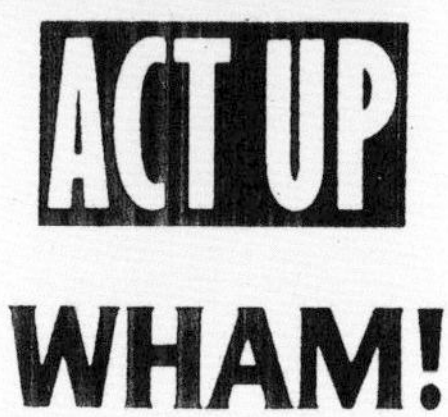

FOR INFORMATION ON THE DEMONSTRATION OR PARTICIPATION IN CIVIL DISOBEDIENCE TRAINING CALL 989-1114.

CARDINAL O'CONNOR
STOP THIS MAN
CARDINAL O'CONNOR
RDINAL O'CO
IDS PREVENT
"MORALITY IS
EDICINE."
MAN
CA
WA
OF
KE
CARDINAL O'CONNOR

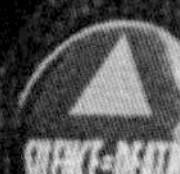
SILENCE=DEATH

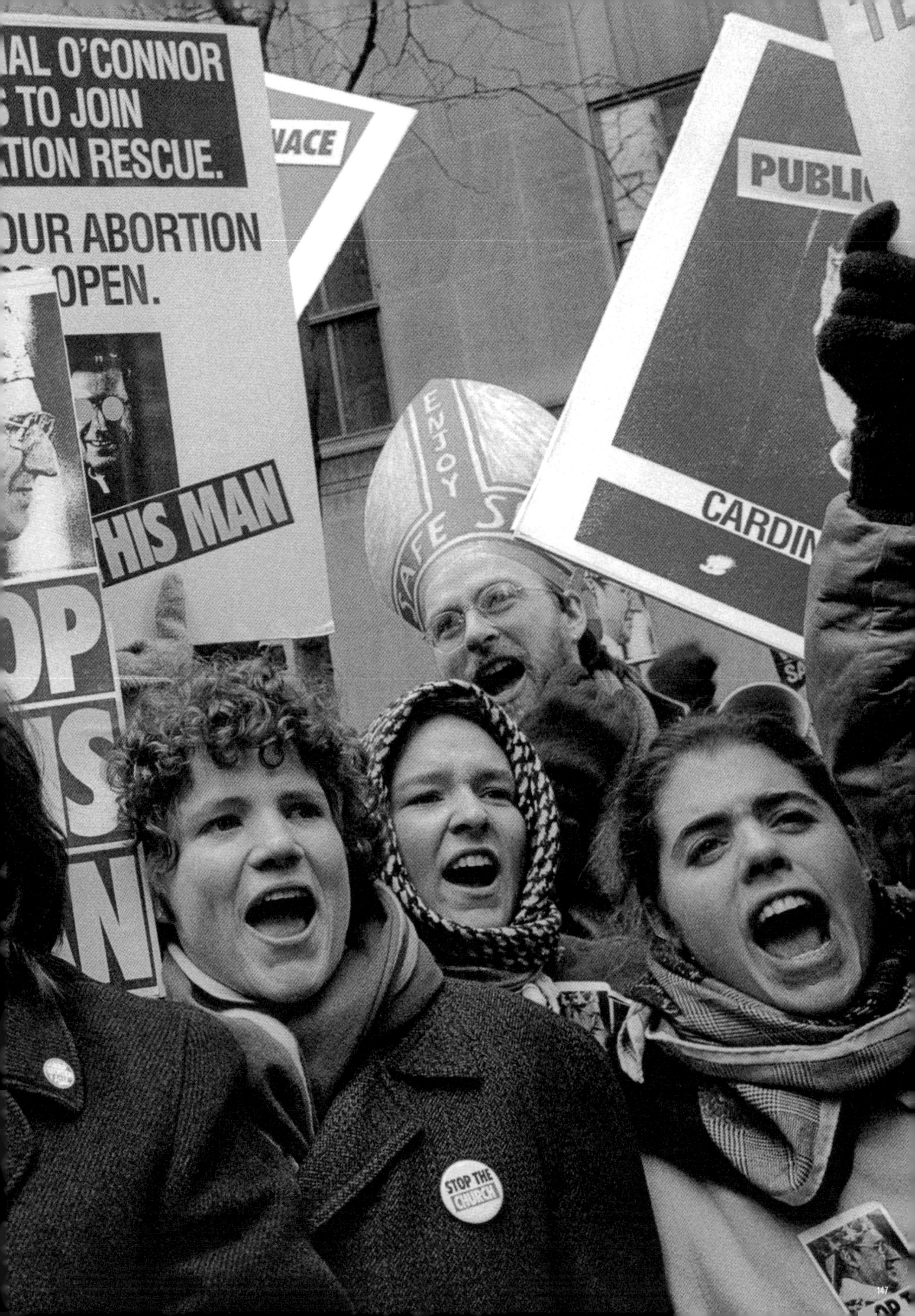

NAL O'CONNOR
S TO JOIN
TION RESCUE.
OUR ABORTION
OPEN.
THIS MAN
OP
S
N
NACE
PUBLIC
ENJOY SAFE S
CARDIN
STOP THE
CHURCH

148
ACT UP
Why We Kiss,
circa 1980s
Offset print on paper,
29.5 × 21 cm

149
T. L. Litt
ACT UP at the New
York City Pride March,
United States, in 1989
Collection of the
artist, Medford,
Massachusetts,
United States

Why We Kiss

WE KISS in an aggressive demonstration of affection. We kiss to protest the cruel and painful bigotry that affects the lives of lesbians and gay men. We kiss so that all who see us will be forced to confront their homophobia. We kiss to challenge repressive conventions that prohibit displays of love between persons of the same sex. We kiss as an affirmation of our feelings, our desires, ourselves.

In simplest terms:

Gay men and lesbians exist. We exist in all cultures. We always have, we always will. What makes us prefer same-sex sex derives from the same source that makes others prefer opposite-sex sex. We are not aberrations, abnormal, maladjusted or misguided. We are not evil; we are not a threat. We are human beings, as capable of love, compassion and all that is best in humanity as are any other human beings.

Yet the society in which we live rejects, ignores and degrades us. We are pressured to deny desire, to remain silent and invisible. Learning to accept and love ourselves in the face of so much disapproval is an uphill battle requiring courage and spirit.

If you don't think homophobia is rampant in America, consider the following:

• Many politicians consider it political death to speak out on gay and lesbian rights issues.

• One in ten lesbians and one in five gay men have been physically assaulted because of their sexuality.

•The media tend to interview us only in formats in which equal time is given to those who oppose our very existence. Imagine serious network time given to Jewish or black community leaders only when Nazi or Ku Klux Klan spokespeople were present to provide a "fair balance" of opinions.

• The Supreme Court recently upheld the Hardwick decision, thereby approving a Georgia stature denying gay men and lesbians engaging in sexual activity in their own homes their constitutionally-guaranteed right to privacy.

• The Helms amendment, preventing federal funding of any **AIDS** educational materials that could be construed to "promote" lesbian or gay sex, passed in the senate by a vote of 96 to 2.

• The federal government has been unconscionably slow to react to the **AIDS** crisis, a slowness tantamount to condoning the deaths of tens of thousands of gay men.

• The Civil Rights Commission is opposing legislation authorizing the gathering of bias-related crime statistics because it objects to the inclusion of sexual orientation as a bias category . This is despite their own admission that crimes against gay men and women, aggravated by perceptions about **AIDS**, are probably the most wide-spread hate crimes today.

What kind of person decides another does not deserve the full scope of human rights and freedoms because of whom he or she chooses to love?
What kind of person tells another her or his love is not real?

We are striving to rid ourselves and others of the mental shackles affixed by a society that rejects same-sex affection. To do this we must acknowledge our own worth. We must refuse to be an invisible minority. We must speak up to those who casually assume we are straight and come out even to those whose rejection we fear most. We must force our presence and our values on all who have hitherto felt confident enough to negate our very existence.

We must celebrate ourselves!

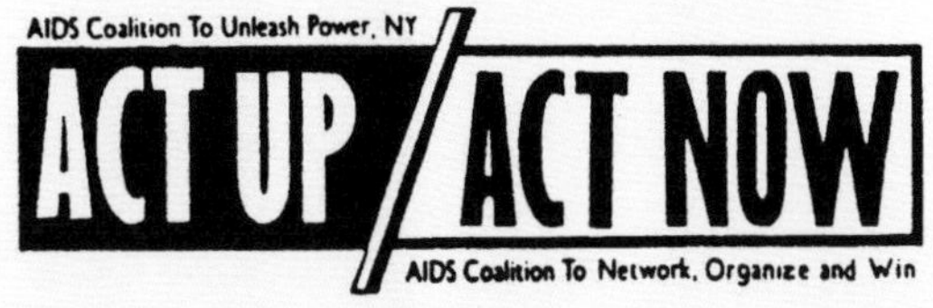

ACT UP is a diverse, non-partisan group of individuals united in anger and committed to direct action to end the AIDS crisis

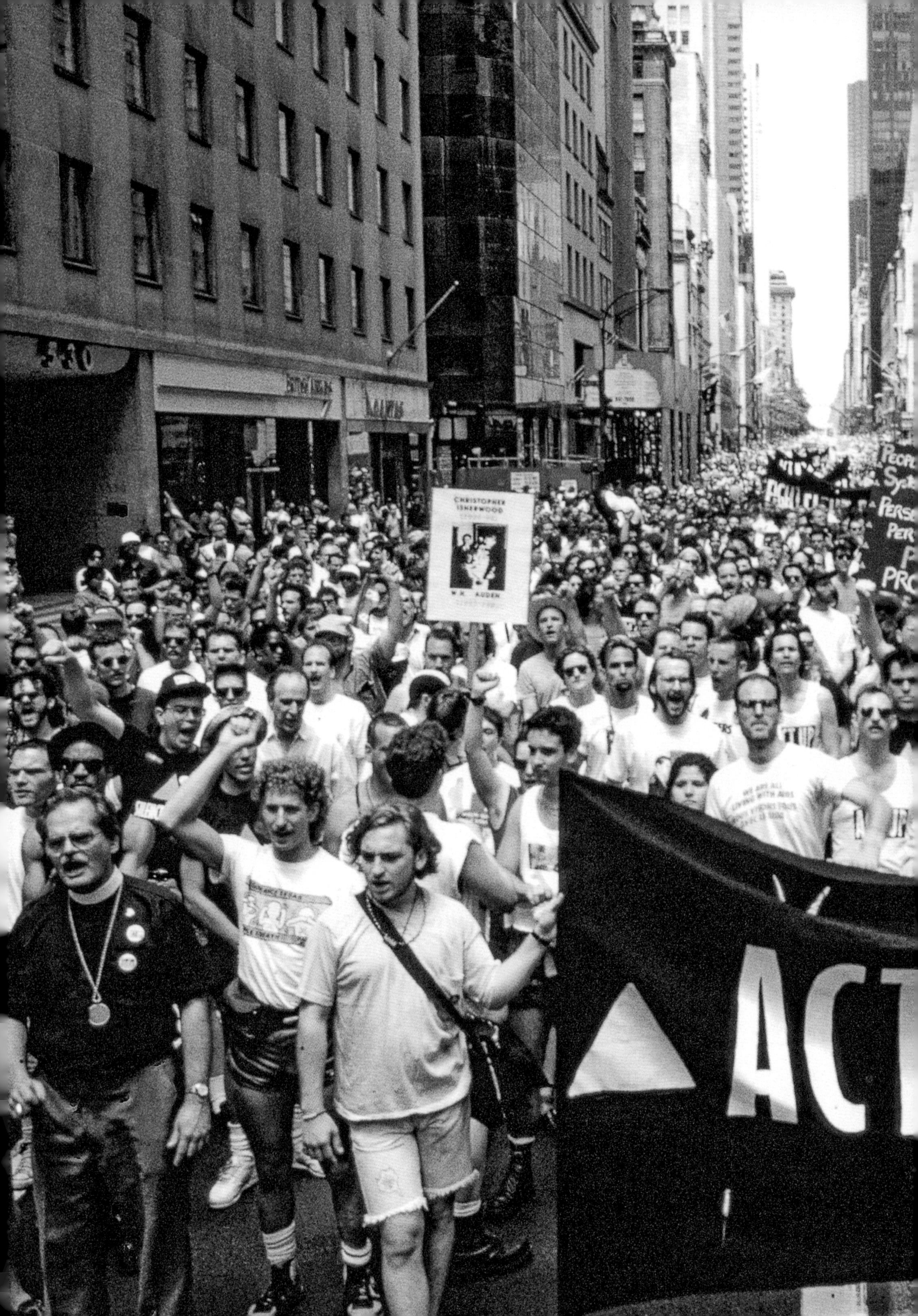

CHRISTOPHER
ISHERWOOD
W.H. AUDEN
ACT

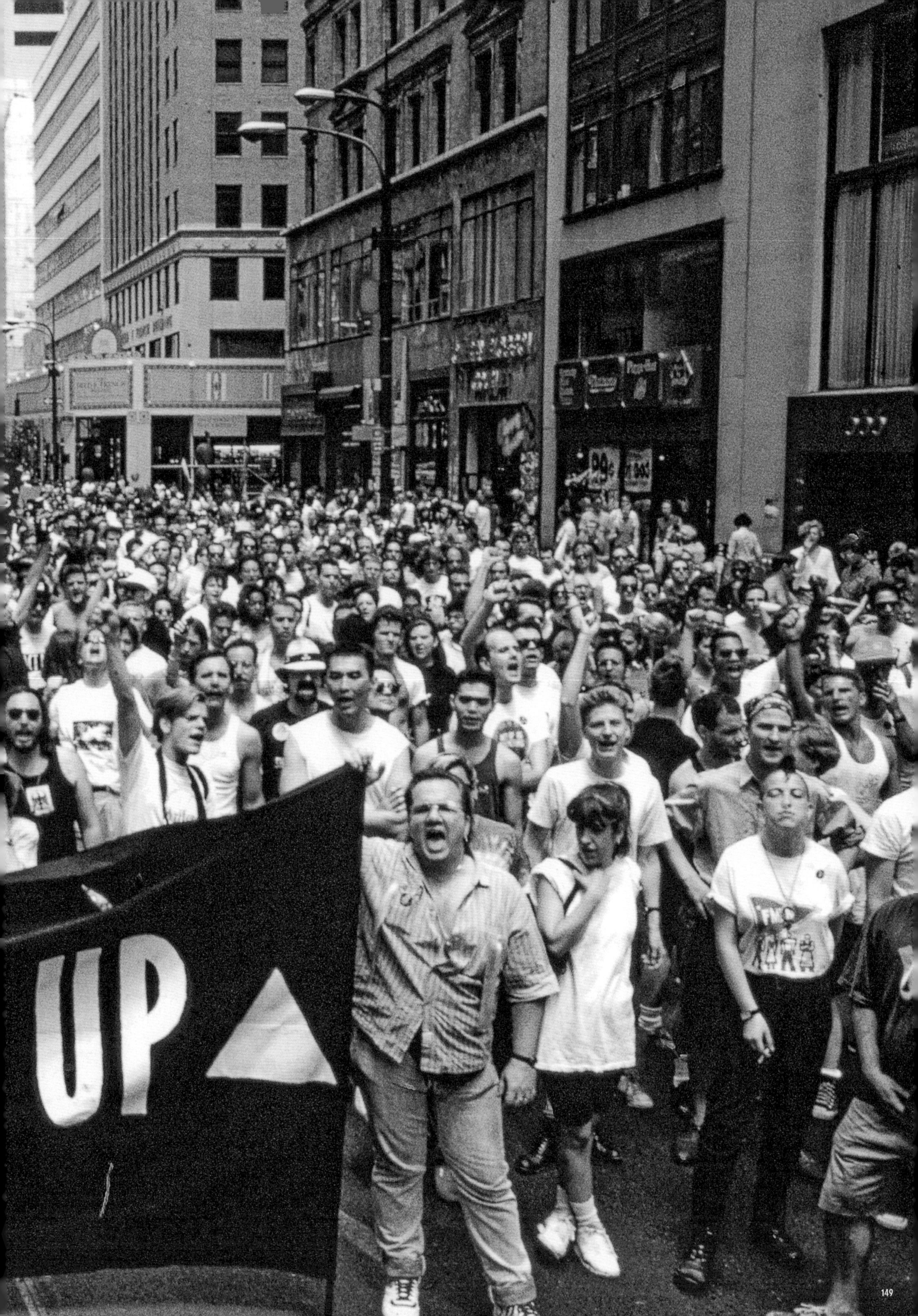

UP

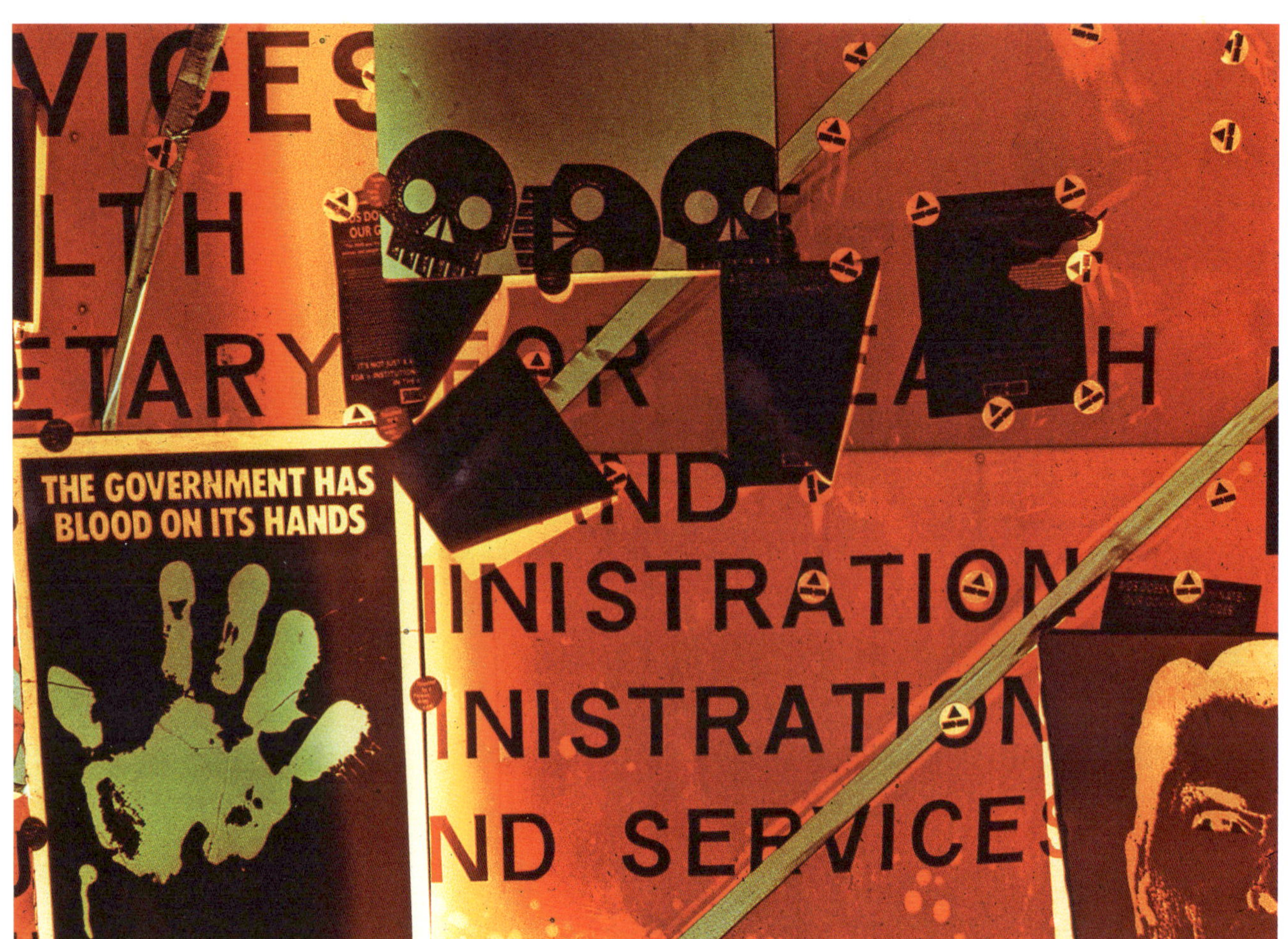

150
Lola Flash
Blood on Its Hands,
1998
Analog photograph,
photographic print
on paper
Courtesy of the
artist, New York,
United States

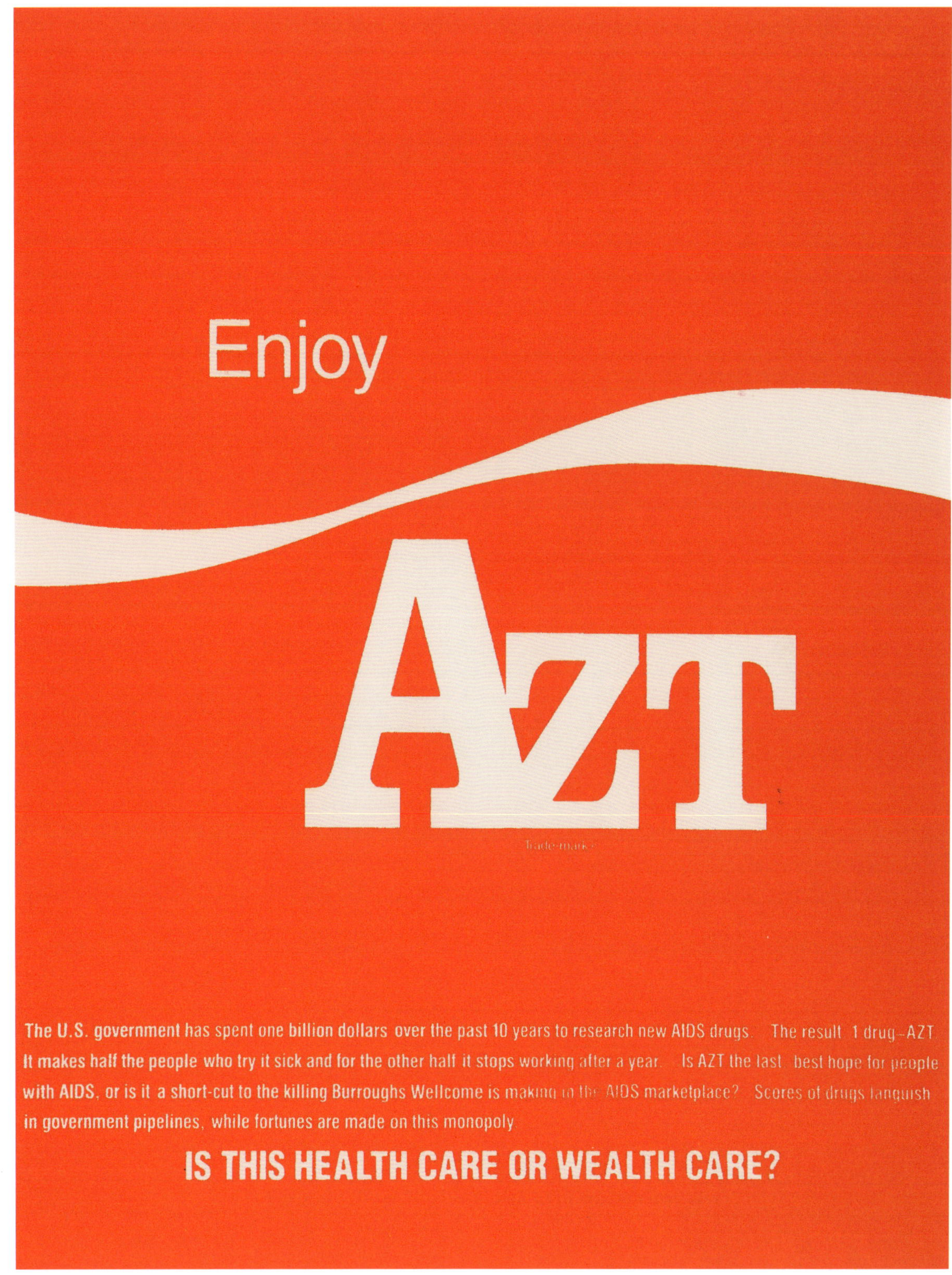

151

151
Avram Finkelstein and
Vincent Gagliostro
Enjoy AZT, 1989
Offset print on paper,
58.5 × 48.5 cm
Avram Finkelstein
Archive, New York,
United States

152

ACT UP
*Bring Your Grief and
Rage about AIDS to a
Political Funeral*, 1992
Offset print on paper,
29.5 × 21 cm

BRING YOUR GRIEF AND RAGE ABOUT AIDS TO A

POLITICAL FUNERAL

in Washington D.C. Sunday October 11 at 1:00 P.M

You have lost someone to AIDS. For more than a decade, your government has mocked your loss. You have spoken out in anger, joined political protests, carried fake coffins and mock tombstones, and splattered red paint to represent someone's HIV-positive blood, perhaps your own. George Bush believes that the White House gates shield him, from you, your loss, and his responsibility for the AIDS crisis. Now it is time to bring AIDS home to George Bush. On October 11th, we will carry the actual ashes of people we love in funeral procession to the White House. In an act of grief and rage and love, we will deposit their ashes on the White House lawn.

Join us to protest twelve years of genocidal AIDS policy.

MEET AT THE STEPS OF THE CAPITOL BUILDING AT 1:P.M· for more information about attending the funeral (with or without ashes) 0r about sending ashes to ACT UP New York for someone else to deliver, call Shane at (212)866-7967 (east coast) or David at (415)252-7401 (west coast)

Sponsored by ACT UP / NY

EXHIBITION CHECKLIST

ACT UP

Let the record show, 1987
Digital print on paper
29.5 × 21 cm
Image 127

*National AIDS Demonstration
at The White House*,
Washington, D.C., United States
1987
Digital print on paper
29.5 × 21 cm
Image 128

AIDS Is Not a Ball Game, 1988
Digital print on paper
29.5 × 21 cm
Image 134

Missing 200,000 New Yorkers,
1988
Digital print on paper
29.5 × 21 cm
Image 135

*Stop Church Interference in
our Lives*, 1989
Digital print on paper
29.5 × 21 cm
Image 146

25,000 Are Dead, circa 1980s
Digital print on paper
29.5 × 21 cm
Image 130

AIDS, Politics, & $$$, circa 1980s
Digital print on paper
29.5 × 21 cm
Image 132

*Que la historia muestre
[Let the Record Show],
circa* 1980s
Digital print on paper
29.5 × 21 cm
Image 136

Why We Kiss, circa 1980s
Digital print on paper
29.5 × 21 cm
Image 148

*Bring Your Grief and Rage
about AIDS to a Political Funeral*,
1992
Digital print on paper
29.5 × 21 cm
Image 152

ACT UP AD HOC

Let the Record Show... (ver.1),
installation view
The New Museum of
Contemporary Art, New York,
United States, 1987
Digital print on paper
15 × 10 cm
Image 117

Let the Record Show... (ver.1),
installation view
The New Museum of
Contemporary Art, New York,
United States, 1987
Digital print on paper
15 × 10 cm
Gran Fury Collection,
Manuscripts and Archives
Division, The New York Public
Library, United States
Image 126

Let the Record Show... (ver.1),
installation view
The New Museum of
Contemporary Art, New York,
United States, 1987
Digital print on paper
15 × 22 cm
Gran Fury Collection,
Manuscripts and Archives
Division, The New York Public
Library, United States
Image 125

**AVRAM FINKELSTEIN AND
DONALD MOFFETT**

Fact or Fiction, 1989
Digital print on paper
65 × 75 cm
Avram Finkelstein Archive,
New York, United States
Image 137

**AVRAM FINKELSTEIN AND
VINCENT GAGLIOSTRO**

Enjoy AZT, 1989
Digital print on paper
58.5 × 48 cm
Avram Finkelstein Archive,
New York, United States
Image 151

BILL STAMETS

Photograph of *Kissing Doesn't
Kill (ver.1)* on train station, 1990
Digital print on paper
22 × 33 cm
Comissioned work for the
project Art Against AIDS:
On the Road, Chicago, United
States
Image 80

BRAD MARKEL

Seize Control of the FDA,
action at the Food and Drug
Administration Headquarters
in Rockville, Maryland,
United States, Oct. 11, 1988
Digital print on paper
30 × 45 cm

BRUNO JAKOB

Installation photographs of
The Pope and the Penis at the
44th Biennale di Venezia, Italy,
1990
Digital print on paper
15 × 22 cm each
Gran Fury Collection,
Manuscripts and Archives
Division, The New York Public
Library, United States
Images 92-97, 119

CATHERINE MCGANN

Seize Control of the FDA,
action at the Food and Drug
Administration Headquarters
in Rockville, Maryland,
United States, Oct. 11, 1988
Digital print on paper
22 × 15 cm
Collection of the artist, Burbank,
California, United States
Image 139

DONALD MOFFETT

He Kills Me, 1987
Digital print on paper
45 × 72 cm
Courtesy of the artist and
Marianne Boesky Gallery,
New York and Aspen,
United States
Image 124

DONNA BINDER

ACT UP demonstration at Federal
Plaza, from left to right: Steve
Gendin, Mark Aurigemma,
Douglas Montgomery, Charles
Stimson, Frank O'Dowd, Avram
Finkelstein, New York, United
States, June 30, 1987
Digital print on paper
20 × 30 cm
Collection of the artist, New
York, United States
Image 129

ELLEN B. NEIPRIS

ACT UP member Gregg Bordowitz
carried away by the police,
Wall Street II, Mar. 24, 1988
Digital print on paper
22 × 15 cm
Collection of the artist, New
York, United States
Image 133

Seize Control of the FDA,
action at the Food and Drug
Administration Headquarters
in Rockville, Maryland, United
States, Oct. 11, 1988
Digital print on paper
45 × 30 cm
Collection of the artist, New
York, United States
Image 144

EUGENE GORDON

Members of ACT UP hold up
signs and placards during the
New York Gay and Lesbian Pride
march, United States, June 26,
1988
Digital print on paper
15 × 22 cm
New-York Historical Society,
Eugene Gordon Photograph
Collection, United States
Image 131

GRAN FURY

Men Use Condoms or Beat It
sticker on brick wall, 1988
Digital print on paper
25 × 37 cm
Gran Fury Collection,
Manuscripts and Archives
Division, The New York Public
Library, United States
Image 69

AIDS Behind Bars, ACT UP, Spring
AIDS Action, 1988
Digital print on paper
90 × 58.5 cm
Image 52

AIDS: 1 in 61, ACT UP, Women's
Committee for the *Cosmopolitan
Magazine* Demonstration, 1988
Digital print on paper
38 × 30 cm
Image 33

AIDS: 1 in 61 (Scared Fags Crap),
1988
Digital print on paper
22 × 15 cm
Gran Fury Collection,
Manuscripts and Archives
Division, The New York Public
Library, United States
Image 34

*All People With AIDS Are
Innocent*, ACT UP, Spring AIDS
Action, 1988
Digital print on paper
90 × 58 cm
Division of Political History,
National Museum of American
History, Smithsonian Institution,
Washington D.C., United States
Image 55

Art Is Not Enough, 1988
Digital print on paper
60 × 38 cm
Poster for a series of events at
The Kitchen, in 1988, New York,
United States
Image 57

*During this Program at least
6 People With AIDS Will Die*,
program insert in The
Bessies, New York Dance and
Performance Awards, 1988
Digital print on paper
10 × 16 cm
Image 60

*Give Me Your Tired, Your Poor,
Your HIV Negative*, ACT UP,
Spring AIDS Action, 1988
Digital print on paper
90 × 59 cm
Division of Political History,
National Museum of American
History, Smithsonian Institution,
Washington D.C., United States
Image 54

Bloody Handprint on Mailbox,
1988
Digital print on paper
15 × 10 cm
Gran Fury Collection,
Manuscripts and Archives
Division, The New York Public
Library, United States
Image 63

Men Use Condoms or Beat It,
1988
Digital print on sticker
18 × 22 cm
Image 68

Berlin Subway with
*When a Government Turns Its
Back on Its People* billboard, 1988
Digital print on paper
22 × 15 cm
Comissioned work for *Full Blown
Image AIDS: An Art Exhibition
about Living and Dying*, neue
Gesellschaft für bildende Kunst,
Berlin, Germany
Image 40

Read My Lips (Men's ver.), ACT UP,
Spring AIDS Action, 1988
Digital print on paper
42.5 × 27.5 cm
Image 118

Read My Lips (Women's, 1 ver.),
ACT UP, Spring AIDS Action, 1988
Digital print on paper
42.5 × 27.5 cm
Image 49

Read My Lips (Women's, 2 ver.),
ACT UP, Spring AIDS Action, 1988
Digital print on paper
42.5 × 27.5 cm
Image 50

Banner *All Pepople With AIDS
Are Innocent*, in front of the
social service agency Henry
Street Settlement, New York,
United States, 1988
Digital print on paper
25 × 37 cm
Gran Fury Collection,
Manuscripts and Archives
Division, The New York Public
Library, United States
Image 56

*Sexism Rears Its Unprotected
Head*, ACT UP Spring AIDS Action,
1988
Digital print on paper
90 × 58 cm
Image 53

*The Government Has Blood
on Its Hands (3 versions)*,
ACT UP, N.Y. City Dept. of Health
Demonstration, United States,
1988
Digital print on paper
42 × 25 cm (each)
Images 64-66

*The Government Has Blood on
Its Hands*, poster on the base of
a traffic light, 1988
Digital print on paper
10 × 15 cm
Image 1

Wall Street Money (10 dollar bill),
1988
Photocopy on paper
9 × 21.5 cm
Images 41, 42

Wall Street Money (50 dollar bill),
1988
Photocopy on paper
9 × 21.5 cm
Images 43, 44

*Wall Street Money
(100 dollar bill)*, 1988
Photocopy on paper
9 × 21.5 cm
Images 46, 47

*When a Government Turns
Its Back on Its People*, 1988
Digital print on paper
90 × 120 cm
Comissioned work for *Full Blown
Image AIDS: An Art Exhibition
about Living and Dying*, neue
Gesellschaft für bildende Kunst,
Berlin, Germany
Image 38

Read My Lips (Women's, 3 ver.),
1988/2012, For ACT UP
Offset print on postcard
10.5 × 15 cm
Image 51

Art Is Not Enough, poster for
the exhibition catalog *AIDS:
The Artists' Response*, at the
Ohio State University, United
States, 1989
Digital print on paper
29.5 × 42 cm
Image 59

Control, Artforum, Oct. 1989
Digital print on paper
26.5 × 26.5 cm
Images 73-76

Welcome to America billboard
in SoHo, at the corner of
Broadway and Houston, 1989
Digital print on paper
25 × 37 cm
Sponsored by the Whitney
Museum of American Art,
New York, United States
Image 88

Kissing Doesn't Kill (ver.1)
billboard on bus, 1989
Digital print on paper
22 × 33 cm
Comissioned work for the
project Art Against AIDS:
On the Road, San Francisco,
United States
Images 78, 79

The New York Crimes, ACT UP,
Target City Hall Demonstration,
New York, United States, 1989
Offset print on newsprint
58 × 38 cm (closed),
58 × 76 cm (open)
Images 70-72

Welcome to America, 1989
Digital print on paper
46 × 100 cm
Image World: Artand Media
Culture, The Whitney Museum
of American Art, New York,
United States
Image 87

Kissing Doesn't Kill (ver.1),
1989-1990
Digital print on paper
60 × 194 cm
Comissioned work for the
project Art Against AIDS:
On the Road, San Francisco,
United States
Image 77

*Art Is not Enough. Seize Power
Through Direct Action*, published
in *The Village Voice*, *circa* 1980s
Digital print on paper
51 × 69 cm
Gran Fury Collection,
Manuscripts and Archives
Division, The New York Public
Library, United States
Image 2

*Art is not Enough
[Over 700,000 Cases of
AIDS Worldwide]*, 1990
Digital print on paper
29.5 × 21 cm
Gran Fury Collection,
Manuscripts and Archives
Division, The New York Public
Library, United States
Image 58

Stills from *Kissing Doesn't Kill*,
1990
Video, 30" (each)
Images 82-86

The Pope and the Penis,
"Aperto 90", 44th Biennale
di Venezia, Italy, 1990
Digital print on paper
120 × 275 cm (each)
Gran Fury Collection,
Manuscripts and Archives
Division, The New York Public
Library, United States
Images 90, 91

Just Do It, (partial support from
Art Matters), 1991
Digital print on paper
25 × 37 cm
Gran Fury Collection,
Manuscripts and Archives
Division, The New York Public
Library, United States
Image 104

Wipe Out, *Bomb Magazine* cover,
n. 34, winter 1991
Digital print on paper
46 × 44 cm
Image 89

Women Just Don't Get AIDS, 1991
Digital print on paper
110 × 75 cm
Public Art Fund, New York, and
The Museum of Contemporary
Art, Los Angeles, United States
Image 101

Je Me Souviens
[I Remember], 1992
Digital print on paper
100 × 65 cm
Musée d'art contemporain
de Montréal, Canada
Image 106

Four Questions, 1993
Digital print on paper
61 × 45 cm
Gran Fury Collection,
Manuscripts and Archives
Division, The New York Public
Library, United States
Image 109

Mark Simpson wheatpasting
Four Questions poster, 1993
Digital print on paper
22 × 15 cm
Image 107

RIOT, 2019
Digital print on paper
88 × 88 cm
Image 36

LA NUOVA VENEZIA

Reproduction of *La Nuova
Venezia* cover with the "Biennale
scandal" abou the installation of
The Pope and the Penis, 1990
Digital print on paper
60 × 42 cm
Image 98

LISA HOWE-EBRIGHT

ACT UP members carrying
Kissing Doesn't Kill (ver. 1)
at Chicago Gay Pride Parade,
United States, June 24, 1990
Digital print on paper
22 × 33 cm
Lisa Ebright Photography,
Windy City Times, Chicago,
Illinois, United States
Image 81

LOLA FLASH

Blood on Its Hands, 1998
Digital print on paper
46 × 67 cm
Courtesy of the artist, New York,
United States
Image 150

MARK HINOJOSA

Gran Fury member Anthony
Viti carried away by the police,
Newsday, March 25, 1988
Digital print on paper
40 × 27 cm
Image 3

SILENCE=DEATH PROJECT

AIDSGATE, 1987
Digital print on paper
84 × 55 cm
Avram Finkelstein Archive,
New York, United States
Image 123

SILENCE = DEATH, 1987
Digital print on paper
84 × 55 cm
Avram Finkelstein Archive,
New York, United States
Image 122

T. L. LITT

Seize Control of the FDA,
action at the Food and Drug
Administration Headquarters
in Rockville, Maryland, United
States, Oct. 11, 1988
Digital print on paper
15 × 22 cm (each)
Collection of the artist, Medford,
Massachusetts, United States
Images 140-143

ACT UP at the New York City
Pride March, United States,
in 1989
Digital print on paper
32 × 55 cm
Collection of the artist, Medford,
Massachusetts, United States
Image 149

Stop The Church, ACT UP and
Women's Health Action
and Mobilization (WHAM!),
Dec. 10, 1989
Digital print on paper
15 × 22 cm
Collection of the artist, Medford,
Massachusetts, United States
Image 147

TOM MCKITTERICK

ACT UP member Joe Ferrari
is carried away by the police,
Target City Hall, New York
against mayor Ed Koch, 1989
Digital print on paper
15 × 22 cm
Collection of the artist,
New York, United States
Image 145

Seize Control of the FDA,
action at the Food and Drug
Administration Headquarters
in Rockville, Maryland, United
States, Oct. 11, 1988
Digital print on paper
15 × 22 cm
Collection of the artist,
New York, United States
Image 138

SELECTED BIBLIOGRAPHY

Compiled by André Mesquita

BALL, Edward. "Publicists to the Epidemic." *New York Magazine*, v. 23, no. 1, Jan. 1990.

BORDOWITZ, Gregg. *General Idea: Imagevirus*. London: Afterall, 2010.

BUSHAK, Lecia. "The Legacy of '80s Art Collective Gran Fury is now part of history, but the work Remains as Furious as Ever," *Capital*, Feb. 28, 2012. Available at https://www.politico.com/states/new-york/albany/story/2012/02/the-legacy-of-80s-art-collective-gran-fury-is-now-part-of-history-but-the-work-remains-as-furious-as-ever-069882. Retrieved Nov. 23, 2023.

CATLIN, Jonathon. "When does an epidemic become a 'crisis'? Analogies between Covid-19 and HIV/AIDS in American public memory." *Memory Studies*, v. 15, no. 6, 2021, 1445–1474.

CLEMENTI, James. "Activism as Art: Gran Fury Gets a NYC Retrospective." *Out*, Jan. 31, 2012. Available at https://www.out.com/entertainment/popnography/2012/01/31/activism-art-gran-fury-gets-nyc-retrospective-nyu. Retrieved Nov. 23, 2023.

COLUCCI, Emily. "Is Art Enough? Gran Fury in Perspective." *Hyperallergic*, Feb. 21, 2012. Available at https://hyperallergic.com/46881/gran-fury-read-my-lips-80-wsenyu/. Retrieved Nov. 23, 2023.

CRIMP, Douglas. *AIDS: Cultural Analysis/Cultural Activism*. Cambridge: MIT Press, 1988.

__________; ROSTON, Adam. *AIDS Demo Graphics*. Seattle: Bay Press, 1990.

__________. "Mourning and Militancy." In: FERGUSON, Russel et al. (Eds.). *Out There: Marginalization and Contemporary Culture*. Cambridge: MIT Press, 1990, 233–45.

__________. *Melancholia and Moralism: Essays on AIDS and Queer Politics*. Cambridge: MIT Press, 2002.

__________. "Gran Fury talks to Douglas Crimp." *Artforum* v. 41, no. 8, Apr. 2003. Available at https://www.artforum.com/columns/granfury-166150. Retrieved Nov. 11, 2023.

DEITCHER, David. "Gran Fury." In: FERGUSON, Russel et al. (Eds.). *Discourses: Conversations in Postmodern Art And Culture*. New York/Cambridge: The New Museum of Contemporary Art/MIT Press, 1990, 196–208.

DRINKALL, Jay. "Gran Fury: 'Read My Lips'." *Afterall*, Dec. 12, 2018. Available at https://www.afterall.org/articles/gran-fury-read-my-lips/. Retrieved Dec. 26, 2023.

DUBIN, Steven C. *Arresting Images: Impolitic Art and Uncivil Actions*. New York: Routledge, 1992.

EXPÓSITO, Marcelo. *Walter Benjamin, Productivist*. Bilbao: consonni, 2013.

FINKELSTEIN, Avram. *After Silence: A History of AIDS Through Its Images*. Berkeley: University of California Press, 2017.

FRANCE, David. *How to Survive a Plague: The Story of How Activists and Scientists Tamed AIDS*. New York: Vintage, 2017.

GOBER, Robert. "Gran Fury." *BOMB Magazine*, n. 34, Winter 1991, 9–13. Available at https://bombmagazine.org/articles/gran-fury. Retrieved Dec. 26, 2023.

GODMER, Gilles; LUSSIER, Real. *Pour la Suite du monde*. Montreal: Musée d'art contemporain de Montréal, 1992.

GOULD, Deborah B. *Moving Politics: Emotion and ACT UP's Fight against AIDS*. Illinois: The University of Chicago Press, 2009.

GRAN FURY. "Control, a Project for *Artforum*." *Artforum* v. 29, no. 2, Oct. 1989. Available at https://www.artforum.com/features/control-a-project-for-artforum-205485. Retrieved Dec. 26, 2023.

__________. *Gran Fury: Read My Lips*. New York: 80WSE Press, 2011.

"GRAN FURY: Read My Lips" Exhibit Documents AIDS Activist Art Collective's Work," *Huffington Post*, Jan. 30, 2012. Available at https://www.huffpost.com/entry/gran-fury-read-my-lips-aids-artexhibit_n_1242106. Retrieved Nov. 23, 2023.

GREEN, Jesse. "When Political Art Mattered." *The New York Times*, Dec. 7, 2003. Available at https://www.nytimes.com/2003/12/07/magazine/when-political-art-mattered.html. Retrieved Nov. 23, 2023.

GROVER, Jan Zita. "Public Art on AIDS: On the Road with Art Against AIDS." In: KLUSAČEK, Allan; MORRISON, Ken (Eds.). *A Leap in the Dark*. Montreal: Véhicule Press, 1992, 58–70.

HARRINGTON, Mark. "AIDS Activists and People with AIDS. A Movement to Revolutionize Research and for Universal Access to Treatment." In: DA COSTA, Beatriz; PHILIP, Kavita (Eds.). *Tactical Biopolitics: Art, Activism, and Technoscience*. Cambridge: MIT Press, 2008, 324–340.

HASSELLE, Della. "NYU Exhibit Features Artists' Response to New York's AIDS Crisis." *DNAinfo*, Jan. 26, 2012. Available at https://www.dnainfo.com/new-york/20120126/greenwich-village-soho/nyu-exhibit-features-artists-response-new-yorks-aids-crisis. Retrieved Nov. 23, 2023.

HELLER, Steven. "How AIDS was Branded: Looking Back at ACT UP Design." *The Atlantic*, Jan. 12, 2012. Available at https://www.theatlantic.com/entertainment/archive/2012/01/how-aids-was-branded-looking-back-at-act-up-design/251267. Retrieved Nov. 23, 2023.

JACOBS, Karrie; HELLER, Steven. *Angry Graphics: Protest Posters of The Reagan/Bush Era*. Lake City: Peregrine Smith Books, 1992.

JONES, Eliel. "Make AIDS Visible: Gran Fury's Provoking Billboards." *Frieze*, Nov. 7, 2018. Available at https://www.frieze.com/article/make-aids-visible-gran-furys-provoking-billboards. Retrieved Nov. 23, 2023.

KALAIDJIAN, Walter. *American Culture Between the Wars: Revisionary Modernism and Postmodern Critique*. New York: Columbia University Press, 1993.

KNAFO, Robert (Ed.). *Public Art Issues: Public Art and AIDS*. New York: The Public Art Fund, 1992.

LAMPERT, Nicolas. *A People's Art History of the United States*. New York: The New Press, 2015.

LOWERY, Jack. *It was Vulgar and it was Beautiful: How AIDS Activists used Art to Fight a Pandemic*. New York: Bold Type Books, 2022.

MCKEE, Yates. *Strike Art. Contemporary Art and the Post-Occupy Condition*. New York: Verso, 2016.

MCQUISTON, Liz. *Graphic Agitation: Social and Political Graphics since the Sixties*. London: Phaidon Press, 1993.

MESQUITA, André; ESCHE, Charles; BRADLE Y, Will (Eds.). *Arte e ativismo: antologia*. São Paulo: Museu de Arte de São Paulo Assis Chateaubriand/Afterall, 2021.

MESQUITA, André. *Insurgências poéticas: arte ativista e ação coletiva*. São Paulo: Annablume/FAPESP, 2011.

MEYER, James. "AIDS and Postmodernism." *Arts Magazine* v. 66, no. 8, Apr. 1992, 62–68.

MEYER, Richard. *Outlaw Representation: Censorship and Homosexuality in Twentieth-Century American Art*. New York: Oxford University Press, 2002.

__________. "This is to Enrage You." In: FELSHIN, Nina (Ed.). *But it is Art? The Spirit of Art as Activism*. Seattle: Bay Press, 1995, 51–83.

MOLESWORTH, Helen. *This Will Have Been: Art, Love, and Politics in the 1980s*. New Haven: Yale University Press, 2012.

PEDROSA, Adriano, MESQUITA, André (Eds.). *Gran Fury: arte não é o bastante*. São Paulo: Museu de Arte de São Paulo Assis Chateaubriand, 2024.

PEDROSA, Adriano; MESQUITA, André (Eds.). *Histórias da sexualidade: antologia*. São Paulo: Museu de Arte de São Paulo Assis Chateaubriand, 2017.

REED, Thomas Vernon. *The Art of Protest: Culture and Activism from the Civil Rights Movement to the Streets of Seattle*. Minneapolis: Univ. Of Minnesota Press, 2005.

RIBALTA, Jorge. *Domini Public*. Barcelona: Centre d'Art Santa Mònica, 1994.

SCHULMAN, Sarah. *Let the Record Show: A Political History of ACT UP New York, 1987–1993*. London: Picador, 2022.

SHEARER, Linda. "Towards an 'International' Perspective?" In: RASPONI, Simonetta (Ed.). *Catalogue General 1990, La Biennale di Venezia*. Venice/Milan: La Biennale di Venezia/Gruppo Editoriale Fabbri S.p.A., 1990, 277–80.

SHOLETTE, Gregory. *The Art of Activism and the Activism of Art*. London: Lund Humphries, 2022.

SPERETTA, Tommaso. *Rebels Rebel: AIDS, Art and Activism in New York, 1979–1989*. Gante: MER. Paper Kunsthalle, 2014.

SUMMERSON, Karen J. *Creating and Re-creating AIDS Activist Art: The Biography of the Gran Fury Poster*. Masters' Thesis. New York: State University of New York, 2013.

WALLIS, Brian; WEE MS, Marianne; Yenawine, Philip (Eds.). *Art Matters: How the Culture Wars Changed America*. New York: NYU Press, 1999.

__________(Ed.). *Democracy: A Project by Group Material*. New York/Seattle: Dia Art Foundation/Bay Press, 1990.

WARNER, Michael (Ed.). *Fear of a Queer Planet: Queer Politics and Social Theory*. Minneapolis: University of Minnesota Press, 1993.

WEINBER, Jonathan. *Ambition and Love in Modern American Art*. New Haven: Yale University Press, 2001.

MASP ENDOWMENT

CHERITABLE PATRONS
Fernão Carlos Botelho Bracher
(*in memoriam*)
Geyze Diniz
Rose and Alfredo Setubal

DIAMOND
Ana Eliza and Paulo Setubal
Luciana and Ronaldo Cezar Coelho
Luis Stuhlberger
Roberto Egydio Setubal

GOLD
Amalia Spinardi and Roberto
Thompson Motta
Família Repucci
Gabriel and Antonio Quintela
Helio Seibel
Marisa and Salo Davi Seibel

SILVER
Carolina and Patrice Etlin
Israel Vainboim
Maria Alice Setubal
Marjore and Geraldo Carbone
Martha and André De Vivo
Mônica and Eduardo Vassimon
Nádia and Olavo Setubal
Neide Helena de Moraes
Paulo Proushan (*in memoriam*)
Sandra and José Luiz Setubal
Sonia and Luis Terepins

PATRONS
Lais Zogbi and Telmo G. Porto
(*in memoriam*)
TVML Foundation

FRIENDS OF MASP*
Daniela Escobari
Frances Reynolds
Geyze and Abílio Diniz
Jana and Bernardo Hees
Patricia and Antonio
Bonchristiano
Patrícia and José Bonchristiano
Priscila and Louis de
Charbonnières
Renata and Claudio Garcia
Rose and Alfredo Setubal
The Helen Clay Frick Foundation

PATRONS

CHARITABLE PATRONS
Ana Salomone
Carlos Jereissati
Geyze e Abilio Diniz
Maria Victoria and Eric Hime
Rose and Alfredo Setubal

DIAMOND PATRONS
Ana Eliza and Paulo Setubal
Cleusa Garfinkel

Nadia and Olavo Egydio
Setubal Jr.
Roberto Setubal
Teresa Cristina Ribeiro Ralston
Botelho Bracher and
Candido Botelho Bracher

GOLD PATRONS
Amália Spinardi and Roberto
Thompson Motta
Flávia and José de Menezes
Berenguer Neto
Frances Reynolds
Guilherme Affonso Ferreira
Henrique Meirelles
José Orlando A. de Arrochela
Lobo
Juliana Siqueira de Sá and
Manuelle Ferraz
Lilian Feuer Stuhlberger and
Luis Stuhlberger
Mara and Cleiton de Castro
Marques
Maria Claudia and Leo Krakowiak
Maria Denise Carvalho Resende
Marina Diniz Junqueira and
Fernando de Almeida
Nobre Neto
Martha and André De Vivo
Mônica and Eduardo Vassimon
Mônica and Fábio Ulhoa Coelho
Paloma and Fersen Lambranho
Regina Pinho de Almeida
Ronaldo Cezar Coelho
Sonia and Hamilton
Dias de Souza
Susana and Ricardo Steinbruch
Susie and Guido Padovano
Tania Haddad Nobre and
Alexandre Nobre
Vania and José Roberto Marinho
Vera Lucia dos Santos Diniz

SILVER PATRONS
Alessandra (*in memoriam*) and
Rodrigo Bresser-Pereira
Ana Karina Bortoni Dias and
Marcos Fernandes Navarro
Ana Lucia and Sergio Comolatti
Ana Maria Igel and Mario
Higino Leonel
Ana Paula Capricho de Azevedo
Motta and Daniel Augusto
Motta
Ana Paula and Sergio Spinelli
Ana Paula Martinez and Daniel
K. Goldberg
Andrea and José Olympio da
Veiga Pereira
Andrea Pinheiro and Newton
Simões Filho
Carolina and Patrice Etlin
Cecília and Abram Szajman
Cristiana and Dan Ioschpe
Eduardo Salomão Neto
Fabiana and Marcelo Marangon

Flávia Camanho Camparini and
Fabio José Camparini
Flavia and Frank Geyer Abubakir
Janaina Dobbeck Fiorini and
Reinaldo Carlos Fiorini
Juliana Freitas Calheiros and
Grenfel Schwartz Calheiros
Julio Roberto Magnus Landmann
Karin Baumgart Srougi and
Thomaz Srougi
Larissa Fortes de Almeida and
Denis Caldeira de Almeida
Lavínia and Ricardo Setubal
Luiza and Marcelo Hallack
Marcia Bossa Graça Scripilliti
and Clóvis Ermirio de
Moraes Scripilliti
Marguerite and Jean Etlin
Maria Alice Setubal
Maria Eduarda and Ricardo
Brito Pereira
Maria Flavia Barbosa Carvalho
and Guilherme Moreira
Teixeira
Maria Luiza and Tito da Silva Neto
Marta and Hecilda Fadel
Paula Pires Paoliello de Medeiros
and Marcelo Medeiros
Paula Proushan
Sandra and José Luiz Setúbal
Sonia and Luis Terepins
Stefania Pelusi Cestero and
Francisco Cestero
Thiago Saddi Tannous
Vera Alves de Lima Parreiras
and Luiz Paulo Parreiras
Vera Novis
Vera Sarnes Negrão
Vicente Furletti Assis
Vivian Jessica Blair Bigoni and
Marcio Verri Bigoni

PATRONS
Alexandra Mollof
Ana Paula Vilela Vianna and
Jose Luiz Vianna
Andrea and Guilherme
Johannpeter
Andréa and Tom Waslander
Angela and Ricard Akagawa
Antonia Bergamin and Mateus
Ferreira
Antonio Almeida and Carlos Dale
Augusto Livio Malzoni
Bruno Baptistella
Camila and Walter Appel
Claudete Brochmann and
Silvano Gersztel
Daniela and Helio Seibel
Daniela Johannpeter
Danielle Silbergleid and Antônio
Pitombo
Eduardo Saron
Fabio Magalhães
Fernanda and Alberto Fernandes
Fernanda Feitosa and Heitor

Martins
Flávia Buarque de Almeida and
Rodrigo Ferreira Leite
Flávia and Jean Sigrist
Gabriela and Adriano Borges
Heloisa and Amos Genish
James Acacio Lisboa
Jane Hayre de Sousa Antunes
and Fábio Lima Mourão
Joan and Jackson Schneider
Karla Meneghel
Liane and Roberto Bielawski
Luisa Strina
Luiz Carlos Schmidt Ritter and
Clelio da Costa Alves
Márcia Fortes, Alessandra
D'aloia and Alex Gabriel
Maria Angela and Roberto Klabin
Maria Monteiro
Mariana Guarini Berenguer
Marilia Razuk e Marcela Razuk
Marina and Marcos Gouvêa
Marjorie and Geraldo Carbone
Marta and Paulo Kuczynski
Max Perlingeiro
Monize Neves and Ricardo
Vasques
Myra Arnaud Babenco
Nara, Alexandre and Daniel
Roesler
Neide Helena de Moraes
Paula Depieri
Paulo Donizete Martinez
Paulo Saad Jafet
Pedro Mendes Ciruffo
Priscilla and Marcelo Parodi
Raquel and Marcio Kogan
Raul Justes Lores
Renata Bittencourt
Renata de Paula David
Renata Tubini
Ricardo Ohtake
Roberta Mendes Pereira Whately
and Wagner Dias Coelho
Sabina and Abrão Lowenthal
Salo Seibel
Sandra and William Ling
Sílvia Teixeira Penteado
Silvio Tini de Araújo
Sonia and Paulo de Barros
Carvalho
Thaissa and Alexandre Bertoldi
Thalita Cefali Zaher
Thiago Gomide Nunes
Titiza Nogueira and Renata
Nogueira Beyruti
Ulisses Eliezer Simonetti Cohn
and Flavio Isaias Simonetti
Cohn
Vilma Eid

YOUNG PATRONS

SILVER YOUNG PATRONS
André Montanholi Mileski
Eliza Correa de Almeida Nobre

Francisco Fernando Correa de
Almeida Nobre
Gabriela Azevedo Forlin
Luiz and Ludwig Danielian
Marcela and Alfredo Nugent
Setubal

YOUNG PATRONS
Alessandra and Guilherme
Simões de Assis
Alexandre Maia de Mello
Ana Clara Medeiros de Almeida
Ana Luiza Tesser Arguello and
Ary Cera Zanetta Neto
Ana Varella and Samuel Varella
Pedrosa
Ananda and Leonardo Lopes
Anne Carolline Wilians
Arthur Jafet
Arthur Masi Uzum and
Maria Helena Loureiro
Masi Uzum
Beatriz Viabone and Thomaz
Henrique Pacheco
Camila Yunes and Conrado
Mesquita
Candido de Azeredo Gomes
and Deyllison Cintra
de Melo
Carolina da Costa Carvalho
and Luiz Carlos da Costa
Carvalho Jr.
Carolina Junqueira Bull and
Edmar Mendoza Bull
Caroline Ficker
Clara Roorda
Dante Alberto Jemma Cobucci
Edmar Pinto Costa
Fabio Pinheiro Molina and Lucas
de Carvalho Tironi
Felipe Calil de Melo and Julia
Suslick
Felipe Hegg and William
Heuseler
Fernanda and Suzana Resstom
Gabriel Affonso Ferreira
Guilherme Nagel and Eduardo
Cherez Pavia
Guilherme Pesenti
Ian Junqueira Duarte Lucas and
Allann de Seabra Camargo
Paulo
Igi Lola Ayedun and Asole
Adelakin de Faria Mello
Isabella Marinho
Isadora Poltronieri Vecchi e
Diogo de Souza Dutra
João Paulo Siqueira Lopes and
Fernando Ticoulat
Juan Eyheremendy
Juliana and Leonardo Gonzalez
Juliana Mamy Suzuki e João
Gabriel Pennacchi
Juliana Versolato dos Santos
and Raphael de Almeida
Fonseca

Leilane Sabatini and Felipe
Sabatini
Lia and Ricardo Pedro Guazzelli
Rosario
Lucas Danicek Borges
Lucas Marques Pessôa
Luis Eduardo Sanchez Maluf
Luiz Augusto de Souza Campos
Junior and Caio Rocha
Correa
Marcela Caio
Marcela Levy Zilberberg and
Eduardo Zilberberg
Marcelo Padua Lima
Maria Carolina Gattaz Caneiro
and Caio Galli Caneiro
Maria Rita Drummond and
Rodolfo Barreto
Nathalie Felsberg
Paula and Bruno Rizzo Setubal
Paula Paes Batista da Silva and
Fernando Cezar Cunha
Spnola Junior
Rafael Moraes
Regina Civolani da Cruz and
Renzo Pasquale Zeglio
Agresta
Renata Alice Lobo Lisboa
Ricardo Von Brusky and Flavia
Waiswol Reitzfeld
Roberto S. Borsic
Rodrigo Hsu Ngai Leite
Sofia Derani
Stephanie Schultz Wenk and
Gabriel Sauer
Susanna Crestani and Marco
Kheirallah
Thais Abujamra Nader and
Luiz Starace Fonseca Ayres
Pimentel
Thomas Ondracek Lemouche
and André Donato Mathias
Valentina Circe Vettori e Rafael
Vettori
Victoria Zuffo and Paulo
Kassab Jr.
Vinicius Veloso

*List of International
Donors: Friends of MASP and
International Council

STRATEGIC PARTNER
Itaú

MASTER SPONSORS
Nubank
Akzo Nobel
B3
Bradesco
Citibank
Klabin
Mckinsey & Company
Renner
Vivo

SPONSORS
Biolab Farmacêutica
Bloomberg
Deloitte
EMS
Goodyear
Grupo Ultra
Unilever

SUPPORTERS
American Express
Banco Votorantim
Chanel
Credit Suisse
Farfetch
Goldman Sachs
Grupo Comolatti
Lefosse
Mattos Filho
Origem Energia
Safra
Singulare
Sotheby's
Talento Gerenciadora
Terra Foundation of
American Art
Ticket
Too Seguros
Unipar
VR

PARTNER COMPANIES
Banco Alfa
Bye Cupim
Comerc Energia
Kaspersky
Poliedro Educação

MEDIA PARTNERS
Boxnet
Buzzmonitor
Canal Arte1
Cult
Estadão
Harper's Bazaar
JCDecaux
Revista 451
Revista Piauí
Zanzar

Every effort has been made for
the mentions of our sponsors,
board members, patrons,
young patrons, and members
of the International Council to
be published correctly. If there
is any error, please inform us,
and we promise to correct in
future editions.

ARTISTIC BOARD
Adriano Pedrosa
Artistic Director

COLLECTION AND CONSERVATION
Pilar Rios
Alejandra Orellana
Aline Assumpção
Camila Zanon Paglione
Juliana Batista
Juliana Peixoto
Luciana Gonçalves
Marina Pelegrini
Nalú Maria de Medeiros
Paula Coelho Lima
Rebeca Felipe
Taynara Lima
Tereza Moura

RESEARCH CENTER
Adriana Villela
Beatriz Yoshito
Bruno Mesquita
Evandro Lima
Filipe Oliveira
Gustavo Bastos
João Vítor Conceição
Pamella Mazucatto
Sara Jesus

COMMUNICATION AND MARKETING
Thais Gouveia
Amanda Sammour
Beatriz Ferro
Laura Jabur
Pablo Mazzucco
Ticiana Gavioli

CURATORS
Edson Kayapó
**Curator at Large of
Indigenous Art**

Kássia Borges Karajá
**Curator at Large of
Indigenous Art**

Renata Tupinambá
**Curator at Large of
Indigenous Art**

Julia Bryan-Wilson
**Curator-at-Large of Modern
and Contemporary Art**

Marcia Arcuri
**Curator-at-Large of
Pre-Colombian Art**

María Inés Rodríguez
**Curator-at-Large of Modern
and Contemporary Art**

Regina Teixeira de Barros
**Coordinating Curator and
Curator of Collections**

Fernando Oliva
Curator

Isabella Rjeille
Curator

Amanda Carneiro
Assistant Curator

Guilherme Giufrida
Assistant Curator

Laura Cosendey
Assistant Curator

Isabela Loures
Curatorial Assistant

Leandro Muniz
Curatorial Assistant

Matheus de Andrade
Curatorial Assistant

Teo Teotônio
Curatorial Assistant

Danilo Cavalcante
Curatorial Internship

Roger Gaspar
Curatorial Internship

PUBLISHING
Carol Ribas
Ana Canellas
Carolina Menegatti
Felipe de Souza
Mariana Trevas
Marina Marcondes
Reniêr Vasconcelos
Tulio Costa

EXHIBITION DESIGN
Juliana Ziebell
Flora Gurgel

MEDIATION AND PUBLIC PROGRAMS
André Mesquita
Curator

Glaucea Helena de Britto
Assistant Curator

Daniela Rodrigues
Curatorial Assistant

David Ribeiro
Curatorial Assistant

Carlos Henrique Martins
Iliriana Rodrigues
Isart Silva
Karolina Vargem
Rafael Figueiredo

Vitória Machado
Vitória Ribeiro

EXECUTIVE PRODUCTION
Marina Moura
Carla Ogawa
Gabriel Belvis
Isaque Vieira
Maicon Ferreira
Maria Rosalem
Marília Amorim
Marina Rebouças
Matheus Gumerato
Victória Dirotildes

FINANCE AND OPERATIONS BOARD

Marcelo Ribeiro
Financial and Operational Director

ENGAGEMENT AND DIGITAL
Beto Gonçalves
Amanda Dias
Daniela Nunes
Davison Cruz
Fernanda Reis
Gabriel Soares
Jefferson Sousa
Mariana Castro
Paulo Cesar Mafra de Matos
Patrick Matias

FINANCE AND ACCOUNTING
Mary Matsumura
Alessandra Silva
Alife Cardoso
Ana Paula Moreira
Anna Beatriz dos Santos
Bruno Araújo
Franciele Cruz
Francisco Rodrigues de Sousa
Heloiza Duarte
Iago Miguel da Silva
João Paulo Gonçalves
Letícia Lisboa
Marina Kolm Sgnotto
Patrícia Martinez
Tânia Aparecida Souza

LEGAL
Mariana Luvizutti
Larissa Neves
Nicole El Murr

MASP STORE
Adélia Borges
Curator-at-Large MASP Store

Milton Schubert
Abraão Rangel
Alailson Melo
Camila Gomes
Kevin Silva
Lohanne Villela
Maíra Carvalho

Mariana Rudiniski
Raphael Ottoni
Tobias Nunnes
William Ferreira

OPERATIONS AND INFRAESTRUCTURE
Karina Del Papa
Adeilton dos Santos Gomes
Alejandra Novaes
Allan Lafitte
Amanda Arantes
Ana Cecília Souza
Andrelito Souza
Andressa Silva
Antônio de Souza Matos
Antônio José dos Santos
Beatriz Pereira
Bianca Ferrari
Bianca Mariano
Bruno Orsini
Charles Reis
Christiane Flores
Clayton Gonçalves Andrade
Cosmes Magalhães
Cristiano Jesus
Damião Barreto da Silva
Danielle Rocha
Denisse Sandovetti
Dionísio Ortiz
Domingos de Jesus dos Santos
Edenice Santos
Elaine Matias
Elaine Neris
Elis Fabro Barreira
Everton Silva
Fábio Silva
Fabiula Lima
Fernanda dos Santos
Flavia Giaconto
Flávia Rosa
Francisco Soares Silva
Gabrielle Ferreira
Geovanna Brandão
Gilberto de Sousa Bezerra
Giulia Rimoli
Gustavo Alves
Henrique Gomes
Hilderlane Oliveira
Jailson Silva Neres
Jéssica Coutinho
Joe Cavalcante
José Nolasco Santana
Lara Duarte
Larissa de Araújo
Luan de Alencar
Lucas Modaneze
Luciano Oliveira
Marcello Israel
Marcelo Nascimento
Márcia Batista
Marcos Pimentel
Marion Novais
Matheus Ferreira
Mikaele Oliveira
Mirian Primo
Mirian Rodrigues

Myrella Marques
Natanael Oliveira
Nicolle Vieira
Rik Castilho
Robinson Xavier Barbosa
Rodolfo Toledo Nogueira
Rodrigo Ferreira
Rômulo Alberto de Oliveira
Severino Cassiano Lopes
Sidiclei dos Santos
Silvano Ferreira
Susana da Silva Morales
Thais Domingues
Thatielly Vidal
Valter Silva
Vinícius Flauaus
Wanda Mirabile

PROJECTS AND ARCHITECTURE
Miriam Elwing
Leonardo Andrade
Lúcia Furlan
Marco Scriboni
Mariele Sebben
Marina Barca

STRATEGIC PLANNING
Fernanda Ferraz Bonini
Victor Serra Lima

HUMAN RESOURCES
Renata Tavares
Dannyele Cavalcante
Elaine Santos
Henrique Rodrigues
Kátia Gomes

SECRETARIAL OFFICE
Paula Zoppello
Débora Ferreira
Gustavo Salla

DEVELOPMENT BOARD

Carolina Rossetti
Development Director

EVENTS, SPONSORSHIPS AND TAX INCENTIVE PROJECTS
Gabriel Di Pietro de Camillo
Ana Beatriz Brayner
Brenda Koschel de Farias
Júlia Weckelmann
Kassandra Lemos
Letícia Petean

NATURAL PERSON PROJECTS
Jussara Nascimento
Ariel de Oliveira
Darlan Lopes
Franciele Teles
Noemia Braz

NEW PROJECTS
Manuela Errera

GRAN FURY: ART IS NOT ENOUGH

MASP, February 23–June 6, 2024

EXHIBITION

Accessibility
Daniela Rodrigues
Isart Silva
Vitória Machado

Accessibility Consulting
Mais Diferenças

Art Handling
Elias Joaquim
Rafael Filipe
Renato Bomfim
Juan Castro

Collection and Conservation
Alejandra Orellana
Aline Assumpção
Camila Zanon Paglione
Juliana Batista
Juliana Peixoto
Luciana Gonçalves
Marina Pelegrini
Nalú Maria de Medeiros
Paula Coelho Lima
Pilar Rios
Rebeca Felipe
Taynara Lima
Tereza Moura

Communication and Marketing
Amanda Sammour
Beatriz Ferro
Laura Jabur
Pablo Mazzucco
Thais Gouveia
Ticiana Gavioli

**Copyediting, Proofreading
and Translation**
Ivan Sousa Rocha

Curator
André Mesquita

With the assistance of
David Ribeiro

Executive Production
Carla Ogawa
Gabriel Belvis
Isaque Vieira
Maicon Ferreira
Maria Rosalem
Marília Amorim
Marina Moura
Marina Rebouças
Matheus Gumerato
Victória Dirotildes

Exhibition Design
Flora Gurgel
Juliana Ziebell

Graphic Design
Pablo Mazzucco

Lighting Design
Fernanda Carvalho

Research Center
Adriana Villela
Beatriz Yoshito
Bruno Mesquita
Evandro Lima
Filipe Oliveira
Gustavo Bastos
João Vítor Conceição
Pamella Mazucatto
Sara Jesus

CATALOG

Copyediting and Proofreading
Bruna Wagner
floresta
Mór Madden
Rafaela Biff Cera

Editors
Adriano Pedrosa
André Mesquita

Editorial Consulting
Karen Marta Consulting

Editorial Coordination
Ana Canellas
Carol Ribas
Felipe de Souza
Mariana Trevas
Reniêr Vasconcelos

Editorial Production
Carolina Menegatti
Marina Marcondes
Tulio Costa

Graphic Design
Bloco Gráfico
Stephanie Y. Shu (assistant)

Production
Todd Bradway

Translation
Adriana Francisco
Lívia Prado Martins

Printing
Artron Art (Group) Co., Ltd.,
China

Fonts
Mallory

Images Credits
© 2023 Digital image, The
Museum of Modern Art, New
York/Scala, Florence 8; © Brecht,
George/ AUTVIS, Brasil, 2024 13;
© Holzer, Jenny/ AUTVIS, Brasil,
2024 114; © Keith Haring
Foundation 12; © Newsday
LLC / Mark Hinojosa. All rights
reserved 3; © The Heartfield
Community of Heirs/ AUTVIS,
Brasil, 2024 111; Barbara Kruger
113; Ben Blackwell 11; Bill
Stamets 80; Bruno Jakob 92-97,
119; Catherine McGann 139;
Courtesy of Gran Fury 6, 19, 25,
26, 31-33, 36-39, 41-44, 46-50, 52,
53, 59, 60, 65, 66, 70-77, 82-87,
91, 98, 108, 112, 115, 117, 118, 127,
128, 130, 132, 134-136, 146, 148,
152; Courtesy of Gran Fury,
photographer unknown 1, 14,
15, 30, 40, 45, 78, 79, 88, 89, 107,
153; Courtesy of the artist and
Marianne Boesky Gallery, Nova
York e Aspen, Estados Unidos
124; Courtesy of the Avram
Finkelstein Archive 7, 122, 123,
137, 151; Courtesy of The Kitchen,
NYC 4, 57; Division of Political
History, National Museum of
American History, Smithsonian
Institution 54, 55; Donna Binder
129; Eduardo Gil 17, 18; Ellen B.
Neipris 133, 144; Eugene Gordon
131; Gran Fury Collection,
Manuscripts and Archives
Division, The New York Public
Library 34, 35, 56, 58, 61-64, 67,
69, 90, 99-101, 103-105, 109, 125,
126; Guerrilla Girls 120; Ken
Schles 10; Lisa Howe-Ebright 81;
Lola Flash 150; Mario Caillaux
20-22; MASP 2, 51, 68, 110, 116;
Mídia NINJA 27, 28; Musée d'art
contemporain de Montréal
106; NGC 5; Pat Kilgore 23,
24; Paula Goldman 102, 121;
Projetação 29; T. L. Litt 9,
140-143, 147, 149; The Museum
of Modern Art, New York/Scala,
Florence 111; Tom McKitterick
16, 138, 145; Watanuki Ltd. |
Toki-no-Wasuremono, Tokyo,
Japan 13

ADDITIONAL CAPTIONS

Dust jacket
FRONT
Read My Lips (Men's ver.)
ACT UP, Spring AIDS Action, 1988
Photocopy on paper, 42.5 × 27.5 cm
Image 64

Mark Hinojosa
Gran Fury member Anthony Viti carried
away by the police, *Newsday*, March 25,
1988

BACK
Gran Fury
The Government Has Blood on Its Hands,
1988
ACT UP, N.Y. City Dept. of Health
Demonstration, United States
Offset print on paper, 80.5 × 54.5 cm
Image 66

pp. 2–3
Gran Fury
The Government Has Blood on Its Hands,
poster on the base of a traffic light, 1988

pp. 4–5
*Art Is Not Enough. Seize Power Through
Direct Action*, published in *The Village Voice,*
New York, United States, *circa* 1980s

p. 8
Mark Hinojosa
Gran Fury member Anthony Viti carried
away by the police, *Newsday*, March 25,
1988

p. 216
Bloody Handprint on public wall and posters,
1987-1995

Edition © 2024 Museu de Arte de São Paulo
Assis Chateaubriand and authors
2.0

Every effort has been made to trace and
contact copyright holders. Any eventual
error and omission will be corrected
in future editions. Please contact us at
editorial@masp.org.br for any doubt.

Cataloging in Publication (CIP)

M986gr
Museu de Arte de São Paulo Assis Chateaubriand
Gran Fury: Art is not enough /
   edited by Adriano Pedrosa;
   curated and edited by André Mesquita;
   texts by André Mesquita... [et al.].
   São Paulo: MASP, 2024.
   216 pp., 153 il. color.

ISBN: 978-65-5777-050-4

Catalog of the exhibition held in São Paulo,
at MASP, from February 23 to June 09, 2024

1. Gran Fury, 1988–1994. 2. Art and sexuality.
3. Art and activism. 4. HIV/AIDS activism.
I. Mesquita, André. II. Martins, Marcos (text).
III. Franco, Vinicius (text). V. Crimp, Douglas (text).
VI. Deitcher, David (text). VII. Título.

CDD (20. ed.): 701.04

Librarian: Sara Ferreira, CRB 8-9366

Printed in China

Distributed by:
ARTBOOK | D.A.P.
75 Broad Street, Suite 630
New York, NY 10004
Artbook.com

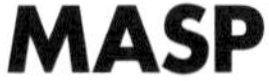

Avenida Paulista, 1578
01310-200 São Paulo, Brazil
www.masp.org.br
info@masp.org.br

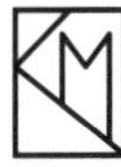

1 University Place, 8F
New York, NY 10003

ISBN 978-65-5777-050-4

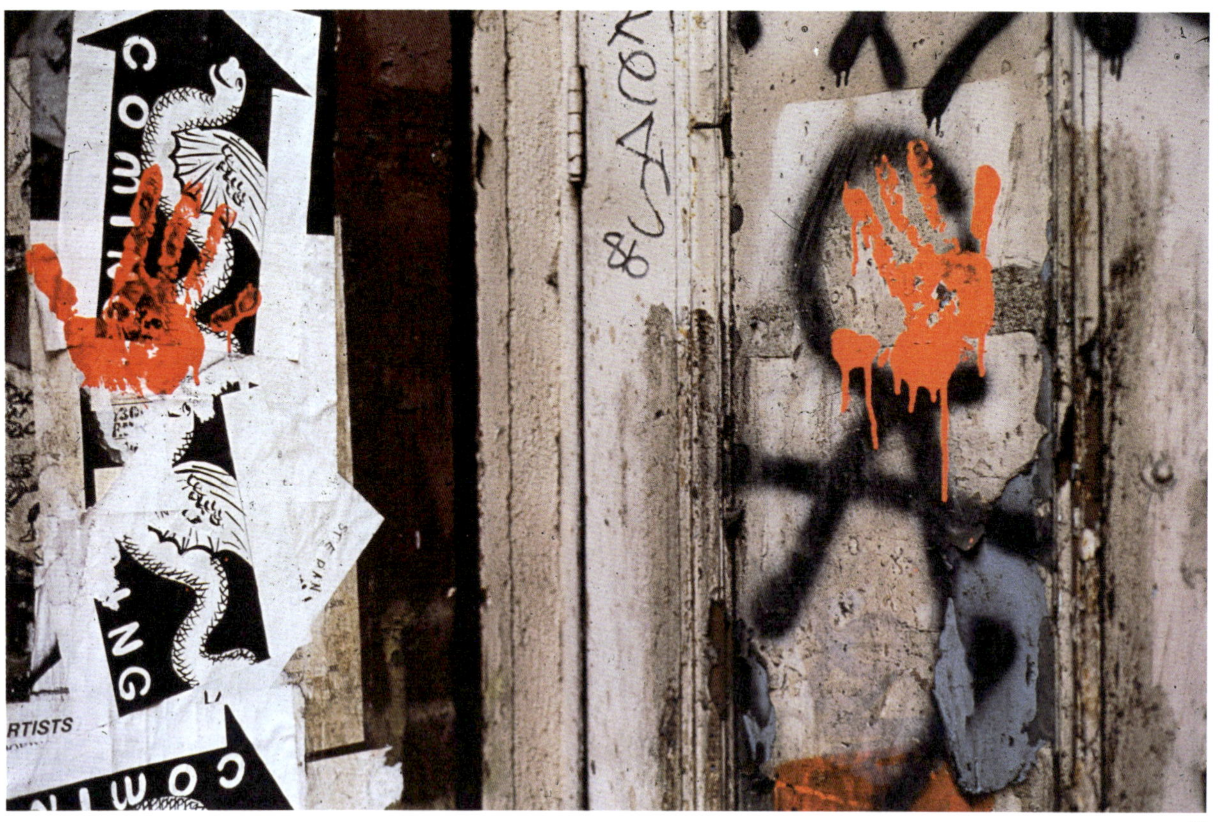

153

MASP, a diverse, inclusive, and plural museum, has the mission to establish, in a critical and creative way, dialogues between past and present, culture, and territories, through the visual arts. To this end, it should enlarge, conserve, research, and disseminate its collection, while also promoting the encounter between its various publics and art through transformative and welcoming experiences.